Shipley Associates

Proposal Guide

For Business Development and Sales Professionals

Larry Newman
Vice President,
Shipley Associates

Shipley Associates
Business Development Services
653 North Main Street
Farmington, UT 84025 USA
888.772.WINS
801.451.2323
Fax: 801.451.4660

Second Edition
Second Printing, 2004

ISBN: 0-9714244-0-3

Shipley Associates' integrated training and consulting services not only ensure success for today's "must-win" contracts but also establish the infrastructure necessary for long-term business development success.

THE SHIPLEY DIFFERENCE

MISSION: We help companies win business

- Established in 1972 with more than 200 associates and consultants worldwide
- Privately owned. Headquarters in Farmington, UT, with international affiliates in the UK, Europe, and Australia

PHILOSOPHY

- Support clients with both consulting and training across the full range of business development
- Leverage clients' existing strengths and resources
- Support clients in a strong, scalable, and collaborative way
- Complete every assignment to client satisfaction
- Leave clients with positive residual value
- Support business development as a profession

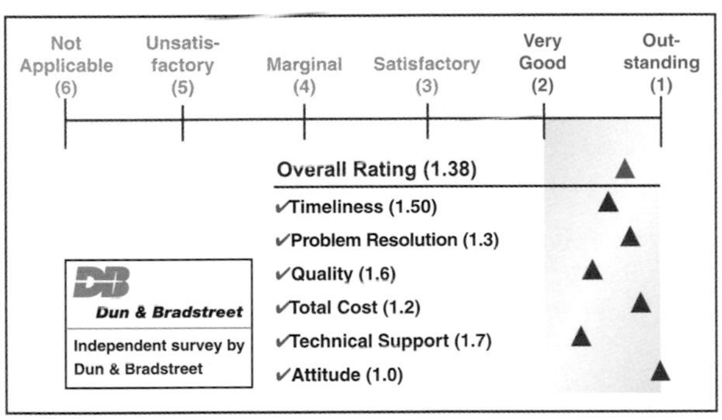

Shipley Performance Rating. *Clients express high satisfaction with our people and services.*

CAPTURE/PROPOSAL CONSULTING

- Full-term proposal management leadership and support—*complete proposal outsourcing!*
- Milestone consulting
  - — Capture/proposal review management
  - — Competitive assessment and win strategy
  - — Orals coaching
  - — Strategic intervention at proposal milestones
- Just-in-time proposal-specific coaching
- Specialized services and subject matter experts
  - — Capture, proposal, and volume managers
  - — Proposal coordinators, writers, editors, graphic artists, and desktop publishers
  - — Experts in Cost-As-an-Independent Variable (CAIV), Integrated Master Plan/Integrated Master Schedule (IMP/IMS), and similar specialties
  - — Engineering, technical, and management services
- RFP Tracking and Compliance

TRAINING SERVICES

- Client-specific capture/proposal programs
- Business development training
  - — *Capture Planning for Strategic Wins*
  - — *Managing Winning Reviews*
  - — *Managing Winning Proposals*
  - — *Opportunity Planning for Strategic Wins*
  - — *Winning Executive Summaries*
  - — *Winning in the Cost Volume*
  - — *Winning Proposal Strategies*
  - — *Winning Through Oral Proposals*
  - — *Writing Winning Proposals*
- Public workshops in business development
- Sales training
  - — *Adaptive Selling™*
  - — *Winning Sales Writing*
  - — *Winning Sales Presentations*

BUSINESS DEVELOPMENT PROCESS CONSULTING

- *Business Development Capability Maturity Model®* Implementation
- Design and development of business capture centers/proposal centers
- Process benchmarking services
- Process design, development, and improvement

Capability Maturity Model and CMM are registered trademarks of the Carnegie Mellon Software Engineering Institute.

*PROFESSIONAL DEVELOPMENT TRAINING**

- Adaptive Leadership Training/Coaching
- Project Excellence
- Team Building: Better Together
- Customer Service: Beyond Gold

** Offered through Professional Development Group (PDG), a division of Shipley Associates*

ASSESSMENT SERVICES AND TOOLS

- JobFIT™ Employee Selection and Screening
- Boilerplate/reuse database development
- Capture/proposal planners, worksheets, templates, and checklists
- Customized manuals and process guides
- Shipley Associates *Proposal Guide*
- Adaptive Sales Index: Online sales style survey

This *Proposal Guide* has three aims:

1. **Help individuals and organizations win competitive business more effectively, efficiently, and consistently**
2. **Offer clear guidance to business development professionals that is practical and easy to find**
3. **Record best-practice guidelines**

Some organizations are 10 times more effective in winning new business than industry averages. How can this be?

The most effective organizations in any market follow framework processes based upon fundamental principles. Less effective organizations follow tightly defined processes but have lost sight of the principles. Their inflexible processes cope poorly with market shifts. The least effective organizations lack both consistent processes and principles.

Help individuals and organizations win competitive business more effectively, efficiently, and consistently

Guidelines in each entry are based upon the fundamental principles of our consulting practice:

- Align your proposal with the customer's evaluation process.
- Use a disciplined business development process that emphasizes up-front planning.
- Schedule to the process and maintain schedule discipline.
- Base your strategy on the customer's perspective.
- Focus your effort early and throughout with an early executive summary.
- Apply proven project management principles to proposal development.
- Use a disciplined, customer-focused writing approach.
- Use reviews to both control and add value to the process.

Organizations implementing these principles, supported by the guidelines in this *Proposal Guide*, will capture more business at a lower cost.

Offer clear guidance to business development professionals that is practical and easy to find

The concept for the *Proposal Guide* originated when individuals in client organizations repeatedly asked the same question:

Is this written down anywhere? Now it is.

Excellent books have been written about sales, business development, and proposals. Most follow a process approach, from beginning to end. But individuals competing for orders against formidable competition need guidance fast. Most training for sales professionals focuses on sales skills and their organization's products and services, but not on how to direct, prepare, or contribute to proposals. When facing a deadline, few sales professionals have time to read a book.

This is the first book designed to be a quick reference for all business development professionals who are seeking practical, clear guidance on how to win competitive business in all markets, large or small, domestic or international, private sector or public.

Record best-practice guidelines

At Shipley Associates, we have observed industry best practices during our more than three decades of proposal training, proposal consulting, research, and business development process reengineering. Fundamental principles of business development exist and can be verified.

We follow these principles in our consulting practice, teach them in our training practice, and share them in this *Proposal Guide.*

This *Proposal Guide* offers guidelines, not rules or laws. Reality encompasses more shades of gray than can be covered in a guide intended to be concise. When in doubt, do what the customer says and be consistent.

Are the guidelines unique? Not usually. Can you find all of these guidelines in any other reference? Not until now.

For individuals needing additional guidance on writing style, grammar, word usage, or punctuation, consider the Franklin Covey *Style Guide for Business and Technical Communication*. This *Style Guide* originated at Shipley Associates, authored by Dr. Larry Freeman, and was a major influence on this *Proposal Guide*. No other style guide is comparable for clarity, accessibility, and applicability to business writing.

Hopefully, you will find this *Proposal Guide* to be a valuable tool that helps you and your organization win more business, more effectively.

The Proposal Guidelines section of the *Proposal Guide* is designed and written to help business development professionals answer routine questions about how to win competitive business more effectively, efficiently, and consistently.

Readers seeking a broad overview of business development, sales, or proposal preparation processes are better served by reading one of the many available process books.

Many of the guidelines involve the preparation of written documents, especially sales proposals. The alphabetical arrangement of the entries allows business development professionals to answer questions easily and rapidly. Numerous examples and suggestions gleaned from industry best practices make the guidelines practical and applicable to real-world competitions.

To assist new users of the *Proposal Guide*, consider the following suggestions when using the Proposal Guidelines:

- Use the alphabetical arrangement to find a specific topic. You may have to try several titles before you find the information you want. If you cannot find a topic, refer to the Index at the back of the book.
- After you have found the relevant entry, review the short summary and the numbered guidelines in the shaded box at the beginning of the entry. Then turn to the guideline that appears to answer your question.
- Read the guideline and following text. Be sure to review the examples to help clarify the guideline. Because individual prospects and competitions are unique, the guidelines are only suggestions rather than rules or legal requirements.
- Consider the context of the guideline and accompanying examples. Check to see if any notes, beginning with the word **NOTE**, add additional information about options or exceptions to the guideline.
- Turn to the cross-referenced entries if you still have questions. Cross-references have this format: *See* **Action Captions**.
- If your question involves the preparation of a document, check the Model Documents section of the *Proposal Guide* for additional applications of the guideline.

  The model documents illustrate best practices in business development and current business English. All documents follow the guidelines as closely as possible, subject to unique aspects of the specific competition.

Different individuals, organizations, market sectors, and countries use similar and potentially confusing terms. The following terms are used in this guide:

- *Bid request* vs. RFP, RFT, RFQ, ITT, or solicitation
- *Commercial* vs. nongovernment or private sector (Not meaning cost or terms and conditions).
- *Prospect* vs. customer, prospective customer, buyer, prospective buyer, or client.
- *Graphics* vs. visuals.
- *Evaluators* applies to people who read any part of a proposal. *Readers* applies to people who read non-proposal documents.

No reference book can answer every question. To help answer difficult, more specialized, or more obscure questions, refer to one of the numerous excellent books, references, or online resources available.

Acknowledgments

My thanks to the many people who generously gave advice, assistance, and support:

- The hundreds of clients from nearly 30 countries who taught me so much while I was trying to help and teach them
- My fellow consultants who patiently reviewed multiple drafts and suggested improvements. I apologize for not being able to name all of you
- My partners at Shipley Associates, who supported the preparation of the Proposal Guide financially

Several people must be both thanked and named:

- Dr. Larry Freeman, for the original inspiration, for setting standards for clarity and economy of writing that I strive to meet, and for his invaluable editorial assistance
- Ms. Patti Ferrin, for fantastic graphics, page layout, and production assistance
- Ms. Nancy Rosen, my wife, and sons Chris and Kevin for their understanding, good humor, and encouragement while I worked on this book

CONTENTS

Winning New Business .... *iii*
Preface .... *iv*
Using the Proposal Guidelines .... *v*
Model Documents 229
Index 277

PROPOSAL GUIDELINES

ALPHABETICAL LISTING

Action Captions 1
Appendices 6
Bid Decisions 8
Capture Planning 12
Choosing Correct Words 17
Color 23
Compliance and Responsiveness 26
Cover Letters 31
Customer Focus 32
Daily Team Management 35
Discriminators 38
Electronic Submittal 41
Executive Summary 44
Features, Advantages, and Benefits 50
Graphics 53
Headings 63
International Proposals 67
Kickoff Meetings 71
Letter Proposals 75
Lists 80
Numbering Systems 83
Oral Proposals 85
Organization 92
Outlining 96
Page and Document Design 103
Photographs 111
Presentations to Prospects 115
Presenting Cost and Price Data 119
Pricing 126
Process 131
Production 139
Proposal Management Plan 146
Question/Response Proposals 151
Relevant Experience/Past Performance 153
Resumes 157
Reviews 162
Risk Management 169
Sales Letters 172
Scheduling 178
Service Proposals 183
Storyboards and Mock-ups 187
Strategy 195
Team Selection and Management 203
Teaming 206
Theme Statements 209
Value Propositions 215
Writing for Grants 219

PROPOSAL GUIDELINES

TOPICAL LISTING

DOCUMENT DESIGN

Action Captions 1
Appendices 6
Color 23
Electronic Submittal 41
Graphics 53
Headings 63
Page and Document Design 103
Photographs 111
Presentations to Prospects 115
Process 131
Resumes 159

PROPOSAL MANAGEMENT

Appendices 6
Bid Decisions 8
Capture Planning 12
Compliance and Responsiveness 26
Cover Letters 31
Customer Focus 32
Daily Team Management 35
Discriminators 38
Executive Summary 44
Headings 63
International Proposals 67
Kickoff Meetings 71
Letter Proposals 75
Numbering Systems 83
Oral Proposals 85
Organization 92
Outlining 96
Presenting Cost and Price Data 119
Process 131
Production 139
Proposal Management Plan 146
Question/Response Proposals 151
Relevant Experience/Past Performance 153
Resumes 157
Reviews 162
Risk Management 169
Scheduling 178
Service Proposals 183
Storyboards and Mock-ups 187
Strategy 195
Team Selection and Management 203
Teaming 206
Theme Statements 209

PRICING AND COSTING

Presenting Cost and Price Data 119
Pricing 126
Process 131
Value Propositions 215

PROCESS DESIGN

Bid Decisions 8
Capture Planning 12
Kickoff Meetings 71
Process 131
Production 139
Relevant Experience/Past Performance 153
Reviews 162
Scheduling 178
Strategy 195

PROPOSAL WRITING

Action Captions 1
Choosing Correct Words 17
Compliance and Responsiveness 26
Customer Focus 32
Discriminators 38
Features, Advantages, and Benefits 50
Graphics 53
Headings 63
Lists 80
Organization 92
Outlining 96
Question/Response Proposals 151
Storyboards and Mock-ups 187
Theme Statements 209
Writing for Grants 219

SALES

Bid Decisions 8
Capture Planning 12
Cover Letters 31
Customer Focus 32
Discriminators 38
Executive Summary 44
Features, Advantages, and Benefits 50
Letter Proposals 75
Oral Proposals 85
Organization 92
Presentations to Prospects 115
Relevant Experience/Past Performance 153
Sales Letters 172
Strategy 195
Value Propositions 215

MODEL DOCUMENTS

Using Model Documents 229

Sales Letter

1. Prospecting 230
2. Follow-up to a Phone Call 231
3. Follow-up to a Meeting 232
4. Invitation to a Sales Event 233
5. Request RFP Modification 234

Executive Summary

6. Informally Solicited Commercial Proposal 236
7. Incumbent's Informally Solicited Services Proposal 238
8. Formally Solicited Government Proposal 240

Cover Letter

9. To Decision Maker with Buying Criteria 241
10. To Decision Maker without Buying Criteria 242
11. To Buyer for Formally Solicited Government Bid 243

Storyboard

12. Formally Solicited Government Bid 244

Proposal Section

13. Formally Solicited Government Bid 246
14. Casually Solicited Commercial Bid 252
15. Question and Response Proposal 257

Capture Plan

16. Major Program, Text Format 258
17. Major Program, Presentation Format 274

Action captions suggest action. Readers of an action caption should accept your ideas and begin to accept your proposal as the best solution to their needs.

NOTE 1: Remember the "10-second Rule." If the reader doesn't get the point within 10 seconds, they will turn the page.

NOTE 2: Labeling all types of graphics "figures" differs from traditional technical writing practice but is increasingly accepted.

While the graphic catches the reader's eye, the caption must deliver the persuasive message. Good captions interpret, inform, and persuade.

A graphic and its action caption enable the evaluator to grasp your key message without having to search the text for an explanation. Many evaluators, especially key decision makers, have little time and will skim your proposal. If the point of a graphic is not obvious, they will simply turn the page.

Place an action caption beside every graphic in your proposal, including photos, drawings, charts, graphs, tables, and even spread sheets. While not universally done in all business documents, labeling all types of graphics *figures* makes it easier for the evaluators and will simplify proposal production.

Both evaluators and writers welcome this simplification because many graphics are combinations of photos, illustrations, tables, and charts. The alternative is to sort through identically numbered figures, tables, exhibits, and charts within the same proposal chapter.

Action Captions

1. **Use interpretative action captions with every graphic in your proposal.**
2. **Draft an action caption for every graphic that contains three parts: the figure number, the title, and the caption.**
3. **Use informative titles rather than *horse titles* that often ambiguously label features.**
4. **Connect a customer benefit to the feature depicted in the graphic.**
5. **Quantify the benefit if possible.**
6. **Place action captions below the graphic.**
7. **Reference all graphics by figure number in prior text.**
8. **Use a different typeface or style for the figure title, the caption, and the body text of the proposal.**

1 Use interpretative action captions with every graphic in your proposal.

Graphics attract the evaluator's eye. Action captions add your "spin" or interpretation. If you do not interpret a graphic, evaluators are left to draw their own conclusion.

Good captions interpret the visual and suggest the benefit to the evaluators' organization:

> **Figure 1. Flexible Voice Messaging System.** *You can end lost orders through dropped customer calls with our graphic operator interface and advanced networking software. Our modular design makes it easy to change or expand, improving your flexibility.*

Evaluators read proposals with much skepticism. Why risk unfavorable interpretations when you can offer a clear, supportable interpretation and explanation?

Note how the action caption in figure 1 increases the believability of the writer's claim by repeating "flexible" in the caption.

One insightful evaluator stated:

> *We went to the graphics and captions for the answer to our questions. If we found the answer, we didn't bother to read the text.*

Many proposal professionals disagree over the proper length of an action caption. One view is to limit captions to a phrase or a single sentence. Unfortunately, short captions may omit important data or force evaluators to search the body text.

Do not worry too much about longer captions. Two to four sentences, while longer than normal, are acceptable and effective if they convey important information to the evaluator and are clear.

Captions are far more likely to be read than body text. Once a point is made in the caption, you do not have to repeat it in the body text. However, key points should be repeated for emphasis in slightly different words.

The following are additional examples of good action captions:

> **Figure 2. Cost of Computer Ownership Is Surprisingly High.** *According to the Gartner Group, the total cost of PC ownership to the average business is approximately $5,000 per year. While the hardware capital cost has decreased, major costs associated with administration, technical support, and end-user operations can be cut up to 30 percent when outsourced to PC Management, Inc.*

Figure 3. Proven Technology for the Bishah Plant. *A few of our most significant design improvements are shown, all proven in production. You achieve a competitive market advantage while reducing operating cost and risk.*

Figure 4. Low-Risk, Six-Phase Implementation. *We have identified the key milestones and deliverables for each phase. The plan, as outlined, is flexible to permit us to incorporate changes based on our mutual review of the prior phase.*

Figure 5. Easy to Use with Minimum Training. *Queries are constructed by simply pointing and clicking on objects representing data tables and raw elements. Graphical Query Language (GQL) allows users to ask questions and receive valid answers after only 8 hours of training.*

Figure 6. Military Design Standards Increase Cost. *While military design standards for ruggedization appear to increase operational life, the low production quantity and added weight both triple acquisition cost and double operational cost versus Commercial-Off-The-Shelf (COTS) alternatives. The minimal increase in operational life does not justify the large cost increase.*

2

Draft an action caption for every graphic that contains three parts: the figure number, the title, and the caption.

NOTE: Some proposal writers and editors prefer to use the detailed section number throughout the final proposal. A compromise is to limit figure numbers to third-order section numbers in final production.

See **Benefits and Features.**

Figure numbers are used to reference graphics in body text. Number figures sequentially in your proposal. On large proposals, number figures sequentially throughout major sections, as illustrated in this *Proposal Guide*.

When your proposal has numbered chapters or sections, insert the chapter or section number followed by the sequential figure number:

Figure 3-1.
Figure 3-2.
Figure 3-3.

Using detailed section numbers is a good idea during proposal development to facilitate coordinating text and graphics from multiple writers. The author of proposal section 3.4.5.1 would number the first graphic as:

Figure 3.4.5.1-1. *Flexible Voice Messaging System.*

However, this long figure number in the final proposal is cumbersome for the evaluator, so limit figure numbers in final proposal production to numbering within the major section. The previous example might change to:

Figure 3–12. *Flexible Voice Messaging System.*

Standard business writing convention is to discriminate figures, tables, charts, exhibits, etc. This practice can be both confusing in the normal proposal evaluation process and more difficult for proposal management and production.

For example, what do you call a spreadsheet with an inset graph or a graph with an inset table? At the risk of upsetting the writing experts, label all graphics as figures or exhibits to make it easier for both evaluators and proposal writers.

Because a proposal is a sales document, follow the figure number with an informative or interpretative title, as discussed in guideline 3.

Follow the title with an action caption that contains features and benefits and links the customer benefit to the relevant features shown in the graphic.

Connecting features and benefits is easier when a full sentence is used, or even several sentences. Phrases often contain only a benefit or only a feature:

Benefit only

Figure 3–12. Flexible Voice Messaging System. *Low cost solution.*

Feature only

Figure 3–12. Flexible Voice Messaging System. *Features graphic operator interface and advanced networking software.*

Benefit and Feature

Figure 8–12. Flexible Voice Messaging System. *Our low-cost solution is due to the graphic operator interface and advanced networking software.*

3

Use informative titles rather than *horse titles* that often ambiguously label features.

See **Headings.**

Labels are often ambiguous. Envision a picture of a horse in your proposal with the following caption:

Figure 7. *Horse.*

While most people laugh at this title, search your own proposals for similar examples:

Figure 8. *Organization Chart*
Figure 9. *PBX*
Figure 10. *Schedule*

While slightly more interpretative, the generic caption for figure 8 is not much better:

Figure 8. Project Team. *Our project teams are generally structured as shown.*

The following example is marginally better:

Figure 9. Project Team. *Our project team is headed by a Project Manager. Five people report to the Project Manager.*

Avoid restating the obvious. Interpret the information in the graphic. Tell the evaluator "Why," as shown in the following example:

Figure 10. Proven Team Organization. *Our project team will be structured as shown, based on the lessons learned from numerous similar previous projects. Our team is managed by a single, on-site, project manager with five direct reports. A larger span of control reduces effectiveness; fewer direct reports increases cost and lengthens response time.*

Figure 1 below shows a "horse title" as the "original" and a model action caption in the "revised" version.

Original

Figure 3-4. Buffalo.

Revised

Figure 3-4. Buffalo No Longer Endangered. *Cattle ranchers in Wyoming and Montana are angry at overgrazing caused by the expansion of buffalo herds leaving Yellowstone and Teton National Parks. Even elk and deer are feeling the effects of overgrazing.*

Figure 1. Avoid "Horse Titles." *The original has a "horse title," stating the obvious: these are buffalo. The revised version has an informative title that is both reinforced and explained in the caption.*

4

NOTE: 1: Action captions are similar to theme statements in structure. Both link benefits and features. Both are stronger when the benefit precedes the feature.

See **Graphics** *and* **Themes.**

Connect a customer benefit to the feature depicted in the graphic.

Following a basic principle of good organization, begin with the most important point to the evaluator. Captions that lead with the benefit are more customer focused than captions that lead with the feature. Benefits attract the prospect's attention. Features support how the benefit is delivered. However, do not get overly concerned if the feature precedes the benefit. Captions comprising a few sentences are short enough that the evaluator will likely see the connection.

If you are struggling to identify the customer benefit, you have two possibilities:

1. You offer no customer benefit. Remove the graphic and caption from your proposal.
2. You do not know what benefits the customer is seeking. Perhaps you should not waste your time and resources bidding.

While a caption should contain both benefits and features, some proposal writers fail to make a clear, plausible connection:

Figure 13. Cost-Effective Switch. *Our in-house design makes the Bogen 480 a low-cost switch.*

Nothing in the caption makes a plausible connection. An in-house design could just as easily increase the cost. Improve the caption by specifying what feature of the in-house design leads to the lower cost. Review captions 1 through 6 in guideline 1 for better examples.

During proposal preparation, ask writers to draft and retain full action captions in their section text files. If writers prepare their own graphics to any degree, ask them to keep all graphics in a separate file, labeled with the detailed section number and the graphic numbered sequentially within the section. The person or persons assigned to produce the proposal are better equipped to insert graphics and captions consistently and efficiently into the final document.

The best way to develop a library of graphics and captions is to collect them from each proposal. Place them on a server that can be accessed by proposal writers and graphics support. A best practice is to develop an indexing and retrieval system that is searchable by key words and an identifying number. Maintain a link between each graphic and potential captions.

NOTE 2: Organizations that produce numerous proposals for similar products or services may often maintain a library file of graphics and action captions. Retrieval is easier, but captions filed as part of the graphic are less likely to be tailored to the opportunity by proposal writers.

If graphics can be reused, place a unique identifying number on each graphic in all proposals to facilitate retrieval. Assign a revision number whenever the graphic is modified. To avoid distracting readers, orient the identifying number vertically to the graphic in approximately 6-point type in the same position relative to each graphic.

Here is another tip to evaluate the captions in a proposal. Extract and print all captions in the proposal. If the captions do not summarize your proposal and tell a persuasive story, they need more words and usually more benefits.

Standard graphics can often be used effectively to make a selling point if the action caption is tailored to each proposal opportunity. When boilerplate or stock graphics are kept with their action caption in the same file, writers seldom tailor them to the opportunity and seldom read them before placing them in the proposal.

5

Quantify the benefit if possible.

See **Theme Statements**.

See **Value Propositions**.

Captions, like theme statements, are more credible when the benefit is quantified and substantiated. Compare the following examples:

Weaker, unquantified action caption

> **Figure 8-12. Flexible Voice Messaging System.** *Our low-cost solution is due to the graphic operator interface and advanced networking software.*

Stronger, quantified action caption

> **Figure 8-12. Flexible Voice Messaging System.** *Users have documented average operating cost reductions of 17 percent due to the graphic operator interface and advanced networking software.*

The second example is also more specific, citing the "average operating cost reductions" versus the more general "low-cost solution."

Much like a value proposition, quantified benefits are more credible when the substantiation, usually supplied in supporting text, includes more of the following elements:

- **Specific**. States what is to be purchased.
- **Measurable**. Tells how much will be purchased.
- **Timed**. Cites the timing of the purchase and the savings or benefits.
- **Results Oriented**. States the result quantitatively, if possible.

Quantify benefits only when you can support your claim. Better to have a benefit unquantified than to lose credibility with prospects.

6

Place action captions below the graphic.

See **Graphics**.

In Western society, most readers read from top-to-bottom, left-to-right. An evaluator who spots a graphic will tend to first look below the graphic for the explanation. Normal practice for most newspapers is to place the caption below the graphic.

In the more sophisticated designs found in some magazines, journals, and books, the caption may be placed above or to one side of the graphic. However, the designer will still usually follow the principle of graphic association: The caption is placed closer to the edge of the graphic than to any other item on the page, causing the reader to associate them. The principle of graphic association is illustrated in figure 2, applied to captions.

In the rapid-response mode typical of most proposal efforts, keep things consistent and simple. Place the caption in the same location relative to the graphic, preferably below, unless you are severely page limited.

7

Reference all graphics by figure number in prior text.

All graphics, with their action captions, should stand alone. The evaluator must be able to get the point that you intended without having to read the body text.

Yet always refer to the graphic in the body text before it appears in the proposal. The approaches shown below are equally acceptable.

> Some of the reasons our voice messaging system is so flexible are shown in figure 3-12.

> Figure 3-12 shows why our voice messaging system is so flexible.

Place the graphic on the same or facing page to enable the evaluator to see the graphic without having to turn the page.

Change the section organization if necessary rather than force the evaluator to search for the graphic. Often evaluators do not search, and your point is lost.

8 Use a different typeface or style for the figure title, the caption, and the body text of the proposal.

Action captions are the theme statements for the graphics. Use a different typeface or style to emphasize and differentiate the caption from body text. Because captions contain key selling points, the change of style increases the chance they will be read and remembered. Captions include the figure number, the figure title, and the explanatory text.

Different caption styles are acceptable for different proposals. Select a style for each proposal and be consistent. Most organizations adopt a consistent style for all proposals unless the style is specified in the bid request.

Using **bold** for the figure number and figure title draws the reader to the beginning of the caption. Informative titles create interest, enticing the reader to read the text in the caption. This convention is illustrated in the *Proposal Guide*.

While action caption styles may vary, consistently follow these guidelines:

1. In captions, the word *figure* should be capitalized. However, when referring to graphics in the text, even if you refer to a specific figure, do not capitalize *figure* unless it begins a sentence:

   As shown in figure 12, . . .

   Our project team organization is shown in figure 3–4.

   However

   Figure 3–4 shows our project team organization.

2. Use periods following captions that are complete sentences but not after captions that are incomplete sentences. If your captions mix complete and incomplete sentences, end all of them with periods.

3. The style of punctuation between the figure number, figure title, and caption text may vary. While all the examples shown below are acceptable, the first is cleanest while the last example is the least preferred.

   Figure 3–12. Flexible Voice Messaging System. *Our low cost solution is due to the graphic operator interface and advanced Networking software.*

   Figure 3–12: Flexible Voice Messaging System. *Our low cost solution is due to the graphic operator interface and advanced Networking software.*

   Figure 3–12.—Flexible Voice Messaging System. *Our low cost solution is due to the graphic operator interface and advanced Networking software.*

   Figure 3–12 Flexible Voice Messaging System *Our low cost solution is due to the graphic operator interface and advanced Networking software.*

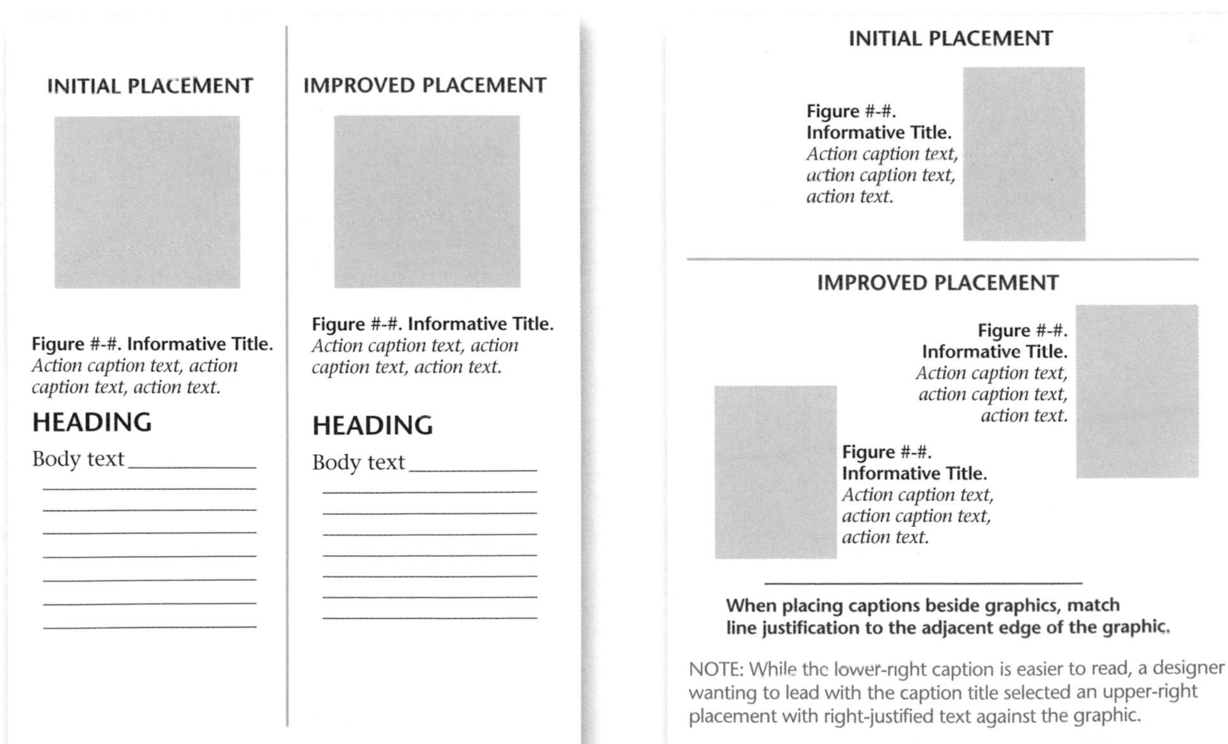

Figure 2. Visually Associate Graphics and Action Captions. *Place action captions closer to the relevant graphic than to any other page element. Placement below the graphic is recommended, but other locations are acceptable in special circumstances.*

Appendices, attachments, and annexes are seen as essentially similar by casual business readers but may have quite specific and different meanings to evaluators. Because each prospect's meaning prevails, ensure your understanding matches the prospect's.

NOTE: Webster's Dictionary, 14th ed., defines the following words as shown:

Annex: section added to a document addendum.

Appendix: additional or supplemental material added at the end of a document.

Attachment: anything added or attached.

Appendices, attachments, and annexes can be used to streamline a proposal, to make it easier to evaluate. Content of interest to most evaluators is included in the body. Content of interest to one or a few individuals is placed in an appendix, attachment, or annex.

An appendix tends to be a self-contained document on a defined topic, attached to the main proposal but containing additional or supporting information.

An attachment tends to be data additions to a proposal, such as company annual reports, marketing brochures, installation lists, parts lists, test reports, requested plans and procedures, past performance testimonials, and resumes.

Annexes tend to have specific meaning to some customers. For example the British Ministry of Defense often uses "annex" instead of "appendix" for similar types of material.

Appendices

1. **Use appendices, attachments, and annexes to streamline your proposal.**
2. **Limit appended material specifically to the information requested by the prospect.**
3. **Treat requests for additional material as a sales opportunity.**
4. **Number or letter appendices sequentially.**
5. **Refer to all appendices, attachments, and annexes in the main body of your proposal.**

1 Use appendices, attachments, and annexes to streamline your proposal.

See **Question/Response Proposals.**

In a proposal, assess whether the information is of interest to evaluators with differing backgrounds. Since most proposals consist of responses to a prospect's questions, provide a summary answer to each question followed by support. If the support is extensive yet needed in the proposal, then consider relegating it to an appendix.

Short proposals are much more likely to be read, especially by senior influencers and decision makers. Government evaluators do not have to evaluate any unrequested material.

2 Limit appended material specifically to the information requested by the prospect.

If the prospect did not ask for the information, leave it out. Account executives and proposal writers often take the supermarket approach to proposal writing. That is, "They might not know we offer a super widget, so let's tell them all about it. We might get lucky."

Instead, include a statement like the following:

> To make your evaluation easier, we have limited our response to the specific items that you requested. Should you need additional information on these or any other services, please contact . . .

List the additional information that you have available and who to contact to obtain the information. Intentionally limiting appended material eliminates the cost of gathering, preparing, and producing material that is seldom read.

If additional material is requested as a result of the evaluation, you can prepare it outside the submittal deadline, leaving more time to devote to the parts of your proposal that are more important.

3

Treat requests for additional material as a sales opportunity.

In many competitions, all seller-prospect contact is prohibited. Treat prospect questions and requests for additional material as a sales opportunity while competitors are locked out.

When additional material is requested, make sure you understand the request, prepare it quickly and concisely, then present it personally, if possible. Exploit any opportunity to relate to the prospect.

4

Number or letter appendices sequentially.

If your proposal sections begin with a number, letter the appendices. The reverse applies.

5

Refer to all appendices, attachments, and annexes in the main body of your proposal.

See **Organization** *for a better understanding of the importance of providing a summary of appendices.*

Include short, informative summaries of the content of each appendix to tell evaluators what they contain:

> Attachment A contains our last three annual reports, as requested in your RFP.

If the appendix is extensive, draft a paragraph that summarizes the key points and previews the content. Most readers will accept your summary and will not read any part of the attachment.

The prior example could be strengthened if necessary to support a key selling point:

> Attachment A contains our last three annual reports, as requested in your RFP. The 50 percent annual increase in sales over the past 3 years demonstrates the increased demand for our services. Please note the stability of our management and financial performance, further supporting our low-risk approach.

Bid decisions are aimed at eliminating opportunities or sales leads that you have a low probability of winning, permitting greater focus on opportunities that can be won. Consider splitting the bid decision into three distinct milestones: pursuit, bid, and bid validation.

For a better perspective on all business development process milestones, see **Process**.

The goal of the **pursuit decision** is to make informed decisions about each opportunity and your ability to effectively pursue it, then to obtain resources for capture development. **A positive pursuit decision initiates preparation of the capture plan.**

The goal of a **bid decision** is to make an informed decision about whether to continue positioning the prospect for the opportunity and to obtain resources for proposal development. **A positive bid decision initiates preparation of the proposal plan.**

The **bid validation decision** is initiated by the receipt of the final bid request. The goal is to identify any requirements that preclude bidding and to ensure the proposal development plan is current. **A positive bid validation decision initiates the final proposal kickoff meeting and the full proposal preparation process.**

Look closely at your bid decision process discipline to see if aspects of the following poor strategies are familiar:

1. Pursuit decisions are made by salespeople with challenging quotas. Management requires all no-pursuit decisions to be justified. Therefore, pursue everything.
2. Bid decisions are initiated by receipt of the bid request. The only valid reason to no-bid is lack of sales support to prepare the bid. Salespeople can prepare the proposal on their own if proposal support is unavailable.
3. While the bid validation milestone does not exist, any reconsideration of a positive bid decision is treated as a bid justification.

Extensive training and coaching to improve proposals can often improve win rates by 15 to 20 percent. However, improvement in bid discipline can double or triple win rates. In fact, some organizations have doubled win rates with good bid discipline without changing anything else.

Bid Decisions

1. **Use the pursuit decision to verify the lead fits your strategic direction and capability and to initiate capture planning.**
2. **Use the bid decision to verify you are positioned to win before committing to an expensive proposal effort.**
3. **Use the bid validation decision to ensure "show stoppers" are addressed.**
4. **Establish clear inputs, outputs, and responsibilities for each decision milestone.**
5. **Make all bid decisions promptly.**
6. **Tailor the process to your organization and the value of the opportunity.**

1 Use the pursuit decision to verify the lead fits your strategic direction and capability and to initiate capture planning.

See **Capture Planning**.

Tools used to aid pursuit and bid decisions include compatibility grids, checklists, weighted matrices, and decision trees. While tools will not make your decision, they often highlight what you do not know.

A positive pursuit decision initiates capture planning and preparation of the capture plan.

A generic compatibility grid is shown in figure 1. Leads are subjectively plotted on a grid according to their relative match with existing products and services on one axis and existing markets and prospects on the other axis. The plot highlights leads outside normal business that often carry higher risk. Typical questions for a pursuit decision checklist include the following:

- *Is the lead within our business area?*
- *Does the lead fit within our strategic plan?*
- *To what extent are we known to the prospect?*
- *Has the prospect budgeted for the purchase?*
- *Do we have local representation?*
- *Who created the prospect's vision for potential solutions?*

- *Do we understand who has the decision power and influence?*
- *Do we have any current or potential "coaches" or sponsors in the prospect's organization?*
- *Is there an incumbent? Are the incumbent or others already favored?*
- *Do we have any competitive advantage, discriminators, or value-added aspects?*
- *How will the lead affect our existing business, positively or negatively?*
- *What resources are required for capture and are they available?*
- *Can we win? How or why could we lose?*
- *Is the lead potentially profitable short-term or long-term?*

Spending prior to the pursuit decision is relatively small. Because industry averages show that 20 percent of bid and proposal (B&P) funds are spent from pursuit to the bid milestone, a positive pursuit decision is essentially authorizing 20 percent of the opportunity's B&P funds for capture activities.

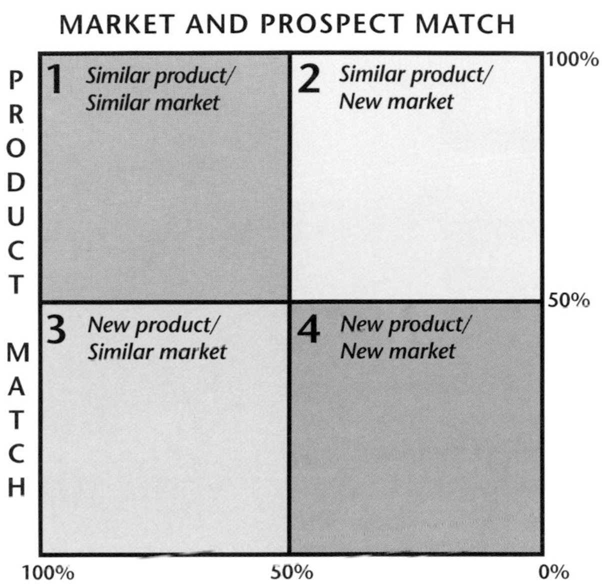

Sector	Match	Pursuit Indication	Probable Action
1	Similar product Similar market	Strong	Know product, market, and customer. Focus on competition.
2	Similar product New market	Caution	Learn the market. Establish your company in the market before focusing on the competition.
3	New product Similar market	Caution	Make sure you have a product to meet the need of your customer base, then focus on the competition.
4	New product New market	Weak, Success unlikely	Drop. If you pursue, it will require a detailed plan and far more resources than leads in sectors 1through 3.

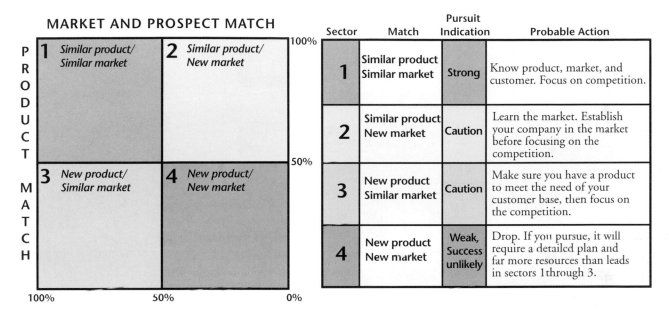

Figure 1. Lead Compatibility Grid. *Subjectively gauge and plot each lead relative to recent delivered orders. Beware of the prospect that says,* "I want another just like the last one, except . . . "

2 Use the bid decision to ensure you are positioned to win before committing to an expensive proposal effort.

See Proposal Management Plan.

Many of the questions asked at the bid milestone are similar to those listed under the pursuit milestone, except decision makers expect a more detailed response.

A positive bid decision initiates preparation of the proposal management plan.

After spending capture money on positioning activities, how successful were you? Consider adding these questions to the earlier list:

- *To what extent have we influenced the prospect's requirements?*
- *Does the prospect rely on us for input and help?*
- *Do we know the competitors and their likely approach?*
- *Are there any surprises in the draft requirements? Do we know why?*

Another approach is to use a bid decision tree like the one shown in figure 2. The usual problem with decision trees is what to do when the answer is not a clear *Yes* or *No.*

Everyone can remember a competition that was won despite negative indicators that suggested a no-bid decision. We conveniently forget the losses. Ignoring no-bid indicators increases the risk of losing. If you must proceed, compensate with more, quality resources.

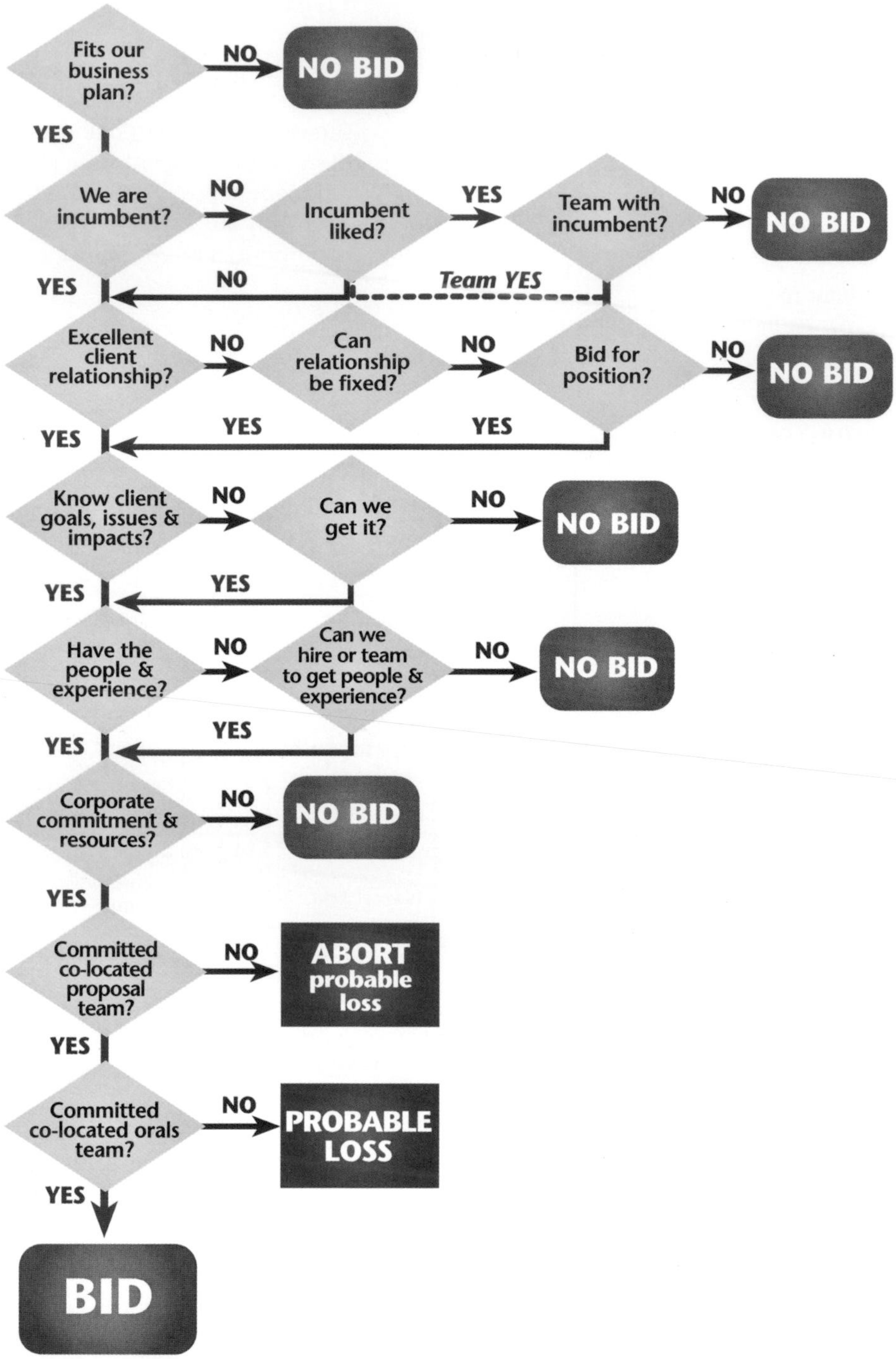

Figure 2. Bid Decision Tree. *Decision trees add discipline to the decision process. Tailor the tree to your organization. Be careful that you do not devolve into adapting the facts to fit the decision you want.*

3 Use the Bid Validation decision to ensure "show stoppers" are addressed.

See **Kickoff Meeting**.

"Show stoppers" include changes in requirements that you cannot meet, unacceptable terms and conditions, unreasonable schedule, unacceptable performance warranties or penalties, or reliable information that the selection is wired. A positive bid validation decision initiates the final proposal kickoff meeting.

4 Establish clear inputs, outputs, and responsibilities for each decision milestone.

The inputs and outputs for the pursuit decision, bid decision, and bid validation decision are summarized in figure 3. All are generic and must be refined for each organization and for the size and value of the opportunity to the organization.

Clearly establish the level of authority required for each decision.

PURSUIT DECISION

Inputs

- Strategic plan
- Annual business plan
- Prospect's strategic direction
- Identified leads/opportunities

Outputs

- Strategic fit agreed
- Capture manager assigned
- Capture plan to be prepared
- Initial budget set
- Tracking and review process set

BID DECISION

Inputs

- Prospect's strategic direction
- Prospect's needs and wants
- Draft bid request
- Current capture plan
- Competitive assessment
- Win strategy
- Positioning effectiveness report

Outputs

- Strategic fit confirmed
- Proposal manager assigned
- Proposal plan to be prepared
- Proposal strategy to be prepared
- Initial proposal budget set
- First draft executive summary assigned
- Solution overview assigned
- Boilerplate and proof to be assembled
- Tracking and review process set
- Risk assessment assigned

BID VALIDATION DECISION

Inputs

- Final bid request
- Current capture plan
- Current proposal plan
- Draft executive summary
- Solution overview
- Boilerplate and proof examples
- Risk assessment

Outputs

- Approved capture plan
- Approved proposal plan
- Draft executive summary
- Writers' packages (assignments) set
- Proposal kickoff set
- Tracking and review process set

Figure 3. Pursuit, Bid, and Bid Validation Decision Inputs and Outputs. *Customize each list for your organization. Revisit any of these decisions if inputs change significantly.*

5 Make all bid decisions promptly.

Establish clear guidelines for time limits and decision authority. Establishing a set time to consider all bid decisions lets everyone know what is required to get a prompt decision. Bid decisions tentatively conveyed to the proposal team lead to halfhearted efforts.

In one competition, a major systems company had delayed the bid decision. They had assigned 20 book bosses, giving them desks in a large bid preparation room. Seldom were more than 4 desks occupied. None of the book bosses thought they would really submit a bid.

6 Tailor the process to your organization and the value of the opportunity.

Commercial organizations with a short sales cycle usually consolidate the bid and bid validation into one milestone. When the sales cycle is 5 to 10 days, compensate by establishing and managing to explicit pursuit and bid parameters.

Organizations lacking clear bid parameters and management oversight exhibit excessive, unproductive proposal activity.

Business capture effectiveness improves when decision authority is clear and proportional to the value of the opportunity. "Value" is a function of the size, profitability, and follow-on potential of the opportunity.

Capture planning is the process of identifying opportunities, assessing the environment, and implementing winning strategies oriented toward capturing a specific business opportunity. Consistently successful capture planning requires a written, action-oriented capture plan.

The aim of capture planning is to position the prospect to prefer your organization and your solution to the exclusion of all competitors or to at least prefer you prior to any proposals being submitted.

See **Bid/No Bid Decision** *and* **Process**.

A majority of industry veterans across all markets agree that the prospect's buying decision is 40 to 80 percent decided before any proposals are submitted.

The term "capture planning" originated in organizations that were primarily focused on large U.S. Department of Defense opportunities.

At the same time, commercial organizations pursuing large, complex opportunities were developing more detailed account or sales planning disciplines. Both were pursuing complex opportunities with the following characteristics:

- High value (millions)
- Buying committee
- Long sales cycle (months or years)

Some commercial organizations use the terms *capture plan* and *account plan* interchangeably. However, many account plans are not opportunity specific and may be merely an allocation of the organization's revenue objective.

A capture planning best practice is to prepare a written, action-oriented capture plan. While the length, complexity, and format may vary, a written plan offers reviewable evidence of the quality of thinking of the planners and the soundness of the plan.

The primary audience for a capture plan is each person who will either manage or execute the plan.

A good capture plan will be realistic and specific, detailing the objective, the action, who is responsible for the action, timing, and the frequency of review.

Organizations that use a formal capture planning discipline are helped in the following ways:

- More realistic understanding of each opportunity
- Improved bid decisions
- Improved solutions and capture strategies
- Greater consensus and information transfer among all individuals pursuing each opportunity
- Saved time, reduced capture cost, and improved win rates

Capture planning is initiated following the pursuit decision process milestone.

A model capture plan in written and presentation formats is included in **Model Documents**, pp. 258-275.

Capture Planning

1. **Implement a capture planning discipline to capture new business more efficiently.**
2. **Use a defined structure for capture plans: external analysis, internal analysis, strategy development, execution, and monitoring.**
3. **Keep the process dynamic, flexible, interactive, and current.**
4. **Maintain a balance between planning and execution.**
5. **Complete the Integrated Prospect Solution Worksheet and the Bidder Comparison Matrix, even when time is short.**
6. **Gain and maintain senior management approval and support.**
7. **Commit the right people to the capture team.**
8. **Assign specific measurable objectives, schedules, and completion dates to department managers by name.**
9. **Establish regular reviews to check progress, resolve conflicts, obtain feedback, make adjustments, and reevaluate pursuit and bid decisions.**
10. **Use the capture plan to jump-start the proposal planning process.**

1

Implement a capture planning discipline to capture new business more efficiently.

Capture planning offers benefits to everyone involved:

- **Sales and business development professionals** who orchestrate organizational resources use the capture plan to specify the needed positioning actions.
- **Senior managers** have a mechanism to leverage limited business development resources to most efficiently win business.
- **Participants** stay committed, knowing their efforts are not being wasted.
- **Employees** keep their jobs, and stockholders make money.

Unlike the top-down, management driven corporate planning process, capture planning is opportunity specific. Capture plans are driven bottom up by the opportunity and the customer, as illustrated in figure 1.

To meet the organization's goals, sufficient specific business opportunities must be won. Thus, the discipline associated with "best-in-class" capture planning aligns organizational objectives and investment with high-probability opportunities within approved strategic business objectives.

Capture planning nests efficiently within the existing business development and planning process, as illustrated in figure 2. Business capture efficiency and effectiveness are improved when all employees have consistent information and communicate consistent messages to prospects. Much of the information in one plan can be reused in subsequent plans.

Figure 1. Planning Hierarchy. *Capture planning is done top down within the context of the overall corporate and sales planning process. However, it is driven bottom up by the prospect's needs specific to each opportunity.*

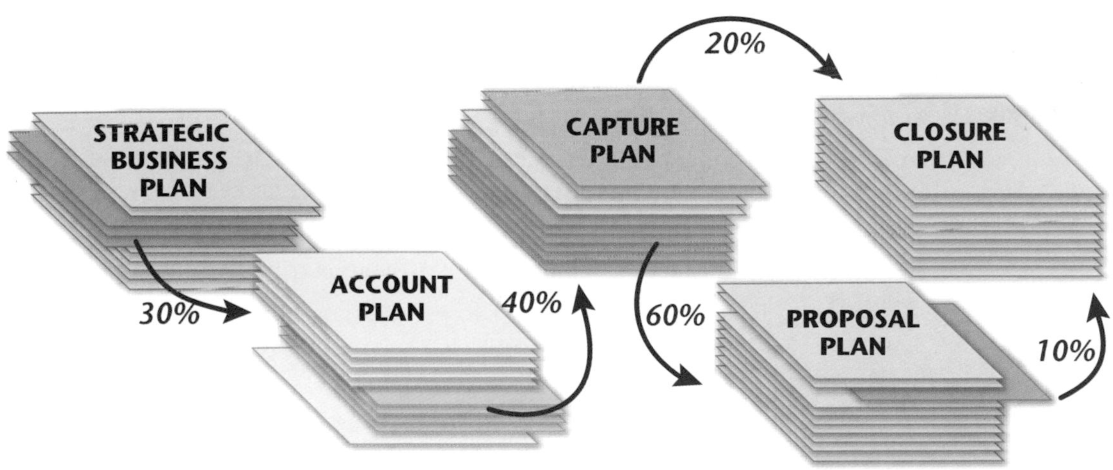

Figure 2. Capture Planning Improves Capture Efficiency. *Much of the data in each plan can be reused; it transfers or flows into the next plan. While the estimates vary, approximately 40 percent of the data from the account plan applies to the capture plan. Up to 80 percent of the capture plan data is needed in the proposal and closure plans.*

2

Use a defined structure for capture plans: external analysis, internal analysis, strategy development, execution, and monitoring.

Each organization must establish a common framework for its capture plans. Figure 3 lists potential contents.

The capture plan structure can vary from a written document to briefing overheads.

Written plans are favored by organizations with more formal management processes and longer sales cycles. Overhead formats are best suited for organizations with less-formal, collaborative management processes and shorter sales cycles.

Using the framework concept, collect and organize data against the topics deemed relevant. Store capture data in files or in a database to permit sharing within the capture team.

External analysis is done in the context of the corporate planning process, including or referencing only directly relevant data. Use the contents list to prompt more comprehensive analysis of the opportunity. Keep your language and terms consistent with established processes.

Internal analysis is focused on early definition of a solution to enable you to influence the prospect's requirements and specifications and to select the best teaming partners.

Strategy development is essentially a series of plans, all aimed at determining what actions will be taken to position your offering against the prospect's needs.

Execution and monitoring are focused on making sure that positioning happens and that results are evaluated and adjustments made.

External Analysis			*Internal Analysis*	*Strategy Development Plans*	*Execution and Monitoring*
Opportunity Description	***Customer Analysis***	***Competitive Analysis***	• Probable solution • Cost & pricing analysis • Past performance • Risk analysis	• Win strategy white paper • Contact/call plan • Intelligence collection • Communication/public relations • Technology development • Risk management • Review milestones • Proposal development • Contingency	• Kickoff • Reviews
• Project name • Background • Connection to mission/vision/ goals/needs • Key requirements • Deliverables & schedule	• Organization & power structure • Buying process • Evaluation process • Issues & hot buttons • Immediate hurts or pain • Buying history & trends • Customer satisfaction feedback	• SWOT (*Strengths/ Weaknesses/Opportunities/ Threats*) analysis • Expected approach & strategy • Integrated Prospect Solution Worksheet			

Figure 3. Potential Capture Plan Contents. *Specific contents of your capture plans will vary depending on the opportunity, your organization, and the value of the opportunity to your organization.*

3

Keep the process dynamic, flexible, interactive, and current.

Keep your capture planning process flexible to permit adjustments depending on the importance of the opportunity to your organization and the resources you can afford to commit.

Build the plan interactively to permit a fast start with reasonable effort and to encourage regular updates.

4

Maintain a balance between planning and execution.

Detailed plans without action are a complete waste of time because they fail to influence prospects' perceptions.

Limit your plans to the resources available. If more resources are essential than your organization will commit to win, reconsider your pursuit decision.

Effective capture planning requires a balance between action and planning.

5

Complete the Integrated Prospect Solution Worksheet and the Bidder Comparison Matrix, even when time is short.

See **Discriminators** *and* **Strategy.**

NOTE: The "gap" is the difference between the prospect's requirement and your available solution.

The Integrated Prospect Solution Worksheet, as in figure 4, is a powerful analysis tool that should be applied throughout the capture process. Early in the process, use it to focus collaboratively with your prospect to define the issues and influence the requirements. If you discover an opportunity after requirements are defined, use it to define the underlying issues driving the prospect's requirements.

Next, extend your analysis to outline your solution, outline your competitors' solutions, identify discriminators, then develop strategy and actions to better position your solution with the prospect.

The Bidder Comparison Matrix, as in figure 5, is used to analyze the prospect's current perception of how your solution compares to various competitors. Use it repeatedly throughout the capture process to measure the strength and effectiveness of your positioning.

NOTE: Additional uses for the Integrated Prospect Solution Worksheet and Bidder Comparison Matrix are discussed in **Executive Summary, Strategy,** and **Teaming.**

INTEGRATED PROSPECT SOLUTION WORKSHEET

Item #	Prospect Issues	Prospect Requirement	Available Solution	Gap	Competitor Solution	Discriminators	Strategy	Action Required
1	System must be available	3-hr. response time	2-hr. resp. time	.1 hr.	3-hr. resp. time	faster response but more expensive?	Emphasize no add'l cost w/ cellular	Show current response time Show photo-service w/ cell phone

Figure 4. Integrated Prospect Solution Worksheet. *Begin by filling down the "issues" column when you are early in the process. If the prospect has already drafted requirements, fill-down the "requirements" column. Then complete each row horizontally, carefully relating each item.*

Issues	Weight	Us Score	Company 1 Score	Company 2 Score
Specific Experience	30	25	20	15
Low Price	20	5	10	15
Familiarity with Manager Named	20	15	10	10
Ability to Meet Schedule	30	25	21	15
TOTAL SCORE	100	70	61	55

Figure 5. Bidder Comparison Matrix. *First list the prospect's issues, then the relative importance of each issue as perceived by the prospect in the "weight" column. Note the total weight always equals 100. Then complete each row horizontally, indicating your estimate of the prospect's perception of each competitor's ability to satisfy that issue. Scores can range from 0 to the total number in the "weight" column.*

6

Gain and maintain senior management approval and support.

Top management must endorse and help communicate the plan to everyone managing and executing the plan as well as those impacted by the reassignment of individuals to the plan.

Management support must begin with the pursuit decision and continue through to a signed contract.

7

Commit the right people to the capture team.

Also see **Team Selection and Management.**

Organizations that value winning competitive business assign their best people to capture teams. Organizations that assign only the people they can spare from other activities to participate on the capture team usually lose the sale.

The capture manager is normally a role rather than a position. In most organizations, the sales or business development lead is given the capture manager role. However, in organizations focused on large Federal prospects, the capture manager role may be assigned to a person from program management, business development, or even line management.

The capture manager role requires a person with customer and market knowledge, sales savvy, proposal experience, leadership skills, broad technical understanding, knowledge of the organization, and positive enthusiasm.

The proposal manager role, while not mutually exclusive to capture manager, requires different skills. Proposal managers lead a team focused on producing a persuasive document within tight deadlines.

Capture team members must be suited to the assigned action, whether direct prospect contact or internal development.

8

Assign specific measurable objectives, schedules, and completion dates to department managers by name.

See **Reviews.**

Most capture team action assignments are part time and for a limited duration. Only the department managers of the assigned individuals can ensure task completion.

Many capture efforts fail because the individuals assigned to the task are expected to complete the task in their spare time.

Either get serious about completing the task, eliminate the task, or no-bid due to lack of resources. The single biggest reason for losing competitive business is the failure to adequately position the prospect prior to proposal submittal.

9

Establish regular reviews to check progress, resolve conflicts, obtain feedback, make adjustments, and reevaluate the pursuit and bid decisions.

To keep reviews short and effective, focus on reviewing the actions taken, the results, and adjustments to future actions.

Recheck the underlying data, assumptions, and analysis only when objectives are not met or additional data is uncovered. Reviews that first focus on the data and analysis usually fail to get to the action.

Remember that changing a prospect's perceptions requires action, not analysis.

As more information becomes available, reevaluate your pursuit and bid decisions. Losing bids are the most costly. No-bid decisions let you apply limited resources to winnable opportunities. In most instances, the capture plan is the sole support for bid and bid validation decisions.

10

Use the capture plan to jump-start the proposal planning process.

As shown earlier in figure 2, approximately 60 percent of the information needed to prepare the proposal management plan can be extracted from a current and complete capture plan.

Relying on the capture plan to quickly prepare the initial proposal management plan both saves time and presents a consistent message to the prospect. In the absence of a capture plan, the newly assigned proposal manager starts from scratch, often with little help and under severe time constraints.

Capture plans and proposal plans have the common elements illustrated in figure 6. Information on the prospect, the requirements, and competitors transfers directly. The capture strategy needs to be extended or converted into a proposal strategy. Only the proposal outline, proposal preparation schedule, and the writer's packages need to be created.

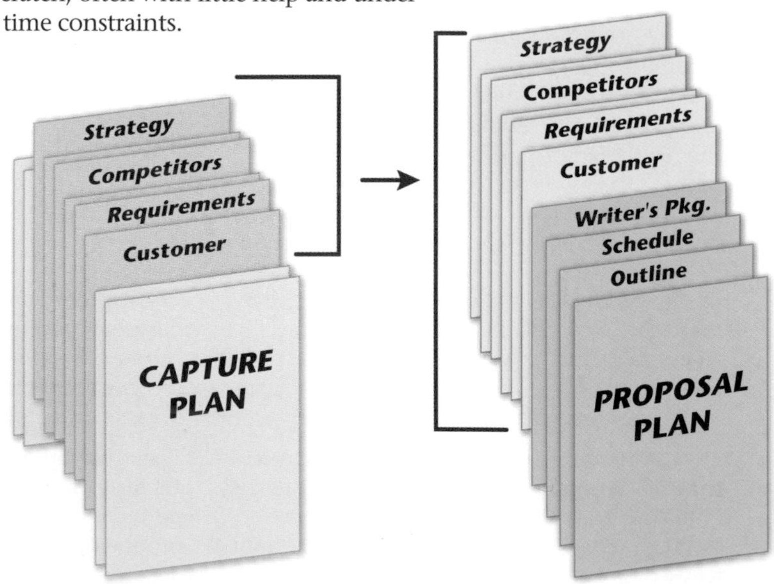

Figure 6. Capture Plans Evolve into Proposal Plans. *A current capture plan effectively front-loads the proposal plan. With approximately 60 percent of the information transferring from the capture plan, you only need to add proposal-specific material. Because the proposal submittal date is set by the prospect, a shorter planning interval prior to kickoff leaves more time to develop a winning proposal.*

Choosing correct words makes sales documents more persuasive, effective, and easier to read. Common word problems include using cliches, gobbledygook, jargon, redundant words, and incorrect words.

Good writers are always looking for resources to improve their writing and word usage. Participants in proposal training workshops often ask, "Can you give me some good words I can use in my proposals?"

No magic formula will turn your sales documents into models of effective persuasion; however, the following guidelines, derived from principles of good writing, extensive proposal writing experience, and recommendations of professional writers, will help you improve your ability to write persuasively.

Choosing correct words is important. Selecting the wrong word has several negative impacts in sales documents:

- Readers question your literacy. If you seem illiterate, then your facts might also be questionable.
- Readers question the possible working relationships. If you cannot communicate clearly in your proposal, perhaps you cannot communicate clearly on the proposed project.
- You increase your project risk when using incorrect or imprecise words in legal documents. Courts tend to support the word on the page, not what the author *claims* to have intended.

A broad range of word problems is discussed in this section. Cliches, gobbledygook, jargon, redundant words, and usage issues trouble writers but are not the same. However, all these word problems reduce the persuasiveness of your sales documents. Writers and editors must recognize these word problems and work to remove them from their documents.

Choosing Correct Words

1. **Understand the differences between cliches, gobbledygook, jargon, and incorrect word usage.**
2. **Eliminate noticeable cliches from your proposals.**
3. **Be as specific as possible while avoiding pompous words and phrases.**
4. **Minimize jargon. Define necessary jargon for nonexpert readers.**
5. **Eliminate redundant words unless used occasionally for emphasis.**
6. **Use "grabbers," transitions, and "clinchers" effectively and appropriately in your proposals and presentations.**
7. **Use the correct word in context.**

1 Understand the differences between cliches, gobbledygook, jargon, and incorrect word usage.

Cliches are worn-out words or phrases that have lost meaning or effectiveness. Writers use them habitually, without thinking. Sales and sales support professionals use the following common cliches to open or close sales documents out of habit, convenience, or to avoid serious thought:

Confirming our conversation . . .
Please do not hesitate to call.
We are pleased to present . . .

Gobbledygook is the use of abstract or pompous words and long, convoluted sentences. The meaning is often unintelligible. Both bid requests and proposals contain gobbledygook, often termed "governmentese."

Not this

In order to bring the proposed uniform facility operational software update plan to final completion, each and every personal desktop computational unit must be inventoried as to its currently installed and operational software.

This

To complete the software update, we will need a list of installed software on each PC.

Jargon has two meanings. First, it means using familiar words in unfamiliar ways.

You have to buy our *hot* new radar.

Second, it means technical or specialized language unfamiliar to a particular reader. Every technical discipline or profession needs a specialized vocabulary. But jargon obscures meaning in sales documents that are read by people with different backgrounds:

Operator efficiency is improved in monitors with a smaller dot-pitch.

The meaning of *dot-pitch* would have to be explained for many readers.

Redundant words or phrases unnecessarily qualify other words or phrases:

absolutely essential
qualified expert
joint cooperation

Incorrect word usage has three aspects. All of the following examples are, at best, confusing as well as incorrect.

1. Using a similar word with a different meaning

The principle problem with the current turbine blade is limited life.

Principle means "belief, moral standard, or law." *Principal* means "main or chief."

2. Using a word out of context

Federal Bank can speed data transfer among branches with a modern ATM network.

Bank executives accustomed to ATM meaning *automatic teller machines* might be confused about a telecommunications proposal referring to networks using *asynchronous transfer mode* protocol.

3. Using a word correctly that may be misunderstood by the reader

All work will be billed bimonthly.

All work will be billed semimonthly.

The ambiguous *bi-* can mean either twice within a time period or every other time period. *Semimonthly* has always meant twice a month but suffers from confusion associated with *bimonthly*. Avoid the confusion by saying *twice a month* or *every other month*.

2 Eliminate noticeable cliches from your proposal.

Noticeable cliches distract the prospect from your message. Others delay the reader from getting to the message, wasting the reader's time.

See **Customer Focus** *and* **Organization**.

Remember two key principles of organization to reduce opening cliches:

1. Begin with the most important point to the reader.
2. Avoid unnecessary or long setups.

Many proposals open with seller-focused cliches:

Global Corporation is pleased to have the opportunity to present this proposal for super widgets.

Thank you for allowing us to submit our proposal for Super Widgets.

Is your gratitude the most important concern of the prospect?

Openings like these evoke images of begging. Professional sellers offering valuable products and services in a complex sale should interact as professionals. Begging debases the professional image you are seeking to create.

Closing with cliches wastes the opportunity to close with power. Readers remember the first thing they read, the last thing they read, and repeated points.

Cut thoughtless, cliched closes like the following:

Please don't hesitate to call.

Instead, prompt action. Suggest the next step. Enable action.

To prompt those who read your executive summary to read your proposal, close with an introduction or preview to your proposal:

Our proposal mirrors the issues discussed in our meetings. Should your requirements change, we welcome the opportunity to discuss further enhancements.

Many sales documents involve additions to existing contracts. If the next realistically achievable step is action, suggest the action:

I will call you June 6 at 2:00 P.M. to answer potential questions and to schedule a follow-up meeting. Please call me anytime at 800-777-0077 for additional information.

While possibly seeming aggressive, this proactive close is more realistic. Most sales professionals know that prospects invited to call seldom do.

Writers often make return calls difficult by omitting a phone number and the name of the contact. Make sure the action suggested is possible:

Please call Frank Fells, our proposed Acme Project Manager, at 800-777-0077 for additional information.

Here are a few favorite (poor) sales and proposal cliches:

Global Corporation is grateful for the opportunity to be a participant in this switching proposal.

We take much pleasure in enclosing our proposal for . . .

The XYZ Team is a force in being.

Additional cliches are listed in figure 1.

3

Be as specific as possible while avoiding pompous words and phrases.

See **Executive Summary** *and* **Sales Letters.**

Being specific improves clarity and credibility. Are you selling a weapon system, an airplane, or an F-22?

When you plan to "interface" with the prospect, do you plan to call, write, meet, teleconference, send an e-mail, or kiss them?

Many writers justify vagueness because they either do not know how to be specific, or they want to avoid being wrong. While understandable, readers may sense the writer is being evasive and cannot be trusted.

Gobbledygook is common in opening sentences of proposals, especially executive summaries. Writers try to be so inclusive that all meaning is lost.

Original version

As we enter the 21st century, the demographics of secondary school students, the attitudes of legislators at all levels of government and parents toward the accountability of schools that their children attend, the increasing demands on teachers and school administrators to improve their performance year-over-year, the discussions over sources of funding, and concerns about the potential for violence and other unhealthy conditions make this an auspicious time to examine a new cohort of high school students in the tradition of the Department of Education's longitudinal data-collection studies, which were first started with the National Longitudinal Study of 1972.

Improved version

National, state, and local policy makers and educators are striving to improve the effectiveness of America's educational system based on facts rather than perceptions. The growing debate about school quality, diversity, standards, and personal safety supports the need to both extend and update the available data.

Concerns about risk have prompted many writers to open with multiple qualifications before making their claim:

Original version

If no major issues arise, existing regulations remain fixed, the required skilled professionals are available, weather remains suitable for construction, war does not commence, all subcontractors and suppliers perform as promised, and all payments arrive as promised, we should complete the vaccine manufacturing facility on schedule.

Improved version

We will complete the vaccine manufacturing facility on time, unless one of the following unlikely events occurs: . . .

Additional examples of gobbledygook are listed in figure 1.

4

Minimize jargon. Define necessary jargon for nonexpert readers.

NOTE: an acronym is a word formed from the initial letters of a title, name or phrase, such as WAC from "Women's Army Corps." An initialism is similar to an acronym except the initial letters are pronounced, such as DoD for Department of Defense. Acronyms and initialisms are all referred to as acronyms in the *Proposal Guide.*

Proposal writers need to use jargon in proposals. Minimize jargon, especially in executive summaries, section summaries, and themes, which are more likely to be read by nonexperts. Writers using jargon may confuse or alienate the prospect.

While not strictly the same, acronyms are often perceived as a type of jargon. In proposals, treat jargon like acronyms; define it the first time the word is used in each major section that is likely to have different evaluators or readers. Using too many acronyms can make a proposal unreadable.

Jargon and gobbledygook are not the same. Gobbledygook can include technical jargon as well as nontechnical words. Good writing can include some jargon if the jargon is defined or understood in context. Good writing never includes gobbledygook.

Ultimately, prospects determine whether jargon is acceptable. Hence, proposal writers must know their prospects well. One prospect may despise common business jargon such as *cost effective, best-in-class, world class,* or the verb *to partner* as a signal that the writer is shallow. Another may expect to see these terms as a sign that the writer is current.

Additional examples of common business and proposal jargon are listed in figure 1.

5

NOTE: Use redundant words when mirroring the naming conventions used in the bid request.

Eliminate redundant words unless used occasionally for emphasis.

Most redundant words can be eliminated. If the meaning is the same after removing a word, do it.

Past experience is redundant because all experience was acquired in the past. *Qualified expert* is redundant because all *experts* surely must be qualified.

Use redundant words in proposals in two circumstances:

- To emphasize a point:

  Planning is absolutely essential to meet every milestone.

- To mirror the bid request:

  Every bidder must include a chapter on past performance.

Call the chapter *Past Performance*, even if the words are redundant.

Do not overuse redundant words for emphasis. The effect diminishes rapidly. Readers see it as hype, and you lose credibility.

Additional examples of redundant words and preferred alternatives are listed in figure 1.

6

CAUTION: Use grabbers, transitions, and clinchers after carefully considering your readers. Any perception of "hype" will reduce your credibility.

Use "grabbers," transitions, and "clinchers" effectively and appropriately in your proposals and presentations.

Grabbers are designed to capture a prospect's attention without offending. Grabbers include headings, slogans, salutations, opening challenges, and theme statements.

Transitions signal a change of topic, link or relate topics, and regain the prospect's attention. Traditional documents place transitions at the end of a topic or section, implicitly assuming the document is read in order. Because proposals are often scanned, transitions in proposals are more effective when placed at the beginning of a section to recapture the evaluator's attention.

Clinchers are closing statements in sales documents that prompt the prospect to take the action that you have requested. Effective clinchers prompt the prospect to act.

Examples of grabbers, transitions, and clinchers are listed in figure 2.

7

See **International Proposals**.

NOTE 1: ***Assure, ensure,*** and ***insure*** (as shown in figure 3) all mean to make certain or guarantee. However, the definitions in this *Proposal Guide* are the usual ones meant in proposals. The usual meaning also changes by country. Use each word consistently in your proposal and define your meaning if necessary.

NOTE 2: ***Will*** and ***shall*** (as shown in figure 3) are often controversial and used interchangeably. Understand each prospect's meaning.

Use the correct word in context.

English is filled with deceptive word-pairs that are nearly identical but refer to unrelated concepts. A few of the word-pairs commonly misused in proposals are listed in figure 3. For brevity, examples of each are not included. Please refer to a good style guide for additional examples, preferably one prepared for business writers.

Words are used out of context in proposals due to the different education, work experience, and the cultural differences of writers and readers.

Education and work experience affect our understanding of words.

Acronyms can be misunderstood:

ATM = Asynchronous Transfer Mode
Automatic Teller machine
Air Traffic Management

Jargon can be used out of context:

Consideration: After due *consideration*, we will complete the project.

A layman might interpret *consideration* as meaning "careful thought." A lawyer might interpret *consideration* as meaning "payment."

Cultural differences lead to the phrase referring to the United Kingdom and the United States as, "Two countries divided by a common language." Native speakers from France and Canada use French differently. Spanish varies greatly among Spain and numerous Central and South American countries. The same applies to Portuguese spoken in Portugal and Brazil.

Confusion may result from English speakers who adopt words from other languages. The original meaning in either language may change over time. Further confusion results from words that sound and may even be spelled identically but have radically different meanings. Marketers have encountered many problems when naming products. An example was the automobile model *Nova*, which was roughly interpreted in some Spanish-speaking countries as "won't go."

CLICHES

A can of worms
A-1
acid test
as a matter of fact
at the end of the day
at this point in time
attached hereto
avoid it like the plague
awaiting further orders

Back to the drawing board
banner week
benefit of the doubt
beside the point
better late than never
bite the bullet
block out
built-in safeguards

Circumstances beyond our control
city fathers
clean slate
come full circle
confirming our conversation
considered opinion
cream of the crop
crying need

Dark horse
dead meat
deliberate falsehood
discreet silence
dog-and-pony show
drastic action

Each and every
easier said than done
enclosed herewith
existing conditions

Feedback loop
feel free to
few and far between
final analysis
food for thought
foregone conclusion

Give the green light to
goes without saying
golden boy
good team player
grave concern

Had me stumped
hammer out a deal
hard and fast
hat in hand
have a field day
heard it through the grapevine
hot pursuit
hue and cry
Ill-fated
in close proximity
in no uncertain terms
in the loop
in this day and age
innocent bystander
iron out the problem
inside track

Keep options open

Last analysis
last but not least
line of least resistance

Man of the hour
marked contrast
moment of truth
moot point
more or less

Narrow escape
needless to say
needs no introduction

One and the same
ongoing dialog
open and shut
out of the loop

Paradigm shift
point in time
point with pride
pushing the envelope

Raising the bar
reinventing the wheel
runnning against the wind/tide
run of the mill

Sacred cow
said and done
second to none
seeing the big picture
select few
serious money
seat of the pants
smoke and mirros
spending a bundle
sweeping changes

Thanking you in advance
thinking outside the box
those present
tie-breaker
too numerous to mention
track record

Unprecedented situation

Wear and tear
without further ado

GOBBLEDYGOOK

Pompous word	*(use)*
Accordingly	(so)
activate	(start)
apprise	(tell)
Cognizant	(aware)
completion	(end)
configuration	(shape, design)
Demonstrate	(show)
disseminate	(distribute)
Fabricate	(make)
function	(work, act)
Heterogeneous	(different)
Interface with	(call, meet, discuss)
Locality	(place)
Manufacture	(make)
modification	(change)
Necessity	(need)
Paramount	(main, chief)
perspective	(view)
proceed	(go)
Ramification	(result)
request	(ask)
residence	(home)
Stonewalling	(lying)
Terminate	(end)
Utilization	(use)
utilize	(use)

REDUNDANT WORDS

a.c. current (a.c. = alternating current)
absolutely complete (complete)
absolutely essential (essential)
actual experience (experience)
after very careful consideration (after considering)
arrive on the scene (arrive)
as a result of (because)
attach together (attach)
at this point in time (now)
at which time (when)

Basic fundamentals (basics)
be cognizant of (know)
black in color (black)

Check up on (check)
combine together (combine)
come to a decision as to (decide)
continue to remain (remain)
contributing factor (factor)

Desirable benefits (benefits)

End product (product)
end result (result)

Final conclusion (conclusion)

Give consideration to (consider)

Heat up (heat)

In spite of the fact that (although)
in the event that (if)
it is often the case that (often)

Join together (join)
joint cooperation (cooperation)

Main essentials (essentials)
make mention of (mention)
make use of (use)
mix together (mix)

New innovation (innovation)

One and the same (the same)
one specific case (one case)
on the grounds that (because)
owing to the fact that (because)

Past experience (experience)
period of time (period)
plan ahead (plan)
plan in advance (plan)

Qualified expert (expert)

Repeat again (repeat)

Same identical (identical)
single unit (unit)
specific example (example)
still remains (remains)
subsequent to (after)

True fact (true)
this is a subject that (this subject)

Ultimate end (end)
unsolved problem (problem)

Visit with (visit)

Ways and means (ways/means)

JARGON

Acquisition streamlining
action plan

Best value

Core business
core competency
cost effective
cutting edge

Downsizing

Empower
enterprise

Headcount

Industry-leading

Joint venture

Knowledge management

Leveraging

Market driven
mission-critical
mission statement

Right-size

Strategic alliance

Task force
telecommute

Uncompensated overtime

Figure 1. Examples of Common Proposal and Sales Document Cliches, Gobbledygook, Jargon, and Redundant Words. *Eliminate cliches and gobbledygook from your proposals. Minimize jargon and redundant words, using them with clear intent.*

GRABBERS	TRANSITIONS	CLINCHERS
Headings and Slogans Can you afford to . . . Proven . . . Compare the difference . . . Switch to . . . Easy to use. The right choice. ***Salutations*** *(other than "Dear . . . ")* Welcome to . . . A special invitation . . . Please attend . . . Join us . . . Proposal to . . . ***Question*** Are your AEs . . . Are you spending . . . Can you afford to . . . Can you . . . ***Statement*** In the 10 seconds it took you to read . . . Most sales managers . . . ***Challenge*** Capture more ____ by . . . Enjoy the . . . See how . . .	After careful study, . . . As you requested, . . . As you witnessed at . . . At less than the cost of . . . Best of all . . . But if you are more concerned with . . . Considering your recent service record, . . . Fortunately . . . If your managers are experiencing . . . In summary, . . . More importantly, . . . Simply stated, . . . So far, so good. So what's the typical result? To illustrate our approach, . . .	Click on ____ to . . . For the fastest response, . . . Go to our website to . . . If you agree that _____, then . . . If you can't wait, call . . . I'll call you at 2:00 p.m. Tuesday to . . . See for yourself by . . . See what others are saying . . . To ensure you get the first selection . . . Waiting could push you into the next . . . With current costs of ____ per day, can you afford to wait?

Figure 2. Use Grabbers, Transitions, and Clinchers Carefully. *Most of these examples are found in advertising copy. Avoid empty claims. Be specific. Like poetry, every word counts in these key persuasive phrases. Blanks (____) or ellipses (. . .) indicate where you would insert appropriate words or phrases for your products and services.*

SELECT CORRECT WORDS

accede	agree to
exceed	to surpass
accept	to receive
except	excluding
adapt	to adjust to
adopt	to accept formally or to take as one's own
affect	*(v)* to influence
effect	*(v)* to bring about, *(n)* result
among	more than two involved
between	two involved
assure	give confidence to
ensure	to make certain
insure	financial guarantee
beside	alongside
besides	also
bimonthly *(avoid)*	twice a month *or* every other month
semimonthly *(avoid)*	twice a month
continual	repeated
continuous	uninterrupted
council	*(n)* a group
counsel	*(n)* advice, *(v)* to advise
discreet	tactful or prudent
discrete	separate or individual
eminent	prominent
imminent	in the immediate future
fewer	numbers
less	amount
flammable	able to burn
inflammable *(avoid)*	able to burn *and* not able to burn
forward	at or near the front
foreword	introduction to a book
imply	to suggest
infer	to draw a conclusion
irregardless	*(do not use)*
regardless	*(adj)* heedless; *(adv)* despite everything
it's	contraction for *it is*
its	possessive
loose	unattached
lose	to suffer loss
precede	to go before
proceed	to begin or continue
presently	soon
at present	now
principal	main, chief, money
principle	rule, belief
shall	obligatory in RFPs
will	best efforts in RFPs
sight	something seen
site	place
stationary	fixed
stationery	writing supplies
superlatives	(Very, extremely) *Remove superlative adverbs and replace with strong words, for example,* **excellent** *or* **outstanding**. *Superlatives tend to be perceived by readers as presumptive and arrogant.*
than	comparison
then	at that time
that *(defining or restrictive)*	**example**: The computer that is broken is on the desk.
which *(nondefining or nonrestrictive)*	**example**: The computer, which is broken, is on the desk.
their	possessive
there	*(adv)* showing location
they're	contraction of *they are*
toward/towards	Different form of the same word; *toward* tends to be American, *towards* tends to be British usage
who's	contraction for *who is*
whose	possessive
would	certain, 100 percent
probably would	very high, 80 percent
could	reasonably high, 50 percent
might	moderate, 30 percent
you're	contraction for *you are*
your	possessive

Figure 3. Select the Correct Word. *While far from complete, many of the words misused in sales documents are listed above. Please refer to a quality style guide or dictionary for a more exhaustive list and more extensive guidance.*

Color adds impact to documents and presentations. Depending on the industry, nearly all presentations and many proposals use color.

Without color, your documents (and, by reflection, your organization) may appear outdated.

Also see **Graphics** *and* **Photographs.**

However, a United States Federal Acquisition Regulation warns that, "overly elaborate proposals may indicate the offeror's lack of cost consciousness and are to be avoided." Many other governments have similar warnings.

The low cost of color printers dates the excessive cost argument when color is used appropriately. Many bidders use color on covers, executive summaries, and frequently throughout a proposal.

Color is effective when it draws attention to the main elements of the graphic. Keep colors the same hue if elements are of equal importance. Use tints to show greater amounts of the same element. Place warm colors (e.g., red, orange, or magenta) in front of cool colors (e.g., blue, green, or tan).

Full color printing on expensive stock for an entire proposal is considered excessive. Keep your approach simple and be consistent.

Color

1. **Use color where it adds the most value.**
2. **Establish color standards as part of your normal style sheet.**
3. **Adjust your color scheme to the medium.**
4. **Follow the recommendations of graphics professionals.**
5. **Consider the emotions and associations evoked by color and possible sight limitations.**
6. **Balance the benefits of color with its increased production time and cost.**

1 Use color where it adds the most value.

Color is a visual emphasis device. Spend your limited color budget to reinforce your strategy, connecting client benefits to key discriminators.

Nearly all proposals use color on the covers. Try to develop a color graphic that conveys the essence of the sale.

When numerous proposals are submitted to a prospect with a largely undefined evaluation process, the engaging color proposal cover may cause it to be read.

Clever proposal covers, packaging, and presentation can have a powerful impact in the right situation, as in these examples:

> A bidder to develop a software package for a large pizza chain submitted a proposal in the chain's box, creating a strong, positive impression.

> An executive summary submitted to a national rental car chain was prepared to look like the color rental folders at the prospect's airport counters.

See **Relevant Experience/ Past Performance.**

> A cover graphic, repeated on the first page of the executive summary, showed color pictures of the desired products superimposed on a declining cost curve. The proposal was to reduce the cost of a critical raw material used to manufacture the desired products.

> A state competing to have a multinational's 2500-employee facility built in its state submitted copies of the proposal in replica Pony Express leather pouches, delivered on horseback in time for the evening news.

Use color in the executive summary, the most important pages in your proposal.

> An executive summary to a frozen food trucking company for information technology (IT) outsourcing used small color photos of the prospect's convenience stores. The executive summary demonstrated understanding of the prospect's business and the added value of IT support in helping the trucking company meet client commitments and maintain product quality.

Color photos or graphics showing the benefits of the product or service are usually more effective than photos of the product or delivery of the services being quoted.

Use color in the rest of your proposal where it adds value. While color logos are OK, fairly standard, and recommended, they add little value and will not discriminate you from most competitors.

Use color graphics to support your claims of experience and offer proof of performance. Photos showing you performing similar work inspire confidence.

2

See **Page and Document Design.**

Establish color standards as part of your normal style sheet.

Set color standards early to save time. Maintaining color standards is easier on larger proposals with professional graphics support.

If many different individuals produce their own proposals, establish one or two style sheets in the software of choice with colors defined. Two standards, one conservative and one more colorful, permit a better match with the prospect's business style.

3

NOTE: On-screen colors often project differently. Either carry your own tested projector and laptop, or try to test the borrowed projector before making your presentation.

See **Presentations to Prospects.**

Adjust your color scheme to the medium.

The high contrast of black print on white paper makes text easy to read. Most proposals are printed on white or near-white paper using dark or colored ink.

Careless use of color sometimes makes a proposal hard to read. Black or dark print on color or shaded backgrounds with little contrast makes reading difficult.

White or reverse print on dark background is also hard to read with extensive text, a common practice in marketing materials.

Presentations must be color adjusted to the medium. Overheads require light or clear backgrounds to be seen in a room with the lights on. While overheads might seem low-tech, they are simple, reliable, and, most importantly, work with the lights on, permitting you to read client reactions.

Laptop screens and TV monitors are more visible with dark backgrounds and light print. Because light print tends to be swallowed by dark backgrounds, select a bolder or wider version of your font to improve readability.

Direct computer projection systems are rapidly replacing overhead projectors. The reduced size and weight, plus the increased clarity and brightness of these projectors, permits use in rooms with full lighting. As with overheads, use light backgrounds and dark text with a quality projector.

4

Follow the recommendations of graphics professionals.

While color selection and document design are usually improved when left to graphics professionals, many proposals and sales documents are created by individuals or small teams without assistance. A few principles will help you use color more effectively.

Begin with the style standards or guidelines of your organization. Follow them or refer to guidelines in published style guides, design books, or the desktop publishing documentation manuals that came with your software. Alternatively, imitate the style of similar documents that appeal to you and the prospect.

A basic color wheel shows colors in different hues. A shade is a darkened hue, created on paper by adding black. Conversely, a tint is created on paper by adding white. The color wheel in figure 1 shows the relationship between hues, tints, and shades.

If the prospect dictates color and styles, follow the prospect's instructions.

5

Also see **International Proposals.**

Consider the emotions and associations evoked by color and possible sight limitations.

Consider your corporate image, the audience, and the objective of your presentation. Colors may cause the emotional responses summarized in figure 2.

Colors evoke different emotions in different cultures, impacting international proposals.

For example, in several Eastern countries white is associated with death and mourning. In the United States, white is associated with purity and innocence. Certain color combinations may evoke unintended associations with holidays, such as orange/black (Halloween), and red/green (Christmas). Check with people from the local culture to prevent embarrassing mistakes.

Consider that 10 percent of the male and 5 percent of the female population are red/green color blind. Being color blind does not mean a person sees in black and white or blue monochrome but may confuse shades of red, green, and brown, or blue and purple. Whether colors are confused depends on the intensity of the hue and the brightness of the light conditions. Consider these guidelines on color design:

- Avoid similar saturations of red, green, brown, gray, or purple next to or on top of each other; do not use these colors together in a gradient blend.

- Create a strong, bright contrast between foreground and background colors for both page text and images. Even totally color-blind readers can differentiate similar colors when contrasted between light and dark.
- Add textures, patterns, or shading to set off special areas. Do not use colors alone in graphics such as bar charts, maps, and navigation bars.
- Use contrasting colors and contrasting saturations to differentiate between important items when you must use color alone.

Use two cool colors for text and graphics on a slide or page. Cool colors are calm and relaxing for most people. Cool colors are:

Blue **Purple** **Cyan**
Green **Brown** **Black**

Use hot colors sparingly: one or two key words, bullets, arrow points, or special effects. Hot colors are stimulating; never use them for text. Hot colors are:

Magenta **Orange** **Red**

6 Balance the benefits of color with its increased production time and cost.

Preparing graphics and printing in color may double time estimates and cost.

Color graphics also result in much larger file sizes. Many organizations send final color printing to an outside vendor, further increasing production time.

See **Production.**

While far beyond explanation in this *Proposal Guide*, be aware of color-matching problems. Different monitors, printers, and projection systems use different color systems. Often the graphic that looks great on screen will print or project with different colors depending on the printer, the projector, and the software.

Color matching can consume inordinate amounts of production time. Use color where it counts.

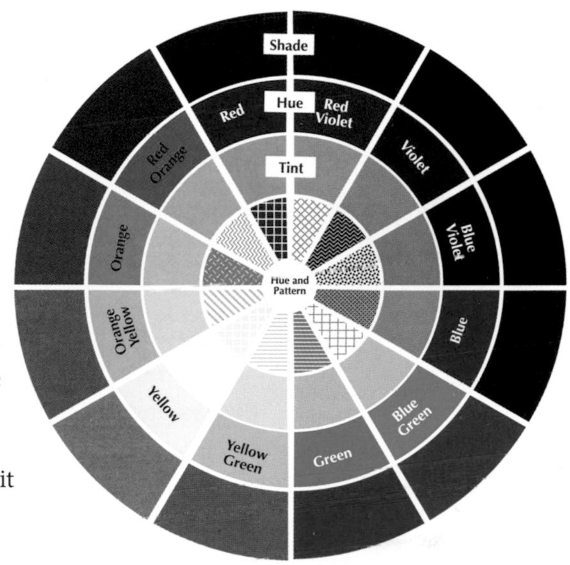

Figure 1. The Color Wheel. *Complementary colors are opposite on the color wheel. Their high contrast is used to grab attention and highlight differences. Harmonious colors are adjacent on the color wheel. Harmonious colors, shades, or tints are used to show subtle variations and to show associations, harmony, or consistency between elements.*

NOTE: Other cultures have entirely different emotions and references attached to colors. In many Eastern societies, red and black are associated with power and good. White is often the color of mourning and death. In Islamic societies, certain shades of green have religious significance.

Be sure to carefully research color use when preparing proposals and documents to international prospects.

COLOR	EMOTIONAL ASSOCIATION	BEST USE
Blue	Peaceful, soothing, cool Authority, power (sometimes)	Backgrounds (90 percent of all business presentations) Dark shades often used for printed headings
White	Neutral, purity, wisdom	Font color choice for dark background
Yellow	Warm, cheerful Caution, warning	Bullets, subheads with dark background
Red	Losses, danger, action Excitement, energy	Bullets and highlights, seldom as background
Green	Money, growth, assertive Warmth, comfort (sometimes)	Highlights, occasionally as a background

Figure 2. Making the Best Use of Color. *In Western cultures, colors tend to have the emotional associations indicated. Remember that persuasion is 50 percent emotion and 50 percent logic. The specific emotional association will vary with the type of audience, individual, and culture.*

Compliance and responsiveness are often confused. Both must be addressed.

Compliance means strict adherence to the prospect's bid request, both the submittal instructions and the requirements.

Responsiveness means addressing the prospect's underlying needs. Proposals can be responsive but not compliant, or compliant but nonresponsive. Confusion reigns.

Compliance with instructions means that you have followed the requested format, answered all questions, completed all forms, and submitted your response to the right person and place on time. Compliance with requirements means that you have agreed to meet all requirements as asked in the bid request.

See **Strategy**.

Government buyers bound by law can use noncompliance as a reason to eliminate your bid. Whether they actually do eliminate your bid gets complicated, often depending on the relative compliance of the other bidders.

Nongovernment buyers, free to do whatever they like, can use noncompliance as the reason to eliminate a bidder.

Assuming a responsive proposal addresses the prospect's underlying needs, your approach could be compliant or noncompliant, depending on whether your approach or solution is specified in the bid request:

A prospect needs the grass cut to a specified height. Their bid request specified a weekly cutting by push mower for the calendar year.

1. A compliant but arguably nonresponsive bidder could agree to cut the grass weekly for 52 weeks, even though the grass might be dormant in winter.
2. A noncompliant but responsive bidder offers to use a robot mowing system that senses grass height and cuts as necessary, thus keeping the lawn at the desired level but reducing the number of mowings and perhaps the total cost.
3. Others could offer to cut the grass weekly with a riding mower versus the push mower, also noncompliant but responsive.

As the examples show, deciding whether to be fully compliant and responsive is an implicit question when determining your solution and strategy.

Compliance and Responsiveness

1. **Do what the prospect asks when you get to the proposal stage.**
2. **Prepare a compliance checklist for all formal bid requests.**
3. **Prepare a compliance checklist for all informally solicited bid requests.**
4. **Use compliance checklist shortcuts with caution and understanding.**
5. **Construct a response matrix early to help plan and track every response.**
6. **Submit a response matrix with your proposal to make evaluation easy.**

---

1 Do what the prospect asks when you get to the proposal stage.

If the prospect asks you to turn in your proposal while standing on your head, practice standing on your head.

Do what the prospect requests. Noncompliance is the easiest way to eliminate an unwanted bidder.

Many popular selling systems advocate noncompliant solutions. These systems suggest that offering a compliant solution puts all power into the prospect's hands, enabling the prospect to compete on price. They recommend offering an innovative, value-added solution that increases the seller's margins.

Noncompliant solutions can win, providing you are early in the sales process when you can influence the prospect to make the specifications less proscriptive or to change the specifications.

After the final bid request is issued, noncompliant solutions are riskier. Your degree of risk depends on the restrictiveness of the buying rules and the relative power of the individuals influencing the buying decision.

---

2 Prepare a compliance checklist for all formal bid requests.

Compliance checklists are lists of bid request requirements and prospect questions that must be answered in your proposal.

Compliance checklists are used to verify that all requests are answered. When proposal responses are formally scored, the added points from many slightly better answers are easily erased by a zero on missing responses.

Proposal writers and managers may not prepare compliance checklists because, "They take too much time when we could be writing the proposal."

For guidelines on handling multilayer bid requests, see **Outlining.**

NOTE: The terms compliance checklist, requirements checklist, and compliance requirements checklist mean the same. A response checklist is different; however, because it includes the response to the compliance requirement.

Preparing compliance checklists and outlines early in the proposal planning process saves more time than they take to prepare.

The procedure to prepare a compliance checklist is listed in figure 1. Compliance checklists are most important for large, multilayer bid requests.

1. Follow the order of topics and paragraphs in the bid request. Within paragraphs, follow the order of sentences.
2. List each requirement as a separate checklist item. If a sentence or paragraph contains two or more requirements, then list each requirement as a separate item.
3. Use the prospect's words and phrases in the checklist. Do NOT paraphrase. Use the prospect's language.
4. Begin each item with the action verb used in the bid request, such as *identify, list, discuss, show, indicate, demonstrate,* and *describe.* These verbs tell the proposal writer what the prospect wants to see in the proposal.
5. Use the compliance checklist as a guide to write each section. Base your section outline on the checklist, and follow the order of topics exactly as it appears in the checklist.
6. Periodically check to see that every requirement has been met.

Figure 1. Compliance Checklists Increase Compliance. *Follow the steps listed to develop a compliance checklist before your initial kickoff meeting. Compliance checklists help you determine writing assignments, estimate page requirements, assess boilerplate applicability, and estimate graphic support needs.*

Note how the following compliance checklist example clarifies precisely what the proposal must contain.

Bid Request Excerpt

What diagnostic tools are built into your system? Indicate those that are available only to the network management personnel. Indicate those that are available only from the central switch site and those that are available from nodes, terminal locations, etc.

Compliance Checklist

✔ Specify the diagnostic tools built into our system.

✔ Indicate the diagnostic tools available only to the network management personnel.

✔ Indicate the diagnostic tools available only from the central switch site.

✔ Indicate the diagnostic tools available from nodes, terminal locations, etc.

3

Prepare a compliance checklist for all informally solicited bid requests.

When you do not have a formal bid request, list the prospect's requirements from meetings, phone calls, prospect file notes, and intelligence resources.

By building the compliance checklist collaboratively with the prospect, you offer a valuable service, you can potentially influence the requirements, and you can reduce surprise requirements and prevent elimination for noncompliance.

Prepare compliance checklists for informally solicited proposals as follows:

1. List the requirements as you understand them.
2. Verify your list and add requirements as you discover them in face-to-face meetings and phone calls.
3. Prioritize your list by categories.
4. Seek final prospect buy-off via a read-through when possible.
5. Submit a copy of the final compliance checklist along with your proposal.

In some instances, this "checklist" may become the basis for a subsequent competitive bid analysis. If so, you have the advantages of more time and influence. For example:

A commercial property manager was sending an unsolicited letter proposal to prospective tenants. A table included in the letter, shown below, suggested features that should be required, what features were available in the offered property, and provided a place to compare competing properties. Based on the features listed, no competing property could be superior. No seller would list a feature that was not available unless the seller knew the prospect did not want that feature.

Recommended features	Sunset Green	#1	#2
Covered parking	✓	____	____
24 x 7 security	✓	____	____
Motorway access < 1/4 mile	✓	____	____
Metro access < 2 blocks	✓	____	____

4 Use compliance checklist shortcuts with caution and understanding.

Many potentially timesaving short cuts are possible. Each carries risk, as summarized in figure 2.

METHOD	ADVANTAGES	DISADVANTAGES
Colored markers used to highlight all *shall's* indicating bidder requirements.	Fast.	• Not all requirements are preceded by a *shall.* More difficult and expensive to distribute to each writer.
Underline or circle, then number each requirement.	Fast, easily photocopied.	• Easy to separate imperative verb from the requirement.
Physically cut requirements from a copy of the bid request. Group by section for writer assignments.	Can be done anywhere, low-tech.	• Can separate imperative verb from the requirement. Lost pieces of paper.
Electronically cut and paste requirements into spreadsheet program. Assign section number and sort list for writers' assignments.	Reliable, available. Imperative verb can be duplicated down a column. No added cost.	• Can take more time than electronic stripping programs.
Proposal preparation software does the stripping electronically and prepares writer packages.	Appears to be easier, especially on large bid requests.	• Can be expensive and hard to operate. • Still requires careful review. • Items can be easily missed.

Figure 2. Comparing Bid Request Stripping Methods. *Your choice of stripping method will depend on the size and number of bid requests to be stripped and the risk of potential errors.*

5 Construct a response matrix early to help plan and track every response.

A response matrix, sometimes called a compliance matrix, is a road map for the evaluator that connects the prospect's individual bid request requirements or questions to each specific response in your proposal.

Response matrices may also include summary responses and indications of compliance or noncompliance.

Prepare response matrices as a routine part of proposal planning prior to the kickoff meeting. Preparing them just before submittal is similar to preparing as-built drawings after the building is complete. Both are time consuming, often incomplete, and easily skipped.

The response matrix shown in figure 3 is the type prepared early in the proposal planning stage. Not all of this matrix would be submitted with the proposal.

An expanded bid request compliance matrix, shown in figure 4, is constructed by the proposal manager to help manage the preparation of individual proposal sections.

VOL II TECH PROPOSAL SEC/PARA	PROPOSAL OUTLINE TITLES	PARA PAGES (SUB TOTAL)	SECTION PAGES (SUB TOTAL)	RESP AUTHOR	MUST COMPLY WITH BID REQUEST REQUIREMENTS					
					PPI	EVAL CRIT.	SOW PARA	SPEC FNCTNL RQMTS.	CDRL	OTHER BID REQUEST REQUIRE-MENTS
2	Technical Discussion		150	Lead	L.043(D)	M.2.0	1			
2.1	TI-SNIPS Concept Selection	0.25	3.00	Arthur	L.043(D)	M.2.1	1.2		4	
2.1.1	Concept Review and Comp	0.25		Arthur	L.043(D)	M.2.1				
2.1.2	Concept Selection	2.50		Arthur	L.043(D)	M.2.1				
2.2	Power System Concept	7.00	67.25	Arthur	L.043(D)	M.2.2			4	WBS 2.04
2.2.1	System Description	0.25		Arthur	L.043(D)		1.3	1.3.2		WBS 2.1
2.2.2	Reactor Subsystem	8.00		B. Bradbury	L.043(D)	M.22a	1.3.1	2.3.3, 1.3.4, 1.3.5		WBS 2.2
2.2.3	Power Conversion Subsystem	8.50		C. Chuck	L.043(D)	M.2.2b	1.3.2	1.2.1, 2		WBS 2.3
2.2.4	Distribution Subsystem	10.50		D. Davidson	L.043(D)	M.2.2c	1.3.3	1.3.4		WBS 2.4
2.2.4.1	Reaction Control	8.00		D. Davidson	L.043(D)	M.2.2c	1.3.3.1	1.2.14		WBS 2.4.1
2.2.4.2	Power Distribution and Cond	4.00		D. Davidson	L.043(D)	M.2.2c	1. 3.3.2	1.2.14		
2.2.5	Heat Rejection Subsystem	7.50		E. Evans	L.043(D)	M.2.2d	1.3.3.3	1.3.3		
2.2.6	Shielding Subsystem	7.00		F. Foe	L.043(D)	M.2.2e	1.3.3.4	1.2.10		
2.2.7	Power System-to-Spacecraft I/F	6.50	10	G. Grand	L.043(D)	M.2.2f	1.3.3.5	1.2.5		
2.3	Design Maturity and Risk Mitigation	0.25		B. Jones	L.043(D)	M.2.3	1.4	1.2.16		
2.3.1	Risk Identification and Red Team	2.75		B. Jones	L.043(D)	M.2.3.1	1.5		2	
2.3.2	Key Technology	1.00		B. Jones	L.043(D)		1.5			
2.3.3	Critical Components	4.00		B. Jones	L.043(D)		1.6			
2.3.4	TI-SNPS Flight Demo Prog	2.00		B. Jones	L.043(D)		1.7	1.2.3	7	
2.4	Projected Performance	0.25	10	T. Hanks	L.043(D)	M.24	1.2	1.2	4	
2.4.1	Performance Requirements	0.25		T. Hanks	L.043(D)		1.2	1.2	4	
2.4.1.1	Power Level	0.50		T. Hanks	L.043(D)		1.2.1	1.2.1		
2.4.1.2	Power Density	0.50		T. Hanks	L.043(D)		1.2.2	1.2.2		
	Total	**81.75**	**90.25**							

Figure 3. Formal Bid Request Compliance Matrix. *A response matrix prepared early in the proposal planning cycle allocates pages to each section and assigns authors. Relevant sections are listed. Tasks are tied to relevant Statement of Work (SOW) sections and Contract Data Requirements List (CDRL).*

PROP SEC/ PARA NO.	PROPOSAL OUTLINES TITLES	PARA PAGES (SUB TOTAL)	SEC PAGES (SUB TOTAL)	RESP AUTHOR	PPI L-2 PARA 3.2.X	PARA TITLE	REQUIREMENT	EVAL CRITERIA M.4	PARA TITLE	REQUIREMENTS
II	Management Proposal		25.0	K Holliway	8.2	Management Proposal	• Describe mgmt structure and processes used to control prog • Describe procedures, methods, tools and facilities you intend to use. • Describe how mgmt methods are proactive and process oriented	3.0 4.0	• Gen Basis for award • Mgmt area	• Mgmt and Tech areas are equal; cost is third • 3 items in Mgmt Area: 1st-Prog Mgmt, Resource Mgmt & Mgmt. Control are less important than 1st and are of equal importance to each other
1	Introduction		2.0		3.2.1	Introduction	• Incl. in matrix form the skills, experience, and qualif. of indiv's who will perform contract tasks, what portion of the work they will perform, and percent of time applied to efforts. Key people resumes req'd			
2.	Program Mgmt Plan	0.25	11.0		3.2.2	Program Mgmt Plan	• Address orgnl structure F&R assignments, procedures, processes & rptg rqrmts for initiation, monitoring control completion, test and validation of tasks, projects & prgms. PMPs/be responsive to draft PCO TL	3.0 4.0	• Gen Basis for award • Mgmt area	• Mgmt and Tech areas are equal; cost is third • 3 items in Mgmt Area: 1st-Prog Mgmt, Resource Mgmt & Mgmt. Control are less important than 1st and are of equal importance to each other
2.1	Mgmt Plan. and Control				PTL 4.1	Task 1 Mgmt Planning & Control	• Establish a prog origin structure, policies, and procedures to ensure all program objectives are met			

Figure 4. Expanded Bid Request Compliance Matrix. *Expanded bid request compliance matrices are used on large, complex responses with multiple writers. Managers, writers, and reviewers find them useful to develop a coordinated, coherent response with minimum revision. Note that many of the words in the requirements column are abbreviated to reduce the size of the table.*

6 Submit a response matrix with your proposal to make evaluation easy.

The bid request response locator, shown in figure 5, is submitted as part of the proposal. Additional columns are often added that summarize whether the response is compliant. If you are worried about being capriciously eliminated for noncompliance, consider the hairsplitting, "Compliant with qualification."

Another best practice is to place a "Why us?" summary on the first page of every volume or major section of a proposal. This summary is usually a table that relates the key prospect requirements, your offering, and your unique discriminator(s). This table helps the evaluator tie your offering to their needs and makes it easy for them to justify selecting your solution. If you cannot convince them in one page, you need to refine your solution.

BID REQUEST REQUIREMENT		PROPOSAL RESPONSE	BID REQUEST REQUIREMENT		PROPOSAL RESPONSE
SECTION	TITLE		SECTION	TITLE	
L.24(b)(3)(i)a.	Technical Approach	2.1	SOW 3.1	Task Completion Schedule	4.2
L.24(b)(3)(i)b.	Understanding of Goals/Objectives	2.2	SOW 3.2	Review Candidate GGSF Exper	2.1.1.1, 3.1.1
L.24(b)(3)(i)c.	Understanding of Configurational . . .	2.3	SOW 3.3	Analyses of Candidate GGSF Exper	2.1.1.1, 2.1.2.1, 3.1.1
L.24(b)(3)(i)d.	Understanding of Goals/Objectives	2.4	SOW 3.4	Identify Facility Subsystems	2.2, 2.3.2, 3.1.1
L.24(b)(3)(i)e.	Understanding of Goals/Objectives	2.1–2.5	SOW 3.5	Assess GGSF and MCPF Tech Area	3.1.1.3
L.24(b)(3)(ii)	Technical Approach/Methodology	3.1	SOW 3.6	Critical Supporting Areas	2.1.1.2, 2.2, 2.5.3, 3.1.1, 3.2
L.24(b)(3)(iii)	Innovation	3.2	SOW 3.7	Issues Requiring Further Study	3.1.1.2
L.24(b)(3)(iv)	Study Plan	4.1	SOW 3.8	Identify Freedom Subsystems	2.4
L.24(b)(3)(v)	Study Schedule	4.2	SOW 3.9	Rqmts for Use of A1 Expert Systems	2.3.2, 3.2
L.24(b)(3)(vi)	Key Personnel	App.	SOW 3.10	Assess Facility Mission Rqmts	2.2, 3.1.1, 4.2
L.24(b)(3)(vii)	Study Manager	5.2, App.	SOW 3.11	Final Report	4.1

Figure 5. Bid Request Response Locator. *Response locators enable the evaluator to easily find answers to the questions in the bid request. Notice that because page numbers are not included, this matrix can be prepared early. Waiting until page numbers are firm puts too much work at the end. Section numbers are sufficient.*

Cover letters are a common part of most proposal submittals. While cover letters have relatively little influence on the evaluation team when compared to the executive summary, they are conspicuous by their absence.

See **Executive Summary.**

Cover letters should reflect the key themes found on the first page of your executive summary but be far less comprehensive. The focus of the cover letter will depend on the reader.

When the person receiving the shipment has a role in selecting the winner, the cover letter presents another opportunity to sell.

For a large, multivolume proposal shipped in several boxes, include a letter of transmittal that serves as a packing list to tell the person who accepts delivery what is included.

Three model cover letters are included in the **Model Documents** *section, pp. 241–243.*

Cover Letters

1. **Use your cover letter to cite your key discriminator, directly tied to a key prospect need.**
2. **Have the cover letter signed by the highest ranking person in your organization who touched the prospect during the capture planning phase.**
3. **In a single page, include two or three powerful reasons to select your offer.**
4. **Close with a short paragraph that points the reader to your proposal, includes the project name and RFP number, gives a contact person and number, and cites terms such as how long your offer is valid.**

1

Use your cover letter to cite your key discriminator, directly tied to a key prospect need.

See **Choosing Correct Words** *and* **Customer Focus.**

Open with a client-focused theme statement like the opening to your executive summary:

> ReadyMaids.com can continue to focus on the explosive growth in home cleaning services by selecting an information technology (IT) support vendor like Global Information Technology (GIT), with an entire division specializing in franchise support.

Avoid opening with the dreaded cliche:

> Thank you for the opportunity to submit our proposal for IT support.

Also avoid this seller-focused opener:

> Global Information Technology is pleased to present our proposal for IT support.

2

Have the cover letter signed by the highest ranking person in your organization who touched the prospect during the capture planning phase.

Skeptical prospects know that a cover letter signed by the CEO of a multibillion dollar organization simply means someone wrote a letter and got it signed.

Draft it early and have it signed by the highest ranking person in your organization that the prospect knows. Reinforce this contact during the capture phase by arranging a meaningful interchange between the signer and a senior person in the prospect's organization. Then reference the meeting in your cover letter:

> In our meeting on October 15, Superintendent Austin indicated that the Sunrise District was looking for a partner that understood the needs of metropolitan school districts.

3

In a single page, include two or three powerful reasons to select your offer.

Cite any value-added aspects of your offer that save time, save money, or reduce risk. Cite any special efforts you have taken to address key prospect concerns. Reinforce any truly unique experience or outstanding performance with the prospect's organization or a similar organization. Carefully avoid using a patronizing or arrogant tone.

4

Close with a short paragraph that points the reader to your proposal, includes the project name and RFP number, gives a contact person and number, and cites terms such as how long your offer is valid.

Avoid closing with a legal-sounding paragraph that essentially says you are not responsible for anything. Consider adding the following to a concise closing paragraph:

- Note what is included in your proposal.
- Include a contact name, address, and number.
- Indicate how long your offer is valid.
- Cite special terms or conditions.
- Cite the contract name and RFP number.
- Indicate the signing person is authorized to make this offer.

Customer focus is a trait that everyone claims but few communicate. When anyone in a business development role is asked, "Are you customer focused?" everyone answers, "Of course!"

What features make one document more customer focused than another document? Do different individuals perceive customer focus differently? Do individuals with different cultural backgrounds or positions perceive customer focus differently?

To determine the answer, individuals were asked to rank the customer focus of five documents. The base document was a 2-page executive summary. For each of the five documents, appearance and content were fixed while writing and organization varied. Figure 1 lists the controlled and variable features of the five test documents. All five versions were by the same seller to the same prospect for the same products and services.

To date, over 1,000 people have completed this exercise in the United States, Canada, United Kingdom, Sweden, continental Europe, Brazil, Mexico, and mixed groups from Latin America, South America, and Asia. The results have been consistent across cultures:

1. Seventy percent ranked the same document as most customer focused.
2. The composite ordinal ranking was consistent from group to group.
3. The least customer-focused version was ranked last by 70 percent of the participants.
4. Only about one-half of the participants could cite specific mechanical aspects of the writing that explained their ranking.

Eight guidelines indicate how to increase the perceived customer focus of a document. Readers rate a document's customer focus higher when more of the guidelines are followed and when the guidelines are followed more frequently.

CONTROLLED FEATURES	VARIABLE FEATURES
• Page layout • Fonts • Visuals • Action captions • Quotes from users	• Cites prospect's organizational vision • Links prospect's vision to the immediate purchase • Cites the prospect's hot buttons • Makes ownership of the hot buttons explicit • Addresses each hot button in the order listed • Names the prospect before the seller • Names the prospect more often than the seller • Cites benefits before features

Figure 1. Customer Focus Research Experiment. *To determine what features of a document affect the reader's perception of customer focus, five test documents were created. The controlled and variable features of the documents are listed. These findings are the basis for the following customer focus guidelines.*

NOTE: These guidelines to improving the customer focus of sales documents are more relevant and important when applied to executive summaries and sales letters than to individual proposal sections.

See **Executive Summary** *and* **Sales Letters.**

Customer Focus

1. **Cite the prospect organization's vision.**
2. **Link the prospect's vision directly to the immediate purchase.**
3. **Cite the prospect's hot buttons.**
4. **Make prospect ownership of the hot buttons explicit.**
5. **Address each hot button in the order listed.**
6. **Name the prospect before the seller in paragraphs and sentences.**
7. **Name the prospect as many or more times than the seller.**
8. **Cite benefits before features.**

1

NOTE: The document ranked as the most customer focused is in the **Model Documents** section, #6. Excerpts are from that model executive summary.

Cite the prospect organization's vision.

Only the top-ranked version cited the prospect organization's vision:

> Cascadia Timber is ranked as the No. 1 company in the world by Forester's Monthly for low cost, innovative forest management. Cascadia Timber Chairman Woody X. Pine set the following strategic direction:
>
> "We have to do everything better, more efficiently from a cost point of view, more effectively from an impact point of view."
>
> *Cascadia Timber Annual Report, 1996*

Too many proposal writers demonstrate their understanding of the prospect's needs by copying a few paragraphs from the bid request, demonstrating only that they can copy.

A significant minority of the participants felt that citing the prospect's vision was pandering. Yet numerous studies of buyers have found that while nearly all bidders are technically qualified, the organization selected was the one that "had the best understanding of the prospect's business."

2

Link the prospect's vision directly to the immediate purchase.

Connecting the prospect's vision to the immediate purchase demonstrates your perspective. After your offer is selected, the direct link to the organization's vision may help the project get funded over other, unrelated but competing projects.

> Cascadia Timber's Forest Management Division
>
> helps improve efficiency and effectiveness by
> *VISION*
> adopting innovative forest management practices.
> *IMMEDIATE PURCHASE*

Buyers sometimes get so close to the immediate project that they lose perspective.

3

Cite the prospect's hot buttons.

Citing the prospect's hot buttons immediately places the focus on what the prospect needs instead of what you are selling. Hot buttons are an amalgam of issues, needs, requirements, and evaluation criteria. To develop a hot button list of two to four items, do the following:

1. List all the major hot buttons you can recall.
2. Group similar hot buttons to reduce the list to two to four items.
3. Restate the grouped hot buttons using the prospect's words.

Note how the following example continues from the previous example connecting the vision and the immediate need, then transitioning into the hot buttons:

> In support of Cascadia Timber's strategic direction, the Forest Management Division verbally requested proposals for 20 ultralight aircraft to be used as a forest management tool. In our meetings with Forest Management and purchasing, individuals cited four primary needs: *IMMEDIATE NEED*
>
> 1. Affordable, portable, and easily transportable,
> 2. All-conditions observation and communication platform
> 3. Safe and easy to fly
> 4. Easy to assemble and maintain in the field
>
> *HOT BUTTONS*

4

Make prospect ownership of the hot buttons explicit.

Make ownership of their hot buttons explicit by citing your source, preferably in the prospect's organization.

The following statement lacks ownership:

> The ideal aircraft must meet four primary needs: . . .

The following makes ownership explicit:

> In our meetings with Forest Management and Purchasing, individuals cited four primary needs: . . .

Even if you have had no contact with the prospect, you can soften the statement by broadening your source:

> In our experience with other, similar forest management organizations, most cited four primary needs: . . .

If your organization has been accused of technical arrogance, you may be making statements like this:

> Cascadia Timber needs to improve forest management by purchasing an aircraft with the following features: . . .

5

Address each hot button in the order listed.

You have announced your document's organization with your hot button list. Follow it, in exact order. Make your subheadings identical to your hot buttons. Use the same words.

See **Model Documents**, *#6, for the complete example.*

Failing to follow your announced organization subtly suggests that you do not keep your word.

The following example shows how a hot-button list is reflected in subsequent subheadings.

Hot button list:

. . . you cited four primary needs:

1. ***Affordable, portable, and easily transportable***
2. ***All-conditions observation and communication platform***
3. ***Safe and easy to fly***
4. ***Easy to assemble and maintain in the field***

. . . .

1. Affordable, Portable, and Easily Transportable
(Section text omitted for brevity)

2. All-conditions Observation and Communication Platform
(Section text omitted for brevity)

3. Safe and Easy to Fly
(Section text omitted for brevity)

4. Easy to Assemble and Maintain in the Field
(Section text omitted for brevity)

6

Name the prospect before the seller in paragraphs and sentences.

Scan the opening sentences of each paragraph in your documents. Do they tend to open with the words "We," "Our," or your organization's or product's name?

NOTE: "Partner" can have positive or negative connotations, depending on the prospect. Avoid using jargon unless the prospect requests "a partner."

See **Choosing Correct Words.**

Seller-focused example

Jenair Sports can reduce Cascadia Timber's cost of forest management in remote, roadless areas by supplying 20 versatile ultralight aircraft and proven Jenair long-term support.

Prospect-focused example

Cascadia Timber can reduce the cost of forest management in remote, roadless areas by selecting a partner to supply 20 versatile ultralight aircraft that also offers proven long-term support.

The seller was not named in the second example. The words "a partner" could have been replaced with the seller's name "Jenair." Since the reader clearly knows whose proposal it is, naming the seller again is not necessary. Both are correct. Using "a partner" softens the tone. When discussing your organization, try to state what others say, not what you say about yourself. Contrast these two statements:

Seller-focused example

Colossal has 75 percent of the widget market.

Prospect-focused example

Seventy-five percent of widgets purchasers selected Colossal.

7

Name the prospect as many or more times than the seller.

Strive to mention the prospect as many or more times than you mention your organization. Include all pronouns in your count.

This measure is quite accurate in an executive summary; the ratio will drop in detailed proposal sections.

8

Cite benefits before features.

Following basic organizational principles, begin with items of greatest interest to the prospect, the benefit rather than the feature.

See **Organization.**

Note the difference in these proposal excerpts:

Jenair Sports is offering 20 Endeavor ultralights for $9,500 each, less than one-half the cost of 3/4 ton 4-wheel drive trucks. This can reduce the cost of forest management. The Endeavor offers a unique combination of features:

- The wings, tail assembly, fuselage, and down tubes are oriented along a slim axis and secured in a rugged transport case for portability.
- Two people can carry the 196-lb. fuselage crate, one carries the 45-lb. engine crate for transportability.

Compare the preceding excerpt with a more prospect-focused version:

Cascadia Timber can reduce the cost of forest management by purchasing 20 Endeavor ultralights from Jenair for $9,500 each, less than one-half the cost of 3/4 ton 4-wheel drive trucks. The Endeavor offers a unique combination of features:

- For portability, the wings, tail assembly, fuselage, and down tubes are oriented along a slim axis and secured in a rugged transport case.
- For transportability, two people carry the 196-lb. fuselage crate, another person carries the 45-lb. engine crate.

Rules 6 through 8 are complementary. Citing benefits first tends to pull in the prospect's name first. Closing with a benefit tends to place the prospect's name last.

Daily team management is focused on efficiently executing the proposal management plan. Detecting deviations from the plan early minimizes the cost of corrective action in a project with a fixed delivery date.

See **Storyboards** *and* **Proposal Management Plan.**

The difficulties of managing a proposal team are compounded when the following conditions exist:

- Large team
- Dispersed team
- Part-time members
- Members from different organizations
- Untrained, inexperienced members

The proposal manager has three key tools to keep the team on schedule:

1. A detailed Proposal Management Plan.
2. Daily stand-up meeting.
3. Proposal Development Worksheets (PDW) or storyboards.

When in the proposal manager role, your primary objective is to prepare a winning document, on time. Any activity that adversely impacts this objective must be identified and eliminated or managed.

Daily team management activities must be tempered by team conditions, size of the proposal, and available budget and resources.

Daily Team Management

1. **Prepare a written proposal management plan.**
2. **Define and document your solution first.**
3. **Confirm that all contributors understand their assignments.**
4. **Conduct daily stand-up meetings with the proposal team.**
5. **Focus team members on their next, immediate task.**
6. **Use storyboards to track the progress of individual writers.**
7. **Review a single aspect of all storyboards each day.**

---

1 Prepare a written proposal management plan.

See **Proposal Management Plan.**

Good proposal plans are detailed and written. Poor plans are in the manager's head. The only evidence of a quality plan is one that is written and can be both reviewed and used as a daily management tool.

The shorter the response time, the greater the need to plan because you have no recovery time.

If you think the proposal plan does not need to be written, then the proposal should not be written. No bid.

For a response time under two weeks, use a quarter of the available time to plan, then execute your plan flawlessly, and you can win.

---

2 Define and document your solution first.

Good proposals are possible with a clear, documented solution. Good proposals are impossible with an unclear, undocumented solution.

Take the time to define your baseline solution first. If you begin writing the proposal before the solution is defined, the result will be a loser full of generic descriptions, boilerplate, and *Trust me* statements, all totally lacking in customer focus.

---

3 Confirm that all contributors understand their assignments.

The kickoff meeting is where contributors to a proposal must receive answers to four basic questions:

1. What is my task?
2. How do you want it done?
3. When is it due?
4. How do I charge my time?

See **Kickoff Meeting.**

Too many organizations mistakenly use the kickoff meeting as a planning meeting rather than to establish clear task assignments.

After giving assignments, immediately follow up with contributors to confirm they understand their assignment in the context of the entire proposal.

A responsibility matrix shown in figure 1 is closely related to the the bid request compliance matrix. Develop a responsibility matrix to allow you to track the status of each writing assignment by author and due date.

The complexity of the matrix will vary with the complexity of the proposal.

Proposal Par #	Proposal Section Title	Relevant Bid Req'st. Par #'s	Author	Page Limit Target	Storyboard Assigned	1st Review Date	Final Review Date	Mock-up Review Date	Pink Team Date	Graphics Due Date	1st Draft Date	Red Team Date
None	Exec Sum	M	S. Ross	4	19 Mar	25 Mar	28 Mar	31 Mar	02 Apr	10 Apr	15 Apr	28 Apr
1.0	Tech Ov	L.2.1	W. Lou	2	21 Mar	26 Mar	28 Mar	31 Mar	02 Apr	10 Apr	15 Apr	28 Apr

Figure 1. Proposal Responsibility Matrix. *Sometimes called a program control matrix, the proposal responsibility matrix is used by proposal managers to assign and monitor the status of each section assigned to each writer. Using spreadsheet software, add a row for each task and a column for each milestone. Keep a current version prominently displayed in the proposal room and review progress in the daily stand-up meeting.*

4 Conduct daily stand-up meetings with the proposal team.

See **Team Selection and Management**.

Keep the focus on the status of the proposal and, specifically, what tasks must be completed near-term.

Hold your 15-minute stand-up meeting at the same time each day, usually the first thing each morning. Take problem-solving discussions outside the stand-up meeting. When issues surface that need discussion, determine who needs to participate, set a time to meet, then move to the next item. Record all actions assigned.

The proposal manager conducts the meeting, supported by the program or solution lead if they are different people. Potential topics include the following:

- Upcoming milestones
- Action items
- Procedural changes
- New prospect information
- Teaming or subcontract considerations
- Solution refinements
- Solution milestones or schedules
- Strategy refinements
- Changes in the bid request, proposal outline, or response assignments
- Graphics, editing, or publication support issues

When managing a dispersed team, compensate for the lack of co-location by daily video or teleconferencing and by e-mail.

Any proposal manager who assumes that everything is on track because "I have not heard about any problems from contributors" is in trouble.

5 Focus team members on their next, immediate task.

See **Scheduling**.

Writers do better with smaller tasks and shorter deadlines than with a few large tasks and longer deadlines. If task deadlines are set by day, authors interpret the deadline to be "close of business" on the due date, burdening management or production support.

Present a high-level milestone schedule showing major events at the kickoff meeting or the next subsequent meeting with the proposal team. Within a few days, turn the milestone schedule into an "inch-stone" schedule. The inch-stone schedule divides major tasks into smaller, clearly defined subtasks. Give everyone a due date and time for each assigned task. Stagger due dates and times to smooth production.

Use the stand-up meeting to reinforce progress, commend excellent work, and remind contributors what needs to be done that day. Make contributors responsible to meet the schedule to the hour. If they cannot meet it, they must reschedule with management and/or trade due times with another contributor. Inch-stones help keep contributors focused on immediate tasks, giving a sense of immediacy and completion.

6 Use storyboards to track the progress of individual writers.

See **Storyboards and Mock-ups.**

While storyboards are primarily a writer's tool, helping writers plan their sections before writing, storyboards are also powerful management tools.

Keep the most current version of each storyboard posted on the proposal room walls. You will quickly spot authors who are falling behind task. Their storyboards are often missing, empty, or do not change from day to day.

7 Review a single aspect of all storyboards each day.

See **Reviews** *and* **Strategy.**

Proposal managers need a method to achieve consistency, coherency, and compatibility across all proposal sections.

Trying to read all the storyboards daily becomes overwhelming. Instead focus on reviewing a single aspect of all storyboards each day.

Select a member of your core team to review storyboards with you, choose one of the following topics, establish your review standards, and review the same topic on each storyboard:

- Theme statements
- Graphics
- Action captions
- Summaries
- Introductions
- Benefit/Feature table
- Risk management
- Relevant experience and past performance
- Compliance
- Content compatibility with other storyboards
- Ghosting

Discriminators are features of your offer or solution that (1) differ from a competitor's offer and (2) are important to the prospect. Both conditions must be met.

The strongest discriminators are true for you and not true for any of your competitors. The weakest discriminators are true for you and not true for at least one of your competitors.

If you are not certain that your discriminators are features, see **Features, Advantages, and Benefits.**

The strength of a discriminator also depends on its importance to the prospect. The CEO of a large defense contractor once said, "We must identify at least one truly unique discriminator to justify bidding."

If the buying organization can discern no discriminators among the various offers, then low price becomes the remaining discriminator. However, most buyers say that relatively small differences between offers become the discriminators among the winner and the losers.

Discriminators

1. **Identify discriminators by understanding your prospect, your competitor, and yourself.**
2. **Identify both positive and negative discriminators and position them as positively as possible.**
3. **Continuously reexamine whether a discriminator still discriminates.**
4. **Develop discriminators by continuing to define them more specifically.**
5. **Emphasize discriminators that focus on people, experience, performance, and understanding of the prospect's business. They are usually the most unique discriminators.**

---

1 Identify discriminators by understanding your prospect, your competitor, and yourself.

When you rent a car, do you ask about the color of the car? No?

When you purchase a car, do you ask about the color of the car? Yes?

If so, paint color is a discriminator when you buy but not when you rent.

Many sellers have either not seen what their competitors offer or rely on obsolete data about their competitors. When you claim to have a unique approach but do not, then you lose credibility with your prospect.

Even worse, many writers know so little about what they offer that they describe it generically:

> We offer an experienced network technician.

Versus the inexperienced network technician you or your competitor usually offers?

Prospects, often not experts in what they are buying, need help to determine the importance of your discriminators. When you do not know specifically what your competitor offers, discriminate your features against other criteria, like national averages, independent study results, or to other approaches that you considered but rejected as inferior.

Consider these good examples:

> Our job site safety record shows that we experience 50 percent fewer lost-time accidents than the national average for comparable construction activity.

> While not all outsourced employees will choose to transition to a new support vendor, independent studies by the Acme Group show that our job offer acceptance rate is 14 percent above the industry average, and that our retention rate long-term is equal to the retention rate of new employees.

> We considered using a fast-track construction approach, which initially appeared to cut four weeks from the construction schedule. However, after studying the local permitting review and approval process, we decided it might offend state regulatory officials and actually increase the risk of expensive schedule delays.

2 Identify both positive and negative discriminators and position them as positively as possible.

Many proposal writers focus exclusively on their positive discriminators. Also identify and deal with your negative ones:

Negative discriminator

Our company manufactures the only seals ever used on submarines that operate below 20,000 meters. Recently a seal failed, endangering the crew. Our client then spent $250 million to determine the cause, with our assistance.

Clearly, the seal failure is a major negative discriminator. A possible reply:

As the only designer and manufacturer of seals for submarines operating below 20,000 meters, and after spending $250 million learning how to improve seal design, can you afford to teach another supplier how to make them?

While possibly too direct for some in a written proposal, articulate the positive side of your negative discriminators.

3 Continuously reexamine whether a discriminator still discriminates.

Many procurements have been lost because the seller assumed that the reason they won the last contract still applied.

Consider these examples:

Decaffinated coffee is far more popular in the evening than in the morning. The power of the discriminator to an individual may be cyclical each day.

A major engine manufacturer won a large order by selling a replacement engine that offered greater thrust. In the next competition they followed the same strategy, offering increased thrust as their key discriminator. They lost when the prospect calculated the life-cycle cost of the additional fuel and judged it more important than increased thrust.

Here the prospect's perceived needs changed. Also, the factions with power may have changed from users to the economic buyer.

4 Develop discriminators by continuing to define them more specifically.

Note the progression from generic to specific:

Experienced manager.

Experienced project manager.

All project managers have a minimum of 10 years of experience.

Fred Jones, our proposed manager, has 10 years of project management experience.

Fred Jones, our proposed project manager, also managed the similar North Cove project to an on-time delivery and within budget.

A writer in a national proposal publication coined the phrase "generic specific," words that sound specific but are really generic. Discriminate by being specific and offering proof.

Generic Specific Language

The program manager will regularly review the risk log with the program team and pursue mitigation actions as needed.

Specific Language Revision

Dave Lee, Program Manager, will review the risk log every Friday and publish corrections on the program website by close of business on the following Monday.

What is the real meaning of a discriminator like the following:

200 years of experience on our team

20 people for 10 years; or 200 people for 1 year? Be more specific by quantifying, if possible.

Consider another example:

Improved fuel economy

We may fail to quantify because we do not know how much fuel economy will improve, we are too lazy to find out, or we do not want to be held accountable.

Be as specific as possible. Oddly enough, the claim of a 14.5 percent improvement is more credible than a 15 percent claim, appearing to be more precise.

5 Emphasize discriminators that focus on people, experience, performance, and understanding of the prospect's business. They are usually the most unique discriminators.

See **Relevant Experience/ Past Performance**.

See **Executive Summary**, *and* **Features, Advantages. and Benefits**.

Each person is unique; even identical twins are not truly identical. If the prospect values the differences in the abilities of the individuals you propose, use these differences as discriminators.

Frequently, sellers throw away the opportunity to use individuals as their discriminators by stating:

All our people are good; it does not matter who you get.

By the time the contract is awarded, we do not know who will actually be available.

We do not have a Big Name like our competitors, so we will not name anyone. We do not play Bait-and-Switch.

Maximize the prospect's interest in the individuals you propose by building a rapport between the prospect and these key individuals before the bid request is issued.

Consider your own purchase of skilled services, such as selecting the person or company to remodel your home. Nearly everyone in this situation wants to know, "Who will actually be in my home doing the work while I am away?"

No two companies have been awarded the same jobs, so your specific experience is different. If you can persuade the prospect to care about the difference, you have a discriminator.

Extend your discussions of experience and performance beyond the appendix or a separate past experience or a past performance section of the proposal. Cite experience and performance throughout your proposal to substantiate all claims. Use the Success Story Template on p. 154 to present your experience and performance in a customer-focused manner.

Most prospects for complex systems and services can readily identify several organizations with sufficient talent, expertise, and resources.

The critical discriminator often becomes the selling organization that demonstrates the best understanding of the prospect's business, vision, and immediate needs, and then shows how the seller can help the prospect achieve this strategic vision.

Discriminate yourself by demonstrating your understanding of the prospect's business throughout your entire proposal. Do not limit it to the executive summary and finals briefing.

Electronic submittal of proposals is increasing, but no common approach has emerged. Electronic submittal for new competitive procurements is often a backup to paper submittal.

NOTE: The technology of electronic submittal will continue to evolve rapidly. This entry may be obsolete prior to publishing. A good source of current information will be various Federal agency websites and the Association of Proposal Management Professionals (APMP), a professional organization which sponsors an Electronic Procurement Task Force. Contact APMP at 909.659.0789; apmpinfo@aol.com; or http://www.apmp.org/national/.

The specified electronic submission format usually does not conform with the format bidders typically use to prepare proposals. Many prospects request text and graphics in combinations of software that do not work well together.

The appropriate submittal format depends on how the electronic submittal will be used. If you can influence the prospect, recommend the following formats, based on the prospect's objectives:

- **To archive,** the seller's format should be sufficient, providing it is prepared with a widely available package.
- **To support the paper-version evaluation,** Adobe® Acrobat® PDF format seems to be the best choice. The free viewer lets evaluators search text, copy, paste, print, and view the entire page with integrated graphics and text.
- **To enable paperless evaluation,** most available commercial packages will generate Acrobat PDF files with the above capabilities.

Submission delivery refers to how the prospect wants the electronic version delivered. Most want a physical media submitted, such as ZIP™ disk or CD-ROM. Submittal via the web raises concerns about security, time stamping, return receipts, file corruption, or simply whether potentially printed and/or viewed copies will appear as intended.

Often purchasers from U.S. government agencies have page limited proposals to reduce the evaluation effort required and the time and cost to prepare the proposal.

Unfortunately, file-size limitations often bear little relationship to the printed size of a proposal. Different software requires different file sizes, and later versions of the same software are usually larger.

Graphics file sizes vary depending on whether they are pixel or raster based. Scanned images can be monsters, depending on the resolution. The graphics inserted into print files often get even larger.

About the only meaningful limitation that is relevant to the individual evaluator is the number of pages, whether physical or viewed onscreen.

Electronic Submittals

1. **Follow each prospect's instructions exactly or do not bid.**
2. **Use the Adobe® Acrobat® PDF file format whenever possible.**
3. **Check and recheck for viruses.**
4. **Use forced page breaks to control pagination.**
5. **Use graphic files that offer adequate resolution for printing.**
6. **Submit on CD-ROM when security is an issue.**
7. **Learn and test all systems early in the preparation process.**
8. **Furnish at least one hard copy, if allowed by the prospect.**
9. **Consider a landscape, three-column, or PDF format for proposals that will be reviewed onscreen.**

1 Follow each prospect's instructions exactly or do not bid.

Following the rules is not an option. Buy the hardware or software required to conform or do not bid. Use the software packages, versions, or releases specified. If none are specified and you do not know what the prospect uses, ask. Use the same hardware platform the prospect uses to reduce problems.

2 Use the Adobe® Acrobat® PDF file format whenever possible.

Files prepared in most common word-processing packages, as well as all leading desktop publishing software can be converted to PDF (portable document format) files. The viewed version is identical on any platform and prints reliably on all printers, including offset press when properly packaged.

3 Check and recheck for viruses.

The last thing you need is to infect the prospect's system with a computer virus. The chances of passing on a virus increase proportionally to the following factors:

- More contributors
- Greater use of boilerplate
- More geographically dispersed teams
- More contributors in multiple countries
- Greater use of web resources

Check for viruses early, often, and just prior to shipping after **all** reviews are complete.

4 Use forced page breaks to control pagination.

Following this guideline will help evaluators see the material as you intended. However, no solution is fool proof.

Pages viewed on-screen may look different on different screens, depending on the screen size and display settings. Even with identical computer hardware and software, different printers with different print drivers or fonts from different type houses might make a page print and/or display differently. Even worse, the different print drivers and font sources can change pagination, making your table of contents and index incorrect.

5 Use graphic files that offer adequate resolution for printing.

The goal is to submit graphic files that require as little memory as possible without producing a "grainy" or "pixelated" appearance. Unless producing the proposal for offset printing, 150 dpi (dots per inch) is generally adequate for most laser or inkjet printers. For on-line viewing, a 72 dpi resolution is adequate.

Reduce file size by creating *.jpeg* or *.jpg* (joint photographic experts group) or *.gif* (graphics interchange format) files. Smaller files make viewing, searching, and printing faster for evaluators.

6 Submit on CD-ROM when security is an issue.

CD-ROM is one of the most compact and cost-effective means of storing and submitting data. They are not affected by magnetic fields and hold more data than disks.

7 Learn and test all systems early in the preparation process.

"Murphy" shows up in every proposal effort. Only the naive fail to test production systems, including the electronic ones.

An "expert" always assures that there will be no problems. Do not bet your job on an expert's reassurances.

8 Furnish at least one hard copy, if allowed by the prospect.

Just in case something does go wrong, a hard copy will ensure you meet submittal instructions. Despite requesting electronic proposals, prospect evaluation teams with multiple members will often have a few who do not like to evaluate on-screen. These evaluators will appreciate having a choice of evaluation media.

9 Consider a landscape, 3-column, PDF format for proposals that will be reviewed onscreen.

See **Page and Document Design**.

NOTE: Some evaluators also evaluate onscreen. With a single monitor, onscreen evaluators may prefer a narrower portrait presentation. Alternatively, they may use an additional monitor or may place the evaluation window above or below the proposal window. If so, the wider page would be preferred.

The best page design for A4 (a metric standard of 210mm x 297mm, or 8.268" x 11.693") or 8.5" x 11" paper may not be the best design for a computer screen. For support, consider the evolution of web pages. Early web pages often were taken directly from paper documents with little modification and were ineffective.

Proposal page designs tend to be portrait, meaning a larger height than width. Computer screens tend to be square or have a larger width than height. Consider going to a two- or three-column format to make your proposal easier to read onscreen. Use PDF format to ensure the viewer sees the content exactly as you intended, regardless of computer platform.

Another option is to send a hyperlinked file, but only if you have the necessary tools and skills. A hyperlinked file contains embedded links to additional files or screens that may contain graphics, supporting data, more detailed explanations, and full-motion video with sound.

A veteran proposal manager for a major defense contractor had noted a dramatic reduction in production costs when proposals were delivered to prospects in the three basic formats: PDF, all text in the prospect's word-processing software, and all graphics in the prospect's presentation software.

Keep the following in mind when preparing electronic submittals:

- Be specific in your requests to prospects to avoid being surprised by their answers.
- Always collaborate with the prospect to understand what will work best for both of your organizations.
- Explicitly follow each prospect's final instructions. Surprises are almost always negative. The best time for constructive collaboration is early in the sales cycle.

The converse of this guideline also applies. Consider submitting an electronic copy on CD-ROM in addition to the hard copy required by the prospect. Consider this true story:

> A multivolume proposal was submitted on both paper and CD-ROM. The print production shop was in the midst of a labor dispute. Copy quality was poor. Some pages were drilled on the wrong side but still inserted in the binders. Poor-quality binders were substituted at the last minute. Volumes were not wrapped, and the binder rings opened, spilling the contents during shipment.
>
> The prospect's purchasing experts decided the proposal met submittal requirements due to the CD-ROM copy. The seller was subsequently given the chance to reassemble the binders.

Executive summaries are the most important pages in a proposal. They set the tone for individual evaluators and are often the only pages read by the decision makers.

NOTE: Three executive summaries are included in **Model Documents**, pp. 236–240.

Readers of your executive summary must clearly understand your solution and its unique benefits and be able to justify recommending your solution over competing solutions.

Effective executive summaries meet the following criteria:

- Connect your solution to the prospect's business vision
- Identify the prospect's needs and make ownership of those needs explicit
- Connect your solution directly to the prospect's needs
- Offer clear proof of your claims
- Show how you offer greater value than the competition
- Be brief but comprehensive by eliminating confusing technical details that are better explained in the body of the proposal
- Indicate the next step, usually by previewing how your proposal is organized

Executive summaries are also powerful internal tools:

- Help refine your bidding strategy
- Become a vehicle to gain senior management endorsement
- Communicate your strategy in-house to all contributors
- Drive proposal development
- Become a model for the complete proposal

Executive Summary

1. **Always include an executive summary.**
2. **Maintain a prospect- or customer-focus throughout.**
3. **Build on your existing sales process and strategy.**
4. **Organize the content to be clear and persuasive.**
5. **Expand the Four-Box Organizer into a single- or multiple-page draft.**
6. **Develop your executive summary based on proven best-in-class practices.**
7. **Follow sound writing guidelines.**
8. **Follow a defined process when preparing on short notice.**

1 Always include an executive summary.

See **Organization.**

If the prospect asks for an executive summary, submit one. If not, do so anyway.

Call it whatever the prospect calls it. Common alternatives are *Management Summary* and *Management Overview.*

Independent of what the prospect calls it, understand the difference between a summary and an introduction. A summary summarizes the essential content of your proposal. An introduction indicates how your proposal is organized. Other terms for introduction are *preview, road map,* and *informal table of contents.*

To include an executive summary when the proposal outline is strictly defined in the bid request, you have several compliant alternatives. One is to include a separately bound executive summary. Place a copy in every volume submitted, either in a pocket in the front or in the binder. Note that in page-limited proposals, the executive summary is considered part of your technical proposal.

An alternative is to make the executive summary the first part of your volume summary in each volume of the proposal.

Summarize at all levels: proposal, volume, section, and question.

2

See **Customer Focus.**

Maintain a prospect- or customer-focus throughout.

Check the focus of your executive summaries against the following criteria:

- States the prospect's vision
- Connects the vision to the immediate purchase
- Cites the prospect's hot buttons, in order of importance or the order listed in their bid request
- Makes the prospect's ownership of the hot buttons explicit
- Addresses each hot button in the order introduced
- Names the prospect more than the seller
- Names the prospect before the seller in the document, paragraphs, and sentences
- Cites benefits before features

3

See **Capture Planning** *and* **Proposal Management Plan.**

Build on your existing sales process and strategy.

To maintain a consistent message with your prospects and to save time, exploit your existing internal information sources as much as possible.

Many organizations have embraced a strategic and/or tactical sales process. Exploit it to develop your executive summary rather than starting over. With a little effort, you can map the information from existing sales templates into your executive summary.

When business development people are asked to draft the executive summary, too many still pull the last one they prepared, do a "search and replace" for prospect and product names, add one or two sentences, and submit. They continue to tailor their last executive summary for subsequent opportunities until the executive summary completely unravels.

Most of the information needed to prepare the executive summary is contained in the capture plan and proposal management plan. The three key templates summarized in figures 1, 2, and 3, are recommended to help assemble and organize the information needed for an executive summary. One example issue is completed to illustrate each template.

The most frequently overlooked portion of strategy statements is how the strategy will be implemented. Note the "how" in the following example:

> We will emphasize our ability to test full-scale components by including a photo of our Manchester test facility.

Using the information in the three templates shown as a source, prepare the Consolidated Prospect Solution Matrix shown in figure 4 with the same hot buttons/issues consolidated from the three templates.

You now have the information needed to begin drafting your executive summary.

INTEGRATED PROSPECT SOLUTION WORKSHEET

Item #	Prospect Issues	Prospect Requirement	Available Solution	Gap	Competitor Solution	Discriminators	Strategy	Action Required
1	System must be available	3-hr, response time	2-hr. resp. time	+1 hr.	3-hr. resp. time	faster response but more expensive?	Emphasize no add'l cost w/ cellular	Show current response time Show photo-- service w/cell phone

Figure 1. Integrated Prospect Solution Worksheet. *The primary focus of this template is to arrive at a competitive solution that is aligned with the prospect's issues and requirements. The strategic messages communicated in sales calls must also be communicated in the executive summary.*

Issues	Weight	Us Score	Company 1 Score	Company 2 Score
Seller's service quality	30	25	20	15
Total Score	100			

Figure 2. Bidder Comparison Matrix. *The primary focus of this template is to discern how the prospect organization perceives your team's solution versus your competitors' as it relates to the prospect's issues. In this example, service quality is seen by the prospect as a strength.*

STRATEGY STATEMENT TEMPLATE

- We will emphasize our strengths in: delivering 2-hr. response
  by: including summaries of our actual service response in the prospect's area.
- We will mitigate our weaknesses in: ____
  by: ____
- We will highlight our competitors' weaknesses in: ____
  by: ____
- We will downplay our competitors' strengths in: ____
  by: ____

©Shipley Associates

Figure 3. Proposal Strategy Statements. *The primary focus of proposal strategy statements is to identify ways you can implement or convey your strategy on paper in a written executive summary and proposal.*

CONSOLIDATED PROSPECT SOLUTION WORKSHEET

	#1	#2	#3	#4
Hot Button	Improve system availability			
Solution	2-hr. response			
Alternatives Considered	3-hr. response			
Discriminators	No addl cost Greater availability			
Proof • *Experience*	List area clients & equipment numbers.			
• *Performance*	Quote records Use quote from XYZ Co.			

©Shipley Associates

Figure 4. Consolidated Prospect Solution Worksheet. *Either complete this worksheet by extracting information from the previous three templates or simply begin with this one.*

4 Organize the content to be clear and persuasive.

Transfer the content that you developed and summarized in the Consolidated Prospect Solution Worksheet into the Four-Box Organizer, shown in figure 5. A completed example is included in the Model Documents section.

See **Model Documents 6, 7, and 8** *for examples of executive summaries in the four-box organizational style.*

The Four-Box Organizer is based on fundamental principles of how to organize a persuasive document.

See **Organization**.

The four-box organizational approach is nearly always more prospect focused than the narrative or mirror approach. The mirror approach is a mini-version of your proposal, most often used when the proposal is formally solicited and the structure is rigidly defined in the bid request.

The Four-Box Organizer includes four primary "boxes," organized around your prospect's hot button issues:

BOX 1

A Thematic Summary: Align with the prospect's vision, summarize needs, preview your solution, and indicate compliance.

BOX 2

A Preview: Introduce the prospect's hot buttons.

BOX 3

The Body: Present your solution aligned with the prospect's hot buttons, including substantiating detail as proof of your claims.

BOX 4

The Summary: Much like Box 1, summarize the needs and your solution, and state the next step.

Use the Four-Box Organizer to draft an executive summary in an organized, expandable structure. Also, use it to prepare other sales documents and presentations.

CONTENT

Box 1–PURPOSE: Recognize prospect's vision, challenges, and objectives, and introduce your solution.

Box 2–PREVIEW: Establish and prioritize prospect's needs (current needs and desired status). This is a preview of what's to come—key points, prospect issues, challenges, etc.

Box 3–DETAILS: Present solutions to the prospect's needs, emphasizing benefits and results. Identify your proof. Maintain the same organizational scheme introduced in Box 2.

Box 4–REVIEW: State why the prospect should select you. Summarize the unique contribution your solution makes to your prospect's success. Indicate the next step.

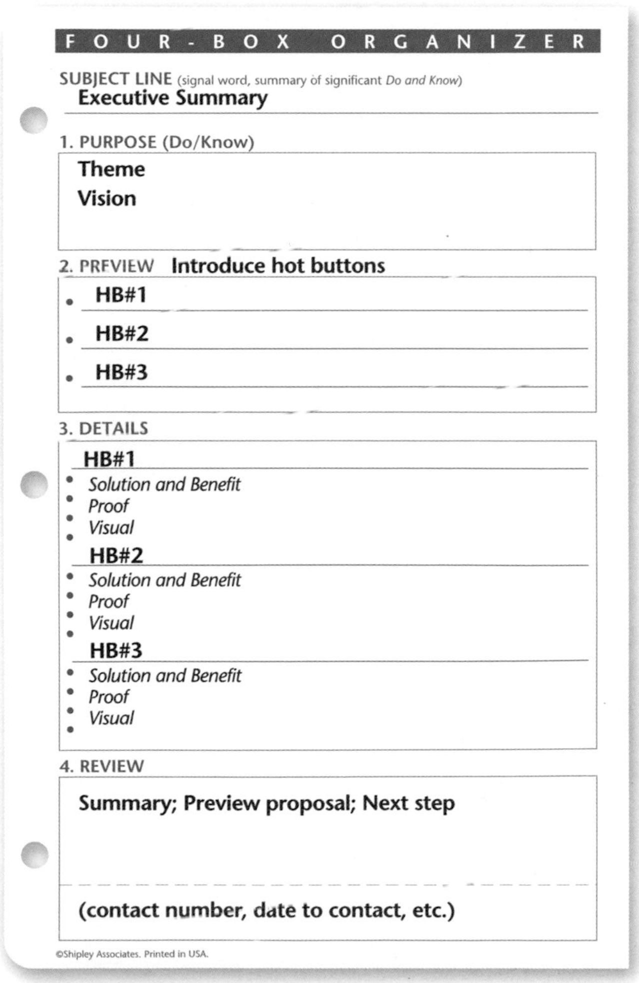
FOUR-BOX ORGANIZER

SUBJECT LINE (signal word, summary of significant *Do and Know*)
Executive Summary

1. PURPOSE (Do/Know)
Theme
Vision

2. PREVIEW **Introduce hot buttons**
- **HB#1**
- **HB#2**
- **HB#3**

3. DETAILS
HB#1
- *Solution and Benefit*
- *Proof*
- *Visual*

HB#2
- *Solution and Benefit*
- *Proof*
- *Visual*

HB#3
- *Solution and Benefit*
- *Proof*
- *Visual*

4. REVIEW
Summary; Preview proposal; Next step

(contact number, date to contact, etc.)

©Shipley Associates. Printed in USA.

PROCESS

1. Brainstorm a high-level strategic theme that encompasses the prospect's strategic direction, this specific opportunity, and your overall strategy to address needs. Write the theme and introduction to the executive summary in Box 1 of the strategy template.
2. Copy the prospect's top hot buttons from the Consolidated Prospect Solution Worksheet into Box 2 of the strategy template. These prospect hot buttons will be the basis for the bullet points.
3. Copy the hot buttons from Box 2 into Box 3 as subtitles.
4. Under each subtitle in Box 3, list the paragraphs that you plan to write to communicate your organization's solution, including:
   - The benefits and features of the solution, emphasizing any applicable discriminators.
   - The visuals of any type that will be included. Think of visuals before text.
   - Proof of claims to be included. Most should be visual.
   - Alternatives and justification of your approach.
5. Restate your overall strategy and summarize your solution and discriminators in Box 4. Suggest the next step as appropriate.

Figure 5. Using a Four-Box Organizer. *The content of each "box" is summarized on the left. Follow the process steps on the right to map your winning sales strategy into your executive summary.*

5

See **Value Propositions**.

Expand the Four-Box Organizer into a single- or multiple-page draft.

The Four-Box Organizer helps you identify key selling points within a prospect-focused, clear framework. Expand the framework into a first draft:

- Develop the visuals.
- Draft action captions for the visuals.
- Draft the text pointing evaluators to the graphics.
- Draft text describing your solutions.
- Draft text describing your experience and proof of performance.
- Summarize your costs/pricing if permitted by purchasing rules.
- Draft text summarizing how your proposal is organized.

Figure 6 illustrates how the Four-Box Organizer is expanded into a 5-page executive summary. Allocate pages in the executive summary according to the relative importance of the topic to the prospect, tempered somewhat by the relative competitive strength of this feature or aspect of your offer. Determining the total length of your executive summary is discussed in guideline 6.

If you develop value propositions as an integral part of your sales approach, summarize them in your executive summary. Present your summary value proposition in Box 1. Introduce individual value propositions in Box 2. Discuss each value proposition against your solution in Box 3. Summarize in Box 4.

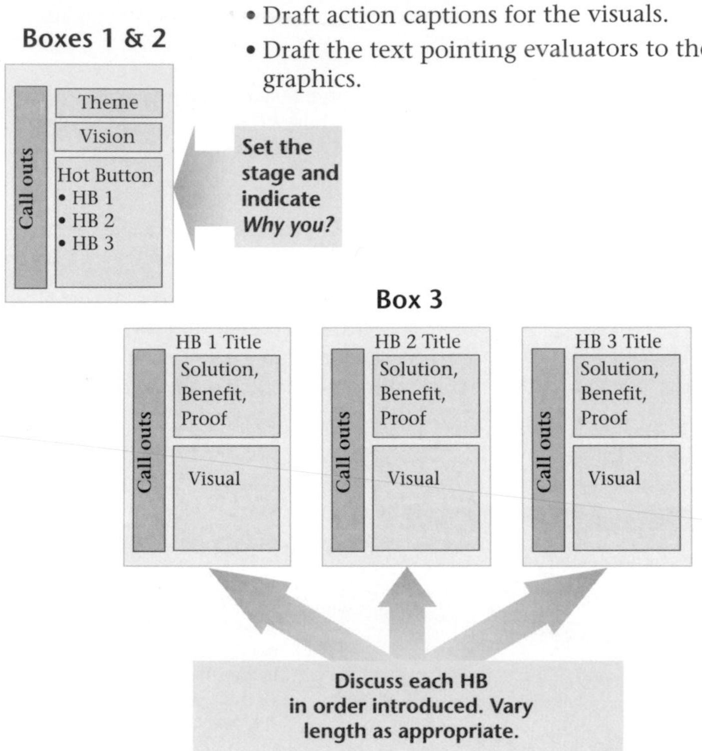

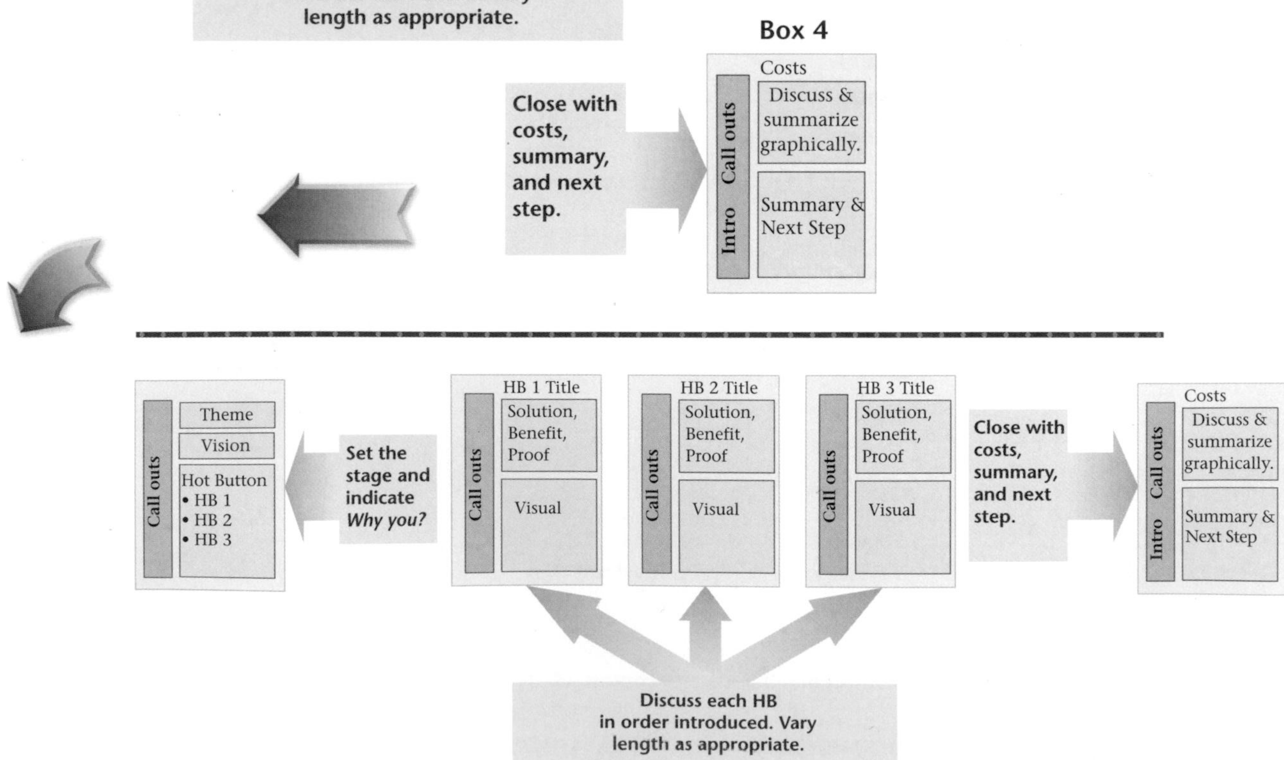

Figure 6. Expanding the Four-Box Organizer into a Multipage Executive Summary. *In this example, Boxes 1 and 2 occupy the first page. Each of the three hot buttons is discussed on a single page, in the order introduced. Visuals are included if appropriate. The last page includes the costs and a brief summary before pointing the evaluator to the rest of the proposal.*

6

Develop your executive summary based on proven best-in-class practices.

See **Presentations to Prospects.**

The following guidelines are based on years of consulting and observation of best practices in organizations with a proven ability to cost effectively win business.

- Sales should complete the first draft of the executive summary prior to the proposal kickoff meeting.
- The proposal manager or sales support should review the draft, add detail on the solution, and complete it early enough to permit review by sales and management.
- Review your draft executive summary with your prospect-coach if possible.
- Limit the total length to 5 to 10 percent of the page length of your proposal, tempered by how much you think this particular prospect's managers will read.
- Make it more visual than the rest of the proposal.
- Use your executive summary as the basis for your finals briefing. Update it if needed and distribute copies to the prospect at the end.
- Maintain your prospect focus from start to finish.

7

Follow sound writing guidelines.

See **Relevant Experience/ Past Performance.**

Follow these writing guidelines to consistently write effective executive summaries. As a manager, use it as a review checklist.

- Except in small proposals (under 20 pages), write the executive summary as a stand-alone document.
- Write executive summaries for upper-level, nontechnical decision makers.
- Make the executive summary brief but comprehensive.
- Include visuals throughout the executive summary.
- Do not assume that readers of the executive summary have been privy to information given during earlier sales calls.
- Organize the executive summary using a prospect-focused framework.
- Clearly state what you are offering and how it benefits the prospect.
- Offer clear proof of your claims.
- Tie major discriminators prominently and explicitly to a prospect issue.

8

Follow a defined process when preparing on short notice.

See **Presentations to Prospects.**

Use this abbreviated procedure when you are out of time or called on to draft an executive summary on short notice.

1. Define the prospect's hot buttons, for Box 2. (Two to five hot buttons.)
2. Allocate all major requirements, high-level aspects of your solution, and your discriminators to at least one hot button, for Box 3. If you have help, assign the drafting of one or more of the hot button portions of Box 3 after completing this step.
3. Draft a paragraph connecting the prospect's vision, the prospect's immediate need, and the most unique aspect of your solution, for Box 1.
4. Summarize the price, your solution, *Why you*, and indicate the next step, for Box 4.
5. Review the content as a team, then edit carefully. Be especially careful if you have multiple contributors.
6. Spend the rest of the time available polishing. Resist changing your solution.

If you have the opportunity to present your proposal to the prospect, use your executive summary as the basis for the presentation. Prepare the slides using your graphics and text, presented in the same order, and leave a copy of the executive summary with your prospect as a written summary of your presentation.

Features, advantages, and benefits are needed to sell effectively in person and in a proposal. Sales and proposal professionals with extensive training about features, advantages, and benefits often omit benefits, fail to link features to benefits, or mention benefits only at the end.

NOTE: Some sales systems stress features, advantages, and benefits while others dismiss them as obsolete. These different views about the importance of features, advantages, and benefits are mostly semantic, resulting from proponents trying to discriminate their sales system.

Features are separate aspects of the seller's product or service, such as speed, schedule, process training, certification, capacity, weight, size, or color. For example: (features in italics):

> The controller has *4MB of memory.*
>
> This model offers *rack-and-pinion steering, 110 horsepower, and a 7-year/70,000 mile warranty.*

Advantages are how, in the seller's opinion, the product or service can help the prospect.

Notice how the features link to advantages in the following examples: (advantages in italics):

> The controller's 4MB of memory allows you to *store more instructions* than your current model.
>
> The rack-and-pinion steering provides a *fast, accurate steering response.*

Advantages are more powerful than features, and are, in fact, potential benefits.

Benefits are advantages that can solve a problem for the prospect. They address the specific issues for which the prospect is seeking a solution. Advantages become benefits only under two conditions:

1. They are linked to the prospect's needs (issues)
2. The prospect wants them

Prospect issues are the perceived impediments to successfully achieving an objective and are also referred to as worries, hurts, or pains. Benefits help the prospect past these impediments to success. In this way, benefits become the converse of issues: if an issue represents a cost or pain, the benefit eliminates the cost and relieves the pain.

Generic examples of benefits that alleviate issues include reduced cost or risk and improved quality, reliability, profit, or safety. (Benefits in italics).

> Our CNC controller with 780MB of memory can meet your need to *electronically download larger CAD instructions.*
>
> Your interest in *avoiding Manhattan's numerous road hazards* is possible when you specify accurate, responsive, rack and pinion steering.

As selling points, features have the least impact on decision makers and can lead to price concerns if overused. Advantages are stronger than features, but if they do not convert to benefits as the sale advances they are likely to weaken the sale and lead to objections, especially in complex sales. This is especially true if the prospect does not value an advantage or views it as negative.

By educating the prospect, you can link your features to advantages, and advantages to benefits. All are important and needed. Prospects must explicitly acknowledge or confirm the value of a feature to convert its advantage into a benefit.

Benefits have the strongest and most lasting impact on prospect's decisions because they are explicitly linked to alleviating issues. In short, prospects buy benefits.

Features, Advantages, and Benefits

1. **Collaborate with the prospect to develop a common vision of the prospect's issues and needs.**
2. **Every member of the selling team must have a common understanding of the prospect's issues and needs before they discuss the features and benefits of your solution.**
3. **Convert advantages to benefits as the sale progresses.**
4. **Emphasize benefits over features in a complex sale.**
5. **Quantify benefits whenever possible.**

1

NOTE: Features linked to benefits become your potential discriminators.

See **Discriminators.**

Collaborate with the prospect to develop a common vision of the prospect's issues and needs.

Benefits cannot be accurately addressed until the prospect and the seller develop a common vision of the prospect's issues and needs and of an acceptable solution. Sellers discussing the benefits of their solution are guessing until confirmed by the prospect. Experienced sellers routinely make educated guesses about what a prospect needs. These guesses can be wrong if the prospect's needs are latent or if this prospect's needs are different from previous prospects' needs.

Consider the following statement to a prospective auto buyer:

> This auto's 4-cylinder engine, rated at 56 miles per gallon, will give you an economical way to commute.

Most proposal writers would cite the *4-cylinder engine* as the feature and *economical way to commute* as the benefit. The *economical way to commute* is a benefit if the prospect is purchasing the auto to commute. If the prospect is interested in racing the auto, this feature is a *negative* benefit. If the prospect is wealthy and unconcerned about fuel economy, the feature is merely an advantage. If the prospect is reimbursed for operating expenses, the economical operation is neither positive nor negative.

Sellers that claim to know the benefits of their offerings before collaborating with the prospect are guessing. When the prospect and seller have a common vision of the solution, the seller can accurately address customer benefits.

2

NOTE: Sales systems that dismiss the importance of features and benefits are dismissing generic benefits. Generic benefits are often advantages at best and negative at worst. To understand this nuance, review the dialog in a commercial or the captions in an advertisement. Note the "benefits" that do not interest you.

Every member of the selling team must have a common understanding of the prospect's issues and needs before they discuss the features and benefits of your solution.

Many sales professionals and their sales support staff misunderstand and misuse features, advantages, and benefits in their sales documents. Consider your proposals:

1. Are they feature-rich and benefit-poor? Prospects buy benefits. They remember benefits well after most features are forgotten.
2. Do they lead with features and close with benefits? Readers often stop reading before they get to the benefits.
3. Are features linked to benefits? Prospects with less expertise than the seller need to see the direct link between the feature and benefit to value the feature.
4. Are the benefits cited generic and only mildly appealing? Did this prospect indicate a need or desire for this benefit?

Frequently sales people accurately identify the benefits but fail to communicate them to their proposal writers. With no direct knowledge of the prospect's issues and needs, writers guess about benefits or ignore benefits. Alternatively, writers discuss what they know best, the features of their products and services. Writers with short deadlines often use previously written material and ignore benefits because it saves time. Consider this example:

> A seller touts a hair restoration product (feature) that promises to create "great hair" (advantage) and suggests an improved social life (benefit). The prospect is a confident, happily married man with great hair.
>
> This seller fails because (1) the prospect already believes he has "great hair," and (2) the prospect does not require "great hair" to improve his social life because he is happily married.

3

NOTE: To review how features and benefits are incorporated into sales planning documents and proposals, see **Action Captions, Capture Planning, Proposal Management Plan, Strategy,** and **Theme Statements.**

Convert advantages to benefits as the sale progresses.

Advantages are only valuable early in a sale because prospects will accept intelligent assumptions made by the seller. As the sale advances, the seller is expected to develop competence about specific prospect needs. Continued reliance on early assumptions indicates a lack of seller competence, i.e., "This seller does not understand what I need."

The discipline of creating capture plans, sales plans, proposal plans, early executive summary drafts, strategy white papers, theme statements, and action captions encourages the sales team to do three things:

- Identify issues
- Convert advantages to benefits
- Connect benefits to a specific feature of its offer

Organizations that rely extensively on previously written material usually submit ineffective proposals. Such proposals are full of features and advantages. Too few advantages are converted to benefits.

4 Emphasize benefits over features in a complex sale.

Complex sales are characterized by multiple buyers, multiple sellers, high values, and long sales cycles. Simple sales have a single buyer and seller, low value, and a short sales cycle.

In complex sales, buyers purchase benefits, not features. For example:

> A major organization is purchasing a $5 million computer numerically controlled machine tool. A detailed analysis of the cost and benefits of available tools and options with each tool is made to determine the bottom-line impact. No one selects machine tools because, "We liked the color."

Features can positively impact simple sales. Personal examples of a simple sale might be a telephone, TV, stereo, or hand tool. Buyers of these items justify their purchase with reasons like the following:

- It looked good.
- I liked the color.
- It fit the available space.
- It had more features than the other model.

Features place emphasis on the seller and the seller's products and services. However, prospects care about themselves and their organizations. They want to know whether the benefits generated by specific features of the seller's solution will address their issues and deliver the benefits they seek.

Prospects faced with mind-numbing lists of features that are not linked to benefits resort to looking for the lowest price.

The following example, common to many computer users and web surfers, illustrates what often happens when features are not linked to the benefit.

> We all hate to wait for our computer to complete a task. We feel the "pain" of wasted time, our issue. We talk to three experts who recommend three different solutions:

EXPERT	FEATURE	ADVANTAGE
1	Upgrade 400 MHz processor to 800 MHz	2x increase in processor speed
2	Upgrade memory from 96MB to 192MB	2 x increase in memory
3	Upgrade 56K modem to DSL connection	10 x increase in data transfer speed

> All three experts assure us that their recommended solution will save us time. We are confused by the diverse recommendations, uncertain whether any of the recommendations will solve our problem, so we don't buy. We fail to see a valid link between the feature, the claimed advantage, and the benefit we seek.

In this example, the prospect's issue is clear—wasted time. The cause, however, is not clear. When the cause is clear to the prospect, the prospect can approve the solution.

5 Quantify benefits whenever possible.

NOTE: Many organizations involved in complex sales routinely train their sales teams to develop *value propositions* for all the reasons just listed. While sales teams struggle to identify and quantify benefits, the process is beneficial. Collaboration is improved, their solution is improved, and the purchase decision is usually easier and quicker.

See **Value Propositions**.

The potential value of benefits ranges from tangible and quantifiable to intangible and perhaps nonquantifiable. Prospects determine value and will not become customers until the value of the benefits being purchased exceeds the price.

Quantifying benefits helps the seller in at least three ways:

- **Forces collaboration:** Because only prospects can determine value, the prospect and seller must collaborate to determine the value of a solution. After the prospect has helped determine the value, the solution seems more acceptable.
- **Sharpens vision:** Quantifying benefits improves the solution. The least beneficial features are dropped and more beneficial features might be added. Both the prospect and the seller gain a clearer vision of the solution.
- **Better justifies a price that is already quantified:** Prospects often make a value judgment that the solution is worth the price. However, as sales become more complex, prospects increasingly need quantitative support for their value judgment. Group purchase decisions are easier when the benefits clearly exceed the price.

Graphics are one of the most effective ways to persuade the prospect to select your solution. Graphics convey both facts and emotion, equally important aspects of effective persuasion.

High-level readers of proposals, those either making or influencing the selection decision, often only skim proposals, looking at the graphics that stand out, then reading the captions, headings, highlight statements, and the executive summary. These readers must be able to see why you should be selected without reading body text.

Detail evaluators reviewing each question and requirement will often get together and ask two questions:

- "Did anyone find anything about . . . ?"
- "Which proposal is the best proposal?"

Effective graphics leave overall positive impressions and can make it easy for evaluators to find detailed answers to questions.

Studies of retention show that after a single reading, evaluators will remember twice as much of what they see in a graphic as what they read in text. In addition, when evaluators both see and read the same point, they recall six times as much. The key elements in retention were repetition and dual modes of acquisition.

Writers of winning proposals tend to both visualize and state why they should be selected.

Too many proposal writers still think that their prospects are different, that their readers might be turned off by graphics. Such writers justify their lack of graphics with statements like, "Our evaluators are scientists, engineers, or accountants. They just want the facts."

Graphics done well are the facts. Poor, inappropriate graphics are an insult to the evaluator.

Today's readers all see professional graphics in business documents, magazines, newspapers, TV, and movies. They also expect to see similar quality graphics in professional proposals.

The wide availability of high-quality graphics, graphics generation software, and color printers make it feasible to create eye-catching, professional graphics and integrate them into proposal text.

The most successful sales people will save time and stay on message by using similar graphics throughout the sales cycle. Reuse essentially the same graphics in sales presentations, white papers, executive summaries, proposals, and finals or short list briefings. Just adapt them to the situation and medium.

Graphics

1. **Select or create graphics that demonstrate your understanding, emphasize your strategy, and highlight your discriminators.**
2. **Conceive the graphics before you write the text.**
3. **Select graphics that best support your message.**
4. **Design or modify graphics until they are understandable by all evaluators.**
5. **Keep graphics simple, uncluttered, and easy to read, with one key idea per graphic.**
6. **Introduce graphics in the text before they appear in the proposal.**
7. **Integrate graphics into the text.**
8. **Orient graphics vertically.**
9. **Minimize cumbersome foldouts.**
10. **Minimize text in graphics. Concentrate text in an action caption.**
11. **Number graphics in order of appearance in major sections.**
12. **Include an interpretative action caption with every graphic.**

1 Select or create graphics that demonstrate your understanding, emphasize your strategy, and highlight your discriminators.

One of the best ways to demonstrate your understanding of the prospect's needs is to visualize what is possible if your solution is selected. People buy benefits, not features, so visualize the benefits—similar to the following good examples:

Laundry soap commercials show happy people going somewhere in clean clothes.

Restaurants show diners enjoying themselves.

Cell phone ads show people talking excitedly, with smiles on their faces, or a person getting help in an emergency.

A photo in an aircraft engine proposal showed a huge, complicated engine with a seven-piece tool kit in the foreground. An informative caption emphasized that the engine could be maintained with the seven tools.

When selling aircraft to the Army, a seller's photo showing battle-ready troops storming out of the aircraft is far more effective than a clean photo of the aircraft without troops.

When selling complex technologies and services, helping the prospect visualize what will happen, as shown in figure 1, is usually more effective than describing your approach in dense text. Note the benefits in the caption.

Prospects are usually purchasing an improvement in their current process. Show potential process improvements in graphs, charts, sketches, or photos. Even when competitors offer the same solution, the one presented graphically appears superior.

Visualize your discriminators to help evaluators remember your differences, while associating your discriminators with the benefits to their organization.

Side-by-side comparisons are particularly effective in highlighting discriminators:

- Current process/proposed process
- Complex process/simplified process
- Old product/new product
- Side-by-side graphs, bar, or pie charts
- Side-by-side scrap bins

Note the side-by-side comparison in figure 2 that compares the current and proposed alignment of a highway. Even the captions are separate to heighten the contrast.

Since graphics are highly emphatic, use them only to convey important information. Do not insert graphics to "break up the text."

The following examples represent poor ways graphics have been used:

A proposal graphic occupied an entire page showing a single finger pressing a single button on a phone set.

Proposals include cliched clip art sketches of clasped hands to represent a proposed partnership (even when not requested), a light bulb to represent a good idea, or smiley faces to represent happy users.

Clip art can be used in graphics but must be used carefully. Note how relatively simple clip art is used effectively in figure 3 to depict how to brew at home.

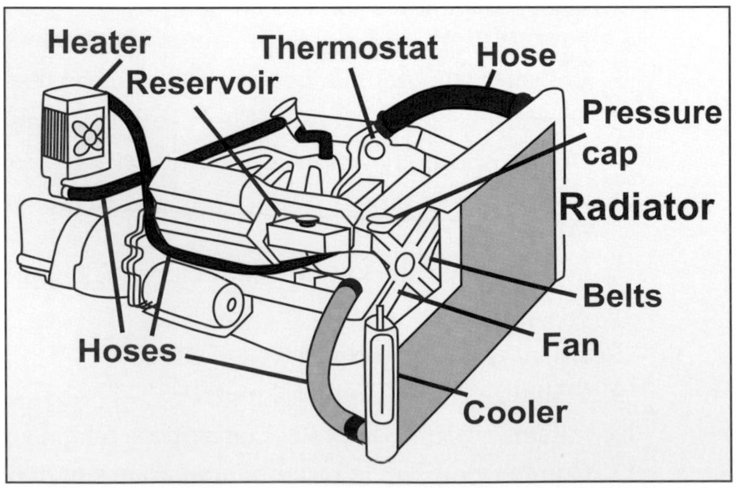

Figure 1. Inside Your Cooling System. *You have high reliability and minimal maintenance with modern auto cooling systems. As your engine reaches its normal operating temperature, the thermostat opens, permitting hot coolant to flow out of the engine block and through the radiator. The relatively cool outside air lowers the coolant temperature before cycling it back to the engine. The heater is essentially another small radiator, which radiates heat to the air inside the car.*

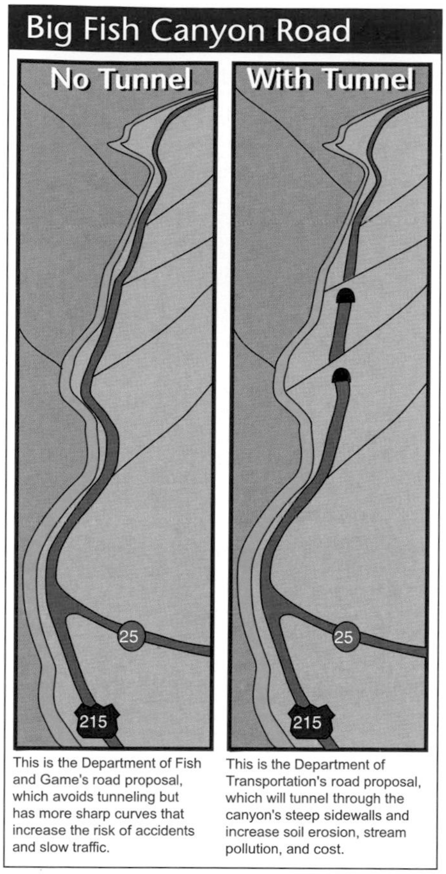

Figure 2. Side-by-Side Comparisons Emphasize Differences. *Graphics like the one above are effective to contrast the current versus proposed approach, alternative approaches, or your approach versus a competitor's approach.*

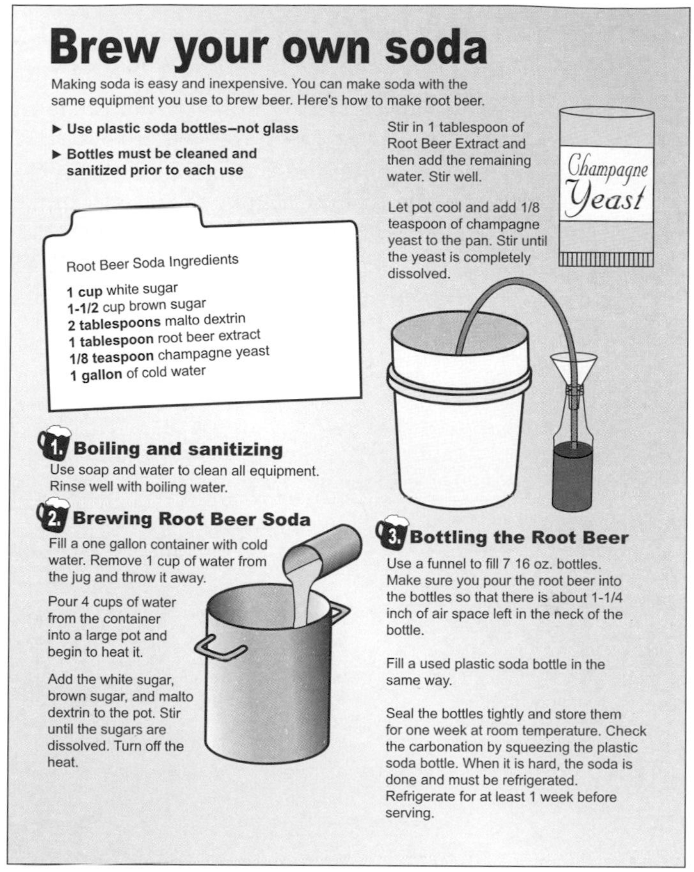

Figure 3. Use Clip Art Carefully. *Considering that many books have been written on home brewing, the relative simplicity of the graphics and text creates the impression that the task is both well understood by the writer and likely to be completed successfully. Note how the slight rotation of the recipe card heightens interest as do the mugs behind the step numbers.*

---

2 Conceive the graphics before you write the text.

Create graphics first. Write the text last. Do the things first that will have the greatest persuasive impact on the evaluator.

Preparing graphics first is a huge time saver, often cutting writing time by one-third. Everyone wants to wordsmith text. A graphic is either correct or not. After completing the graphics, writers often find they have much less text to write.

See Storyboards and Mock-ups.

If text is drafted before the graphic is developed, most writers stubbornly resist deleting the now-redundant text.

Proposals often contain long descriptions of processes that would be better depicted in a graphic. Figure 4 shows how black ice forms on roadways. Text descriptions could take pages. The graphic uses a fraction of the page and is clear.

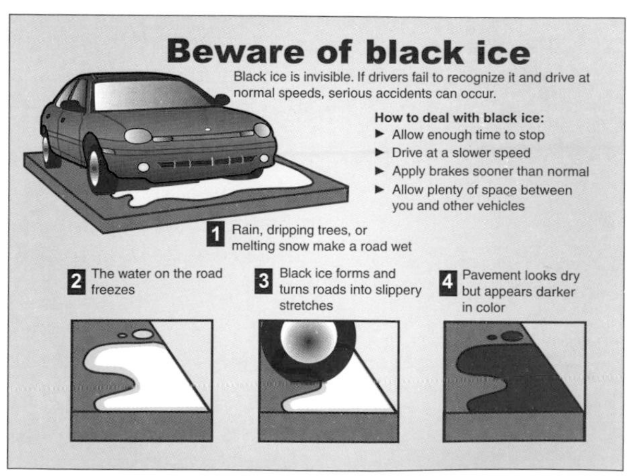

Figure 4. Depict Processes Graphically. *This four-part graphic explains a process much more easily, clearly, and briefly than could be done using only text. Prepare similar graphics to explain complex technical processes and eliminate the cumbersome and ineffective text descriptions that most sellers use.*

Many proposals are for technical services. The written descriptions of these services are frequently too complex to be understood and the complexity suggests greater risk.

Instead, depict your service processes graphically as shown in figure 5. Every information technology support contractor has to perform essentially the same process. Often the only discriminator between contractors is the clarity of the explanations of their services.

Another bonus—you can reuse these graphics in every proposal for the same services and eliminate pages of boring text.

Evaluators often say, "We looked at the tables, charts, and graphics first. If we found the answers, we did not bother to read the text."

The entire storyboarding process used to create winning proposals is focused on designing proposal sections graphically in response to the bid request and then conceiving appropriate graphics.

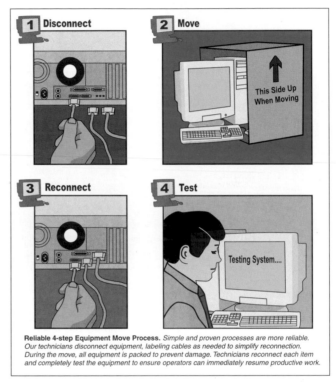

Reliable 4-step Equipment Move Process. *Simple and proven processes are more reliable. Our technicians disconnect equipment, labeling cables as needed to simplify reconnection. During the move, all equipment is packed to prevent damage. Technicians reconnect each item and completely test the equipment to ensure operators can immediately resume productive work.*

Figure 5. Use Graphics to Sell Your Processes. *This graphic shows an excellent way to eliminate tiresome prose or bullet points describing a process. Once developed, graphics like this can be used in multiple proposals. Clarity implies simplicity, which suggests low risk.*

3

Select graphics that best support your message.

The type of graphic you select should depend on the point you want to make with the evaluator. Figure 6 summarizes which types of graphics can be used to best support your message.

Do not select graphics simply because they are available. Keep the following selection guidelines in mind:

- Charts show relationships or the flow between items.
- Graphs show correlations, trends, or comparisons, depending on whether it is a line, bar, or pie graph.
- Photos show realism, that the item exists.
- Illustrations show specific features and eliminate extraneous detail that could be confusing in a photograph.
- Maps and drawings show relationships, often to scale.
- Tables emphasize actual numbers. When the absolute value of the number is most important, use a table. When a comparison or trend is most important, use a graph.

For example, when discussing your salary, do you want to see a graph (trends in salaries) or the amount you will be paid (table of comparable salaries)? For most, comparability is more important than the trend. If you start low enough, the trend looks great, but you are still underpaid.

TYPES OF GRAPHIC	Advantage Disadvantage [1]	Cause/ Effect	Chronology	Compare/ Contrast [1]	Costs Prices	Decisions Alternatives	Designs Compo-nents	Organizational Relationships	Processes	Policies Procedures	Trends
Bar Graph	✔		✔	✔	✔	✔					✔
Blue-print							✔				
Combination	✔	✔	✔	✔	✔[3]	✔		✔	✔	✔	✔
Flow Chart		✔	✔			✔		✔	✔	✔	
Illustration	✔	✔	✔[2]	✔		✔	✔		✔[2]		✔
Line Graph		✔	✔	✔	✔						✔
Map/Site Plan						✔	✔				✔
Photograph	✔	✔	✔[2]	✔			✔		✔[2]		✔
Pie Graph	✔			✔	✔	✔					✔
Schematic Drawing							✔				
Table	✔	✔	✔	✔	✔	✔		✔		✔	✔
Tree Diagram						✔		✔	✔	✔	

1 Almost any side-by-side comparison can show advantages/disadvantages.
2 Photographs or illustrations can be presented in a series.
3 Excellent cost combinations are tables with an inset graph, or a graph with an inset table.

Figure 6. Support Your Strategy with Appropriate Graphics. *Different types or styles of graphics will support your strategy, purpose, or intent better than others. Use this table to help you select more appropriate graphics. The footnotes offer further recommendations.*

4 Design or modify graphics until they are understandable by all evaluators.

See **Executive Summary.**

Choose graphics that are appropriate to the readers of that section of the proposal. Executive summary graphics must be understandable by all potential readers, including nontechnical ones.

Within a proposal and within proposal sections, you can increase the technical complexity of both graphics and text. Begin with a succinct, clear summary that is broadly understandable. Then increase the complexity as needed to satisfy your more technical evaluators. The less technical evaluators will have quit reading and jumped to the next section. Apply this guideline to both graphics and text.

While highly technical proposal sections will have more complex, technical graphics, only include sufficient technical detail to make them correct. Proposals are not technical treatises, and readers often perceive overly technical graphics as technical arrogance.

Some of the most useful stock materials for a proposal writer are boilerplate graphics. But always tailor boilerplate graphics for the evaluators of each proposal.

5 Keep graphics simple, uncluttered, and easy to read with one key idea per graphic.

Like good paragraphs, good graphics have one key point. If you realize that you have several points, divide them into several graphics.

When brainstorming graphics, ask yourself these questions:

- What is the overall point I am trying to make?
- What is the most important idea that I must communicate?
- What is the central concept?
- How are we different in this area?
- What is unique, desirable, or beneficial?

Many large organizations bidding Federal government programs have prepared elaborate macro graphics that portray the entire program. These graphics are understandable after they have been explained for 30 minutes. They do not work well in a proposal with a single paragraph caption. Very few evaluators have the patience to figure them out.

Keep the 10-Second Rule in mind. If the evaluator cannot get the point in 10 seconds, they will turn the page. Does the graphic in figure 7 pass the 10-Second Rule with you?

Clean up your message
Proposals and sales tools
Training materials
Product and system documentation
Policy and procedures
801 531-1631
www.mckinnon-mulherin.com
McKinnon Mulherin

See **Customer Focus.**

Figure 7. Use the 10-Second Rule to check Your Graphics. *All but your most technical graphics should pass the 10-Second Rule. did the graphic capture your interest? Did you get the message within 10 seconds?*

See **Color.**

A better approach is to explain complex concepts through a series of graphics that build to your point.

> A proposal writer was assigned to explain the management structure for a 2,600-employee contractor-operated government facility. He developed a five-page foldout that extended from the company president to first-level supervisors and through all 12 business units. The draft caption title was, "Top Management Visibility."
>
> The complexity of the organization chart and the large number of levels between the president and the proposed organization contradicted the message in the caption.
>
> The fix was one graphic showing the senior management link to the proposed facility manager, a second graphic showing the 12 operating departments, and a third graphic showing each department.
>
> The final series of 14 charts told the management story simply and convincingly. Each graphic had an extended caption, some taking 1/4 to 1/3 of a page. No additional body text was needed beyond the section summary and introduction.

Some graphics cannot be saved; they must be reconceived and recreated, as shown in figures 8 and 9. In figure 8, the help desk process is outlined in the smallest type. The circle suggests a continuous cycle, and the graphic is cluttered with numerous department names.

The intent was to emphasize that a single call would lead to the resolution of a customer's problem. Figure 9 emphasizes the single call to the help desk while downplaying the source of help. Figure 8 is seller focused; figure 9 is customer focused.

To reduce rework, decide on the finished size of your graphic before it is drawn. Frequently graphics are drawn in one size, then reduced to fit, making lettering hard to read or line width inappropriate.

When writers have graphics assistance, ask each writer to specify an approximate finished size, such as full-page, half-page, or quarter-page. Alternatively, specify column inches, depending on your page design.

Well-designed graphics have a foreground, middle-ground, and background. Foreground objects are centered or slightly off-center, appear in front, have greater line width, or are more visible through the use of color or size.

Middle-ground items show the overall object or concept. These items are usually sketched with medium-weight lines and are less brightly colored.

Background items are used to establish context, enhance realism, and add balance. Background items are behind or to the side of fore- and middle-ground objects and are sketched with lighter, narrower lines in more neutral colors.

Nothing stands out when graphics are drawn with the same line width and color throughout, as illustrated in the poor graphic in figure 10.

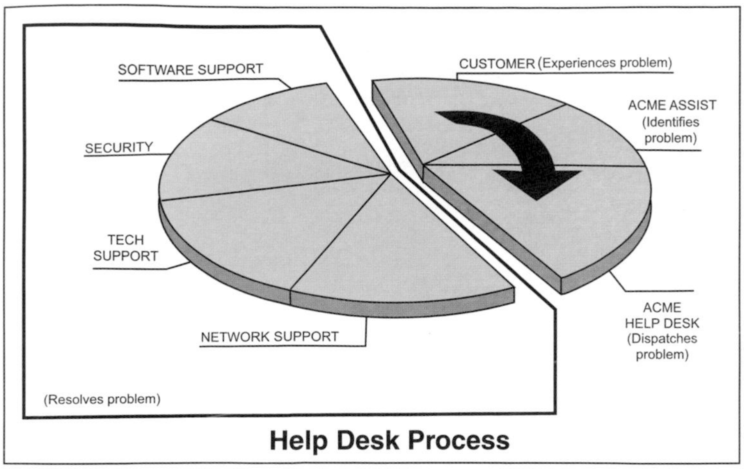

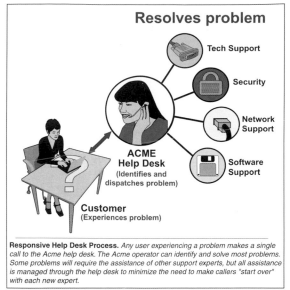

Figure 8. Seller-Focused Graphic with "Horse Caption." *If you bother to figure out this graphic, you might get the impression that calling the seller's help desk leads to a runaround response. While perhaps realistic, this was not the message intended.*

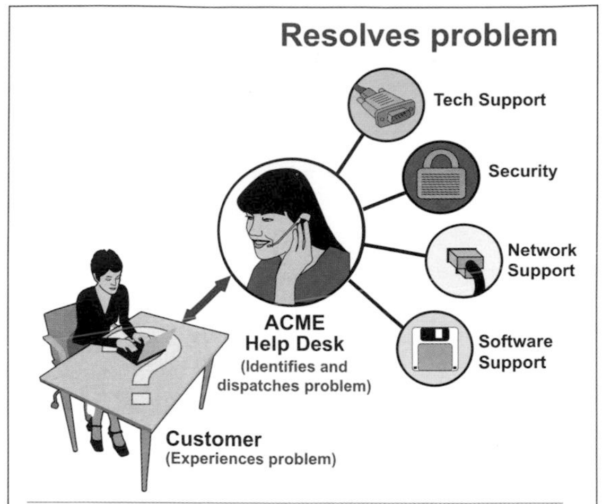

Responsive Help Desk Process. *Any user experiencing a problem makes a single call to the Acme help desk. The Acme operator can identify and solve most problems. Some problems will require the assistance of other support experts, but all assistance is managed through the help desk to minimize the need to make callers "start over" with each new expert.*

Figure 9. Prospect-Focused Graphic with an Action Caption. *In contrast to figure 7, the title adds "responsive" to emphasize the benefit to the prospect. The action caption explains the process, including features and benefits.*

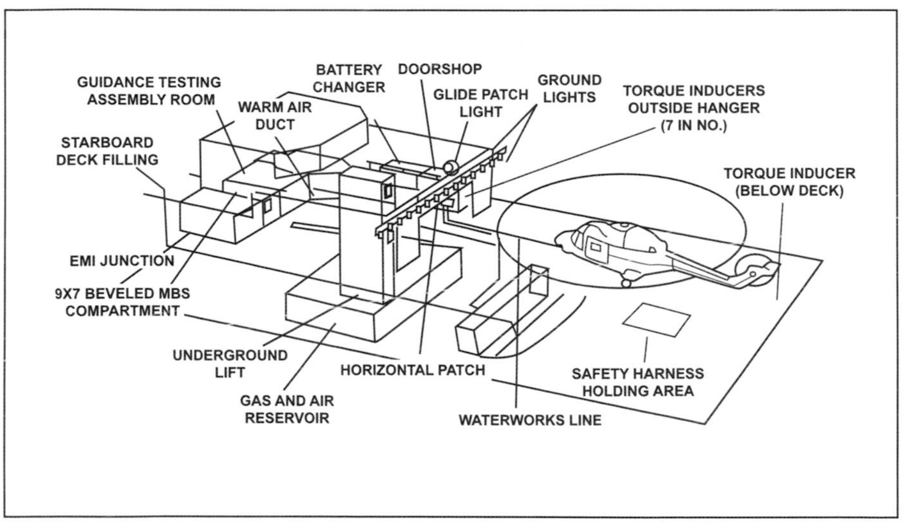

Figure 10. Poorly Designed Graphic. *The uniform line width, lack of color, and excessive labeling of irrelevant details ensure that nothing stands out. The complete lack of a caption in the original graphic ensured that the evaluator did not get the point intended.*

6 Introduce graphics in the text before they appear in the proposal.

Introduce every graphic in the text before it appears in the proposal. Readers encountering a graphic that has not been introduced may get confused.

Introduce the graphic by telling how it fits with or supports other proposal content. You do not have to repeat the content of the graphic in your text. For reinforcement, make the same point in different words.

Make your introduction informative and specific:

> Figure 3 indicates how we helped a major services company in Sweden raise its capture percentage to 68 percent.

> Our 24 x 7 national call center in Salt Lake City is shown in figure 4.

Avoid noninformative introductions like this:

> See figure 5.

> Our organization chart can be found in figure 6.

Like a good action caption, a good introduction puts the spin on the graphic that you want, helping the evaluator interpret its meaning. While we joke about political spin doctors, action captions put the spin on our graphics.

Recognize some exceptions where graphics may not be introduced in prior text. With careful page design, graphics can be so well integrated into the text that introductions can be omitted. A professional executive summary is the most likely part of a proposal to meet this criterion. Eliminating introductions of graphics in proposals is higher risk than in other business documents because the writing and production are done by different individuals under tight time constraints.

See **Action Captions, Executive Summary, and Page** *and* **Document Design.**

Another exception might be when a graphic appears at the top of a page in a new section or in the left-hand margin. Also avoid unnecessarily breaking columns of text to insert a graphic if the reader could be confused about where to read next. Such confusion is common in proposals with multiple column page designs, as illustrated in figure 11.

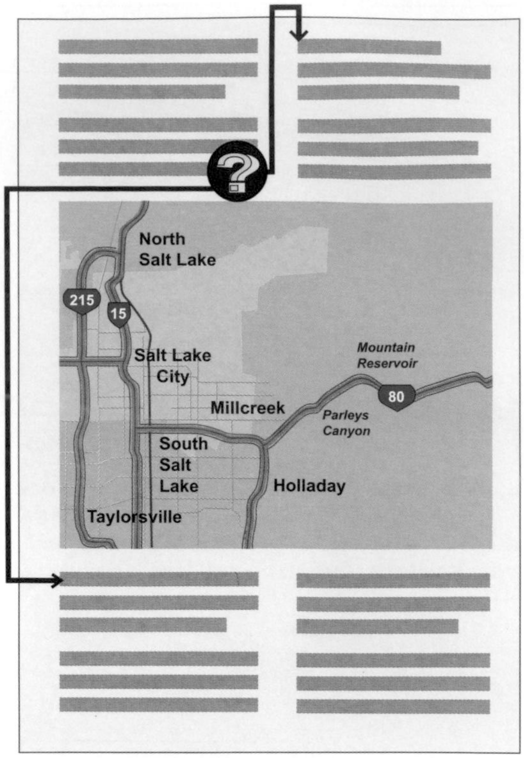

Figure 11. Where to Next? *Minimize evaluator confusion by placing the graphic at the top or bottom of the page. Placing graphics in the middle of text columns as shown may confuse your readers.*

7 Integrate graphics into the text.

See **Appendices and Attachments.**

To enable evaluators to refer to a graphic without turning the page, place graphics on the same or the facing page. Evaluators asked to turn to another page, or worse, an appendix, usually do not.

Avoid referring to refer to graphics in mass:

> Our approach to facility construction is shown in figures 1 through 14.

Technical and scientific writers traditionally place all graphics at the back for the convenience of the writer. Make your proposal easy to read for the evaluator by integrating your graphics into the text.

8 Orient graphics vertically.

Design your proposal to enable the evaluator to read it without rotating or steering the book. Avoid any action that interrupts the flow of ideas from the document to the reader.

If you have numerous graphics better suited to a horizontal or landscape page, consider orienting the entire volume in the same direction. Cost volumes full of spreadsheets are a common example.

9 Minimize cumbersome foldouts.

Foldouts have numerous drawbacks:

- Take extra time for the evaluator to unfold and refold
- Make your proposal look much thicker
- Lead to larger, complex graphics that are harder to understand
- Often get torn, removed, or lost from handling
- Require a separate production process followed by error prone insertion in each volume at the last minute

Use foldouts when needed; typically for the following types of graphics:

- Project schedules
- Staffing charts
- Cross-reference matrices
- Engineering drawings

10 Minimize text in graphics. Concentrate text in an action caption.

Concentrate the text with your primary message in the action caption where you can use word processing tools like spellcheck, search, and replace. Production costs are also reduced by letting word processing handle the text and letting the artists do graphics.

Excess text clutters the graphic and distracts from the message intended. Figure 10 is an example of text cluttering a graphic with the excessive numbers of labels.

Insert keys and legends that enable evaluators to understand the graphic, but try to group them to reduce clutter rather than inserting them wherever you have space.

When given the choice of using direct labels on items or a key, use direct labels unless the excessive number of labels clutters the graphic. Remove labels from items not being addressed.

By minimizing text in graphics, graphics are easier to tailor for subsequent proposals without embarrassing inclusions of the wrong client or product name.

Minimizing text in graphics is a guideline with many exceptions. The graphic in figure 12 has extensive text, however, the text is grouped and organized for maximum clarity. Note the simplicity of the graphics in figure 12.

While having skilled graphics support is a great aid to preparing winning proposals, you can use relatively simple graphics to attract a reader's attention, as shown in figure 12. Anyone can find a picture of a car. The car attracts the reader, the text conveys the message.

Another exception is shown in figure 3 where a visual page is inserted as a graphic. Consider the following similar examples, all used in proposals:

- Table of Contents—to show the contents of a plan
- Letter of Commendation—to show excellent, relevant experience
- Certificate—to show compliance with established standards
- Procedure—to show an approach or evidence of a proven approach
- Template/Form—to demonstrate the item already exists
- Sidebar—to label specialized content

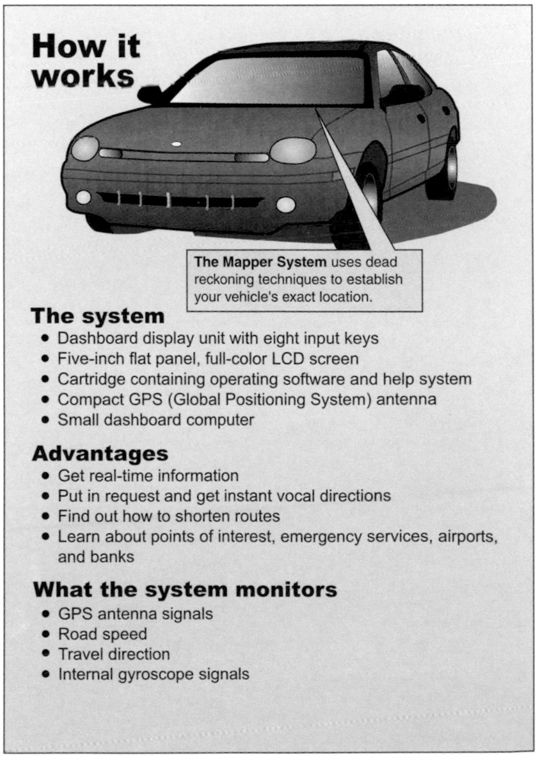

Figure 12. No Artist—Still No Excuse. *Some graphics just draw attention to the text message. In this example, any car graphic (including clip art) would have worked. Do not let the lack of a skilled artist stop you from using graphics in proposals.*

11 Number graphics in order of appearance in major sections.

To make evaluation easy, refer to all graphics as figures or exhibits and number them consecutively within major sections of your proposal.

Refer to both tables and figures as figures. With many forms of blended graphics, such as tables inserted within a figure, adopt a single naming convention to simplify the process for both the evaluator and yourself.

In a short proposal, label all graphics consecutively. In proposals with multiple sections, label them consecutively within sections. Use the section number, an en dash, then the figure number.

Figure 3–2. Informative Title. Full sentence(s) action caption.

To facilitate matching graphics with section drafts, use the complete section number during proposal development. Then simplify section numbers when control of section drafts is transitioned to the production coordinator.

During proposal development	During production
Figure 3.2.4-1	Figure 3–10
Figure 3.2.4-2	Figure 3–11
Figure 3.2.4-3	Figure 3–12

Place a complete list of all figures at the beginning of your proposal, immediately after the table of contents.

In multivolume proposals, place a list of figures in every separate binder. Include either the complete list of all figures in the proposal or just the figures contained in that volume. Place the list of figures immediately behind the table of contents for each volume.

12 Include an interpretative action caption with every graphic.

See **Action Captions** *and* **Features, Advantages, and Benefits.**

Action captions interpret the graphic for the evaluator. They impart your spin.

All action captions include three parts:

1. Figure number
2. Informative heading
3. Complete sentence(s) explaining the relevance of the graphic to the evaluator, including both benefits and features

Some graphics are simply inappropriate for the proposal. Figure 13 shows appropriate (on the left) and inappropriate (on the right) graphics for an ultralight airplane proposal targeted for use by foresters.

Sometimes a caption cannot save a graphic. The graphic in figure 8 has a "horse caption." Even if the caption in figure 9 is used with the figure 8 graphic, the graphic is still not effective. The primary focus is on the seller and not the prospect.

The message intended is redrawn and accompanied by a more effective caption in figure 9. When graphics just do not seem to work, even with a good action caption, reconceive the message intended.

Figure 13. Select Appropriate Graphics. *In a proposal targeting foresters as users, the left graphic is more appropriate than the right graphic. The graphic on the right shows recreational users driving a Jaguar. Recreational use could imply light duty. The Jaguar implies a lack of understanding or lack of relevant experience.*

Headings are essential features of a good proposal. They enable evaluators to quickly find answers to their questions.

Headings make a proposal easier to evaluate, and proposals that are easy to evaluate get higher scores.

Informative headings are one of the best ways to convey key selling points. Unlike formal theme statements, which are sometimes not read by evaluators, informative headings are nearly always read.

Headings enable formal evaluators, those looking for answers to specific evaluation questions on a score sheet, to rapidly locate answers. Informal evaluators, those skimming for content on specific topics, can also rapidly identify content of interest.

Like graphics and white space, headings help break up bleak masses of text, making your proposal more readable.

Headings

1. **Use the exact heading dictated in the bid request.**
2. **Use telegraphic headings to label major sections.**
3. **Use informative headings in all other instances.**
4. **Limit numbered headings to three levels unless dictated by the bid request.**
5. **Use verb headings to convey action; use noun headings to signal your purpose.**
6. **Make the bulleted list of contents and section subheadings identical in proposal sections with an informal table of contents.**
7. **Signal the level of heading by placement on the page, size of type, type appearance, and section number.**

1 Use the exact heading dictated in the bid request.

Headings may be directly dictated or implied in a bid request.

EXCEPTION: If they misspell "potatoe," you should not repeat the misspelling in your document.

Directly dictated

Bid request excerpt:

2.0 Management Plan

1. Organization and Facilities. Include a current organization chart and a brief description of operational function. Describe your organization in terms of size and organizational stability. Identify relevant facility resources (e.g., word processing, graphics generation, DTP, and printing).

Proposal section headings:

2.0 Management Plan

2.1 Organization and Facilities

If the bid request refers to *Project Management*, then do not change it to *Program Management*, even if that is your organization's usual term. Call it what the prospect calls it. If the prospect hyphenated the title, *Integrated-Systems Engineering*, then you hyphenate it, however unconventional.

2 Use telegraphic headings to label major sections.

See **Executive Summary.**

Recommended telegraphic headings in a proposal include major, expected, or standard sections:

Executive Summary
Management Summary
Technical Proposal
Cost Volume
Appendix

Most of these will also fall under the first guideline, headings dictated in the bid request.

Telegraphic headings are generally less desirable because they are not very interesting and are less likely than informative headings to capture the attention of busy readers. However, telegraphic headings clearly label content.

3 Use informative headings in all other instances.

Informative, specific headings enable evaluators to immediately determine both the contents of a section and often the benefit to their organization.

Informative headings are like newspaper headlines. They convey the essence of the story and create interest before you read the story. Good informative headings make any document more user friendly, enabling the evaluators to make an informed choice about what and how much they read depending on their interests and needs.

See **Discriminators** *and* **Theme Statements**.

Many proposal section headings are boring, general, and not informative:

Introduction
Organization
Design
Implementation

While these headings qualify as good telegraphic headings, use them primarily when dictated by the bid request instructions. More informative versions would be:

How Our Proposal Is Organized to Ease Your Evaluation

Our Flat Organizational Structure Reduces Overhead Cost

T700 Bearing Design Based on Successful Demonstration Program

Continuous Support Through a Three-Phase Implementation

Make informative headings inclusive. Inclusive headings signal that only material mentioned in the heading will be covered in the section. Proposal writers using boilerplate often violate this recommendation.

Busy, skeptical evaluators are more likely to read an informative heading than a formal theme statement. Exploit this by giving your informative headings many of the features of good theme statements:

1. Link a benefit to a feature
2. Cite features that are discriminators

Emulate these examples of informative, inclusive headings that contain both features and benefits:

Cut Bearing Lubrication Downtime 20 Percent with Our Unobtanium, Tapered Design

Detecting Malignant Tissue in Real Time Using Biotec's Laser Probe

DOE Has Unlimited Access to All Proposed Sites to Speed the Phase II Permitting Process

Gain Comprehensive IT Expertise in the Financial Industry

Avoid Start-up Fees by Continuing the Current Contract

Maximize Business Capture Effectiveness by Selectively Outsourcing Proposal Management

Many proposal writers worry that their informative headings become too long when they follow these recommendations. While evaluators have made negative comments about long theme statements, they have never complained about informative headings being too long.

4 Limit numbered headings to three levels unless dictated by the bid request.

Proposals are accessed rather than read. Evaluators search for answers to questions, either formally or informally.

See **Compliance and Responsiveness**.

NOTE: Cross-reference matrices often do not contain page numbers because the page number is not known until the final document is published. Including page numbers in the cross-reference matrix is desirable but optional.

Two devices help evaluators find the information they want:

- Numbered or lettered headings
- Cross-reference matrix or compliance matrix

Use a numbering system with your headings on all but the shortest proposals, approximately five pages or less.

The cross-reference matrix links the specific question in the bid request to the proposal section number and heading where the question is answered.

If your cross-reference matrix does not contain page numbers, your subsection number should direct evaluators to within three pages of the answer. Then an informal table of contents at the beginning of the section and matching unnumbered, run-in subheadings should take the evaluator to the paragraph with the answer.

Using run-in subheadings is an effective way to facilitate evaluation by indicating content without adding more numbered headings.

A Run-in Heading. When you do not use punctuation, make the heading visually distinct from the rest of the text. Use **boldface** type or a larger typeface.

Always follow the client's bid request numbering and heading system, regardless of level. One such proposal required heading subsection levels 8, 9, and 10.

The levels of headings may be indicated by the numbering system, placement, size, or appearance of the heading. When given the choice, use numeric decimal numbering systems instead of alpha numeric systems to minimize potential reader confusion:

4.2.3.7 vs. IV.B.3.g

Generally, the less technical your readers, the fewer levels you should use.

Large, formally solicited government proposals often need four to five numbered heading levels. If you cannot direct the evaluator to within a few pages of the answer, add another level. Ease of evaluation is more important than limiting heading levels.

5 Use verb headings to convey action; use noun headings to signal your purpose.

See **Parallel Lists**.

When given a choice, keep headings parallel in structure. Parallel headings use the same grammatical structure. Parallel verb headings begin with a verb in the same tense. Verb headings tend to be more active and persuasive.

3.1 Cut Bearing Lubrication Downtime 20 Percent with Our Unobtanium Tapered Design

4.2.1 Detect Malignant Tissue in Real Time Using Biotec's Laser Probe

5.3 Gain Comprehensive Computer Expertise in the Financial Industry

8.7.4 Avoid Start-up Fees by Continuing the Current Contract

Noun headings begin with a noun or noun clause and tend to be more useful when answering the bid request question in the heading to avoid forcing evaluators to read the text.

7.2 DOE Has Unlimited Access to All Proposed Sites to Speed the Phase II Permitting Process

8.1 All Systems Operate on 220 Volt 50 Cycle Current

Limit or entirely avoid using question headings in proposals. Question headings may leave the impression with some evaluators that you do not know the answer.

2.0 Can Global Corporation Cut IT Costs?

2.3 How Does Titanium Hold Up in Space?

3.3 Is It Possible to Retrain Existing Personnel?

5.1.1 Can Enemy Missiles Be Detected in Time?

6 Make the bulleted list of contents and section subheadings identical in proposal sections with an informal table of contents.

See **Organization**.

Writers that follow the fundamental principles of sound section organization often list topics in their section introduction, then draft informative headings for the subsequent subsections.

Introduction

In our meetings over the past 3 months, your medical technicians said the tumor diagnostic system must have the following characteristics:

Accurate
Available
Cost effective

Subsection headings

Test Accuracy Increased from 98 to 99.9 Percent

Availability Demonstrated at 95 Percent Over Two Years of Clinical Use

Beta Users Show Six-Month Payback

While all the headings reflect the same topic and convey important messages, skimming evaluators might not see the immediate connection. Either make the topics announced in the introduction more informative and match them in the subheadings, or at least begin the subheadings with identical words:

Accurate to 99.9 Percent

Available 95 Percent of the TIme During Two Years of Clinical Use

Cost-Effectiveness Demonstrated by Six-Month Payback

Headings introduced in bulleted lists do not need to be numbered in the subsequent subheadings. However, if the subheading titles have section numbers, then use those same section numbers in the introductory list as illustrated below.

3.0 Introduction

In our meetings over the past 3 months, your medical technicians said the tumor diagnostic system must have the following characteristics:

3.1 Accurate
3.2 Available
3.3 Cost Effective

Subsection headings

3.1 Accurate to 99.9 Percent

3.2 Available 95 Percent of the Time During Two Years of Clinical Use

3.3 Cost-Effectiveness Demonstrated by Six-Month Payback

Be especially careful about making introductions and subheadings identical in the following situations:

- Extensive boilerplate is used to prepare the proposal.
- Multiple writers contribute to the proposal.
- Writers have limited training in or understanding of the basic principles of organization.

When extensive boilerplate is used, additional material is often inserted in section text but not introduced. Conversely, a writer eliminates material that is not relevant to the immediate proposal but forgets to change the introduction.

With multiple writers, a writer may decide to add or delete material without also realizing that the material is previewed in the introduction. A poor solution is to eliminate all introductions or previews. Unfortunately, this solution may be worse than the original lack of agreement between the introduction and the order of subsequent section content.

7

Signal the level of heading by placement on the page, size of type, type appearance, and section number.

Placement variations include centering, flush left, indented, and run-in.

A Centered Heading

A Flush-Left Heading

An Indented Heading

A Run-in Heading. The text begins following the period or colon and one or two spaces.

See **Page and Document Design.**

Size variations are possible by varying the point size of the lettering. Larger lettering indicates a higher level.

A 24-pt Heading

A 18-pt Heading

A 14-pt Heading

A 12-pt Heading

Make the size variation large enough to be obvious. Consider changing from **Bold** to Normal at about 24-point, depending on the font.

Appearance variations include the following, generally in the order listed:

1. Point Size
2. **Boldface**
3. Color
4. *Italics*
5. **Font change**
6. ALL CAPITALS
7. Underlining

Multiple appearance changes raise the level of the heading. However, changes like color and font will depend on the choice made. Generally, try to avoid using ALL CAPITALS and Underlining, as they are harder to read and are outdated, typewriter-like conventions.

Capitalize headings using the same conventions as for titles of books, articles, and other documents. An emerging trend is to capitalize only the first word in a heading, to make the heading more readable.

The most common font style for headings has been sans-serif with serif styles for body text. That convention has been followed in this *Proposal Guide*; however, designers may have sound reasons for other choices.

An emerging trend in many newspapers and magazines is to use serif fonts in headings "because they are easier to read." In this instance, the designer may have chosen to emphasize readability over emphasis. However, emphasis may be enhanced by increasing point size more significantly, using a different color, or using a noticeably different serif font.

Avoid using too many different types of fonts. For greater consistency, use the same font for all headings, and perhaps, a different font for body text. Some designers choose to use the same font for both headings and body text to "make everything look like it is from the same document." Often designers will choose a font created in both serif and sans-serif versions. For example, the fonts used in this *Proposal Guide* are both from the ITC® Stone® font family.

The decision of how to apply fonts is usually subjective. Set your style and be consistent.

International proposals and international business correspondence are radically different from domestic proposals. Standards and practices that you normally use at home with great success may cause you to lose business internationally.

NOTE: Every country has different acquisition systems. International proposals take on many forms and variations. Bidders must be acutely tuned to specific business practices, customs, standards, and laws.

A study by the Parker Pen Company revealed that language problems are the root of many, if not most, international business misunderstandings.

The trend is for international governments and business organizations to encourage more competitive bidding and more structured evaluation and decision making.

Political considerations, socioeconomic arrangements and investments, protectionism, and teaming with local organizations all play larger roles when acquisition rules are not tightly defined.

Numerous excellent references have been written about specific international differences. These guidelines are generic and limited largely to the writing and production of the proposal document.

International Proposals

1. **Respect the customs of prospects' countries.**
2. **Understand your prospects and their evaluation approach.**
3. **Use your normal capitalization, spelling, and punctuation when writing to a foreign contact in English.**
4. **Use prospects' spelling conventions when replying to formal bid requests.**
5. **Keep your writing clear, short, and concise.**
6. **Use more graphics, but keep them simple.**
7. **When in doubt, overpunctuate.**
8. **Recognize that English usage varies significantly when taught as a second language.**
9. **Use translation services cautiously.**
10. **Adjust your proposal preparation schedule.**
11. **Offer a "read-through," oral presentation, and/or Question and Answer session to ensure your proposal is understood.**

1 Respect the customs of prospects' countries.

The conventions surrounding proposals and business development vary widely between countries, cultures, and organizations. Meticulously observe the usage and practices of each country.

Most business guides emphasize what you *should not do*:

- Do not criticize your contact or the person's country.
- Do not impose your pace or schedule on them.

What you *should do* is also significant. Find out what you can do to proactively create a positive impression. Local employees or representatives are vital.

Locals will know the customs and can help you avoid awkwardness, embarrassment, or perhaps directly insulting the prospect. Consider this example:

A Scottish businessman working for a UK corporation was pursuing business in Hong Kong, China. After working closely with a local representative and the local office staff, he impulsively decided to buy a simple gift valued at £10 sterling for a Hong Kong staff person who had put in many hours of overtime on their proposal. When presented with the gift, the staff person became extremely upset and immediately left the room.

This businessman later learned that in the Chinese culture, gifts of any value are *exchanged*, not given unilaterally. His gift had caused a loss of face because the staff person had no return gift immediately available.

2 Understand your prospects and their evaluation approach.

Consider any document that you use to advance the sale to be a proposal. Understand how it will be used and what they expect; then design your document to exceed their expectations.

Many international proposals are both directly compared among the evaluators and shared with other bidders. Confidentiality is loose.

Evaluators and decision makers are not only available but may expect to be contacted as an indication of your interest. **The only rule is that the prospect rules.**

3 Use your normal capitalization, spelling, and punctuation when writing to a foreign contact in English.

With no other rules defined, prospects expect you to be yourself. Use your normal approach for informally solicited proposals as well as the other business and sales documents that surround the proposal.

Be careful when mixing written material with American spelling and a UK English speaker, or conversely, UK English spelling and an American speaker.

An American presenting American materials in a foreign country is usually acceptable. However, an Englishman presenting the same American materials in the same country might not be equally accepted.

Always follow the style prospects use for their titles, names, company name, and address.

4 Use prospects' spelling conventions when replying to a formal bid request.

Follow the particular dialect. Most of us recognize the differences in word usage and spelling between American, British, Canadian, and Australian English. Yet many languages have multiple dialects.

For example New South Wales, Australia, tends to use the Macquarie dictionary while the other Australian states and territories use the Oxford English dictionary. Usage and spelling differ.

While using the same spelling convention, you do not have to use the same format and font as was used in the bid request *unless directed to do so by the prospect.*

The capitalization, punctuation, and spelling style that you use is not as important as being consistent. While consistency is needed to avoid appearing careless and unprofessional, it is mandatory to avoid creating confusion and misunderstanding in foreign readers.

5 Keep your writing clear, short, and concise.

Use short and simple words, sentences, and paragraphs but not necessarily simple concepts. In international proposals, complexity can cause translation difficulties as well as confusion and misunderstanding.

Also see **Choosing Correct Words.**

Whenever possible, choose a short word over a long, complex, unfamiliar, or abstract word.

A fellow consultant noted: "English has a relatively simple structure, Subject-Verb-Object. If you change the order, you have to understand punctuation."

Any sentence having more than 20 words is more difficult to understand. An easily readable newspaper, like *USA Today,* averages about 15 words per sentence and fewer than two sentences per paragraph.

Too many short sentences tend to make the writing seem choppy, so writing instructors advise varying sentence length and using transition words. However, choppiness is not the primary concern in international proposals. If your proposal is translated, it will probably seem choppy, independent of how the original sentences were written.

Sentence fragments cause severe difficulties for international readers. Delete fragments or rewrite them as a complete sentence. Evaluators struggling to understand your meaning are unlikely to absorb content.

Evaluators repeatedly say that they favor proposals that are easy to read and evaluate. Clear, short, concise words, sentences, and paragraphs make international proposals easier to read.

6

See **Action Captions** *and* **Graphics**.

Use more graphics, but keep them simple.

Graphics are more universally understood, summarize information and concepts quickly, and reduce the total size of a proposal.

However, complex graphics force the evaluator to search body text to be understood.

Simplify all graphics as much as possible and include complete action captions.

7

When in doubt, overpunctuate.

Punctuation is important in all types of writing, but it is mandatory in international documents. Without punctuation, the probability of the evaluator getting lost increases dramatically.

Overpunctuate international proposals, even though the trend is to under punctuate in domestic correspondence. The intent of punctuation is to add clarity, so make sure your overpunctuation is correct.

While usage will vary slightly, most common punctuation marks such as periods (.), quotation marks (""), and commas (,) are understood. Exclamation points (!), ellipsis points (. . .), and virgules (/) are less understood and should be avoided.

8

English usage varies significantly when taught as a second language.

Drop the notion that English is English everywhere in the world. Most are aware that U.S. and UK English vary, with many identical words having different and potentially embarrassing meanings.

Japanese English often does not distinguish between singular and plural words because Japanese speakers do not have singular and plural in their own language and may not be used to making such distinctions.

Egyptian English deviates from U.S. English by treating certain adjectives as nouns: *He is from the Egyptian* [delegation].

Often words considered singular in the U.S. are considered plural in the UK. Professional sport teams or clubs, organizations, and government are often plural, even though when asked, most UK speakers admit they are singular.

The government are meeting. . .

Manchester United are pleased to win. . .

British Telephone are entering the wireless market throughout Europe.

The difference between U.S. English and UK English largely involves different spellings of the same word, different meanings for the same word, and different words for the same meaning.

Consider the following examples:

U.S.	UK
bathroom	lavatory
biscuit	scone
center	centre
cookie	biscuit
defense	defence
dessert	pudding or sweet
elevator	lift
pavement	road
potato chip	crisp
program	programme
realize	realise
sidewalk	pavement
table (put aside)	table (act on now)

These examples illustrate how differences in understanding of the same language can lead to trouble or embarrassment. Be aware if you intend to propose successfully to people who are more fluent in UK English than in U.S. English.

9

Use translation services cautiously.

If the prospect requires translation or you decide to translate all or portions of your proposal, proceed cautiously. Be very fussy about the translator's credentials.

Language in other nations evolves just as English evolves. Your translator must be current and familiar with regional differences.

Due to the high risk of incorrect translation, try to stick to English unless delivering a translated proposal is part of your strategy. At best, an error can be embarrassing; at worst, it can kill the deal.

Review translated work carefully, especially names, numbers, and statistics. Consider having particularly sensitive portions back-translated to verify the translation has remained true to the original.

Computerized translation is improving rapidly but is not yet sufficiently reliable.

Design graphics and pages with translation in mind. Depending on the language, allow 20 to 30 percent more space for text expansion.

Expand your running glossary of acronyms and unique terms to aid the translator.

Translation requires more time. Allow 2,000 English words per day per translator. Overall quality variations will increase with more translators.

Translation costs vary, depending on language and location:

Language	Cost per word U.S. $
W. European/S. American	$ .18 – .27
Asia	$ .22 – .28
Scandinavian	$ .30 – .44
E. European	$ .22 – .33

Note that the absolute cost of translation will change, but the relative cost to translate different languages should remain accurate.

10

Adjust your proposal preparation schedule.

See **Scheduling.**

While many international prospects are more relaxed about deadlines, do not depend on a relaxed attitude. Any prospect can use missed deadlines as the reason to eliminate your proposal. Varying languages, time zones, cultures, technologies, and laws usually increase the time required to produce a winning proposal.

Translation often applies to many of the bid documents as well as the proposal. Discrepancies in the translated documents take more time to resolve.

NOTE: Most countries outside the U.S. use A4-size paper, a metric standard that is 210 mm x 297 mm (8.268 in. x 11.693 in.).

Different time zones usually increase the time required. While many people have visions of writers in different time zones working around the clock, you still have the same number of writers available, and the communication time overlap might be narrow.

Many proposal managers who have managed writers in broadly different time zones say they would rather not do it again.

Each country has different utility standards, environmental requirements, and laws. Differences affect your solution and how your writers work.

Management reviews become more complex and reviewers are less likely to be co-located, thus leading to conflicting recommendations. Limits on technical transfer may require time for an outside Commerce Department or regulatory review.

Production time might increase with changes in paper size (A4) or the need to deliver electronic copy. Shipping takes longer and is subject to customs problems.

11

Offer a "read-through," oral presentation, and/or a Question and Answer session to ensure your proposal is understood.

Prospects managing international competitions are acutely aware of and worried about the risks of misunderstanding all sellers' proposals. Offering to make or even sponsor a "read-through" will both reduce prospects' risk and potentially improve your position. Read-throughs give you the chance to observe prospects' understanding and to clarify your offer.

An oral presentation followed by questions and answers is a good alternative to the read-through and takes less time. Note that all these options will raise proposal preparation costs, require more time, and require more resources.

If the competition is rigidly managed, all sellers will be given the same opportunity. If the competition is loosely managed, you may be the only seller allowed to present, giving you a significant advantage.

Kickoff meetings are critical milestones that require careful core team planning followed by professional execution. Good ones inspire teams; poor ones demoralize teams.

See **Proposal Management Plan**.

See **Capture Planning**.

Kickoff meetings should be motivational, informative, and directive. Kickoff meetings have the following objectives:

- Initiate the proposal effort for all contributors
- Answer questions about the opportunity
- Make writing assignments
- Coordinate upcoming activities
- Create a cohesive team

Kickoff meetings range from carefully planned and executed large-team efforts to loosely structured teleconference calls. Resist the urge to have a kickoff meeting as soon as you receive the bid request. Premature kickoff meetings offer only the illusion of progress and lead to more rework and a less competitive proposal.

The proposal manager should run kickoff meetings , supported by the capture manager.

Large-team proposals may have four kickoff meetings:

1. The teaming or subcontractors' kickoff follows the formal commitment to team or subcontract. The purpose is to establish clear roles, responsibilities, and assignments.
2. The proposal kickoff follows two events: (1) bid decision and (2) subsequent planning that enables the core team to issue clear task assignments to each proposal contributor.
3. The proposal update kickoff follows the Bid Validation milestone, prompted by receipt of the prospect's final bid request, and redirects each contributor's efforts based on changes in the prospect's bid request.
4. The cost kickoff establishes estimating ground rules, procedures, guidelines, schedules, costing strategy, and task assignments.

Fewer than 10 percent of all proposals have multiple kickoff meetings.

Do not confuse your initial proposal planning meeting with a kickoff meeting. The event called the kickoff meeting for many non-Federal organizations is actually an initial planning meeting, conducted in a conference call. These misnamed meetings loosely cover the following topics:

- Client requirements and perhaps motivators and hot buttons.
- Available solution, incorrectly termed *our strategy*.
- Broad area assignments, such as, "Fred has the technical, Mary takes the management, Jim's group can do the production."
- Schedule, "We'll talk again next week. Your completed proposal section is due on . . . "

To make proposal team kickoff meetings more successful, these guidelines stress (1) planning before the kickoff meeting, (2) execution in a single setting, and (3) execution via tele-conference. Teleconference kickoff meetings are the only option for many organizations. If this is the case in your organization, carefully read guideline 7.

Nearly all materials distributed at the kickoff meeting are part of the Proposal Management Plan (PMP) or its appendices and attachments.

Kickoff Meetings

1. **Allocate approximately 15 percent of the available preparation time to core team planning prior to the kickoff meeting.**
2. **Invite the right people.**
3. **Prepare a complete but concise agenda.**
4. **Prepare a comprehensive kickoff package in advance.**
5. **Review operational guidelines for proposal development.**
6. **Establish a tone of competent, professional proposal leadership and management.**
7. **Establish additional ground rules for teleconference kickoff meetings.**

1

Allocate approximately 15 percent of the available preparation time to core team planning prior to the kickoff meeting.

See **Scheduling.**

A 10-day effort would allow 1 to 1.5 days to plan the meeting. A 45-day effort would allow approximately 1 week.

Preparation time will depend on draft bid request availability, your organization's willingness to commit to capture planning and core team planning, and your Proposal Management Plan completeness.

2

Invite the right people.

Invite the people whose work will be affected by the proposal, either by direct contribution, temporary loss of resources, or consequences:

- Senior managers who support and help motivate the team
- Program or product managers who own the solution
- Capture, sales, and/or marketing leads who represent the prospect and align the proposal to sales efforts
- Proposal manager who is tasked to produce a winning proposal
- Volume managers or book bosses who manage portions of the team
- Writers and contributors who develop content
- Proposal specialists or coordinators who help the proposal manager coordinate section drafts and graphics
- Production or print shop supervisor who will format, publish, and copy the proposal
- Editors and graphic artists assigned to support the proposal
- Managers who are committing or losing resources to the proposal effort
- Teaming partners and subcontractors who provide text or pricing, providing they are exclusive to your bid and have signed teaming and nondisclosure agreements

See **Team Selection and Management.**

Every proposal of any size requires a sponsor or owner—ranging from a management executive to the account executive. An executive sponsor for the proposal effort will help you get the right people for your proposal, from planning the kickoff meeting to submittal and negotiation. Major proposal efforts that cannot attract an executive sponsor should be stopped.

Best-in-class business organizations view winning new business as a critical activity worthy of assigning their best employees. Less-effective organizations tend to assign individuals they can spare or who are available. Think of this as "making the right people available" rather than rationalizing that the "available people are right."

3

Prepare a complete but concise agenda.

See **Daily Team Management.**

Target no more than 2 to 3 hours for a kickoff meeting with 10 to 30 contributors. Make the kickoff meeting informative and professional. Do not let it turn into a problem-solving event. Like daily stand-up meetings, when problems surface, limit discussion to who needs to be involved and when that group can meet.

A typical kickoff meeting agenda is shown in Figure 1. Since everyone does not need to attend the entire meeting, arrange the agenda to permit the unneeded participants to leave early.

Establish a professional tone by distributing a copy of your agenda with the invitation to attend.

TIME (min)	PERSON	TOPIC
5	Proposal Mgr	Welcome everyone and introduce participants
5	Senior Mgr	Deliver motivational remarks and indicate organizational commitment
10	Sales, Capture, or Marketing Lead	Give background on the prospect and the opportunity
45	Proposal Mgr	Distribute and discuss the Proposal Management Plan (PMP), including outline, executive summary, Work Breakdown Structure (WBS), writers' packages, and storyboards (when used)
10	Break	. . . .
5	Tech Vol Mgr	Outline technical approach
5	Mgmt Vol Mgr	Outline management approach
5	Cost Vol Mgr	Outline costing approach
15	Proposal Mgr	Discuss daily proposal operations and schedule
15	Proposal Mgr	Answer contributor's questions and dismiss meeting

Figure 1. Plan a Concise Kickoff Meeting. *Keep your kickoff meeting short, informative, and professional. Focus on being informative over being inspirational. Excuse people early who do not need to hear sensitive information or details about the solution, individual assignments, or daily team management. Teaming partners who have not yet signed a teaming agreement should usually be excluded.*

4 Prepare a comprehensive kickoff package in advance.

See **Proposal Management Plan.**

Determine exactly what material you need to distribute at the kickoff meeting. Start with the Proposal Management Plan (PMP).

Managers of smaller proposals in less structured markets and organizations should carefully review the recommended kickoff meeting materials listed in figure 2 and select those most relevant to your proposal

See **Strategy, Scheduling,** *and* **Outlining.**

See **Storyboards and Mock-ups.**

See **Strategy.**

See **Executive Summary.**

REQUIRED ITEMS	CONTENT/FUNCTION
Proposal Project Summary	Information about the opportunity, contract type, value, official name, relevant dates, key contacts, scope, primary deliverables. All or relevant portions of the bid request.
Customer Profile	Customer needs, issues, hot buttons, evaluations process, and perception of your organization.
Proposal Strategy	Overall strategies, themes, and discriminators. Includes key messages and how they are to be implemented in the proposal.
Proposal Operations	Establishes approach, formats, protocol, resources, and approaches to review.
Proposal Schedule	Sets dates for key milestones.
Proposal Outline	Defines section numbers, headings, page allocation, responsible person, and incremental task deadlines.
Writers' Packages	First page of Proposal Development Worksheet (PDW) or storyboard, which includes the writer assigned, page limits or guidelines, information from the proposal outline relevant to each writer, along with the compliance checklist items assigned to that section
RFP	Relevant parts or pointers to an electronic source.
DESIRABLE ITEMS	**CONTENT/FUNCTION**
Competitive Analysis	Competitor profiles, Integrated Prospect Solution Worksheet, Bidder Comparison Matrix
Roles and Responsibilities	Team members, location, contact info, role, expertise, cost center, and hours authorized
Draft Executive Summary	Provide contributors with the overall perspective on prospect's needs, proposed solution, and win strategy. Models good themes, graphics, action captions, and format
WBS/WBS Dictionary	Breaks the proposal work into tasks, defining the hardware and data that will be delivered and services that will be performed

Figure 2. Recommended Kickoff Meeting Materials. *To prevent serious misdirection of your proposal team, conduct the kickoff meeting after preparing most of these materials.*

5 Review operational guidelines for proposal development.

Establish clear operational guidelines at the kickoff meeting to minimize rework later.

The simpler you can make it for contributors to follow your guidelines, the more likely they will actually follow them. For example:

> At a kickoff meeting for a major systems contractor, the production coordinator was handing out a 12-page set of formatting instructions to each contributor, including different handwriting samples to help writers estimate the amount of finished text they would have when handwriting their drafts. When asked, "Why so long?", The reply was, "The writers never seem to get it, so we have added more detail."
>
> Writers ignored the handout. When asked why, one said, "I'm not a typist. I don't need it."

Give writers a word processing file template on disk or over your intranet. Writers asked to read long instructions and correctly set up a file will usually ignore the instructions.

Clear operational guidelines will help achieve the following aims:

- Assess assigned task status
- Facilitate inputting, editing, developing and integrating graphics, and reviewing
- Coordinate writing tasks among writers
- Update and disseminate new information
- Develop and roll up cost data
- Verify consistent task descriptions and costs
- Increase senior management review and endorsement
- Identify and close gaps early to stay on schedule
- Verify drafts are complaint, responsive, and supportive of your strategy

6 Establish a tone of competent, professional proposal leadership and management.

Contributors enjoy working on a team that has senior management visibility and support, is professionally led, has a clear win strategy, has adequate resources, and has a good chance of winning.

You cannot fool your team into thinking you are competent when you have failed to plan before asking for their help.

7 Establish additional ground rules for teleconference kickoff meetings.

Teleconference kickoff meetings often have these major business development weaknesses:

- No defined process to do proposals
- Unclear understanding of roles and responsibilities
- Little consequence for late task completion
- Rewards go primarily to the nonparticipants
- General view that proposals are not important
- Proposals are free—those deciding to bid do not pay for the proposal or do the work

Establish these practices:

- Separate the initial core team planning call from the proposal kickoff call. A small core team can resolve issues and make decisions faster without wasting contributors' time.
- Establish lines of authority. The ranking person on the call from each participating organization must make and stand by their decisions. No one is permitted to go back to their organization for approval. Any organization that fails to participate must abide by the decisions of those who did.
- Establish a detailed, written agenda and distribute it early enough to permit participants to prepare.
- Take the time to poll participants for acceptance after each agenda item. Obtain closure on each item and summarize the decisions.
- As tasks are assigned, ask the responsible individuals to restate their understanding and acceptance.
- Assign someone other than the person chairing the call to keep detailed minutes. E-mail a copy of the minutes to all participants and their managers a few hours after the call is completed. Ask them to confirm their acceptance in writing, usually by e-mail.
- Check progress of a dispersed team more frequently than when your team is co-located. No news is bad news when your team is dispersed.
- Test your submission process for hardware and software compatibility. Before drafts begin, ask each participant to submit sample text and one graphic in each of the file formats they plan to use.

Letter proposals are short proposals, often not formally solicited, ranging from 1 to 20 pages. When acceptable to the prospect, use letter proposals to minimize competition and to reduce or eliminate proposal preparation and evaluation costs.

See **Executive Summary** *and* **Sales Letters**.

Structure letter proposals, executive summaries, and sales letters similarly. Keep them customer focused and structured around the prospect's hot buttons or key issues.

Too many letter proposals are deemed boilerplate documents that incorporate standard descriptions of the proposed products and services.

Instead, regard every document sent to a prospect as a proposal. Each sales document must convince the prospect's organization to agree to take the next step toward your overall sales objective.

Letter Proposals

1. **Clarify the prospect's expectations before preparing an unsolicited letter proposal.**
2. **Use the flexible Four-Box organization.**
3. **Use an informative subject line and incorporate a signal word.**
4. **In Box 1, connect your solution to the prospect's organizational objectives, your prior work with the prospect's organization, and the prospect's immediate objectives for this purchase.**
5. **In Box 2, preview the proposal's organization, arranged according to the prospect's hot buttons.**
6. **In Box 3, align your proposed solution to the prospect's most relevant hot button.**
7. **In Box 4, close with a short summary and a clear indication of the next realistically achievable step.**
8. **Use graphics with captions to discriminate your letter proposal.**
9. **Include an executive summary comprising no more than 5 to 10 percent of the proposal.**
10. **Limit attached or appended materials to items specifically requested by the prospect or essential to specialist readers.**

1 Clarify the prospect's expectations before preparing an unsolicited letter proposal.

NOTE: All sales professionals are trained to win the prospect's business without submitting a proposal. In fact, many leading sales disciplines say having to submit a proposal is a sign of failure.

Explicitly discuss what information your prospect will need in your proposal to make a decision. How can you meet your prospect's expectations unless you know what they are?

Use language similar to one of the following examples to clarify prospects' expectations:

Approach 1: You said that you will need a proposal before you can make a final decision. To make sure you get what you need, let's talk about what you would like to be included in our proposal.

Approach 2: You have used our products/services for years. To simplify your evaluation, how about if we eliminate all the usual corporate background and history and focus specifically on what we plan to do on this project?

Approach 3: If we agree to limit the proposal to 20 pages on the specifics of this project, we can eliminate 100 pages of background, corporate history, and standard product descriptions and deliver the document that you expect in 4 days. Would this be acceptable to your evaluation group?

While getting the order without a proposal is ideal, remember that purchasing professionals are trained and purchasing processes are designed to require a proposal. Competition often both improves the quality of the solution and reduces the cost.

2 Use the flexible Four-Box organization.

Use the Four-Box organizational structure to prepare persuasive, clearly organized, and expandable letter proposals. The Four-Box organizational structure is based on fundamental principles of document organization.

The Four-Box structure for any type of sales document includes a heading and four distinct boxes. The heading is treated as a separate component and not included in box 1.

Broadly viewed, the objective for each of the four boxes in a generic sales document is as follows:

- **Box 1:** Summarize the document.
- **Box 2:** Preview the document's organization, arranged according to the reader's hot buttons or needs.
- **Box 3:** Link the hot buttons to the writer's solution or key information. This is the body or main part of the document.
- **Box 4:** Summarize the document and suggest the next step.

See **Executive Summary, Organization,** *and* **Sales Letters.**

While letter proposals, executive summaries, and sales letters should all follow the Four-Box organizational structure, each will vary depending on the seller's objective, the targeted evaluators or readers, and the complexity of the information.

The greatest differences among letter proposals, executive summaries, and sales letters are in the contents of Box 1. The suggested content for each of the four boxes for the three types of sales documents is compared in figure 1. Guidelines 4 through 7 discuss the content of each of the four boxes of a letter proposal.

NOTE: Some of the listed elements will be excluded from some letter proposals depending on your history and relationship with the prospect.

The Four-Box organizational approach is flexible in several ways. First, some of the suggested content might be either omitted, appear in a different order, or be placed in a different box. For example, the statement of compliance might be omitted because it is implied in other text, or it might be placed in Box 3 or 4 because it is relatively less important than other information.

COMPONENT	TYPE OF SALES DOCUMENT		
	Letter Proposal	Executive Summary	Sales Letter
HeadingType	*Informative* *"Proposal to . . ."*	*Telegraphic* *"Executive Summary"*	*Informative* *"Invitation, Request, etc."*
BOX 1			
Theme Statement	Yes	Yes	Not needed
Vision Statement	Yes	Yes	Not needed
Linking Statement	Yes Vision-to-need	Yes Vision-to-need	Yes To previous event
Preview Solution	Yes "solution"	Yes "solution"	Yes *"Request . . ."*
Statement of Compliance	Desirable	Desirable	Not needed
BOX 2			
Introduce hot buttons	Yes	Yes	Yes
Explicit Ownership	Yes	Yes	Yes
BOX 3			
Ordered as in Box 2	Yes	Yes	Yes
Link hot button to content	Yes	Yes	Yes
Discuss Price	Mandatory	Desirable	Not applicable
BOX 4			
Summary	Yes	Yes	Yes
Suggest next step	Yes, to negotiate?	Yes, to read the proposal	Yes, to agree to seller's request

Figure 1. Comparing Letter Proposals, Executive Summaries, and Sales Letters. *All three types of sales documents should follow the Four-Box organization. The content of each box will vary depending on the specific sales objective, the targeted evaluators or readers, and the complexity of the information required to make or support the seller's point.*

Another type of flexibility with the Four-Box approach is that documents can be expanded or reduced to better match the importance of the information and the necessary level of detail. Figure 2 shows the Four-Box organizational approach applied to both 1- and 20-page letter proposals.

One-Page Narrative Letter Proposal

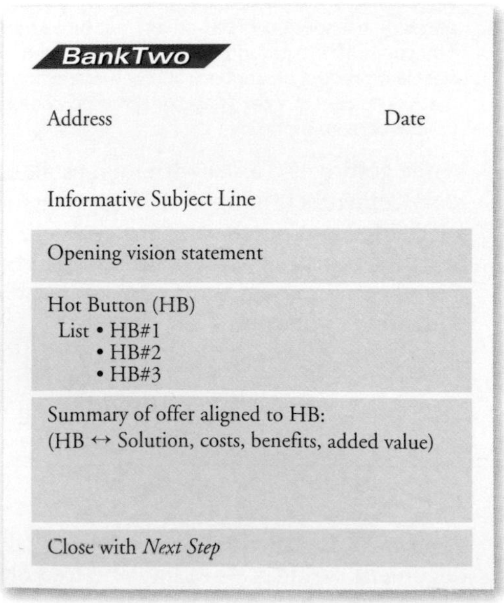

BankTwo
Address
Date
Informative Subject Line
Opening vision statement
Hot Button (HB)
List • HB#1
• HB#2
• HB#3
Summary of offer aligned to HB:
(HB ↔ Solution, costs, benefits, added value)
Close with Next Step

Typical 20-Page NarrativeLetter Proposal Outline

Page	Content
1	Cover Page
2	Contents
3	Summary & Introduction
4	Introduce hot buttons
4-7	Hot button 1 discussion
8-10	Hot button 2 discussion
10-12	Hot button 3 discussion
13-14	Hot button 4 discussion
15-17	Summarize Offer & Schedule
18-19	Cost Justification with Quantified Client Benefits
20	Closing Summary

Figure 2. Expandable, Flexible Four-Box Organizational Approach. *Expand or contract the same structure as appropriate. Allocate space according to the relative importance of the topic to your prospect.*

3

Use an informative subject line and incorporate a signal word.

Also see **Headings.**

Like a well-crafted headline, informative subject lines both summarize your key message and interest or engage the reader. Make the first word a "signal word" that immediately announces the purpose of your letter:

- Proposal
- Recommendation
- Request
- Invitation
- Contract
- Statement of Work
- Analysis
- Final Report

When you omit these elements, prospects often stop reading.

Whether you want to label your proposal as a proposal depends on your sales strategy. If the prospect requested a proposal, call it that. If you want to emphasize your consultative role, you might begin with one of the other signal words.

Informative subject lines include benefits when possible. Benefits immediately interest prospects. Effective subject lines open with a signal word that defines the document's purpose for the reader:

- Proposal to Supply Rail Cars at One-half of Current Cost
- Recommendation to Immediately Contract for Legal Benefits to Enhance Executive Retention
- Invitation to Contract for FY 2002 Desktop Support
- Contract Provisions Approved August 1, 20XX

4

In Box 1, connect your solution to the prospect's organizational objectives, your prior work with the prospect's organization, and the prospect's immediate objectives for this purchase.

NOTE: Statements of compliance are somewhat controversial. Some professionals say they are required. Others say compliance is implied when a bid is submitted unless exceptions are stated in the bid.

See. **Theme Statements.**

As listed in figure 1, Box 1 of a letter proposal may include a theme statement, vision statement, linking statement, preview of the solution, and a statement of compliance. Several of these items may be combined in a single sentence to be concise.

The theme statement summarizes everything you want to say in one sentence. Tie the benefit to your key discriminator. Vision statements demonstrate how well you understand the prospect's overall direction and need. A prospect will purchase from sellers who best demonstrate their understanding of the prospect's business and immediate needs.

Linking statements that tie prospect's immediate needs to the organization's objectives demonstrate your understanding and support funding this project versus competing projects.

The preview of your solution is often only a phrase. In the first Box 1 example shown below, the preview of the solution is in the theme statement, "*. . . supply 20 versatile ultralight aircraft* [with] *long-term support.*" In the second example, the solution is summarized in the first and last sentences, "*. . . contracting with Able IT . . .*" and "*. . . an IT support partner . . .*" Sales and sales support professionals often voice two objections:

1. Don't they already know their need?
2. What if I get it wrong?

First, of course they know. They need to be reassured that you know. Second, if you cannot get it right, you should not be bidding and do not deserve to win.

Note how the two examples link the prospect's organizational objectives and immediate objectives to the offer and cite prior work.

Cascadia Timber Annual Report

THEME STATEMENT
Cascadia Timber can reduce the cost of forest management in remote roadless areas by selecting a partner to supply 20 versatile ultralight aircraft that also offers long-term support.

ORGANIZATIONAL VISION AND OBJECTIVES
Cascadia Timber is ranked as the No. 1 company in the world by *Foresters' Monthly* for low cost, innovative forest management. Cascadia Timber Chairman, Woody X. Pine, set the following strategic direction:

We have to do everything better, more efficiently from a cost point of view, more effectively from an impact point of view.

LINKING STATEMENT TO THE IMMEDIATE OBJECTIVE
During our discussion over the past 6 weeks, you have indicated that Cascadia Timber's Forest Management Division helps improve efficiency and effectiveness by adopting innovative forest management practices.

THEME STATEMENT
Bank Two can cut IT support cost by 30 percent by contracting with Able IT, Ltd.

ORGANIZATIONAL VISION AND OBJECTIVE
Having emerged from the recent industry consolidation, Bank Two is now the second largest and fastest growing bank in the Northwest. Bank Two's board challenged management to increase ROI by 25 percent.

IMMEDIATE NEED
In our initial meeting 2 months ago, you stated that Bank Two's Operations Department would contribute to ROI improvement by seeking proposals for an IT support partner that can reliably deliver support at a 30 percent cost reduction.

5

In Box 2, preview the proposal's organization, arranged according to the prospect's hot buttons.

Box 2 introduces the prospect's hot buttons for the current purchase. Brainstorm an extensive list of needs, issues, hot buttons, key requirements, and evaluation criteria. Then consolidate or group them into three to five distinct items. Use the prospect's words.

Prioritize them in one of two ways:

1. Order of importance to the prospect
2. Order stated by the prospect

Ideally, the prospect states the hot buttons in order of importance. If you are not sure which hot buttons are more important, follow the order stated in the bid request, in other prospect documents, or in discussions with the prospect.

This becomes your hot button list. Now introduce the hot buttons, making prospect ownership explicit:

Poor example ***(NO PROSPECT OWNERSHIP)***

The ideal aircraft must meet four primary needs:

1. Affordable, portable, and easily transportable
2. All-conditions observation and communication platform
3. Safe and easy to fly
4. Easy to assemble and maintain in the field

Good example ***(EXPLICIT PROSPECT OWNERSHIP)***

In our meetings with Forest Management and Purchasing, you cited four primary needs:

1. Affordable, portable, and easily transportable
2. All-conditions observation and communication platform
3. Safe and easy to fly
4. Easy to assemble and maintain in the field

All too frequently writers are asked to draft a letter proposal when they lack adequate prospect contact or knowledge about the prospect's needs. When this happens, set up the prospect's hot buttons based on what you do know:

Good example

Our experience with customers in the forest products industry has indicated that most cite four primary needs:

1. Affordable, portable, and easily transportable
2. All-conditions observation and communication platform
3. Safe and easy to fly
4. Easy to assemble and maintain in the field

Note how the softer setup avoids being arrogant, gives you an out if you have the needs wrong, and validates your industry experience.

6

In Box 3, align your proposed solution to the prospect's most relevant hot button.

NOTE 1: If the hot button takes more than one page, insert a short introduction or preview between steps 1 and 2.

NOTE 2: Occasionally you will have some additional content that must be included but that clearly does not fit against any of the hot buttons. First, verify that it is relevant, then introduce it between Boxes 3 and 4.

NOTE 3: Link pricing and costing information to a relevant hot button or place it between Boxes 3 and 4. The following hot buttons are typically relevant to pricing:

—Reduce Operating Cost
—Increase Market Competitiveness
—Deliver Operational Plant Within Budget
—Payoff Within 2 Years

To keep your letter proposal brief but comprehensive, you must link all of your points to one of the prospect's hot buttons, the ones listed in Box 2.

Make first-level subheadings in Box 3 identical in wording and order to the hot buttons introduced in Box 2. Prospects are confused when either the wording or order changes.

Figure 2 illustrates how to identify and allocate your letter proposal content to a single section under one hot button. First, make lists of information you need to include in the proposal. Then, find a reasonable place for each item under one of the hot buttons.

Organize your response to each hot button in the following manner:

1. Succinctly state your solution to the requirement.
2. Provide supporting details, either graphically or in text.
3. Offer proof of experience and/or performance.

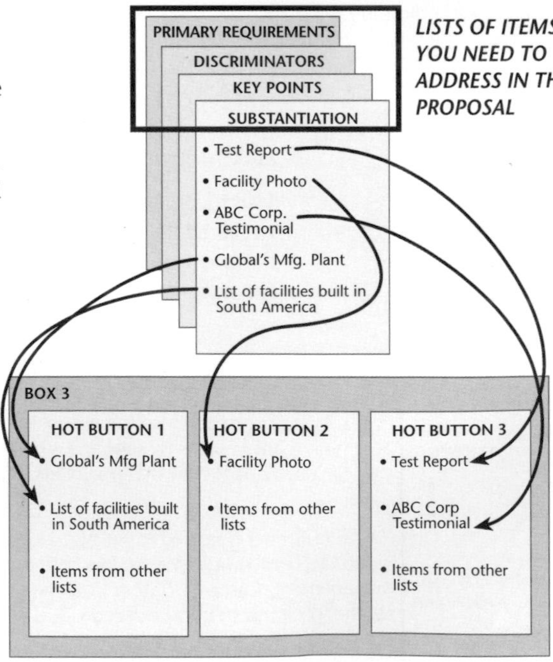

Figure 2. Organizing Box 3. *First, list the primary prospect requirements that you must address, your primary discriminators, key points, and relevant substantiation. Then allocate all items from each list in some reasonable manner under one of the hot buttons. As there is no single, correct allocation, try to group similar items and present them logically.*

7

In Box 4, close with a short summary and a clear indication of the next realistically achievable step.

Summarize the benefits the prospect will enjoy from your solution. List them in the order presented, as concisely as possible.

Then proactively suggest the next step, usually a phone call or meeting to resolve any questions and to finalize the contract.

The following Box 4 example summarizes the seller's offer in the first two paragraphs, then reinforces the seller's compliance and flexibility and suggests the next step in the last paragraph.

Cascadia Timber has kept on the leading edge of innovative forest management techniques. Jenair Sports welcomes the opportunity to supply 20 ultralight aircraft, flight and maintenance training, and long-term maintenance and inspection support to further Cascadia's leadership.

While many ultralights are used for recreation, the Endeavor's unique 10-year use by Special Forces personnel over similar terrain and more difficult conditions reduces the risk of use in continuous operation.

Our proposal addresses all issues discussed in our meetings. Should your requirements change, we welcome the opportunity to discuss further enhancements. We will call you in 1 week to resolve any open items and to agree on the next step.

8

See **Action Captions** *and* **Graphics.**

Use graphics with captions to discriminate your letter proposal.

Few sellers use graphics in letter proposals. Emphasize the clarity of your thinking by using graphics with complete action captions in your letter proposal.

Consider using the following types of graphics in a letter proposal:

- Photos showing the product being used or the service being delivered
- Photos of reference sites
- Reference lists
- Organization chart of the delivery team
- Photos of the prospect using or observing the product
- Brief schedule
- Pricing table

9

NOTE: The recommended structure is intentionally repetitive. As Jim Beverage noted in *The Anatomy of a Win*, "A good proposal is a summary of a summary of a summary."

Include an executive summary comprising no more than 5 to 10 percent of the proposal.

Even with short letter proposals, include an executive summary.

Your executive summary need not be labeled. When using the Four-Box organization, the informative heading and Box 1 constitute the executive summary.

Executive summaries, previews, and closing summaries are intentionally repetitive because people remember the first items they see, the last items they see, and repeated items.

Few proposals, including letter proposals, are completely read from beginning to end. Repetition increases the probability that they will get your key points.

10

See **Appendices and Attachments.**

Limit attached or appended materials to items specifically requested by the prospect or essential to specialist readers.

Attaching extensive materials to a letter proposal dilutes your message and negates the primary objective of submitting a letter proposal—to reduce the time and cost of preparing and evaluating proposals.

If you must attach materials, follow the guidelines for appendices.

List the additional materials that are available but not included to ease their evaluation. Regard subsequent requests for materials as an opportunity to call on the prospect when your competitors cannot.

Lists serve two important functions in proposals: (1) emphasize important points and (2) preview direction.

Readers are more likely to remember information presented in a list, especially a display list.

Evaluators searching proposals for answers to their questions use display lists to spot information and to point them to where the information is discussed in body text.

Guidelines for the optimal use of display lists in proposals are more specific and restrictive than in other business documents.

Proposals are read and accessed differently than most other business documents. Virtually no one reads them completely or continuously.

Evaluators are skeptical. They are trying to detect the spin in your message; what information has been slanted, omitted, or even deliberately misrepresented.

Unfortunately, many proposal writers use lists as a dumping ground for information. They put unrelated items in a list because the information is available and when they do not have a clear message in mind.

Lists

1. **Make all items in lists parallel in structure. Begin each item with the same kind of word (noun, verb, adjective, or adverb).**
2. **Name each list.**
3. **Place the name of the list immediately in front of the list.**
4. **Limit list contents to the items named.**
5. **Limit your use of display lists to items deserving emphasis.**
6. **Minimize or eliminate confusing nested lists.**
7. **Begin display lists with numbers or letters if you are mimicking the bid request numbering system or if you refer to list items in subsequent text. Otherwise, use bullets or dashes.**
8. **Capitalize the first word in each item. End all items with a period only if at least one item is a complete sentence.**

1

Make all items in lists parallel in structure. Begin each item with the same kind of word (noun, verb, adjective, or adverb).

Items listed must be consistent in form and structure. Each item begins with the same kind and type of word, e.g., verbs in the same tense.

Verb lists are the most effective type of lists in proposals because they convey a sense of action.

Verb list

The Party 2000 music system empowers DJ's to perform the following actions:

- Play any cut in random order
- Set play time for each cut
- Suppress voice tracks for Karaoke applications
- Adjust individual speaker volume

Adjective list

The Party 2000 music system includes the following features:

- Random play
- Variable play time for each cut
- Voice suppression for Karaoke use
- Adjustable volume for individual speakers

Noun list

The Party 2000 music system includes the following features:

- Amplifier with 200 watts
- Storage of 200 CDs
- Karaoke
- Speaker with individual volume adjustments

2

Name each list.

Naming a list makes your proposal easier to understand when evaluators skim read or search for answers to their questions. Naming a list also increases the probability that the list is parallel. In an unnamed list, the reader must read the list and determine what the items are.

Unnamed list

Our project manager will:

- Plan all work
- Set quality standards
- Report progress weekly

NOTE: In addition to naming a list prior to the list, some writers name the list in the prior heading. Naming the list in the heading is not possible when the headings are dictated in the bid request.

See **Headings.**

Unnamed lists often become a dumping ground, especially when boilerplate is used extensively and deadlines are short.

The following named list is easier to understand:

Named list

Our project manager will complete the following tasks:

- Plan all work
- Set quality standards
- Report progress weekly

---

3 Place the name of the list immediately in front of the list.

Sometimes the introduction to items in the list becomes so long that the reader forgets what was supposed to be in the list.

Named list with long setup (difficult to read)

When initiated by a call to the Help Desk, actions taken by our service technician will include the following unless the service call is initiated outside our normal business hours, 8:00 AM to 5:00 PM, EST:

- Review the service request
- Determine probable cause using our proprietary Dr. Bug™ software
- Schedule service call with the initiator
- Make the call and fix the problem

Named list with name before the list (easier to read)

When initiated by a call to the Help Desk unless the service call is initiated outside our normal business hours, 8:00 AM to 5:00 PM, EST, our service technician will take the following actions:

- Review the service request.
- Determine probable cause using our proprietary Dr. Bug™ software.
- Schedule service call with the initiator.
- Make the call and fix the problem.

While the setup is too long in either case, the second is easier to understand because the named action preceeds the list.

---

4 Limit list contents to the items named.

See **Features, Advantages, and Benefits.**

Many lists found in proposals are both not the items named and not parallel in structure.

Our project manager will complete the following tasks:

- Plan all work.
- Set quality standards.
- Project managers cannot begin out-of-scope work unless approved by Purchasing in writing.

The third item is not a task. Such explanatory detail should be placed in a following sentence or omitted. Other lists are parallel in structure but do not contain the items named.

Our solution offers the following benefits:

- 24 x 7 service
- ISO 9000 certification
- Operational cost reductions
- 99.92 percent availability

The first two items are features, the third is clearly a benefit, and the fourth is probably a benefit.

Calling a feature a benefit suggests you do not understand your prospect's needs and that you may be trying to sell them something that they do not need, thus increasing the cost. Incorrectly confusing features and benefits is a major problem in many proposals.

---

5 Limit your use of display lists to items deserving emphasis.

See **Page and Document Design.**

Prospects care about the benefits to them and their organization. In complex sales, features are relatively less important. Notice how features are emphasized over benefits:

The Endeavor is the ultimate in ultralight aircraft on the market today. Cascadia Timber can improve forest productivity and the efficiency of individual foresters with Jenair's comprehensive solution. In the attached proposal, you will see the following products detailed:

- Endeavor aircraft
- Pilot training
- Maintenance training
- Spare parts
- Radios
- Transportation and packing
- Disassembly/assembly approach
- Maintenance support
- Standard warranty
- Manuals

Notice how the benefit, "improve forest production and the efficiency of individual foresters," is presented before the features (good) but buried in the middle of the second sentence (poor). The list of features gets the most emphasis by being surrounded by white space. Skim readers may only see the list of features. A more persuasive organization would begin with the second sentence, bullet list the benefits, then discuss the benefits in order. The features should be aligned with the appropriate benefit.

6

Minimize or eliminate confusing nested lists.

Nested lists are lists within lists. They are confusing, cumbersome, and sometimes border on the ridiculous.

Nested List (confusing)

All systems are shipped with these items:

- 17" monitor
  - –.22 dot pitch
  - –1 million colors
  - –Swivel stand
- Apple G4 CPU
  - –Rage card
  - –800 MHz processor
  - –30 GB IDE hard drive
- 1200 x 600 flat bed scanner
- 10 ppm color printer
- Coffee cup
  - –Aluminum
  - –Double insulated
  - –Handle
    - √ Black
    - √ Plastic
    - √ Detachable

7

Begin display lists with numbers or letters if you are mimicking the bid request numbering system or if you refer to list items in subsequent text. Otherwise, use bullets or dashes.

Readers assume that items in lists are placed in decreasing order of importance. Follow that convention.

Using bullets, dashes, or similar nonordered marks does not mean items are of equal importance. If you want the reader to know that all items are of equal importance, tell them.

8

Capitalize the first word in each item. End all items with a period only if at least one item is a complete sentence.

Many proposal writers incorrectly punctuate items in a display list like items in a paragraph list. Do not place commas at the end of display list items or a period at the end of the last item in the list.

Incorrectly punctuated display list (poor example)

Our project manager will complete the following tasks:

- Plan all work,
- Set quality standards, and
- Report progress weekly.

Correctly punctuated display list (good example)

Our project manager will complete the following tasks:

- Plan all work
- Set quality standards
- Report progress weekly

Punctuate a displayed list when the items in the list complete an introductory statement.

Correctly punctuated display list (good example)

You may identify potential boilerplate material for your proposal by

1. Calling up the search screen,
2. Entering a word or topic, followed by striking the "return" key, and then
3. Reviewing the potential material that appears in the next window.

NOTE: This style of punctuation in displayed lists is increasingly rare and outdated. Less than 10 percent of current editors retain this style.

Traditional practice is to end all list items with a period only if at least one item is a complete sentence. This includes imperative commands when the first word is a verb and the noun is understood.

However, the current trend is to reduce unnecessary punctuation as much as possible. Some editors recommend making all list items either phrases or complete sentences. Make your choice and be consistent.

Many more punctuation variations are possible than have been discussed in this *Proposal Guide*. If you need further detail, refer to a writing style guide or manual of style.

Numbering systems are used with the table of contents, cross-reference matrix, and headings to show the proposal's organization and allow evaluators to rapidly locate the answers to the questions asked in the bid request.

See **Outlining**.

Ideally, your numbering system takes the evaluator directly to each answer. The compromise on large proposals is to balance the number of heading levels used with how closely the subsection number takes the evaluator to each answer.

The two basic numbering systems are the traditional or alphanumeric system and the decimal system.

Traditional System

Traditional outlines use the following numbering and lettering conventions:

I.
  A.
    1.
      a.
        (1)
          (a)
            1)
              a)

Decimal System

In the decimal system, successive decimal points indicate levels of subordination:

1.0
  1.1
    1.1.1
    1.1.2
    1.1.3
      1.1.3.1
      1.1.3.2

2.0
  2.1
  2.2
    2.2.1
    2.2.2

Some bid requests simply skip numbers, reserving a section in case they need it later. Clearly, many people who write bid requests have never read this *Proposal Guide*. Some place periods after the last number. Some drop in a letter when they want to use a single place and nine is not enough places.

For example, the author of a bid request wants bidders to discuss 11 items within section 3.2.4. Bidders may select any of the three following numbering options:

1	2	3
3.2.4.1	3.2.4.01	3.2.4.a
3.2.4.2	3.2.4.02	3.2.4.b
⋮ ↓	⋮ ↓	⋮ ↓
3.2.4.9	3.2.4.09	3.2.4.i
3.2.4.10	3.2.1.10	3.2.4.j
3.2.4.11	3.2.4.11	3.2.4.k

The concern with approaches 1 or 2 is that someone will insert a decimal point between the last two numbers. Sometimes the field only allows a single digit. Assuming base-10 numbering, a single space permits 1 through 9. When letters are used, 26 places are possible—A through Z.

Numbering Systems

1. **Mirror the numbering system of the bid request when possible.**
2. **If given a choice, select the decimal system over the traditional system.**
3. **Limit numbered subheadings to three levels plus an additional unnumbered sublevel, unless you are mirroring the bid request.**

---

1 Mirror the numbering system of the bid request when possible.

See **Outlining**.

See **Compliance and Responsiveness**.

No matter how poor the numbering system in the bid request, use it. Imagine how difficult evaluation is when each bidding company invents its own system. Often the evaluator did not prepare the bid request.

Place helpful notes in your proposal and your cross-reference matrix to make it easy for evaluators to correlate the bid request and your proposal.

Good Example

2.3 Intentionally blank. This section was skipped in our proposal to maintain identical section numbers between your RFP and our proposal.

Our proposal section numbers mirror the RFP section numbers except the L.21 prefix on every number was dropped for simplicity. For example:

RFP Para. #	Proposal Pars. #
L.21.1	1.0
L.21.1.1	1.1
L.21.3.3	3.3
L.21.3.3.1	3.3.1

2

If given a choice, select the decimal system over the traditional system.

The decimal system is instantly understandable. Three numbers means it is a third-level section. Additionally, the reader does not have to rebuild the real reference caused by an "a)" that goes with a "1" that goes to an "A" two pages previous, etc.

Assuming the traditional system, few readers instantly know "a" is a fourth-level heading—I.A.1.a.

Ever find yourself or see others saying the alphabet to determine which letter comes next? That seldom happens with numbers.

While the convention is established, does every potential reader know the correct order for "a.", "(a)", or "a)"? Also, while increasing indentation at succeeding levels is most common for traditional systems, it can leave unusually wide left margins when combined with multicolumn page designs.

3

Limit numbered subheadings to three levels plus an additional unnumbered sublevel, unless you are mirroring the bid request.

NOTE: Guideline 1 *always* overrides guideline 3.

The greater the number of levels in the proposal, the harder it is to follow. If your numbering system can get the evaluator to within three pages or closer, your numbering system is probably adequate.

Use introductions and unnumbered or run-in subheadings to direct evaluators within subsections longer than one page. Either of the following examples is acceptable. The one on the left numbers all subsections. The one on the right uses unnumbered or run-in subheadings.

All Subsections Numbered

Proposal Outline

2.0 Management Plan
  2.1 Organization Structure and Facility Resources
    2.1.1 Current Structure and Operation
      2.1.1.1 Project Team Structure
      2.1.1.2 Project Team Management
    2.1.2 Organizational Size and Stability
    2.1.3 Relevant Facility Resources
      2.1.3.1 Fire Protection Plan
      2.1.3.2 Seismic Protection Plan

Unnumbered Subsections

Proposal Outline

2.0 Management Plan
  2.1 Organization Structure and Facility Resources
    2.1.1 Current Structure and Operation
      Project Team Structure
      Project Team Management
    2.1.2 Organizational Size and Stability
    2.1.3 Relevant Facility Resources
      Fire Protection Plan
      Seismic Protection Plan

Oral proposals were approved in 1995 by the U.S. Office of Federal Procurement Policy (OFPP) as a substitute for information traditionally provided in written form under the cover of the offeror's proposal. In contrast to most oral sales presentations, the oral proposal is not a direct restatement of information in the written proposal.

See **Presentations to Prospects.**

A type of oral proposal has been used in non-Federal competitions for years, often for professional services. Most entailed a written prequalification proposal, short-listing, then the winner was selected after a presentation that was specific to the prospect's need.

OFPP believed that oral proposals would help achieve the following objectives:

- Reduce procurement time
- Improve information exchange to select the most advantageous offer
- Reduce buyer and seller costs
- Increase competition

The U.S. Navy released the following comparison of two procurements:

Measure	*Conventional*	*Oral Proposal*
Time to award	30 mos.	3 mos.
Navy procurement head count	15-40	4
RFP length	1000 pages	3 pages
Cost to Navy	$6M USD	$NA

The twist with oral proposals is the unusually detailed written bid request instructions for the presentation that must be followed precisely.

Many agencies use oral proposals, including DoD, DOE, DOT, FAA, GSA, IRS, NASA, and NRC. Usage is increasing, and the formal approach is likely to spread to other governments and commercial organizations.

Previously, when a presentation followed a written proposal, the team would focus first on the written document, then the presentation.

Now, the timing and extent of the oral proposal and the written proposal, if any, vary. Often both must be prepared in parallel, requiring a different and potentially more demanding preparation process. Bid requests normally specify the time, location, presentation facilities, length of presentation, visual aids, and who may present.

Note that while the intent was to replace the written proposal with an oral proposal, agencies frequently require both.

Typical proposal sections included in oral proposals include the following:

- Sample tasks and other tests
- Requirements understanding
- Capabilities
- Approaches
- Experience
- Quality and transition plans

Typical proposal sections excluded include the following:

- Cost information
- Representations and certifications
- Personnel resumes
- Performance history
- Contractual commitments

Oral Proposals

1. **Prepare for an oral proposal by understanding the similarities and differences between written and oral proposals.**
2. **Develop a style that presents your nonverbal messages so they reinforce your verbal messages.**
3. **Plan your entire approach before preparing your presentation.**
4. **Organize your presentation by using the Oral Proposal Planner (OPP) to map content from the Proposal Development Worksheet (PDW) into the presentation.**
5. **Create effective visuals.**
6. **Rehearse early, realistically, and often.**
7. **Orchestrate the entire presentation.**
8. **Prepare a lessons-learned analysis to understand your win or loss and to improve subsequent proposals.**

1 Prepare for an oral proposal by understanding the similarities and differences between written and oral proposals.

Oral and written proposals have similar requirements:

- Pre-positioning with the prospect
- Making a good bid decision
- Understanding the audience
- Complying with bid request instructions
- Preparing a Proposal Management Plan
- Preparing and conducting the kickoff meeting
- Designing and implementing your strategy
- Adhering to schedule
- Storyboarding the proposal

Oral proposals have several fundamentally different requirements:

- Planning and developing written and oral proposals simultaneously
- Selecting, training, and rehearsing credible presenters
- Designing fewer but more critical graphics
- Rehearsing realistically
- Preparing to handle extemporaneous questions

Instructions for oral proposals vary by agency and procurement official:

- Delivery is at your site or theirs.
- Delivery is taped or live.
- Written proposals, submitted prior to or at the presentation, may or may not be required.
- Media, handouts, and props may be specified and limited.
- Presentation materials are often limited and must be submitted in advance with no subsequent modifications.
- Presentation time is usually limited and structured.
- Presenters and their roles are often specified, especially when teams are being tested.

2 Develop a style that presents your nonverbal messages so they reinforce your verbal messages.

Nonverbal messages can reinforce, replace, or contradict the verbal message. Your goal should be to control your nonverbal messages so that they reinforce your verbal message. Reinforcing your verbal messages requires congruence of the verbal and nonverbal elements.

The verbal elements of a speaker's message are the words. The nonverbal elements include visual and vocal cues. Visual cues are the way the speaker appears, stands, moves, gestures, and looks at the audience. Vocal cues are the way the speaker says the words.

The nonverbal aspects of oral communication are vital to being clear, credible, and persuasive. Nonverbal elements affect clarity because approximately 70 percent of the information absorbed in oral communication stems from the nonverbal elements.

NOTE: If you have any doubts about the presentation skills of those who will be delivering your company's presentation, seek professional coaching.

Your credibility is questioned when the verbal and nonverbal elements of your oral communication conflict. When this happens, audience members are more likely to trust the nonverbal elements when they determine the meaning of the message.

Effective persuasion is conservatively estimated to be 50 percent facts and 50 percent emotion. Emotion in a presentation is conveyed primarily by nonverbal elements, as shown in figure 1.

Presenters need to develop and display competent, acceptable nonverbal presentation skills. Evaluators do not expect stars. Assess the following nonverbal skills of your presenters and use rehearsals to minimize their negative impact.

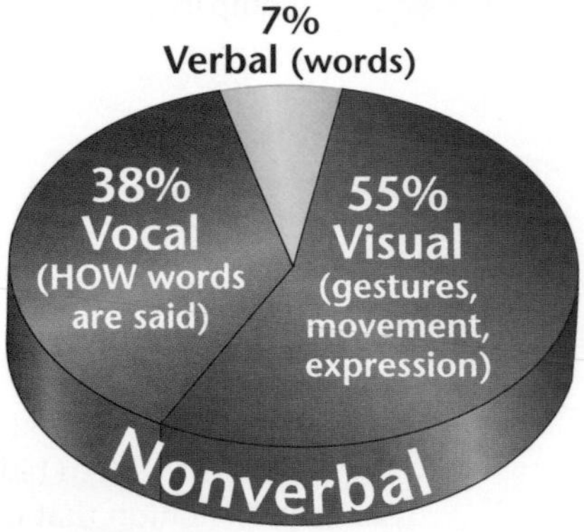

Figure 1. Importance of Nonverbal Communication to Persuade. *Research by Dr. Albert Mehrabian at UCLA demonstrated the importance of nonverbal communication to communicate emotion. He determined that 93 percent of the emotional content of a message is conveyed nonverbally by visual and vocal cues.*

Nonverbal Skills

1. **Eye contact** is one of the best ways to hold a listener's attention. Use specific drills to accustom presenters to hold eye contact for three seconds with individual audience members.

   Try this drill to improve a presenter's eye contact with the audience. Ask individuals in the audience to hold their hands up until the presenter has maintained continuous eye contact with them for three seconds. The presenter's objective is to get all arms down during their short presentation.
2. **Facial expressions** must naturally reflect your message. Smiling does not detract from a serious message. Most inappropriate facial expressions, such as frowns, sneers, smirks, etc., are eliminated through rehearsal.
3. **Appearance** should be appropriate, neat, and similar among presenters but not necessarily identical. Appropriate dress helps presenters feel confident.

Appropriate dress will depend on the country, culture, location, season, and industry. Try to dress slightly better than the audience. Groups of presenters should dress similarly, to look like a team, but not identically unless uniforms are normal dress. Discuss dress options during preparations and preview all presenters' dress at a "dress" rehearsal.

4. **Posture** demonstrates confidence and self esteem. Gestures between the waist and shoulders are strongest and project confidence. If using a podium, stand beside it, not behind it. Try to eliminate anything that blocks the audience's view of the speaker from the waist up.
5. **Enter and exit confidently.** Movement draws the eye of the audience and commands attention. Use movement to signal a change of topic. Move closer to the audience when emphasizing a point or addressing a question.
6. **Gestures** are an extension of movement. Practice gesturing, not gestures. Gestures that are studied look studied. Gestures will vary by presenter and will become more natural with rehearsal.

   Audiences will accept a wide variety of speaking styles. Your primary objective should be to coach presenters to eliminate distractive mannerisms, not to turn them into robots. For example, if a presenter persists in placing a hand in a pocket, make sure there is nothing in the pocket that might rattle or jingle. If a presenter tends to bend pointers, click pens, or fiddle with markers, take those items away. Markers can be tied to charts; pointers can be placed on overhead projectors instead of the screen. Seek solutions that minimally impact the presenter.
7. **Voice delivery,** not the words, carries 38 percent of the emotional impact. Vary voice volume, speed, and pitch. Pause for attention or emphasis. Enunciate carefully, especially when discussing complex points. Repeat key or complex points.

3 Plan your entire approach before preparing your presentation.

NOTE: Common aspects to planning oral and written proposals are covered in greater detail in the **Proposal Management Plan** and are only briefly listed here:

- Analyze the bid request
- Create a compliance checklist
- Complete the PDW
- Develop an annotated outline

Both oral and written proposals require careful planning before preparing the presentation or drafting sections. A unique aspect of oral proposal planning is assessing the presentation situation.

Vital aspects of the presentation situation are the time, setting, and occasion.

Time aspects include the time allowed, the time of day, and the order of presenters.

Regarding the **setting**, determine the location and physical layout of the room, the number of evaluators present, and the resources available.

The **occasion** requires you to understand the situation in context; what outside events could affect your presentation?

4 Organize your presentation by using the Oral Proposal Planner (OPP) to map content from the Proposal Development Worksheet (PDW) into the presentation.

Use the OPP, shown in figure 3, to build a presentation that is logical, responsive, consistent, and persuasive. Use the OPP to plan every major topic:

- Identify the time allotted to the topic.
- Identify applicable evaluation criteria.
- Show how strategy will be implemented.
- Structure topic introductions.
- Develop content point by point.
- Summarize key benefits and features.
- Close with power.

NOTE: The overall organization is similar to that recommended for executive summaries.

See **Executive Summary** *and* **Storyboards and Mock-ups**.

When the prospect requires a written and oral proposal, use the PDW to develop content. Then map the content from the PDW to the OPP to save time and maintain consistency. Data flows from the PDW, shown in figure 2, to the OPP, shown in figure 3.

If no written proposal is required, you could begin with the OPP. However, content planning is not as thorough and important points are easily missed.

Order your main points in the same order as they were listed in the bid request. If no order is specified, order them in decreasing order of importance to the prospect.

Use the Triple-S presentation formula to present each main point:

1. **State**
   My first point is. . .
   My second point is . . .
2. **Support**
   Let's define . . .
   What this means is . . .
   For example, a previous client with. . .
   The president of Acme said . . .
   Imagine that . . .
   Here is a picture of . . .
   Independent testers found that . . .
3. **Summarize**
   To summarize . . .
   In essence . . .
   What we are saying is . . .

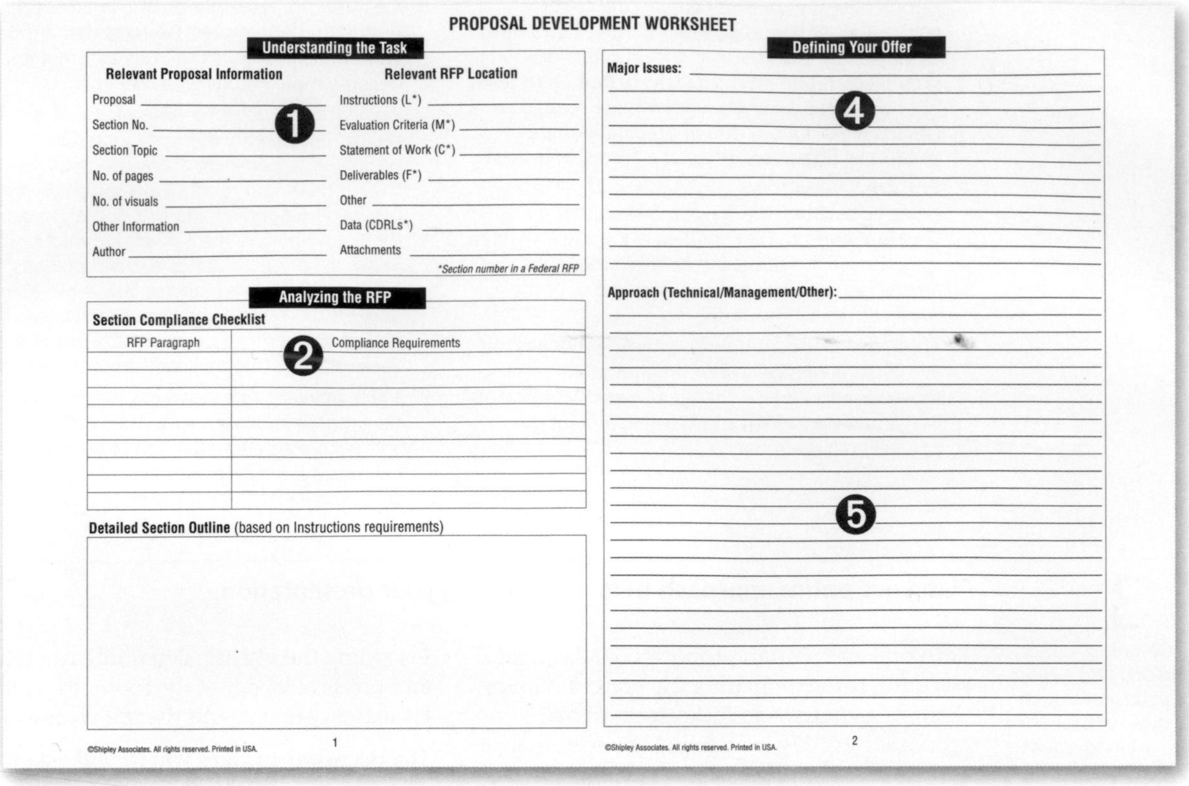

PROPOSAL DEVELOPMENT WORKSHEET

Understanding the Task

Relevant Proposal Information	Relevant RFP Location
Proposal	Instructions (L*)
Section No. ❶	Evaluation Criteria (M*)
Section Topic	Statement of Work (C*)
No. of pages	Deliverables (F*)
No. of visuals	Other
Other Information	Data (CDRLs*)
Author	Attachments

*Section number in a Federal RFP

Analyzing the RFP

Section Compliance Checklist

RFP Paragraph	❷ Compliance Requirements

Detailed Section Outline (based on Instructions requirements)

©Shipley Associates. All rights reserved. Printed in USA. 1

Defining Your Offer

Major Issues: ❹

Approach (Technical/Management/Other): ❺

©Shipley Associates. All rights reserved. Printed in USA. 2

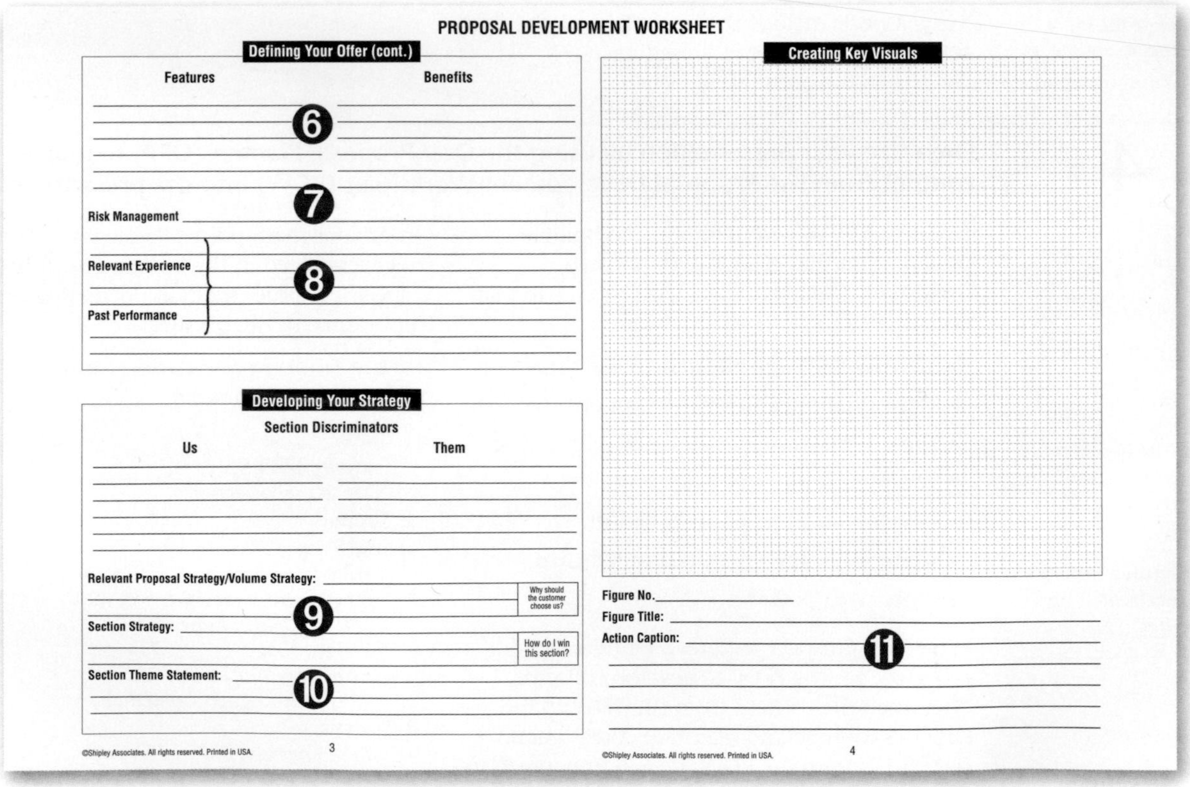

PROPOSAL DEVELOPMENT WORKSHEET

Defining Your Offer (cont.)

Features ❻ Benefits

Risk Management ❼

Relevant Experience ❽

Past Performance

Developing Your Strategy

Section Discriminators

Us | Them

Relevant Proposal Strategy/Volume Strategy: (Why should the customer choose us?)

Section Strategy: ❾ (How do I win this section?)

Section Theme Statement: ❿

©Shipley Associates. All rights reserved. Printed in USA. 3

Creating Key Visuals

Figure No.

Figure Title:

Action Caption: ⓫

©Shipley Associates. All rights reserved. Printed in USA. 4

Figure 2. Flow of Data from PDW to OPP. *Note how the data developed in the PDW for responsiveness, customer focus, strategy, risk, past performance, and themes flow into the OPP shown in figure 3, indicated by the common numbering system.*

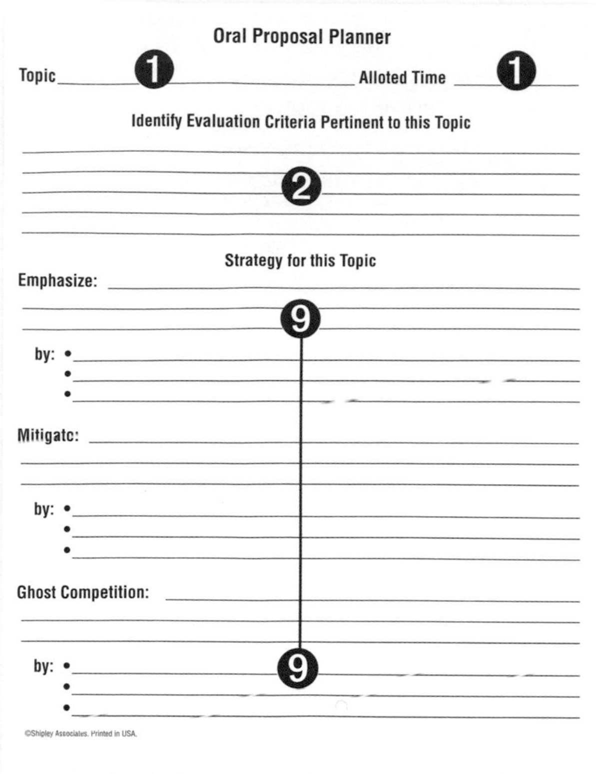
Oral Proposal Planner

Topic ___ 1 ___ Alloted Time ___ 1

Identify Evaluation Criteria Pertinent to this Topic

2

Strategy for this Topic

Emphasize: ___ 9

by: •
•
•

Mitigate: ___

by: •
•
•

Ghost Competition: ___

by: • ___ 9
•
•

©Shipley Associates. Printed in USA.

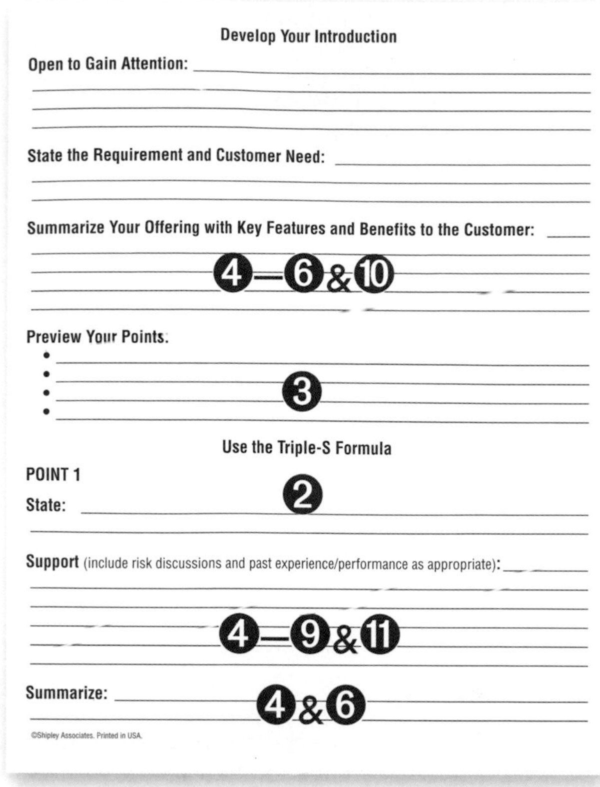
Develop Your Introduction

Open to Gain Attention: ___

State the Requirement and Customer Need: ___

Summarize Your Offering with Key Features and Benefits to the Customer: ___ 4–6 & 10

Preview Your Points:
•
•
• ___ 3
•

Use the Triple-S Formula

POINT 1

State: ___ 2

Support (include risk discussions and past experience/performance as appropriate): ___ 4–9 & 11

Summarize: ___ 4 & 6

©Shipley Associates. Printed in USA.

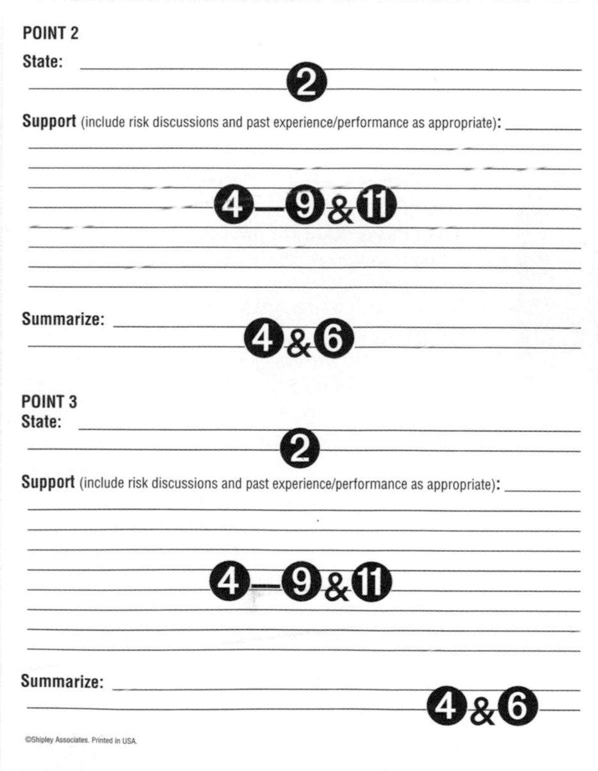
POINT 2

State: ___ 2

Support (include risk discussions and past experience/performance as appropriate): ___ 4–9 & 11

Summarize: ___ 4 & 6

POINT 3

State: ___ 2

Support (include risk discussions and past experience/performance as appropriate): ___ 4–9 & 11

Summarize: ___ 4 & 6

©Shipley Associates. Printed in USA.

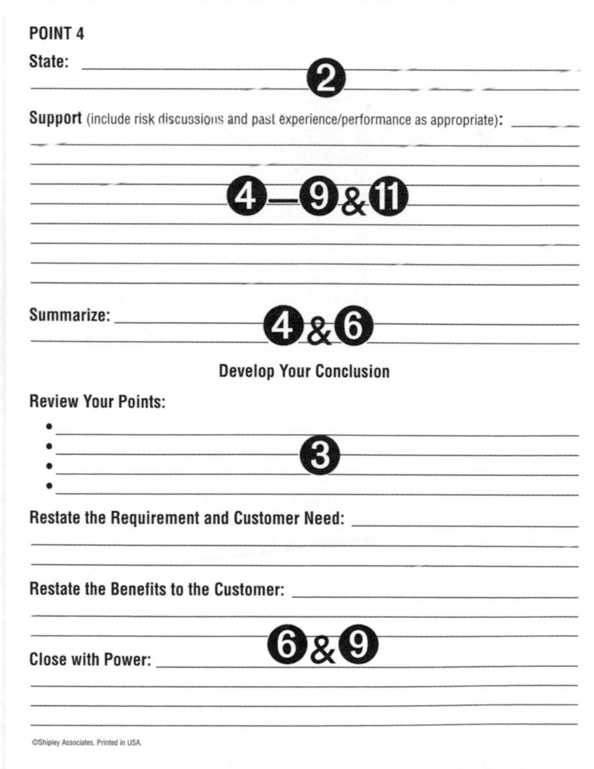
POINT 4

State: ___ 2

Support (include risk discussions and past experience/performance as appropriate): ___ 4–9 & 11

Summarize: ___ 4 & 6

Develop Your Conclusion

Review Your Points:
•
•
• ___ 3
•

Restate the Requirement and Customer Need: ___

Restate the Benefits to the Customer: ___ 6 & 9

Close with Power: ___

©Shipley Associates. Printed in USA.

Figure 3. Use the Oral Proposal Planner. *The planner lends structure and logic to develop powerful presentations that are easily followed and understood. The original content is developed in the Proposal Development Worksheet (PDW) or storyboard shown in figure 3. The numbers show the flow of data from the PDW to the OPP.*

With the core of the presentation complete, develop the introduction and summary.

Introductions have mandatory and optional functions:

Mandatory

- Gain attention
- State the requirement and prospect need
- Summarize your offering/response and the associated benefit
- Preview your main points

Optional

- Establish credentials
- Define key terms
- Offer background
- Set the tone and establish rapport
- Introduce key program personnel
- Overview requirements

Gain attention in your introduction with a prospect-focused statement of need, a shocking fact, challenge, quotation, illustration, story, or rhetorical question.

Like introductions, conclusions have mandatory and optional functions:

Mandatory

- Review main points
- Restate prospect's requirements/needs
- Close with power

Optional

- Transition to the next speaker
- Open to questions

Mirror your introduction in your conclusion. If you started with a challenge, quotation, or surprising fact, close with it.

5 Create effective visuals.

For guidelines on creating proposal visuals, see **Color** *and* **Graphics**.

Carefully selected visuals have a powerful effect on evaluators. Effective visuals help them remember your key messages, often after a series of presentations presented in one mind-numbing day or several days apart.

According to the Industrial Audio Visual Association, people remember what they see and hear better than if they learned in only one mode, as summarized in figure 4.

NOTE: Always test visuals on the actual delivery media, slides, transparencies, or projector. Colors may shift significantly in hue or intensity from computer monitor to projected image or printed transparency. Projectors also have variations in color and brightness depending on model and light or power output.

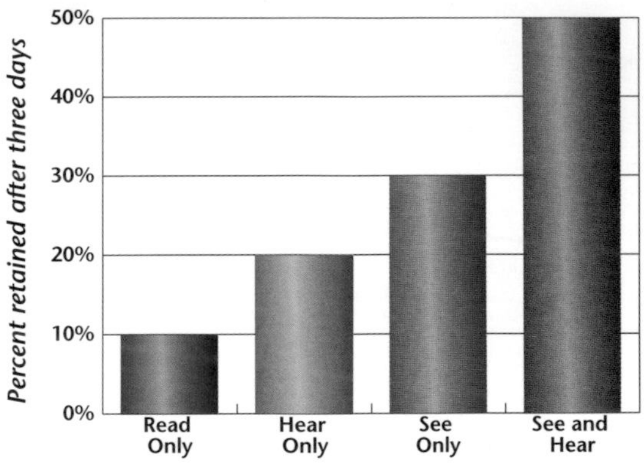

Figure 4. Memory Retention Based on Delivery. *The combination of repetition and multiple intake modes increases memory retention.*

The purpose of this guideline is to focus on and identify appropriate graphics for an oral proposal and how to present them effectively. For brevity, a discussion of the pro's and con's of different media was eliminated.

With limited time and resources, use an organized process like the following to identify appropriate graphics:

1. Identify the number of visuals allowed. Two to three per minute is a maximum; add time if you need to comment on them.
2. Determine your key strategies and how you could depict each.
3. Review the evaluation criteria and major issues; then brainstorm what graphics tell compelling stories or offer proof of performance about each.
4. Review your PDWs for useful graphics.
5. Identify risks and visually depict risk mitigation approaches.
6. Visualize ways to portray added value.
7. Prioritize your visuals, one to three, low to high.
8. Retain the three's and as many two's as you have time to present.
9. Review the sequential logic of your visuals. Remove or add visuals as needed.
10. Do this quickly. Do not agonize. You will learn much more as you rehearse using the visuals.

Use the following guidelines to present effectively:

- Check sight lines to ensure everyone can see.
- Place the screen to one side of the room at a 45-degree angle, space permitting.
- Use a flat pointer laid on the overhead projector to point instead of pointing at the screen.
- Touch the screen, turn to the audience, then talk to the projected images. Pointers or light pencils poised in midair show every tremor and suggest nervousness.
- Rehearse with your visuals and always talk to the audience, not the visual.
- Use animation or progressive reveal to limit reading ahead.
- Summarize complex visuals; expand on simple visuals.

6

Rehearse early, realistically, and often.

Capitalize on your strengths and minimize your presentation weaknesses. Most of us are painfully aware of our weaknesses. Extensive practice with skilled coaching can make anyone much better.

Practice individual parts of your presentation. Then rehearse the entire presentation before a live audience while you time it.

Practice progressively. Initially, practice in nonthreatening situations; then add peers, videotaping, your boss, and final dress rehearsals.

While most oral proposals do not specify a question period, prepare for one anyway. Much of the real testing of a proposal team is during the question period.

Anticipate tough questions; prepare your answers, and rehearse answering them. Handled properly, the question period is an important opportunity to reinforce key ideas, clarify points, establish a rapport with individual evaluators, and generally discriminate your team and offer.

Learn a consistent method to address questions. Practice following these guidelines:

1. Respond to one question at a time.
2. Listen to the full question carefully.
3. Focus on the questioner:
   - Face the questioner.
   - Lean forward or move toward the questioner.
   - Establish eye contact.
   - Indicate active listening.
4. Do not interrupt.
5. Listen to the content (words) and for the intent (ultimate purpose) of the question.
6. If you do not know the answer, admit it or defer to someone else on your team.

Essentially similar to the *State, Support, Summarize* approach to present main points, follow these guidelines when answering questions:

1. Restate the question.
2. Concisely state your summary answer.
3. Support your answer.
4. Summarize or restate your original answer.
5. Ask if the questioner is satisfied.

For negative questions, do not restate the question. Agree with the questioner if possible. Try to address the positive side of what has been done.

As part of your preparation, develop two or three specific and Very Important Points (VIPs). They usually flow from your strategy as expressed in your executive summary and are no more than 20 seconds long.

When you must deny an accusation, bridge or transition to one of your VIPs. When questions are hostile, restrict negative, nonverbal language, such as touching your head or face or shifting your weight.

7

Orchestrate the entire presentation.

Try to control as much of your presentation as possible. Appoint one person to be a facilitative leader, much like an MC.

Prepare backup materials and approaches. Anticipate what could go wrong and devise a solution.

Prepare handouts for distribution at the end, if permitted. Refer to them at the end, not the beginning. Offer electronic copies when appropriate.

8

Prepare a lessons-learned analysis to understand your win or loss and to improve subsequent proposals.

As with all proposal efforts, prepare a lessons learned analysis after each oral proposal.

Ask each participant to submit a short self-assessment and team assessment. Collect and combine them into a format report, and debrief the team so that everyone learns from the experience.

Request and attend a customer debrief as soon as the customer allows, win or lose. Summarize their comments in writing, add it to your formal report, and pass appropriate comments to all presenters and contributors.

Organization is the key writing principle for all types of business documents, including proposals. A sound, well-conceived organization will make the actual writing easier, especially for writers with limited confidence in their writing skills. Nothing can save a poorly organized proposal.

NOTE 1: The principles of organization discussed here underlie the guidelines for **Appendices and Attachments, Client Presentations, Cover Letters, Executive Summary, Lists,** and **Oral Proposals**.

NOTE 2: These organizational guidelines for proposals are stated in order of precedence. Conflicts are common. For example, guideline 1 overrides all other guidelines.

Evaluators read proposals much differently than other types of documents. Few evaluators read the entire proposal, and virtually no one reads the proposal sequentially, start-to-finish, like a novel. Instead they search for answers to their questions.

Recall the last time you lost something. Why do you always find the item in the last place that you look? Because you stop looking after you find it.

Similarly, evaluators with limited time search for answers to their questions. Why would they keep reading after finding the answer? They simply score the answer, then look for the answer to their next question.

Principles of organization differ slightly from document to document, depending on the type of document, the readers, the content, and the writer's purpose.

After you review these guidelines, you will see many similarities to national and regional newspapers and magazines. All are designed to be flexibly used and easily understood by diverse readers with limited time available.

Well-organized proposals have common features:

- They announce their organization and follow it.
- The ideas are clear and understandable for the intended evaluators.
- They are customer-focused, conforming to the evaluators' sense of what is important to them.
- They use multiple stylistic devices to enable evaluators to access the document virtually at random and quickly understand the organization and locate the information they need.

Organization

1. **Organize your proposal the way the prospect tells you to organize it in the bid request.**
2. **Organize information to make your proposal easy to evaluate.**
3. **Group similar ideas.**
4. **Order your points in decreasing order of importance to the prospect or evaluators.**
5. **Summarize at all levels.**
6. **Adjust the writing style and graphics in each section of the proposal to the anticipated needs of the evaluator.**
7. **Use templates to help organize your messages before drafting text.**

1

Organize your proposal the way the prospect tells you to organize it in the bid request.

NOTE: For a more detailed description of how to build your proposal outline from a bid request, see **Outlining**.

Mirroring the bid request's organization in your proposal might violate other recommendations in this *Proposal Guide*; your goal is to prepare an easily evaluated proposal, not necessarily a logical one.

Everyone's logic varies. Imagine how difficult multiple proposals are to evaluate when each proposal follows the offeror's unique logic.

Often the evaluator did not prepare the bid request and is as frustrated with the imposed organization as you are. Live with it.

Your top-level organization will vary depending on whether you have a bid request with specific instructions, a bid request with no instructions on proposal organization, or an orally solicited request with no written bid request.

2

Organize information to make your proposal easy to evaluate.

See **Compliance and Responsiveness.**

See **Headings.**

Make it easy for evaluators to find the answers to their questions and easy for them to give you a maximum score. Consider these recommendations:

- Group a series of answers in a table or matrix. One U.S. Air Force evaluator said, "We went to the tables and graphics first. If we found the answer, we didn't have to read the text."
- Answer questions in informative headings.

Requirement

DOE must have unlimited rights of entry to all proposed sites during the site survey period.

Response

All Site Owners Agree to Unlimited Rights of Entry

We have obtained signed agreements from all twelve property owners within the proposed site indicating . . .

- Include a compliance matrix at the beginning of the proposal and perhaps at the beginning of proposal sections.

No one enjoys reading proposals. You should not care if they read every word of your proposal as long as they give you the highest score and select your solution.

3

Group similar ideas.

See **Storyboards.**

Separating similar ideas creates confusion and chaos. Grouping similar ideas in a proposal can be difficult:

- Bid requests scatter similar questions.
- Different questions require similar support.
- Multiple authors are unaware of the overlap.
- Authors draw answers from the same boilerplate (previously written materials).

Using storyboards to plan and review content before drafting helps writers group similar ideas.

Proposal managers have the primary duty to detect and resolve redundancies. Writers may also detect them by reviewing section drafts posted on proposal room walls.

How you deal with redundancies depends on the size of the proposal. Do not insult the intelligence of the evaluator by inserting identical text without an explanation.

To eliminate cross-referencing between volumes, repeat the answer to the same question asked in different volumes. Tell them that you repeated your answer:

We answered this question earlier in Volume 1, Section 1.2.3, and have repeated it here for your convenience.

Cross-referencing within the same volume is generally acceptable. Answer the question fully the first time it is asked. The next time the same question is asked, introduce your answer as shown:

We answered this question earlier in Section 1.2.3, and have summarized our response here for your convenience. For greater detail, please refer to Section 1.2.3.

4

Order your points in decreasing order of importance to prospects or evaluators.

NOTE 1: The base principle supporting both the managerial and scientific formats is the same: Place the most important idea to the reader first.

Also see **Lists.**

Most newspapers, magazines, technical journals, and professional business documents use the opposite, managerial format, i.e., they state their conclusion or result, then support it.

In a fast-paced business environment, readers value the result over the support. Managers usually value results over process. A *Wall Street Journal* study found that 10 percent of their readers stopped reading per column inch of copy. Six inches into a story, one-half of the readers have quit reading.

Proposal evaluators have a similar reading pattern; they read until satisfied, score the question, then look for the answer to the next question.

Additionally, most writers write like the documents they read. Technical people tend to use a technical or scientific format. Scientists know that a result is useless unless the proper process was followed. Hence, in the scientific format, process is more important than the result and comes first in the document.

Proposal writers with technical backgrounds tend to lead to, rather than from, major ideas. Such writers build their case logically, fearing sceptical evaluators will not believe them unless they build their case.

When writing any proposal or business document, ask yourself, "If the evaluator or reader stopped reading at any time, have I placed my ideas or points in decreasing order of importance to the reader?" If not, reorder them.

5 Summarize at all levels.

NOTE: Many sellers outside the U.S. object to the idea of launching immediately into their message. They say this is very American and not acceptable in their culture. Yet when asked to evaluate proposals and other sales documents, they nearly always prefer the proposals that open with the seller's key messages.

See **Executive Summary** *and* **Theme Statements.**

The first sentence of any part of your proposal is the most important. The last sentence is potentially the second most important, but only if you assume evaluators will read it. When preparation time is limited, focus on the first sentence.

The opening theme statement in your executive summary should state the most important point you want every evaluator to remember. The executive summary should open with your overriding theme statement, a statement of the prospect's vision, a link between the prospect's vision and immediate need, an overview of your solution, and a statement of compliance, all within the first few paragraphs.

Evaluators can choose to quit reading at any time. Give evaluators your most important points before they quit reading by summarizing at all levels, the proposal, volume, section, subsection, and paragraph.

The executive summary should summarize your entire proposal, and volume summaries should summarize each volume. Open every section and subsection with a summary, and open individual paragraphs with summary sentences.

Opening any portion of a proposal with an introduction implies that you and the prospect have never met. Instead place introductions, previews, or informal tables of content immediately after the summary to tell the evaluator what will follow.

6 Adjust the writing style and graphics in each section of the proposal to the anticipated needs of the evaluator.

Choose graphics and a style of writing appropriate to the evaluators of that section of the proposal. For example, executive summary graphics must be understood by all evaluators, including nontechnical ones. Highly technical proposal sections can contain more complex, technical graphics, but only include sufficient technical detail to make them correct.

See **Choosing Correct Words** *and* **International Proposals.**

Adjust your style of writing similarly. Larger paragraphs, sentences, and words are acceptable in more technical proposal sections. However, proposals are not technical treatises.

Evaluators often perceive overly technical writing and graphics as technical arrogance.

Within a proposal and within proposal sections, you can increase the technical complexity. Begin sections with succinct, clear summaries that are broadly understandable. Then increase the complexity as needed to satisfy the more technical evaluators. The less technical evaluators will have quit reading and jumped to the next section.

Apply this guideline to both graphics and text.

7

Use templates to help organize your messages before drafting text.

Use templates customized for the type of document being written to encourage writers to follow a process approach.

When asked to write, most people think about drafting text. You will produce more successful documents if you follow a writing process:

1. Analyze the audience.
2. Define your objective.
3. Brainstorm, group, and prioritize your key ideas or points according to your judgment about each prospect's priorities.

When confronted with different templates, remember that following the process is more important than the exact content, form, or format of the template.

This *Proposal Guide* contains many of the templates listed in figure 1.

TEMPLATE	FINAL DOCUMENT	LOCATION IN PROPOSAL GUIDE
Proposal Development Worksheet (PDW) or Storyboard	*Proposal Section*	**Storyboards and Mock-ups**
Oral Proposal Planner	*Oral Proposal*	**Oral Proposals**
Four-Box Template	*Cover Letter* *Executive Summary* *Finals Presentation* *Letter Proposal* *Sales Letter*	**Cover Letters** **Executive Summary** **Presentations to Prospects** **Letter Proposals** **Sales Letters**
Proposal Management Plan	*Proposal Management Plan*	**Proposal Management Plan**
Capture Planner	*Capture Plan*	**Capture Planning**
Integrated Prospect Solution Worksheet	*Capture or Proposal Plan*	**Strategy, Capture Planning, and Executive Summary**
Bidder Comparison Matrix	*Capture or Proposal Plan*	**Strategy, Capture Planning, and Executive Summary**
Success Story Template	*Proposal Section*	**Relevant Experience/Past Performance**

Figure 1. Use Templates to Organize Your Messages. *Using a template to develop and review content before writing saves time and improves the effectiveness of the final document. Remember that following the process is more important than the exact content, form, or format of the template.*

Outlining is a crucial proposal management activity. All subsequent work is based on the initial outline.

See **Compliance and Responsiveness, Customer Focus, Headings, Numbering Systems, Organization, Proposal Management Plan,** *and* **Storyboards and Mock-ups.**

Outlines are important in individual proposal writing efforts and essential in team writing efforts. The outline forms the basis for the table of contents, serves as a proposal management tool, and helps writers see their task as it relates to the entire proposal.

Recommendations on developing sound proposal outlines are based on the principles of customer focus and organization. By following the prospect's instructions and organization, no matter how illogical, you demonstrate that you listen to your prospects and give them exactly what they request. By following sound document organizational guidelines, you demonstrate your ability to meet the prospect's needs.

Developing a compliant outline is often difficult. Nearly every bid request is confusing on the first reading. The difficulty increases with complex and poorly written bid requests, management pressures to start writing immediately, and individual pressure to use another organization because it is *more logical* or better matches something already written.

Outlining

1. **Develop your proposal outline as the prospect suggests, either in the bid request or verbally.**
2. **Prepare a top-level, topical outline that follows the prospect's organizational priority. Mimic the numbering system, naming conventions, and order listed in the bid request.**
3. **Assign or allocate all other response requirements within the topical outline.**
4. **Use informative headings at section levels below those specified by the prospect.**
5. **Allocate pages according to the relative importance of the topic to the prospect.**
6. **Develop outlines for unsolicited proposals (1) collaboratively with your prospect, (2) based on discussion with your prospect, or (3) logically.**
7. **Annotate outlines as needed to guide writers.**
8. **Extend your outline into a Proposal Responsibility Matrix to help manage the proposal.**
9. **When you have to deviate from the bid request, always explain your deviation to the evaluator.**

1

Develop your proposal outline as the prospect suggests, either in the bid request or verbally.

See **Compliance and Responsiveness.**

First, follow the prospect's proposal organization instructions precisely, even if they seem illogical. Then, apply sound organizational principles at succeeding levels.

Prospects frequently direct or at least suggest how offerors' proposals should be organized. A common organization makes the task of comparing proposals easier.

Detailed proposal preparation instructions are required for U.S. Federal bid requests issued under the Federal Acquisition Regulations, FAR Part 15. The FAR requires the bid request structure shown in figure 1, with Instructions to Offerors in section "L."

Acquisitions under other parts of the FAR are not as prescriptive, but most bid requests will have some type of preparation instructions.

International central and local government agencies of all types often include a relatively less detailed set of instructions on how to organize your proposal. Large companies that routinely compete in these market sectors tend to follow similar procedures.

The complete lack of organizational instructions usually reflects a lack of established purchasing procedures or experience on the part of the people requesting the proposal. Treat this as an opportunity to favorably influence the bid request by collaboratively developing the proposal requirements and outline with the prospect.

RFP	DESCRIPTION	TYPICAL CONTENT
A	Solicitation/Contract form	RFP table of contents, contact information, due date, submittal location, serves as contract when signed by offeror and government
B	Supplies or services and prices	Contract Line Items (CLINs) listing what is to be priced and how
C	Statement of work	Describes work required, i.e., specification
D	Packaging and marketing	Product packaging and marketing required
E	Inspection and acceptance	Product/service inspection and acceptance criteria
F	Deliveries or performance	When products or services are required
G	Contract administration data	Contract requirements not on solicitation form
H	Special contract requirements	Items not in Section I or other sections of the contract
I	Contract clauses	Clauses required by law or included in contract
J	List of attachments	Data requirements and organization, anything that did not fit elsewhere, and occasionally organizational instructions not included in L to permit using an otherwise "standard" RFP
K	Representations, certifications	Acknowledgment forms that must be signed and submitted with the proposal
L	Instructions, conditions, notices	Instructions for proposal preparation, format, organization, content, length
M	Evaluation factors for award	Process, evaluation factors, and relative importance of the factors used to evaluate offers

Figure 1. How U.S. Federal Bid Requests Are Organized. *FAR Part 15, Contracting by Negotiation, prescribes this bid request structure for major competitive and negotiated procurements to simplify proposal preparation and evaluation for offerors, contractors, and contract administrators.*

See Numbering Systems.

If you have a bid request with no instructions on how to organize your proposal, mirror the organization of the bid request as closely as possible. Number, order, and name sections as was done in the bid request. When all else fails, make an assumption, state it clearly, and get on with proposal development.

State your assumptions explaining how your proposal is organized in your compliance matrix, table of contents, and introductions at all levels. This style choice conveys a helpful, reader-friendly tone.

The following two examples show how organizational assumptions can be stated in both formal and question and response bid requests:

Assumption stated in the contents and/or response matrix

All proposal instructions were followed explicitly. Our numbering system is identical to bid request Section L. Other requirements were inserted within the "L" dictated outline where they were most relevant. All responses to bid request requirements can be located in the Response Matrix.

Assumption for a non-Federal question and response style

All sections of the bid request and all questions with sections were answered in the order asked. Short summaries at the beginning of major sections establish perspective.

Many leading sales trainers recommend never accepting prospects' initial vision of the solution or requirements. Instead, they recommend reengineering their vision or redefining their requirements. The sales trainers' recommendation is based on the premise that reshaping a prospect's vision puts you in the leading position and makes a uniform, low-price selection more difficult.

Reengineering a prospect's vision is valid earlier in the sales process but usually not after a final bid request is issued. If you find that to win you must reshape the prospect's vision after the final bid request is released, look for another opportunity.

2 Prepare a top-level, topical outline that follows the prospect's organizational priority. Mimic the numbering system, naming convention, and order listed in the bid request.

Many bid requests are written by different people, with different knowledge and interests, over months or years. Follow the organizational priority set by the individual(s) who manage the evaluation process.

For a U.S. Federal bid request, develop your outline based on the following organizational priority:

1. Section L: Instructions, conditions, notices
2. Section M: Evaluation factors
3. Section C: Statement of Work
4. Section B: Supplies or services and prices
5. All other sections

NOTE: On a large proposal effort or on a complex proposal, prepare a 2nd-level outline first and get consensus among management and key team members. Then create a 3rd- or 4th-level outline and try to keep it there. Avoid further substantial changes.

For all other written bid requests, look for similar instructions:

- Organizational instructions
- Evaluation criteria or hot buttons
- Statement of Work tasks
- Separately priced items or tasks

These recommendations are consistent among proposal professionals and based on who has control of the evaluation process. Different sections are often written by different types of people. "L" is prepared by the people running the procurement. "M" is prepared by the group making the selection decision. "C" is written by the people who understand the services or products or by their consultants, as much as 3 to 5 years earlier. They may or may not be users of the services or products. "B" is prepared by an accounting or financial person.

To emphasize compliance, retain and extend the numbering system used in the bid request.

Keep identical naming conventions. Capitalize the same words, hyphenate the same words, and spell them the same unless the word is misspelled.

Maintain the same order as listed in the bid request, even if the order is not logical to you.

Figure 2 shows how a top-level, topical outline is prepared from a bid request excerpt typical of any market sector. The bid request directly indicates the numbered, second-level topics, e.g., *2.1 Organization Structure and Facility Resources*.

Adding the third- and fourth-level subsections depends on their page length. Generally, use a subsection number if the length exceeds two pages. Note the lower-level topics are included as unnumbered items but would not be listed in the table of contents.

If you are lucky, these sections are similar. When they are different, look to guideline 3.

RFP Excerpt

2.0 Management Plan

1. Organization Structure and Facility Resources. Include a current organizational chart and a brief description of operational function. Describe your firm's organization in terms of size and organizational stability. Identify facility resources (e.g., word processing, ADPE, etc.), which may be used for this project.

2. Relevant Corporate Experience. Relate two recent (within the last 3 years) successful corporate experiences in Software Development and Implementation Engineering, Data Base Management and Integration, User and System Integration, and Network Operation. For each completed project cited, provide the following information: project name, hardware and operating systems involved, user, description of work performed, experience in data communications and packet-switching, period of contract, contact point, subcontractors with contact name and phone number, description of subcontractor's involvement . . . .

Proposal Outline

2.0 Management Plan

2.1 Organization Structure and Facility Resources
2.1.1 Current Structure and Operation
2.1.2 Organizational Size and Stability
2.1.3 Relevant Facility Resources
2.2 Relevant Corporate Experience
2.2.1 Software Development and Implementation Engineering Projects
2.2.1.1 ABC Project
—Project name
—Hardware and operating systems
—User
—Description of work performed
—Experience in data communications and packet-switching
—Period of contract
—Contact point
—Subcontractors with contact name and phone number
—Description of subcontractor's involvement
2.2.1.2 DEF Project
2.2.2 Data Base Management and Integration
2.2.2.1 GHI Project
2.2.2.2 JKL Project
2.2.3 User and System Integration
2.2.3.1 MNO Project
2.2.3.2 PQR Project
2.2.4 Network Operation
2.2.4.1 STU Project
2.2.4.2 VWX Project

Figure 2. Developing a Top-level, Topical Outline. *Mimic the numbering system, naming convention, and order of the topics listed in the bid request. The items listed under 2.2.1.1 are shown to illustrate subsection content under each project description but would not be included in the topical outline or table of contents.*

3 Assign or allocate all other response requirements within the topical outline.

After placing all response requirements embedded within the proposal instructions in your outline, you must assign or allocate all other requirements within the same topical outline. Augmenting the original topical outline with additional subsections and requirements is more difficult when different bid request sections have different structures.

A single-level bid request, like the example in figure 2, is relatively simple to outline. Multilevel bid requests are more complex.

Multilevel bid requests have the organization and requirements established at the top level plus additional overlapping requirements at one or more lower levels.

Multilevel bid requests are similar to a couple purchasing a house. Each partner establishes his or her own requirements; some are the same, some are unique, and some conflict.

Figure 3 illustrates how additional bid request sections other than the proposal instructions are incorporated into the proposal outline. Since there is no single *correct* answer, your compliance or response matrix becomes even more important.

When you extend the topical outline, aim for balance. For example, if you go only to 2.1 in one section, try to avoid going to 2.2.X.X in another section. Such differences imply an unbalanced response.

A disturbingly common approach is to develop the topical outline, and then instruct all contributors to "Read the bid request, identify the additional requirements relevant to your section, and address each one in your draft." The results are orphans that no one addresses and redundancies that several people address differently. Making the problem worse, redundant items may be double costed.

Bid Request Excerpt: Statement of Work

5.2 Management Reporting. Contractor shall maintain a current organizational structure for the assigned project team indicating all people assigned, a description of their duties, and how they are to be contacted. All proposed changes must be reviewed and approved by the Contract Administrator.

5.3 Facility Compliance. All facilities proposed must comply with all Federal, state, and municipal zoning and building requirements, including continuing licensing and permitting standards. Contractor will maintain proof of compliance on site.

Zoning Regulation

Fire alarms must be tested weekly, and evacuation procedures practiced monthly.

All buildings must meet applicable seismic codes, including a posting of compliance displayed prominently in the primary entrance area.

Proposal Outline

2.0 Management Plan
- 2.1 Organization Structure and Facility Resources
  - 2.1.1 Current Structure and Operation
    - 2.1.1.1 Management Reporting
      - — Project Team Structure
      - — Project Team Management
  - 2.1.2 Organizational Size and Stability
  - 2.1.3 Relevant Facility Resources
    - 2.1.3.1 Facility Compliance
      - — Fire Protection Plan
      - — Seismic Protection Plan
- 2.2 Relevant Corporate Experience

Proposal Outline

2.0 Management Plan
- 2.1 Organization Structure and Facility Resources
  - 2.1.1 Current Structure and Operation
    - 2.1.1.1 Project Team Structure
    - 2.1.1.2 Project Team Management
  - 2.1.2 Organizational Size and Stability
  - 2.1.3 Relevant Facility Resources
    - 2.1.3.1 Fire Protection Plan
    - 2.1.3.2 Seismic Protection Plan
- 2.2 Relevant Corporate Experience

Figure 3. Extending a Topical Outline for Multilevel Bid Requests. *Adding to the example shown in figure 2, a lower-level Statement of Work (SOW) section shown in blue lists requirements relevant to the Management Plan. The SOW further references zoning regulation in paragraph 5.3, which are excerpted in red type. The colored text shows how the additional requirements are folded into the proposal outline. The alternate approaches show two acceptable ways the outline could be prepared, depending on the length of each subsection.*

4 Use informative headings at section levels below those specified by the prospect.

See **Headings.**

Informative headings can impart a positive message. In the example shown in figures 2 and 3, the headings in *black* are all telegraphic and identical to the bid request. Some of the headings in *blue* and *red* can be improved by making them informative:

Telegraphic heading

Project Team Structure
Project Team Management
Fire Protection Plan
Seismic Protection Plan

Informative Heading

Proven Team Structure Reduces Risk
Responsive Team Management Improves Service
Proactive Fire Risk Management Cuts Loss
Earthquake Preparedness Is a Priority

Avoid combining theme statements and informative headings. These combinations are cubersome and repetitive.

5 Allocate pages according to the relative importance of the topic to the prospect.

Allocate pages based on the page limitations or recommendations in the bid request or suggestions from the prospect. If none are given, attempt to discover the prospect's expectations through a collaborative discussion. Attempt to reduce page-length expectations to optimize preparation time and cost unless a shorter proposal conflicts with your proposal strategy.

After determining or estimating the total page count, allocate pages according to the relative importance to the prospect, tempered by your proposal strategy.

Determine relative importance based on the following indicators, in the order listed:

1. Evaluation criteria
2. Discussion with the prospect
3. Judgment

Often evaluation criteria are both broadly stated and stated in order of relative importance. Use your judgment to allocate the page count among the first-level topical outline, then extend your allocation to subsections until all contributors have a clear page limit or guideline for their assigned sections. The approach is shown in figure 4.

RFP INSTRUCTIONS TO OFFERORS

All proposals are limited to 100 pages, excluding preface pages. Attachments are not included nor are they encouraged.

All proposals should contain the following sections:

1. System Hardware—Describe all hardware that will be supplied and how it connects with existing hardware. Include appropriate system diagrams.
2. System and Network Software—Indicate the software to be supplied, its capabilities, upgradability, and warranty.
3. Project Management—Indicate how the project will be managed, naming all proposed personnel judged "key" to this project's success. Include a first- and second-tier schedule that links to your proposed WBS and SOW. For all personnel, indicate the percentage of their time devoted to this project.
4. Training—Include a training plan for all operators and maintenance technicians. Indicate the additional support available and its cost.
5. Pricing—Include a complete pricing breakdown of all hardware, software, and services identified in the SOW.

EVALUATION CRITERIA

Proposals that fail to respond fully to all requirements as listed may be rejected without further consideration. Selection will be based on the evaluation team's judgment of the offer that affords the best value. The following evaluation factors are listed in decreasing order of importance: (1) Technical, (2) Management, (3) Cost.

In the Technical area, hardware is one-half as important as software but twice as important as training.

Figure 4. Establishing Page Count Guidelines. *Allocate pages according to their relative importance to the evaluator. Make the initial page allocation based on the evaluation criteria.*

ESTIMATED WEIGHTS AND PAGE ALLOCATION

Criterion	Category	Weight	Proposal Section	1st Cut Page Allocation
1	Technical	50		50
			1. System Hardware	14
			2. System and Network Software	28
			4. Training	8
2	Management	30	3. Project Management	30
3	Cost	20	5. Cost	20
			Total	**100**

ADJUSTED PROPOSAL OUTLINE

#	Section	Page Allocation	Comments
	Executive Summary	6	Approximately 5 to 10 percent of total
1	System Hardware	12	Reduced, not a discriminator
2	System and Network Software	27	Equal to weight less executive summary
3	Project Management	32	Increased; discriminator for us
4	Training	10	Increased; hot button of key evaluator
5	Cost	8	Decreased; use tables extensively
	Total	**95**	
	Contingency	5	In case someone runs over
	Page Limit per RFP	**100**	

Figure 4. Establishing Page Count Guidelines (continued from previous page). *Allocate pages according to their relative importance to the evaluator. After your initial page allocation, adjust it based on the number required and your strategy. Allocate 5 to 10 percent for the executive summary and 5 to 10 percent for the contingency that someone might exceed the limit.*

6 Develop outlines for unsolicited proposals (1) collaboratively with your prospect, (2) based on discussion with your prospect, or (3) logically.

When you do **not** have a formal bid request, discern the prospect's requirements collaboratively in meetings or phone calls. Refer to previous proposals deemed acceptable by the prospect, prospect file notes, and intelligence resources.

Prepare a response checklist.

In some instances, this "checklist" may become the basis for a competitive bid. If so, you have influenced the requirements, giving yourself an advantage.

Follow these steps:

1. List the requirements as you understand them.
2. Verify your list and add requirements as you discover them in face-to-face meetings and phone calls.
3. Prioritize your list by categories.
4. Seek final prospect buy-off via a read-through when possible.
5. Submit a copy of the final requirements checklist along with your proposal.

7 Annotate outlines as needed to guide writers.

If you want writers to include certain information, use a specific example, or follow a set strategy, tell them by annotating the proposal outline. Too frequently proposal managers ask writers, "Why didn't you discuss the ABC Project?" The usual answer, "You didn't tell me to," or, "I didn't know about it."

Avoid rework by annotating your proposal outlines.

8

Extend your outline into a Proposal Responsibility Matrix to help manage the proposal.

NOTE: The proposal responsibility matrix shown in figure 5 is also discussed in ***Daily Team Management.***

Extend your proposal outline into a Proposal Responsibility Matrix. Most proposal managers use a spreadsheet program, enabling them to add columns to track additional tasks associated with the development of each proposal section in the outline.

Proposal Par #	Proposal Section Title	Relevant RFP Par #'s	Author	Page Limit Target	Storyboard Assigned	1st Review Date	Final Review Date	Mock-up Review Date	Pink Team Date	Graphics Due Date	1st Draft Date	Red Team Date
None	Exec Sum	M	S. Ross	4	3-19-00	3-25-00	3-28-00	3-31-00	4-2-00	4-10-00	4-15-00	4-28-00
1.0	Tech Ov	L.2.1	W. Lou	2	3-21-00	3-26-00	3-28-00	3-31-00	4-2-00	4-10-00	4-15-00	4-28-00

Figure 5. Proposal Responsibility Matrix. *Sometimes called a Program Control Matrix, proposal managers use it to manage and monitor the status of each section assigned to each writer. Using spreadsheet software, add a row for each task and a column for each milestone. Keep a version prominently displayed in the proposal room and review progress in the daily stand-up.*

9

When you have to deviate from the bid request, always explain your deviation to the evaluator.

NOTE: Explanatory comments are in addition to always including a compliance or response matrix in every proposal. For unsolicited proposals, consider adding a topic index, directing evaluators to all significant topics.

When you are deviating from the bid request or you do not understand their intent, insert explanatory comments, like those in figure 6. This stylistic choice signals your desire to make things easier for the evaluator and suggests that your organization will be easier to work with if you win the contract.

At a proposal debriefing, the buyer said, "It was like you were reading our mind. We found 80 percent of the answers where we expected to find them." If 80 percent is mind reading, imagine what evaluators normally face.

At the beginning of compliance matrix

Our proposal mirrors your bid request organization and numbering system. The *L.21* prefix was dropped for all proposal section numbers.

In a cost volume

All items costed correspond with tasks described in our technical volume.

This page is intentionally blank.

Section number x.x.x was intentionally skipped to maintain agreement with the bid request.

Figure 6. Explain Any Deviation from Bid Request Instructions. *Help evaluators understand how your proposal is organized by inserting short explanations. Insert explanations at the beginning of major sections, on the compliance matrix, or any other place where your organization might be unclear.*

Page and document design impact whether your proposal is read, how it is read, and whether it is remembered. The physical design of your proposal pages emphasizes or de-emphasizes your messages much like body language, word dynamics, and facial expressions in conversation.

A good page layout promotes clear, persuasive communication even though evaluators may not be conscious of the page layout techniques used. A well-organized, visually appealing page reflects your organization's professionalism.

Never underestimate the importance of the proposal's appearance. When competitors' offers differ minimally, the appearance of the proposal can make the difference. Consider these comments from an evaluator:

Every answer was where we expected to find it. After we read it, we found that you did not fully comply with our requirements. But it was too late; everyone liked it too much.

A well-designed document and page layout make the evaluator's job easier. Answers are easy to find, the organization is easy to follow, key points stand out, graphics are clear and conveniently placed, and the text is easy to read.

Your document and page design should consider the following elements:

- Page format
- Type size and font
- Color
- Covers and binding system
- Graphics type, size, style, and quantity
- Production requirements

Many proposal professionals in the Federal sector cite the Federal Acquisition Regulation warning "Overly elaborate proposals may indicate the offerors lack of cost consciousness" as a justification for dull, plain proposals. With the cost of a computer, software, and color printer under $1,000, intelligent, attractive page and document design are not expensive.

The greater danger is to use a page and document design that suggests your organization is out of date. Claims of leading-edge technology and world-class products and services cannot counter a visually outdated proposal.

Design tools will not make most of us designers. Use a professional to develop one or two quality, standard proposal designs. Reassess those designs every 2 or 3 years. Then use the specific design most appropriate to each competition.

Page and Document Design

1. **Follow the prospect's page and document design instructions.**
2. **Use a style sheet for every proposal.**
3. **Select a document and page style appropriate to your prospect's organization, your industry, and your organization.**
4. **Use white space to guide the evaluator and to emphasize key points.**
5. **Use headers and footers to help evaluators navigate through your proposal while maintaining customer focus.**
6. **Select a page-column design that balances page limits, production requirements, readability, and graphics size flexibility.**
7. **Select complementary font styles, sizes, and leading.**
8. **Establish a consistent system for headings, themes, action captions, lists, and other page design features.**
9. **Choose and place graphics for maximum impact and readability.**
10. **Avoid overusing emphasis devices.**
11. **Use left-justified text.**

1 Follow the prospect's page and document design instructions.

Many bidders do not. Consider the following examples.

A major computer company, highly regarded for its sales training, had training materials that said, "Our proposals should include these sections: . . ." and included a fixed list of topics. No mention was made to first follow prospect's proposal instructions. How could they claim to be customer focused while ignoring prospect's proposal instructions?

A contractor bidding to manage a large facility misinterpreted instructions to use pica type. Pica type gives 10 characters per inch, or 10 pitch. The contractor thought 10 pitch was the same as 10 point. The government evaluators said that they estimated 30 percent more characters were on a page, so they removed the last 30 percent of the pages in their page-limitedproposal.

Bidders trying to get around page limitations used foldout pages. Instructions were amended to count any page larger than 8.5″ x 11″ as two pages.

Follow preparation instructions precisely. Ask for clarification if needed. Bid request preparation is often rushed, and mistakes are common. Prospects never try to trick bidders to see who is the cleverest or most astute.

Consider submitting a sample page for approval. The worst possible result is that the prospect refuses to answer.

---

2 Use a style sheet for every proposal.

Style sheets are essential and they reduce preparation time. Whether you have single or multiple contributors, using a style sheet will give the proposal a consistent appearance, making it easier to evaluate.

A good style sheet both shows and tells writers the page layout; font choice, point size, and line spacing for body text and graphics text; and the colors to use. Figure 1 shows a style sheet for an asymmetrical two-column page design (also called one-third/two-third layout) with the narrower left column reserved for themes, callouts, and small graphics.

NOTE: Many proposals need two style sheets. The simple version shown in figure 1 serves the needs of writers. Final production/designers will need a far more detailed and comprehensive style sheet.

The person in the production management role should build a list to document all style decisions. Most are common to all proposals, but some are unique to each proposal.

Establish an electronic template style sheet in the software of choice, and limit the physical style sheet, like the one in figure 1, to a single page. Longer style sheets tend to be ignored by many writers.

A best practice on proposals with multiple writers and a production support group is to give each writer a simplified style sheet or template, either at the kickoff meeting, via e-mail, or over your intranet site. This simplified style sheet is easier for writers to use and cuts the time spent on formatting.

Production people generally strip out formatting before imposing their more complex style sheet, so production time is also reduced.

Regardless of deliverable format, some veteran proposal managers prefer to complete the proposal using their preferred layout software, then convert it to the prospect's required format at the end. If you adopt this approach, test the conversion to ensure it works.

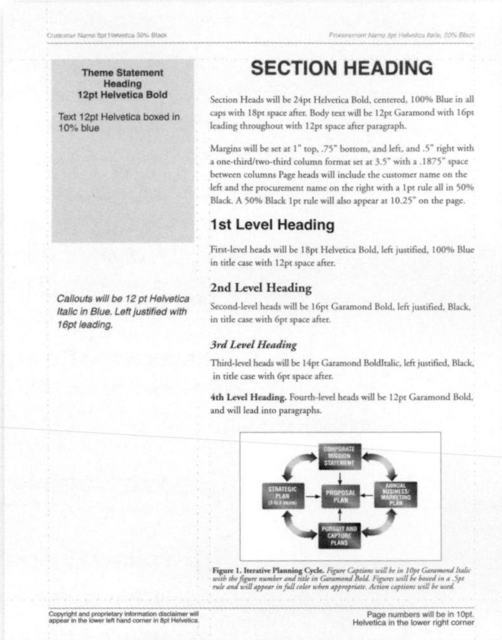
Customer Name 8pt Helvetica 50% Black
Procurement Name 8pt Helvetica Italic, 50% Black

Theme Statement Heading 12pt Helvetica Bold

Text 12pt Helvetica boxed in 10% blue

SECTION HEADING

Section Heads will be 24pt Helvetica Bold, centered, 100% Blue in all caps with 18pt space after. Body text will be 12pt Garamond with 16pt leading throughout with 12pt space after paragraph.

Margins will be set at 1" top, .75" bottom, and left, and .5" right with a one-third/two-third column format set at 3.5" with a .1875" space between columns Page heads will include the customer name on the left and the procurement name on the right with a 1pt rule all in 50% Black. A 50% Black 1pt rule will also appear at 10.25" on the page.

1st Level Heading

First-level heads will be 18pt Helvetica Bold, left justified, 100% Blue in title case with 12pt space after.

Callouts will be 12 pt Helvetica Italic in Blue. Left justified with 16pt leading.

2nd Level Heading

Second-level heads will be 16pt Garamond Bold, left justified, Black, in title case with 6pt space after.

3rd Level Heading

Third-level heads will be 14pt Garamond BoldItalic, left justified, Black, in title case with 6pt space after.

4th Level Heading. Fourth-level heads will be 12pt Garamond Bold, and will lead into paragraphs.

Figure 1. Iterative Planning Cycle. *Figure Captions will be in 10pt Garamond Italic with the figure number and title in Garamond Bold. Figures will be boxed in a .5pt rule and will appear in full color when appropriate. Action captions will be used.*

Copyright and proprietary information disclaimer will appear in the lower left hand corner in 8pt Helvetica.

Page numbers will be in 10pt. Helvetica in the lower right corner

Figure 1. Establish a Style Sheet for Every Proposal. *Good style sheets both show and tell writers how proposal pages will look. They define the fonts, point size, color, and spacing for all text and graphics. Simple visual style sheets like the one shown help writers visualize the appearance of their draft.*

---

3 Select a document and page style appropriate to your prospect's organization, your industry, and your organization.

Document style refers to the overall look and binding, or packaging, of the proposal. Page style refers to the size and orientation of individual proposal pages.

Proposal managers often think that competitors' proposals look much like their own proposals. Package your proposal to make it easy to identify, and design it to make it easy to evaluate while supporting your overall strategy. Consider these examples to broaden your perspective:

A company bidding to governments in the Middle East always packaged their executive summary in separate leather folios with a gold-plated pen inside.

The executive summary for a proposal to a rental car company was prepared to mimic the prospect's folders used at pickup counters.

A cost volume, full of large spreadsheets, was presented in landscape format to better fit the typical spreadsheet layout.

A bid to a company whose current public advertising image was a western express rider on horseback was packaged in replica Pony Express leather pouches. To capture media attention, one set of the proposal was delivered on horseback, timed to hit local evening TV news.

NOTE: Creative proposal packaging and submittal activities might appear to be "cute" or artificial. However, prospects are usually more receptive to creative packaging than some conservative members of the bid team. Carefully consider the prospect's likely reaction. Use sound judgement. Slick packaging with little content will reduce your win probability.

A company competing to supply business software development services to a pizza chain delivered their proposals in the same boxes their prospect used to deliver pizzas.

A mobile radio manufacturer had an audio voice-chip device, similar to ones used in greeting cards. The chip began in a voice filled with background static, then switched to a clear, CD-quality voice to emphasize the difference between analog and digital radio systems. Embedding the chip in the cover tempted evaluators to push the button until the battery died.

A woman was applying for a position as editor of the employee newsletter for a large, health care chain. Structuring her resume in a newsletter format to demonstrate her capability got her an interview.

See **Graphics** *and* **Resumes**.

Get the page size correct. North America uses a page standard of 8.5" x 11", often packaged in three-ring binders. Europe and much of the rest of the world use the A4 size, (a metric standard of 210mm x 297mm, or 8.268" x 11.693"), packaged in four-ring binders. Getting the size wrong tends to emphasize a foreign origin and a potential lack of compatibility.

Different packaging systems afford different cover art options. Ring binders offer a spine that can display titles, art, and text—features not possible with other types of binding systems. However, ring binders are difficult to store in filing cabinets, and pages can be removed or shuffled.

Ring binders are one of the easiest systems for rapid page changes during production. Conversely, one contractor noted that they did not use ring binders because they could be changed by prospects.

Your packaging should be inviting and attractive to prompt the prospect to read your proposal. Consider how proposals will be handled. Some packaging systems will look better than others after extensive handling.

One nongovernment evaluator described how packaging influenced the selection decision for a $50,000 branch store computer system:

> *I had 15 proposals and little time to evaluate. One cover caught my attention, and I remembered that the account representative for that organization was competent. I opened their executive summary and found the price was within my budget. I gave them the contract. I had no requirement to open the other 14 proposals.*

Unless your proposal has fewer than 20 pages, use double-sided printing. Thinner proposals are less daunting to evaluate, and graphics are easier to integrate on the same page or a facing page.

Minimize foldouts unless they are required for larger graphics or response matrices, like the one shown in figure 2. Large graphics requiring foldouts include wiring diagrams, schedules, and some personnel charts.

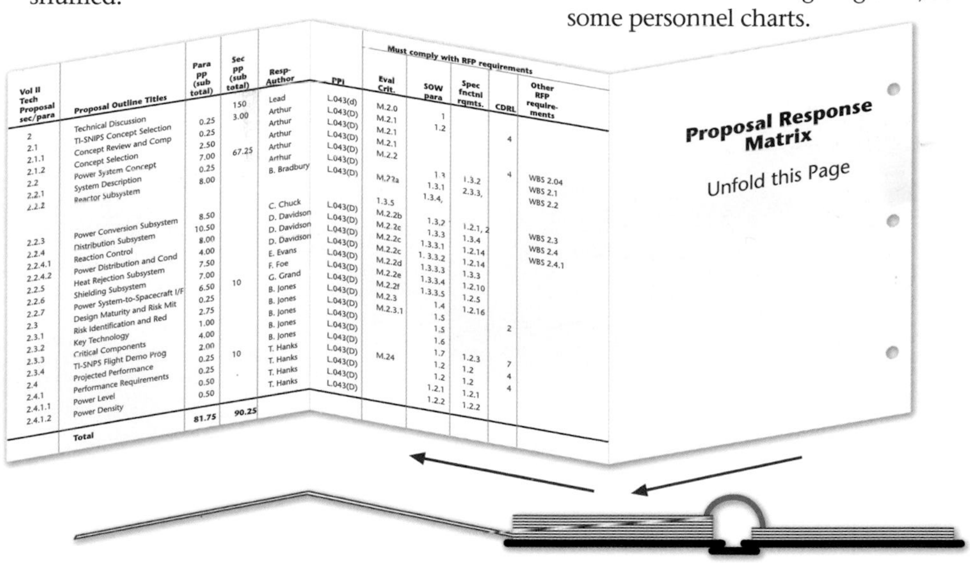

Figure 2. Using Foldouts for a Response Matrix. *The response matrix shown, placed at the front of a binder, has the matrix on the back side of the foldout that extends beyond the normal page. Evaluators can turn proposal pages without obscuring the response matrix. Similar response matrices can be placed in the back of the binder, but some evaluators miss them, even when referenced.*

4 Use white space to guide the evaluator and to emphasize key points.

Using white space to emphasize and link points is like using a spotlight to highlight a performer on stage. Two principles are involved:

1. **Emphasis**—The more white space around a page element, the greater the emphasis.
2. **Association**—Page elements are associated with nearby page elements.

Page elements include text, paragraphs, headings, bullet lists, tables, graphics, and even the edge of the page. Using white space for emphasis in lists is illustrated in figure 3.

Figure 4 illustrates the visual association of page elements applied to both headings with text, and graphics with captions.

Many of the decisions about how different page elements relate are implicit in the style sheet and are not evident to proposal writers. Even with a good style sheet, all proposals benefit by using desktop publishing assistance to produce a professional proposal that reflects your professional capabilities.

Version A

In the attached proposal, you will see the following products detailed: Endeavor aircraft, pilot training, maintenance training, spare parts, radios.

Version B

In the attached proposal, you will see the following products detailed:
- Endeavor aircraft
- Pilot training
- Maintenance training
- Spare parts
- Radios

Version C

In the attached proposal, you will see the following products detailed:

- Endeavor aircraft
- Pilot training
- Maintenance training
- Spare parts
- Radios

Version D

In the attached proposal, you will see the following products detailed:

- Endeavor aircraft
- Pilot training
- Maintenance training
- Spare parts
- Radios

Figure 3. Using White Space for Emphasis. *White space is used to emphasize a graphical element. This series of examples shows how increasing white space around the bullet list increases emphasis and thus, memorability. All versions are acceptable.*

Poor Example ***Better Example***

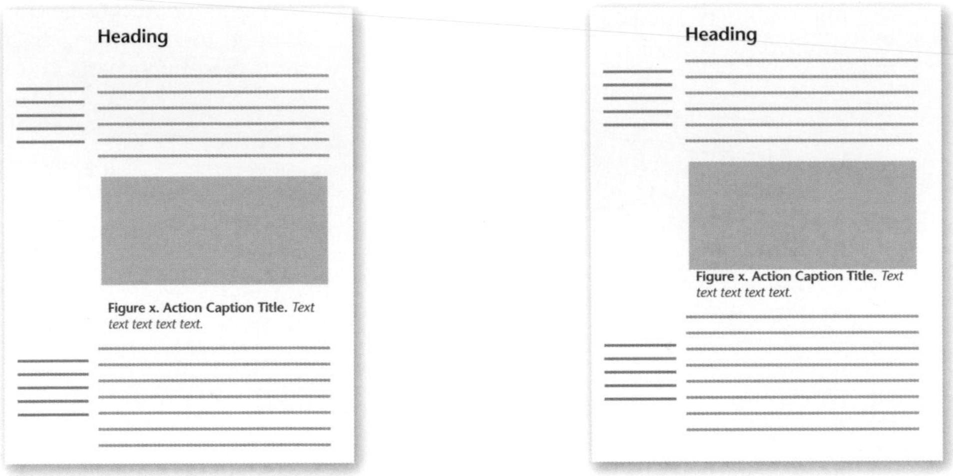

Figure 4. Using White Space to Associate Page Elements. *Readers can more easily track through a document when related elements are visually associated. Heading should be closer to the text than any other visual element. Captions should be closer to the related graphic than any other visual element. In the poor example, the heading is closer to the edge of the page than the relevant text, and the caption is equidistant between the graphic and the text.*

---

5 Use headers and footers to help evaluators navigate through your proposal while maintaining customer focus.

Evaluators would like to be able to open a proposal at random, page backward or forward to a major section heading, and readily understand where they are in the document. For maximum focus on the prospect, place the following information in the header:

- Prospect name and logo (left)
- Procurement name and number (right)

Place the following information in the footer:

- Offeror's name and logo
- Volume and page number
- Nondisclosure statements
- Win theme, slogan, or tag line
- Section name and number
- Date submitted
- Draft or final

NOTE: Check your printer to ensure that everything prints. Many printers clasp the paper at the top or bottom, potentially cutting off page numbers placed too near the edge.

With this much potential information, headers and footers can become cluttered. Try to group information, leaving more of the margins empty. Keep information in the same place, especially the parts that change, like page numbers and section names and numbers.

Use color, font style, and size to emphasize the most important information, while minimizing less important items like nondisclosure statements.

With double-sided printing, you can make right- and left-hand pages identical or make them mirror images. Identical right and left pages makes adding or removing pages easier, reducing production time.

In Western cultures, we read from top to bottom, left to right. Make the top rule heavier than the bottom rule to draw the eye to the top of the page. The rule is the line running across the page from margin to margin.

6 Select a page-column design that balances page limits, production requirements, readability, and graphics size flexibility.

See **Electronic Submittal** *for guidelines on proposals that will be viewed and evaluated on-screen.*

Most proposal pages are designed with an underlying grid pattern, most frequently one to four columns. Figure 5 shows some of the typical arrangements. Note that a four-column design does not necessarily mean there are four columns of text.

Multiple columns offer more flexibility in page layout and make reading easier. Readability study results suggest limiting lines of text to 40 to 60 characters. While influenced by font choice and leading or spacing between lines of text, readers tend to lose their place when text lines get too long.

Ever wonder why contracts are written in tiny print with the lines of text crammed tightly together across the entire page?

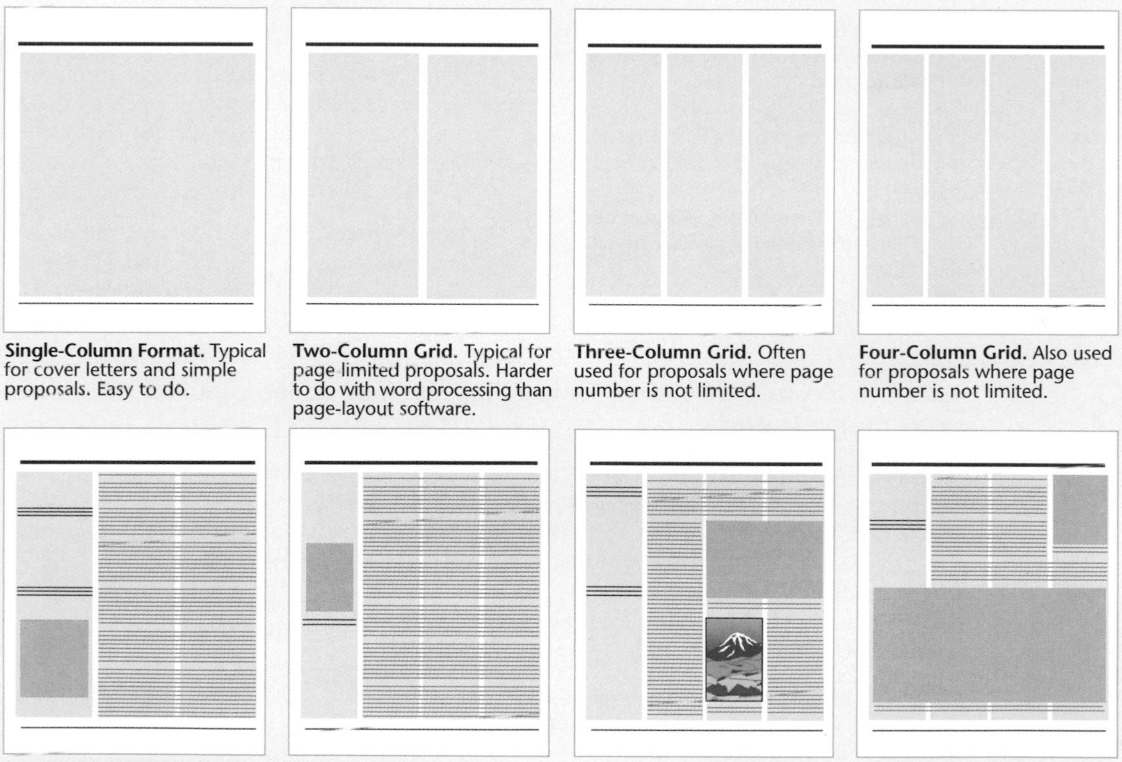

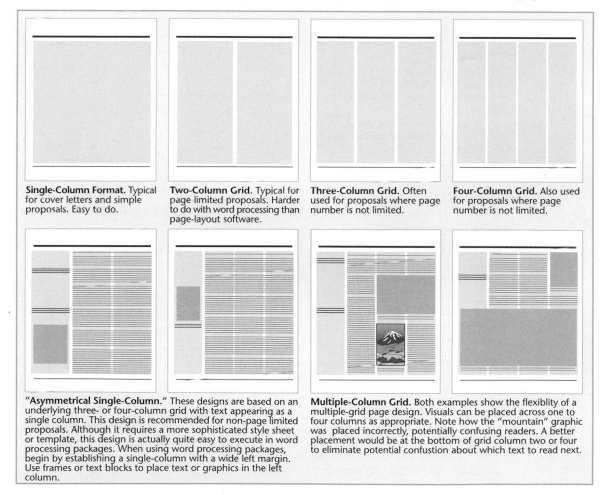

Single-Column Format. Typical for cover letters and simple proposals. Easy to do.

Two-Column Grid. Typical for page limited proposals. Harder to do with word processing than page-layout software.

Three-Column Grid. Often used for proposals where page number is not limited.

Four-Column Grid. Also used for proposals where page number is not limited.

"Asymmetrical Single-Column." These designs are based on an underlying three- or four-column grid with text appearing as a single column. This design is recommended for non-page limited proposals. Although it requires a more sophisticated style sheet or template, this design is actually quite easy to execute in word processing packages. When using word processing packages, begin by establishing a single-column with a wide left margin. Use frames or text blocks to place text or graphics in the left column.

Multiple-Column Grid. Both examples show the flexiblity of a multiple-grid page design. Visuals can be placed across one to four columns as appropriate. Note how the "mountain" graphic was placed incorrectly, potentially confusing readers. A better placement would be at the bottom of grid column two or four to eliminate potential confustion about which text to read next.

Figure 5. Using Underlying Grid Patterns to Design Pages. *Using multiple columns in your page design increases both flexibility and complexity. The leading approaches are a two-column format for page-limited proposals and a one-third/two-third style format using a three- or four-column grid for proposals without page limits. Place graphics toward the edges of pages to avoid confusing reading patterns that unnecessarily interrupt columns of text.*

7 Select complementary font styles, sizes, and leading.

NOTE: In this *Proposal Guide*, serif fonts are used in body text and captions. Sans-serif fonts are used for guidelines and examples as well as most text within graphics.

See **Electronic Submittal.**

Fonts or typefaces are divided into two broad groups, serif and sans serif (also called "gothic"). Serif is usually more compact, has "feet" or flared ends on the type, and is typically used for body text. Serif is easier to read in mass.

Sans serif is usually less compact, has squared ends, and is typically used for headings and labels. Sans serif is more authoritative.

Try to limit a document to two fonts unless you have a designer available. Use the variations of styles within the font, such as normal, italic, and bold.

Designers can be quite emotional about fonts. The following are only guidelines to help those without design background who do their own proposals:

- Avoid ALL CAPITAL LETTERS. They are harder to read.
- Use **bold text for emphasis** rather than underlining. Underlining is harder to read and looks outdated.
- **Avoid overusing bold or any other emphasis technique. Too much emphasis means no emphasis.**
- Use *italic for lighter emphasis than bold* but limit use to short pieces of text or quotes. Long passages of italic text are harder to read than normal text.

  Use italic to quote the prospect's bid request. Readability is less important, and italic type suggests a quote, which it is.

Type must be large enough to be comfortably read. Fonts are measured in points with 72 points equalling 1 inch. The point measuring system dates from the days of lead type.

Use 10- to 12-point fonts, depending on a number of factors:

Font choice—Fonts differ in width and x-height, x-height being literally the height of an "x" in the font. 10-point in one font may be nearly as easy to read as 12-point in another font.

Printer and paper quality—Printers with a higher dot per inch capability and coated paper will render clearer print, enabling smaller letters.

Copying—If your printed proposal is photocopied or if your prospect is likely to photocopy your proposal, use larger type.

Older readers—Many readers appreciate the readability of larger type.

Line length and leading—The longer the lines of text and the narrower the leading or spacing between lines of type, the larger the font required to maintain readability.

With more prospects requiring electronic versions of proposals, select commonly available fonts that are identical across all platforms. Inappropriate font substitutions can ruin the look of your proposal. Embed fonts in the PDF files when submitting electronic proposals.

Generally, a safe choice for the proposal body text is 12-point in a font like Times or 10-point in a serif font with a larger x-height.

8 Establish a consistent system for headings, themes, action captions, lists, and other page design features.

See **Action Captions, Headings, Lists,** *and* **Themes.**

Proposal headings divide and label content, helping evaluators find answers to their questions. Frequent headings at multiple levels help evaluators quickly find information of interest without having to read large blocks of text. Frustrated and confused evaluators give lower scores.

Where possible, use informative rather than telegraphic headings to convey a more complete message.

As part of your style sheet, establish a consistent system for headings, themes, action captions, and lists that include font, type style, type size, color, placement, and other emphasis devices such as borders or shading.

Too many proposal writers use long themes, short headings, and short captions. Strive for the opposite.

Consider replacing themes at lower section levels with informative headings. While evaluators may not read themes, they nearly always read headings.

Be cautious about using screens or shades to emphasize text. As the contrast between the text and the screen diminishes, the text becomes much harder to read.

Many copiers and some printers print screens differently, either fading out or becoming much darker than intended. Check your printer or copier. Also consider whether prospect copying of your proposal will add to the problem.

Be particularly cautious when using a dark background with reverse print. Dark backgrounds tend to swallow light print, requiring a larger and bolder font and type style.

Another caution is warranted for backgrounds with progressive screens, both in proposals and presentations. Legible type at one side of the screen might become illegible on the other side.

Print on photographs may be hard to read. Both regular and reverse print become illegible as photograph colors change. Place print on a white background to improve print clarity.

Establish quality and style criteria for headings, themes, action captions, and lists should extend beyond appearance to include content. Evaluators make negative inferences when emphasized items offer no discriminating content.

9 Choose and place graphics for maximum impact and readability.

See **Graphics.**

NOTE: Some complex technical graphics will not meet the 10-second rule. Strive to make technical graphics as clear as possible. Consider adding more information to the captions of complex technical graphics.

Use graphics to help evaluators remember your main points. The larger a graphic, the greater the emphasis. Both color and white space around a graphic increase its emphasis on the page.

Select an appropriate type of graphic to support your strategy and key point. Too many proposal writers use a graphic simply because it is available or because it is the only type of graphic they know how to create.

Consider the following contrasting guidelines:

- Use a **chart** or **graph** when emphasizing relationships or trends. Use a **table** when the absolute values of the numbers are important.
- Use a **photograph** to show that something is real, that it exists. Use a **sketch** or **line drawing** to emphasize specific details. Photographs show everything, and often the details of interest are not as easy to see.
- Use **display lists** for greater emphasis. Use **paragraph lists** when the items are not as important.

NOTE: To eliminate the possibility of missing or substituted fonts and graphics, create a PDF file of your document for submission. A PDF will contain all the elements of your document in a self-contained file. You can touch up any spacing problems or missing graphics using the complete version of Adobe® Acrobat® software.

See **Electronic Submittal.**

Keep the following suggestions in mind when placing graphics in your proposal:

- Introduce the graphic in body text before it appears in the proposal.
- Orient graphics vertically to the text so that evaluators do not have to rotate the page.
- Integrate the graphic so the evaluator can see the graphic without turning the page.
- Ensure evaluators can get the point you intended by attaching an action caption to every graphic.
- Observe the 10-Second Rule: Readers must be able to get your point within 10 seconds. If they cannot, consider dividing the single graphic into several graphics.
- Emphasize the right points. All but the simplest graphics should have a fore-, middle-, and background to make the graphic easy to interpret. Use line widths, color, and shading to differentiate the separate graphic elements.
- Remove anything in your graphic that does not contribute to your point.

In addition to the recommendations offered, consider the following observations gleaned from reviewing hundreds of proposals:

- Most U.S. Federal proposals contain graphics that are too complex.
- Too few proposal graphics have captions; those that do are generally too short.
- Sales professionals who would refuse to make an overhead presentation from slides that contain only text seem perfectly happy to give prospects nonproposal sales documents totally devoid of graphics.
- Proposals outside of large, custom bid requests tend to contain graphics that feature logos and clip art (the only color available), and tables and spreadsheets (the only type of graphic the writer knew how to make).
- Organizations should focus more on developing boilerplate graphics and less on developing boilerplate text.
- Boilerplate, both text and graphics, is generally used poorly.

Be sure all graphic files are included when submitting an electronic proposal. Missing graphics will display poorly or not at all. Certain programs will not open until the appropriate graphic links are located.

10

See **Organization**.

Avoid overusing emphasis devices.

Too much emphasis is no emphasis. Too many different emphasis devices are confusing and distracting.

White space at the end of a column or page is not only acceptable, but also desirable. The fundamental principles of organization must be followed.

Emphasize the points most important to your prospects; then tie these points to the most important reasons for them to select your solution and your organization. Avoid emphasizing relatively minor points.

11

NOTE: Using left-justified text is a recommendation and not a rule. If a senior manager insists on both left and right justification, do not risk your career. The difference is relatively minor.

When a page is created to show four or more columns of text, many designers will use full justification to create a more ordered page. For example, most newspapers printed in a five- to eight-column page layout use full justification. The same newspaper may use left-only justification for columns or op-ed pieces to visually discriminate these items from regular news stories.

Use left-justified text.

Use left-justified text rather full-justified text. Full justification has several undesirable attributes:

- Uneven spacing between words and letters creates more eye fatigue and may distract readers from your message. Readers sometimes pause on a poorly spaced word and think "That word looks funny. I wonder if it's misspelled?"
- Uniform line endings increase the probability that readers may accidentally skip a line or reread the same line of text.

Both of these problems interfere with the clear flow of information to the prospect.

Left-justified text with ragged-right line endings offers several advantages:

- Text is more readable.
- Words and letters are spaced more evenly.
- Gutters (space between columns) appear wider.
- Pages of multicolumn text are more varied, interesting, and appealing.

Photographs convey realism and authenticity. Readers tend to trust photographs, perhaps based on their own experience taking straightforward pictures with relatively simple cameras.

Skilled photographers have, for years, been taking photographs that distort reality, as was emphasized in the PBS television documentary, *American Photography: A Century of Images*. Aside from any photographic cleverness, the production discussed how Edward Curtis, a 19th century American photographer, traveled with a large trunk full of Native American clothing to dress Native American subjects who did not "look like Indians."

Photos are still persuasive, but evaluators realize that they can be manipulated. As with writing, present your case positively but honestly. Distortions destroy the prospect's trust.

Use a photograph to show what exists. Use a sketch or illustration to show what is possible or to emphasize a specific feature in isolation.

Typically, too few photographs are used in proposals. Photographs can be expensive, but hours of graphic artists' time can be even more expensive. Worse yet, engineers' drawings of marginal quality are even more costly, but none are as costly as lost orders due to boring, dense, text-heavy proposals.

These guidelines suggest ways to use photographs more effectively in sales documents. Techniques to either take or compose photographs are left to other sources.

Photographs

1. **Visualize what your prospect wants to see, then select images that support that vision.**
2. **Select photographs that support your overall strategy.**
3. **Collect photographs throughout the entire sales process.**
4. **Use prospects' and existing or past clients' photographs.**
5. **Go digital, but use the resolution appropriate to the finished size.**
6. **Use color to add realism, add information, and increase interest.**
7. **Establish the size, scale, and orientation of objects in the photograph.**
8. **Develop a searchable and retrievable boilerplate photographic and graphics library.**
9. **Balance the use of photographs with increased production time and cost.**

1 Visualize what your prospect wants to see, then select images that support that vision.

See **Graphics** *for a further discussion of how benefits are visualized.*

Visualize the benefits your solution offers. Then plan or select photographs that make the benefits seem real. The reality of a photograph emotionally reinforces your message and implies a lower risk. Imagine what the prospect wants to see after making a purchase, as discussed in these examples:

> A prospect selecting a design-build contractor for a distribution center wants to see photographs of a similar, complete distribution center with a caption citing success measures.

> Parents selecting schools for their children want to see photographs of happy students; clean, bright classrooms; caring teachers; and elated graduates.

When the sales approach extends beyond citing features to stressing benefits, service and product sales are identical. Both products and services enable the prospect to do or experience something different and presumably better. Skilled marketers sell benefits. Select photographs that do the same for your proposals.

2 Select photographs that support your overall strategy.

Prospects make or justify their selection decisions by identifying differences in offers that relate directly to their issues.

Portray these differences, your discriminators, and directly tie them to the prospect's issues.

State these differences and issues, using the prospects' words.

For example, if a prospect is worried about whether you can do what you say, then your strategy could be to emphasize your experience.

See **Discriminators** *and* **Strategy**.

A visual showing you doing what you propose for another organization would emphasize your experience. A quote from the satisfied client would bolster your claim.

Figure 1 offers an extended example of using photographs to support a bidder's strategy. The competition was to prequalify only two organizations to provide $500 million annually in construction services. The prospect listed three hot buttons in their bid request:

- Reduce capital cost
- Reduce cycle time from inception to production
- Streamline project planning

The winning two-page executive summary included two small photographs to support the first and third hot buttons. The photographs and quotes have been slightly altered to protect confidentiality.

Note how the first hot button, "reduce capital cost," is directly supported at the end of the Drugs-R-Us quote, ". . . and significantly under budget." The third hot button, ". . . streamline project planning," is supported by the statement, "In 6 months your team is 2 months ahead of schedule . . ." Both photos showed the completed facility, shots that are commonly available to constructors.

Sometimes you may not be able to get a photo of the actual object. One solution is to create a high-quality graphic or scale model. Then photograph the graphic or model to make the conceptual item look and feel more real to the evaluator.

Scale models or prototypes have been used for demonstrations for years. Including photographs of a prototype in the proposal permits the evaluator to view the prototype that they cannot view live.

Do not misrepresent photographs of graphics or prototypes as real. If the prospect feels you are being deceptive, you lose your credibility, the sale, and often subsequent sales.

"In 10 years of doing projects throughout the U.S. and Europe, this has been the best so far. The Global Constructors difference is the people—uniquely qualified, energetic, and team oriented—they consistently exceeded my expectations and completed the project ahead of schedule, with outstanding quality, and significantly under budget."

Drugs-R-Us
Corporate Headquarters

"Trying to describe what your Global team has accomplished during the past 6 months is difficult. Words such as astounding and astonishing are insufficient. In 6 months your team is 2 months ahead of schedule, under budget, achieved a perfect safety record, and the quality of construction work is outstanding."

World Chemicals Health
Division Laboratory

Figure 1. Using Photographs That Support Your Strategy. *The photographs and client quotes were selected to reinforce the seller's ability to address the prospect's issues of reduced capital cost, reduced cycle time, and streamlined project planning.*

3

Collect photographs throughout the entire sales process.

When you have to write the proposal, you seldom have time to go back and take photographs. Collect them throughout the sales process.

All sales and service people, site managers, and project managers should travel with a camera, whether film or digital. Observe all prospect or client restrictions. Even when the inner facilities are proprietary, you can often take photos of the outside or perhaps the sign at the front gate.

Photos taken during demonstrations or site visits either remind the evaluator of the experience or reinforce that members of their organization have seen proof of your performance.

To broaden your vision of possible photographs, consider these examples:

Photos of stages of facility construction enrich a project schedule.

Photos of implementation enrich a transition plan.

Group photos of proposed individuals support claims of teaming experience.

Adjacent before-and-after photos emphasize change.

Photos of your own facilities emphasize capacity and ready capability.

4

Use prospects' and existing or past clients' photographs.

Photos collected from the prospect or taken at the prospect's facilities demonstrate client focus.

Many photos are directly available from an organization's marketing, public relations, or investor relations departments.

Web sites are another source, although the resolution is usually limited.

Gather copies of the prospects' and clients' annual reports, marketing brochures, and employee newsletters. Observe all restrictions on the rights to reuse or change the photos.

5

Go digital, but use the resolution appropriate to the finished size.

Writers without skilled publishing support often insert digital photos but are disappointed with the poor quality. To increase your success, observe the following guidelines:

- Web photos and graphics typically have a 72 dpi (dots per inch) resolution, marginal in a printed document. Use 72 dpi photos at their actual size or smaller.
- The maximum acceptable enlargement for any digital photo is about 20 percent before the print becomes too "grainy."
- Aim for 150 dpi when printing on typical office laser or ink jet printers. Higher resolutions increase file sizes with minimal increases in print quality.
- The minimum acceptable dpi resolution for offset printing is 300 dpi. Figure 2 compares the various file sizes for a single 3″ x 5″ scanned photo using different resolutions, file formats, and degrees of compression. Multiple photos create immense files. Printers generally require TIFF or EPS file formats.
- Scan in RGB (Red-Green-Blue), the additive visible light spectrum. RGB files are smaller and easier to manipulate in programs like Adobe® Photoshop™.
- When submitting electronic proposals, embed RGB graphics for on-screen viewing.
- When printing proposals, convert the RGB files to CMYK (Cyan-Magenta-Yellow-Black) or scan directly in CMYK for truer color print quality. WYSIWYG (What You See Is What You Get) does not apply to color viewing on screen versus color printing. Print a trial version before full production.
- Observe all copyright restrictions and licensing agreements when using stock photos, scanned photos, or photos off the Internet. Rules vary widely.

SCANNED RESOLUTION	300 DPI			600 DPI		
File Type	JPG	JPG	TIFF	JPG	JPG	TIFF
Compression	none	Med	none	none	med	none
File Size	2.5MB	370KB	4.1MB	9.5MB	1.3MB	16.5MB

Figure 2. Scanned Files Can Be Large. *A 3″ x 5″ scanned photo resulted in file sizes of 370KB to 16.5MB. Variables were scanning resolution, degree of compression, and file format.*

6

Use color to add realism, add information, and increase interest.

NOTE: Make a black and white copy of color art. If you cannont read it, revise your color scheme to increase the contrast between colors.

See **Color.**

Until recently, color was considered too expensive in proposals. Color is now common in best-in-class proposals.

The highest-value places to use color are in your executive summary and in emphasizing your discriminators in the proposal.

Too often proposals simply use color where color is convenient for the writer and production people. Typical but poor uses for color are the seller's logo, the prospect's logo, and header and footer lines. When these design elements get the greatest emphasis, you de-emphasize your strategy and discriminators.

Limit color photos when your proposal is likely to be photocopied. The best approach is to advise the prospect that you will use color in your proposal and ask if the number of copies requested is sufficient to eliminate the need for the prospect to make photocopies.

7

Establish the size, scale, and orientation of objects in the photograph.

When the size, scale, or orientation of a photo or graphic is not obvious, include rulers, a human hand, or common objects. A car key, coin, coffee cup, or a person will establish scale.

Use arrows to establish orientation, linear movement, or rotation.

8

Develop a searchable, retrievable, boilerplate photographic and graphics library.

The greater effectiveness and higher cost of photographs when compared to text suggests that more organizations should develop a boilerplate photographic and graphics library.

For each photograph, collect relevant information and sample action captions. As with other boilerplate materials, assign someone to verify that all materials remain valid.

Another best practice is to attach a unique tracking number to each photo or graphic, including the revision number or date when appropriate. As in figure 3, print the tracking number with the photo in the proposal to facilitate rapid retrieval for subsequent proposals.

Figure 3. Assign Graphic Tracking Numbers. *Attach graphic tracking numbers to all photos and graphics to facilitate reuse. To be less obtrusive, print the numbers vertically in a small point type.*

9

Balance the use of photographs with increased production time and cost.

See **Scheduling.**

Most proposal pages with color photos are individually printed instead of photocopied. Double-sided printing compounds problems. Then each page must be inserted correctly in every copy, increasing production time and cost. Use color photos only where they count.

Presentations to prospects are intimately related to written proposals. Both are planned and structured to advance the sale. Any disconnect or conflict between what you say and what you submit in writing creates dissonance and confusion, reducing your chances to advance the sale.

Prospect presentations usually have one of the following primary objectives:

1. To persuade
2. To convey information

A secondary objective is to solicit feedback and new information.

Successful persuasion is based 50 percent on emotion and only 50 percent on logic and facts. Many technical presenters are overly reliant on logic and data. Your personal belief, enthusiasm, and commitment are essential to persuade prospects to accept your ideas and solutions.

Presentations to Prospects

1. **Maintain consistency throughout the sales process.**
2. **Keep a balance between content and delivery.**
3. **Identify the next realistically achievable sales objective.**
4. **Analyze your audience and present logically according to their priorities and needs.**
5. **Consider the parameters and environment.**
6. **Include evidence to support your points.**
7. **Use effective graphics to support your message.**
8. **Deliver with confidence.**
9. **Establish the ground rules, then follow them.**

1 Maintain consistency throughout the sales process.

See **Customer Focus.**

Complex sales involve multiple sellers and presentations. Unexplained changes in your message cause dissonance, doubt, and objections.

By organizing all of your presentations and documents in the same prospect-focused manner, you will save time, be more consistent, and be more successful in achieving your objectives.

2 Keep a balance between content and delivery.

When you plan a presentation to a prospect, spend as much time developing your content as you spend practicing your delivery.

Writers use graphics, color, lists, fonts, white space, and style for emphasis. Presenters rely on gestures, voice dynamics, eye contact, posture, movement, and facial expressions. These nonverbal messages can either reinforce or contradict the verbal message.

When verbal and nonverbal messages conflict, the listener tends to trust the nonverbal elements to determine the meaning.

3 Identify the next realistically achievable sales objective.

Begin by answering two questions:

1. What is your objective?
2. What would you like the prospect to agree to do next?

The answer to the first is usually broad, to persuade the prospect to buy your idea, product, or service.

The answer to the second is far more focused, to agree to change a specification, for example, or to commit to attend a product demonstration.

Then state your objective in your presentation:

> Today I will demonstrate how outsourcing network support can save $240,000 annually and free your managers to focus on Global's core activities.

4 Analyze your audience and present logically according to their priorities and needs.

See **Customer Focus, Executive Summary,** *and* **Oral Proposals.**

To present effectively, you must understand your prospects' priorities and needs. When presenting, state your understanding of their needs and ask for confirmation.

> In your (bid, phone request, initial meeting) you asked us to address the following issues:
>
> *(List the issues.)*
>
> Have we gotten them correct? If so, with your agreement, we will address each one in order.

If you are too early in the sales process to have a basis to state their issues, then either ask them or cite your understanding and the basis for your understanding.

> We agreed to meet today to discuss how we might help you establish bottling facilities in South America. Our experience with other organizations developing manufacturing facilities in South America suggests that most are concerned about the following issues:
>
> *(List the issues.)*
>
> How would yours be similar or different?

Presentations organized around the seller's key points are rarely persuasive and successful.

Organize in order of importance to the prospect, unless directed otherwise by the prospect. Presentations can be logically organized by order of importance, time, cause and effect, or spatially.

Use your draft executive summary as the basis for prospect presentations throughout the sales process to maintain a consistent sales message, save time, and be customer focused.

The similar organization of prospect presentations and the executive summary is shown in figure 1. Note two differences:

- Presentations require more emphatic summaries and transitions among main points.
- Graphics will have to be adjusted for the medium.

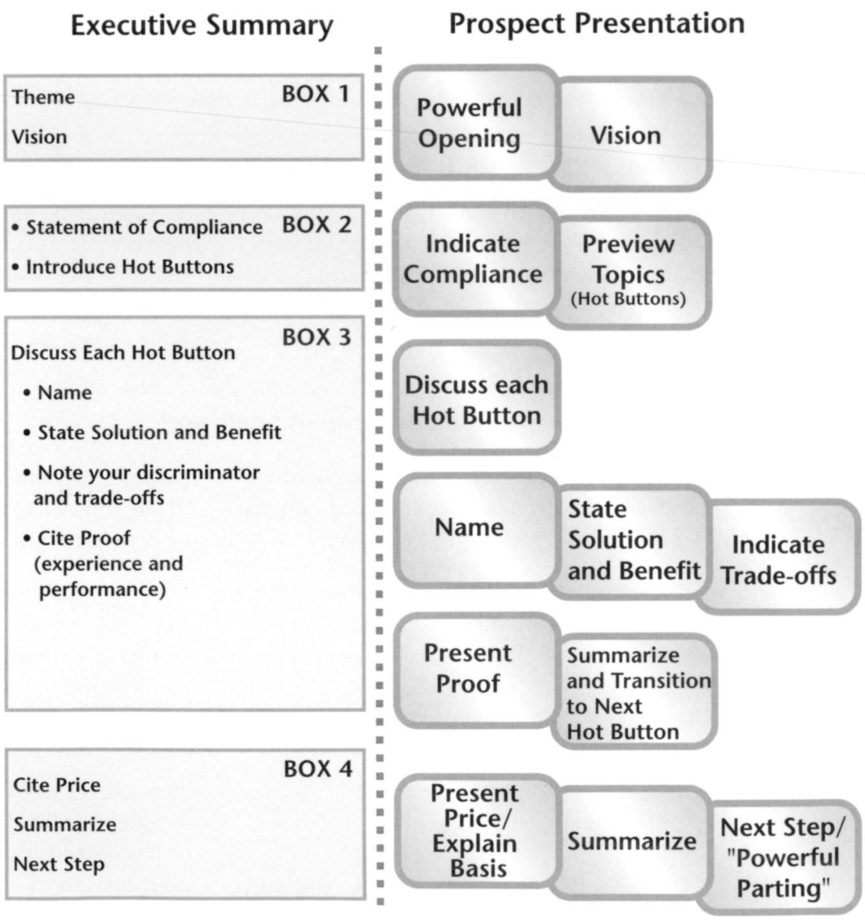

Figure 1. Use the Same Organization for Your Prospect Presentation and Executive Summary. *Note how the Four-Box organization directly maps to slides in a presentation or sections in an executive summary. If you organize your prospect presentations as shown, you will save time preparing the executive summary and maintain a consistent message. If your executive summary is prepared first, simply add slides as needed, following sound slide preparation guidelines.*

5 Consider the parameters and environment.

The *location* will determine the physical distance to your prospects and often the presentation aids that you can use.

The *time* available will affect the depth of content.

The *number* in the audience will affect the visual medium selected and the design of your graphics.

The *occasion* will affect the expectations, motivation, enthusiasm, and level of expertise of the audience.

6 Include evidence to support your points.

NOTE: Proof of performance is from post-sale experience.

See **Relevant Experience/ Past Performance.**

Develop adequate support for each main point. Remember evidence of support is not necessarily proof in a scientific sense. Support includes definitions, evaluation criteria, explanations, experience, proof of performance, and testimonials.

Definitions establish a common basis of understanding and *evaluation criteria* establish a basis for judgment or comparison.

Explanations are nearly always necessary, but match them to the expertise of the audience.

Experience is the proof that your organization has done this before or has completed similar tasks. When experience is not identical, relate parallel experience from similar subtasks.

Proof of performance is about results. When you completed the task, what was the benefit to the customer or impact on the customer's process?

Testimonials or *references* offer independent proof that the experience and performance cited are real. Testimonials carry emotional persuasive impact in addition to the facts.

7 Use effective graphics to support your message.

See **Color** *and* **Graphics**.

Effective graphics are simple, clear, and uncluttered, keeping the primary focus on the presenter.

Graphics should highlight key messages, not display every point. Think of them as billboards, not text ads.

Keep the following in mind when designing your presentation graphics:

1. Keep text simple.

- Keep to one thought, concept, or idea per slide.
- Limit text slides to six lines and six words per line.
- Use upper and lower case. All caps are hard to read.
- Capitalize only the first word per line.
- Use one or two fonts or typefaces (at the most).
- Highlight with bold, italics, or color. Highlight key numbers.

2. Keep the graphics uncluttered.

- Show only key numbers when the actual number is important.
- Show only trend lines when the trend is your key point.

3. Guide eyes to the main point.

- Use larger type.
- Use an arrow.
- Use a build, motion, or (with caution) a video clip.

4. Follow these additional suggestions:

- Use a landscape style, permitting longer phrases that are easier to read.
- Use 24-point or larger type but also check the room size.
- Use simple typefaces, usually sans-serif.
- Keep the grammatical structure of bullet points parallel, making content easier to understand and present.
- Proof carefully; do not rely exclusively on spell check.
- Use numbers in display lists when you may want to refer to a few specific items.
- Use phrases, not sentences.
- Leave plenty of blank space. Builds permit denser slides.

Choose colors and templates carefully. Sometimes audiences will comment on the background or motion while missing the presenter's point.

When selecting a template, consider your corporate image, the audience, and the objective of your presentation.

8 Deliver with confidence.

See **Oral Proposals** *for information on the nonverbal aspects of delivery.*

Confident delivery demands rehearsal. Professional comedians and actors rehearse extensively to develop a natural delivery.

Rehearsals enable you to test six critical aspects of your presentation:

Timing—Does it match the prospects' expectations?

Intonation and Emphasis—Do you hit each point correctly?

Technology—Can you use all hardware, software, lights, and screens? Do the visuals project correctly and clearly for all viewers?

Confidence—Have you rehearsed to enable you to focus on your prospects and to adjust to their reactions?

Audience Reaction—Does the test group get your message?

Questions and Answers—Are questions allowed during or after your presentation? Do you want to encourage questions? How will questions affect timing?

9 Establish the ground rules, then follow them.

See **Compliance and Responsiveness** *and* **Oral Proposals.**

Follow prospects' ground rules or establish them if the prospect hasn't stated them. If permitted, encourage participation and collaboration to promote acceptance.

In less formal situations, frequently check the prospects' understanding and acceptance. Participation keeps the prospect's attention.

Presentation experts differ on how and when to allow questions. No single approach is best in all situations. One approach is to ask the audience to hold questions for the end. With this approach, nervous presenters can stay on topic and on schedule. However, interactivity is lost, and the presentation can end dully when questions abruptly cease.

Another approach is to encourage questions during the presentation to involve prospects, gauge reaction, and tailor content. With this approach, presenters must be skilled enough to stay on topic and on schedule. Allow interruptions if you have adequate presentation skills.

Retain enough time with either approach to summarize and close with power and enthusiasm.

Presenting cost and price data is routinely neglected in different ways in different markets. Federal government bidders see it as a time-consuming process of completing numerous forms and spreadsheets. Commercial bidders may hide their price in the back of their proposal, thinking that will force the prospect to read their proposal and discover their added value.

Some perspective on the differences between government and commercial markets is needed to understand the following guidelines. Many governments have cost disclosure requirements similar to the U.S. Federal government.

Because governments make large purchases from a few bidders, they tend to require full disclosure of the bidder's cost and pricing data above defined dollar thresholds. The U.S. government defines cost and pricing data as all facts at the time of agreement on price that can be expected to affect price negotiations significantly.

If cost and pricing data are not disclosed, the government can demand a refund. Price adjustments never happen in the contractor's favor. If the data were intentionally not disclosed, the government can send bidders to jail for fraud.

As a result, governments get so much cost and pricing data, literally boxes full of paper, that no one but specialist cost analysts look at it. This creates an opportunity for bidders to gain a competitive advantage by presenting their cost and pricing data clearly and concisely in a cost volume summary.

In commercial markets, 90 percent of all bidders think that their price is higher than their competitors, so they try to hide their price. Instead, disclose your price early in the executive summary. To limit the prospect's ability to negotiate, include detailed price breakdowns only when required.

Presenting Cost and Price Data

1. **Include pricing in the executive summary unless prohibited.**
2. **Explain and quantify, where possible, your added-value components instead of just claiming to offer added value.**
3. **Present cost and price data graphically to engage senior management, promote rapid understanding, and establish perspective.**
4. **Substantiate cost or pricing with past performance data.**
5. **Present relative cost comparisons in the technical proposal when actual cost data is not permitted.**
6. **Prepare a cost volume summary for markets where costs are prohibited in the technical proposal.**

1 Include pricing in the executive summary unless prohibited.

NOTE: If you wonder whether price is important, consider how your account executives spend their time when the proposal is being prepared. Do they spend more time seeking a price cut or reviewing the proposal?

Sales professionals who get the opportunity to present their proposal to their prospect usually say they keep the prospect's attention for about 5 minutes, then the prospect begins turning through the proposal, looking for the price.

Keep the prospect's attention by putting your price in the executive summary, unless prohibited.

Seldom will a sales professional say that price is not important. Even when price is not the most important factor, price invariably falls into the prospect's top four hot buttons.

Even if price is a minor selection factor, everyone has a budget. Price is a rapid elimination factor as long as several bidders are within the prospect's budget. Consider the following examples:

A company was bidding an IT support contract to a large city, priced at approximately $1 million. The price was placed on the front page of the executive summary in bold type larger than the text. The seller's comment, "We offered excellent value for money. Why hide our price?" The prospect's comment, "We appreciated having the price on the first page. Everyone else hid theirs."

A buyer of a retail store computer system valued at $50,000 made the following comment, "I had 15 proposals and little time to evaluate. One cover caught my attention, and I remembered that the account representative for that organization was competent. I opened their executive summary and found the price was within my budget. I gave them the contract. I had no requirement to open the other 14 proposals."

2

Explain and quantify, where possible, your added-value components instead of just claiming to offer added value.

Most sellers claim to offer added value. Many government bid requests cite "best value" as an award criterion. Yet few explain or attempt to quantify their added value.

Added value is essentially quantified cost-benefit selling. Figure 1 illustrates the concept.

Price to the seller is simply the cost plus profit, assuming the sale is profitable. However, the prospect sees the price as the cost. These terms change as the perspective changes.

Added value to the prospect is the difference between the value of the benefits of the solution less the prospect's costs. The prospect's costs include both the purchase cost and potential implementation costs.

Prospects trying to obtain maximum added value must determine the difference between the value of each seller's solution and the total cost to the prospect of each seller's solution.

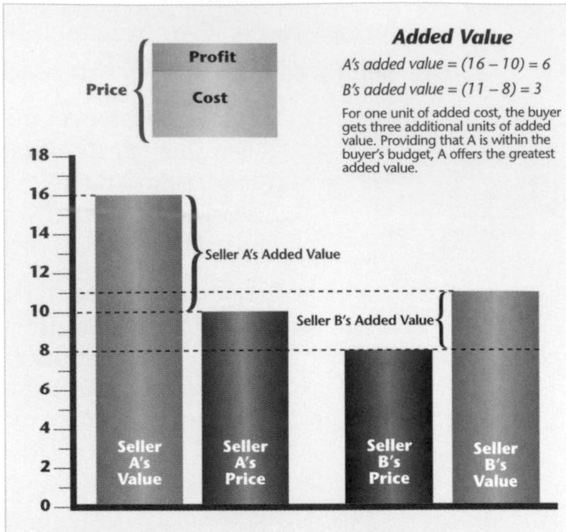

Figure 1. Understanding the Concept of Added Value. *Most proposals claim to offer greater added value but never attempt to explain or justify their claim. Credible explanations require an intimate understanding of the prospect's business and collaboration with the prospect to understand their cost and value structure.*

3

Present cost and price data graphically to engage senior management, promote rapid understanding, and establish perspective.

Graphic presentation of cost and pricing data elevates the analysis to the level where best value decisions can be made. Examine your proposed costs or prices from the point of view of the prospect's senior management.

Senior managers are interested in the following cost or price-specific items:

- How is the cost spread among products and services?
- What are the major cost drivers?
- What is the spending pattern over time both in total and by major cost category?
- Which costs are at risk, and what is being done to manage that risk?
- Which items are subcontracted?
- Who are the major subcontractors, and where are they located?

Potential ways of presenting different cost elements are listed in figure 2. Review the mocked-up cost volume summary in figures 3 through 14 for more examples.

TYPE OF COST DATA	POTENTIAL PRESENTATION METHODS
Cost distribution among cost elements	Pie or bar chart.
Major cost drivers	Table; pie or bar chart.
Spending pattern or profile	Line chart over time, one line for each category. Sum can be additive.
Higher risk cost elements	Line chart showing standard deviations; tables citing the category, amount at risk, and risk management approach.
Subcontracted vs. in-house sourced	Pie or bar chart.
Subcontractors by location	Combination map and pie chart, perhaps accompanied by a table insert.

Figure 2. Present Costs and Pricing Graphically. *Succinct, graphical presentations of costs are more likely to influence decision makers. Place similar graphics in your executive summary and cost volume or pricing summary.*

4

Substantiate cost or pricing with past performance data.

See **Relevant Experience/ Past Performance.**

NOTE: Vendor quotes, cited by many estimators as the most reliable, are negotiated and purchased at a lower price. Analysts apply a negotiation decrement to vendor quotes.

When costs or prices have to be justified, cite past performance data. Enhance credibility by citing how this data has been adjusted for future conditions.

Understanding how government cost analysts evaluate cost proposals will help proposal writers in all markets. Cost analysts begin with two primary assumptions:

1. **Nothing is new. Everything has been done before.**

   Even if the overall task has never been done, the subtasks, when sufficiently segmented and defined, have all been done before.

2. **The accuracy of cost estimates is directly related to the basis of the estimate.**

   Cost analysts rank the following bases of cost estimates from most accurate and credible to least accurate and credible:

   a. Firm negotiated price by future delivery date

   b. Actual past price paid, escalated for future delivery based on an accepted cost index

   c. Vendor quote

   d. Engineering judgment

On seeing "engineering judgment" as the basis of estimate, one cost analyst said, "I offer them 25 to 50 percent of their quoted price and see what they can do to justify any amount above that figure."

5

Present relative cost comparisons in the technical proposal when actual cost data is not permitted.

Relative cost comparisons in the technical proposal help justify your approach compared to alternative solutions when direct cost figures are not allowed.

Evaluators are trying to compare approaches and want to know that a bidder considered all feasible alternatives. Many technical people complete an exhaustive analysis of alternatives, select one, then describe only the selected approach in their proposal. Evaluators get the impression that only one approach was considered.

When costs cannot be included in your technical proposal, present relative cost comparisons as follows:

1. Cite your selection criteria.
2. List the alternative considered.
3. Cite cost differences in relative terms.
4. Justify your selected approach.
5. Explain why others were not selected.
6. Note potential changes in your selection if the selection factors changed or the importance of the selection factors changed.

6

Prepare a cost volume summary for markets where costs are prohibited in the technical proposal.

Beginning the cost volume with a cost volume summary is a best practice in Federal proposals. This means going beyond preparing a Standard Form 1411, the top-level cost summary form for U.S. government proposals.

See **Executive Summary.**

Evaluators of the cost volume rarely make the selection decision, and decision makers rarely look at the cost volume because it is too difficult to quickly understand. A good cost volume summary can be read and understood by the decision makers and senior influencers and positively sets up the cost analysts' evaluation of the cost volume.

A cost volume summary uses the graphical presentation methods outlined in guideline 3 in this section to present a clear, easily read summary of your costs for the prospect's senior management and decision makers.

Federal cost analysts must prepare a summary document, a Price Analysis Report, to summarize their evaluation. Think of the cost volume summary as the draft of the report you would like the cost analyst to present to the source selection authority or decision maker.

Place a copy of your executive summary in the front of the cost volume. Place it directly in the binder or place a copy in the pocket in the binder cover. Make it available to every cost analyst.

Prepare a cost volume summary that meets as many of the following objectives as possible:

- Projects overall proposal themes
- Overviews your approach
- Discusses total prices or costs in graphics and words
- Discusses price and cost implications of your approach while ghosting alternative approaches
- Emphasizes how costs are fair and reasonable
- Summarizes exceptions taken to the RFP
- Summarizes your estimating approach
- Summarizes how costs are accurately tracked and controlled
- Demonstrates sound logic
- Indicates your cost system has been audited and approved by the appropriate agencies
- Contains approximately 50 percent graphics and 50 percent text
- Comprises no more than 12 pages

An open mock-up of a cost volume summary for a large, multiphase systems program is shown in thumbnail version in figures 3 through 14. As shown in figure 14, the cost volume comprised eight chapters, all in separate binders.

Evaluators look favorably at proposals that are easy to evaluate, giving them higher scores. The last portion of the cost volume summary, figures 12 and 13, sets up the evaluation, telling cost analysts how the cost volume is organized. A 40-year veteran of cost proposal evaluation made the following comment:

> *A well-organized cost proposal is trackable. I should be able to open the cost volume at random, page backward or forward to the beginning of any subsection, and directly see where it ties to other sections. I can see where these costs are supported in greater detail and where they roll up to the next cost level.*

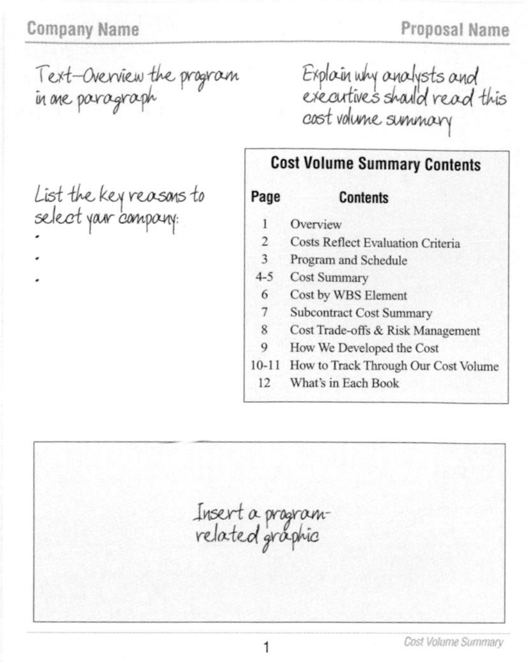
Company Name Proposal Name

Text—Overview the program in one paragraph

Explain why analysts and executives should read this cost volume summary

List the key reasons to select your company:
-
-
-

Cost Volume Summary Contents

Page	Contents
1	Overview
2	Costs Reflect Evaluation Criteria
3	Program and Schedule
4-5	Cost Summary
6	Cost by WBS Element
7	Subcontract Cost Summary
8	Cost Trade-offs & Risk Management
9	How We Developed the Cost
10-11	How to Track Through Our Cost Volume
12	What's in Each Book

Insert a program-related graphic

1 Cost Volume Summary

Figure 3. Summary Page. *Overview the entire program in one paragraph followed by the key reasons to select your organization. Insert a graphic that summarizes the overall program. Explain how this cost volume summary will aid cost analysts, then preview how the cost volume summary is organized.*

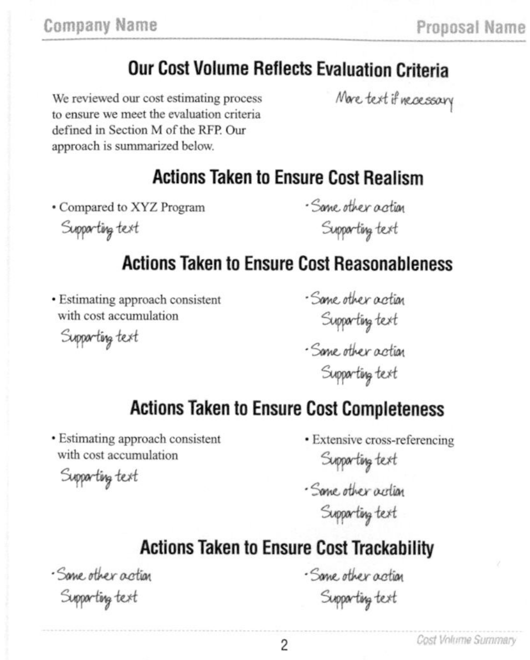
Company Name Proposal Name

Our Cost Volume Reflects Evaluation Criteria

We reviewed our cost estimating process to ensure we meet the evaluation criteria defined in Section M of the RFP. Our approach is summarized below.

More text if necessary

Actions Taken to Ensure Cost Realism

- Compared to XYZ Program
  Supporting text
- Some other action
  Supporting text

Actions Taken to Ensure Cost Reasonableness

- Estimating approach consistent with cost accumulation
  Supporting text
- Some other action
  Supporting text
- Some other action
  Supporting text

Actions Taken to Ensure Cost Completeness

- Estimating approach consistent with cost accumulation
  Supporting text
- Extensive cross-referencing
  Supporting text
- Some other action
  Supporting text

Actions Taken to Ensure Cost Trackability

- Some other action
  Supporting text
- Some other action
  Supporting text

2 Cost Volume Summary

Figure 4. Reflect the Cost Evaluation Criteria. *Summarize how your costing approach reflects the prospect's bid request cost evaluation criteria. Stress responsiveness as well as compliance. You are essentially presenting your costing strategy, drafting a justification that the cost analyst can later use to help justify supporting your approach.*

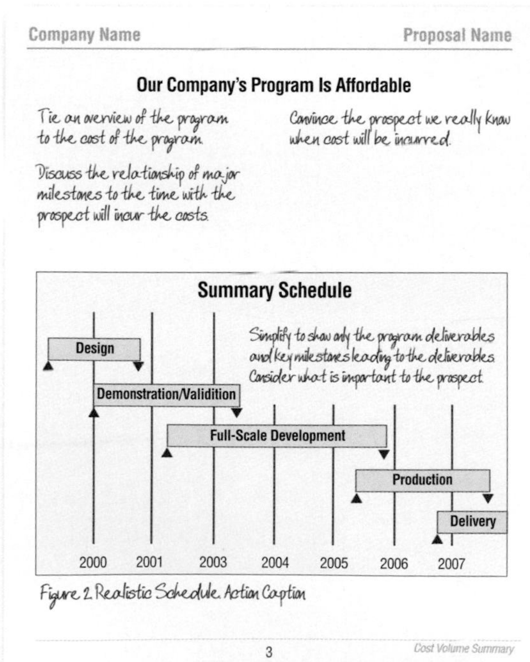
Company Name Proposal Name

Our Company's Program Is Affordable

Tie an overview of the program to the cost of the program.

Discuss the relationship of major milestones to the time with the prospect will incur the costs.

Convince the prospect we really know when cost will be incurred.

Figure 2. Realistic Schedule. Action Caption

3 Cost Volume Summary

Figure 5. Stress Affordability Tied to Your Schedule. *Use this page to present an overview of the program schedule, the first opportunity for the cost analyst to see the relative costs of different parts of the program over time.*

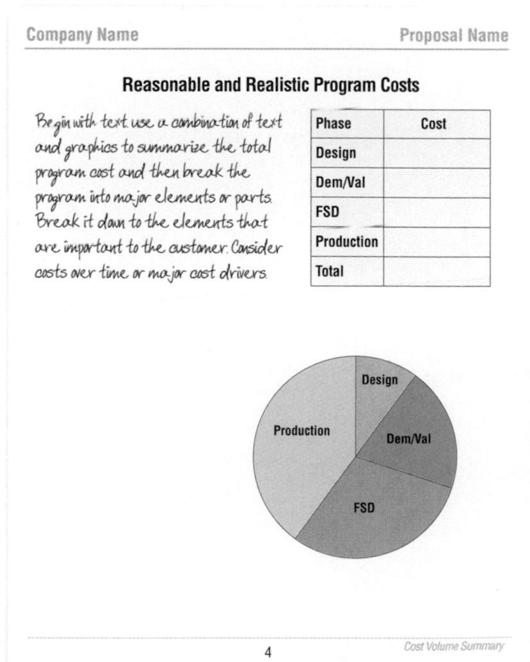
Company Name Proposal Name

Reasonable and Realistic Program Costs

Begin with text use a combination of text and graphics to summarize the total program cost and then break the program into major elements or parts. Break it down to the elements that are important to the customer. Consider costs over time or major cost drivers.

Phase	Cost
Design	
Dem/Val	
FSD	
Production	
Total	

4 Cost Volume Summary

Figure 6. Stress Your Cost Reasonableness and Realism. *This page gives each reader some perspective on the major cost drivers, whether by component, task, or program phase.*

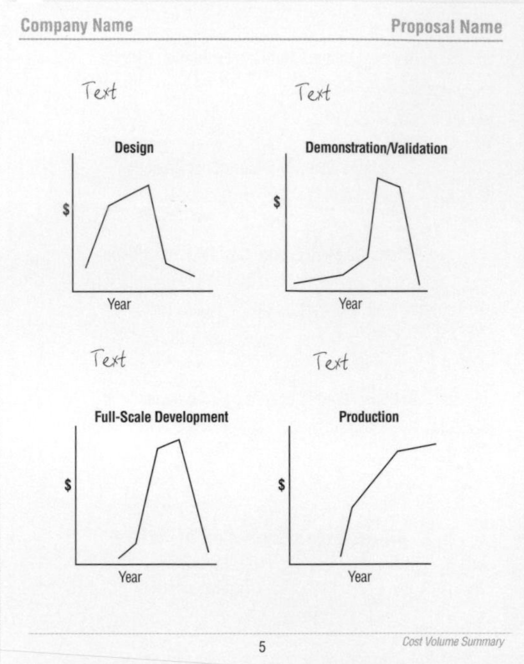

Figure 7. Cost by Phase Over Time. *Present your cost profile, so the cost analyst can easily compare it to the funding profile. The funding for complex programs often comes from different sources with different restrictions. For example, maintenance money may have to be spent within a fiscal year, while capital expenditures are usually allocated for longer periods.*

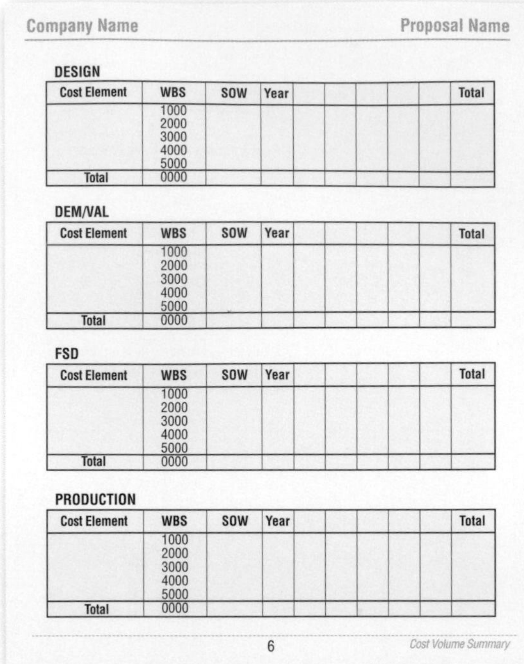

Figure 8. Cost Summary by Element. *This is the most detailed presentation of costs in the cost volume summary. Present costs by phase, cost element, Work Breakdown Structure (WBS) tracking number, Statement of Work (SOW) task, and year.*

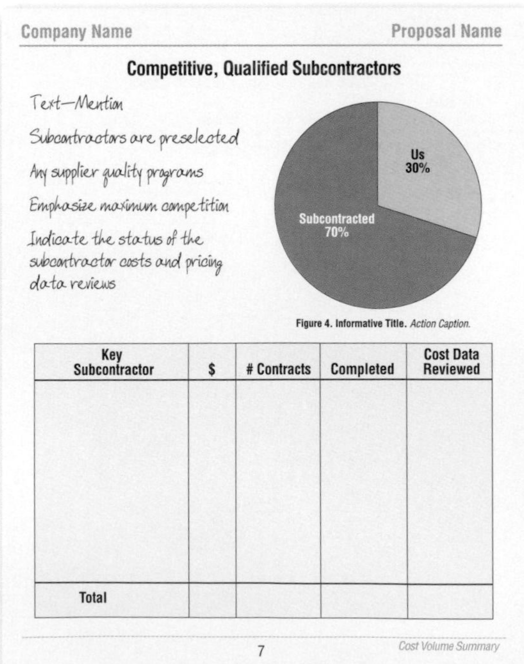

Figure 9. Summarize the Costs of Team Members and Subcontractors. *Who is doing what work and where they will do the work is important to cost analysts and their managers. Funding sources want to make sure that they get their share of work. For example, congressmen want work in their state, and export prospects want a fair share of the work in their country under coproduction agreements.*

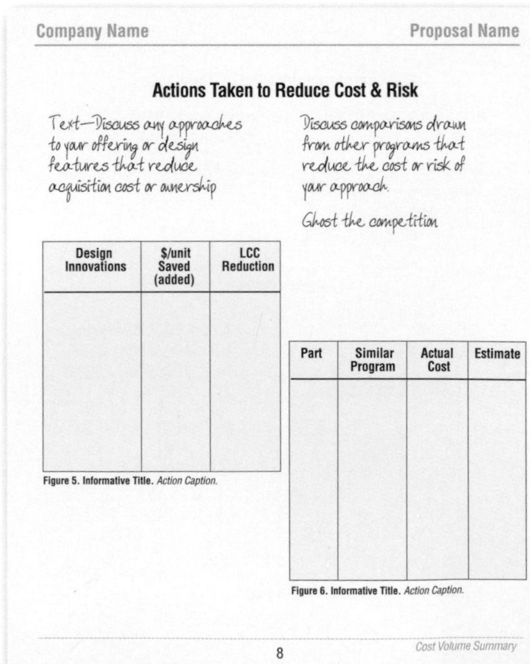

Figure 10. Reflect Strategies That Reduce Cost and Risk. *Technical proposals are full of claims of superior approaches. Summarize the actual cost impact of each of these claims, cross-referencing the cost analyst to the appropriate pages in your technical proposal.*

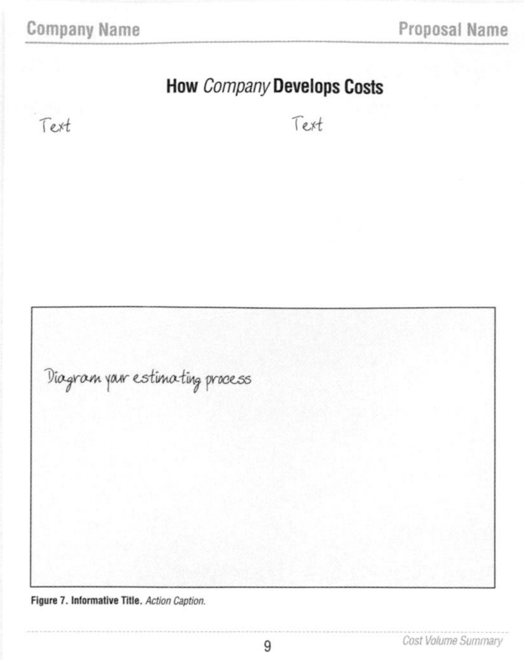

Figure 11. Summarize Your Costing Approach. *Use both text and a graphic to summarize your costing approach. Summarize and justify any changes in your approach. If you have calculated new labor standards, justify why. For example, one cost volume manager justified a high engineering cost per hour by noting that all drafting and computer support costs were wrapped into the engineering overhead rate.*

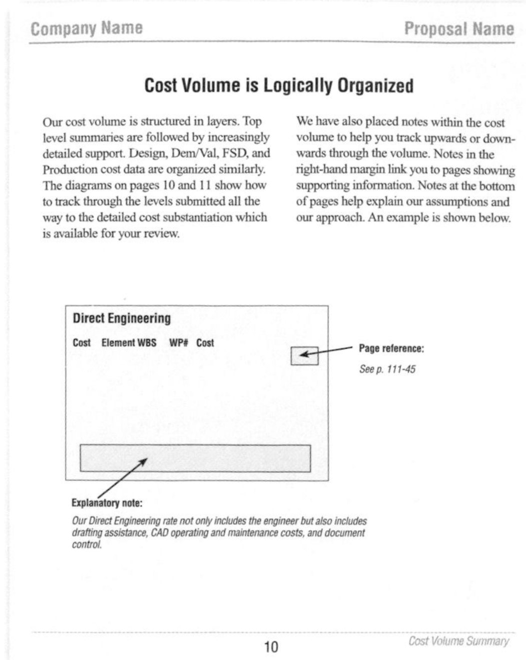

Figure 12. Explain Your Cost Volume Organization. *Cost analysts are often forced to spend a lot of time just trying to figure out how cost volumes are organized. Eliminate this wasted time and improve cost analysts' evaluation perspective by clearly explaining your approach.*

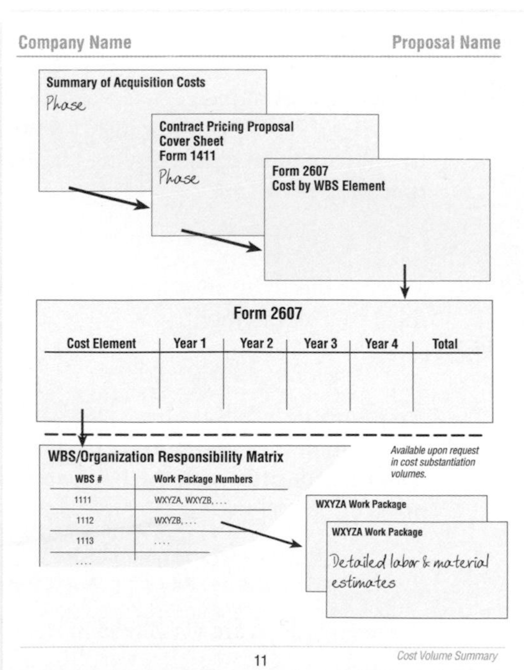

Figure 13. Graphically Show the Organization of Your Cost Volume. *Emphasize the traceability of costs through the cost volume, emphasizing the relationship between the various forms either required in the bid request or used by your organization.*

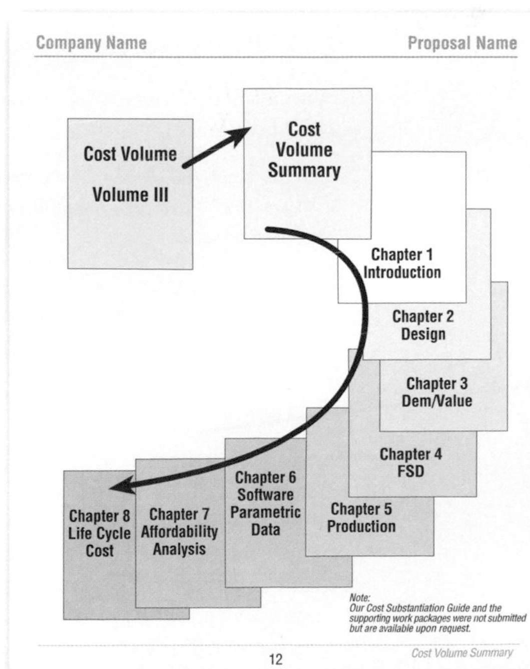

Figure 14. Overview Major Elements of Your Cost Volume. *Until you see the boxes of paper submitted with some major government procurements, few individuals would understand the value of the last four pages suggested. While numbers are objective, the credibility of numbers is pretty subjective. Cost analysts tend to believe bidders who make their jobs easier.*

Pricing requirements vary by market and are unique to every organization. In government markets, pricing is often regulated. In a market with one prospect and few sellers, prospects might be required to base their prices on a defined set of costing rules plus an allowable profit margin.

In open markets with many prospects and sellers, cost is only one of many factors that are used to set the price. The price offered in the proposal will be negotiated before purchase.

Consider this paradox:

- Most sellers say prospects in their market select the solution with the lowest price.
- Most prospects say they seldom select the solution with the lowest price.

The reality is that most prospects try to select the best value solution within their budget.

Pricing

1. **Differentiate value and price.**
2. **Develop should-costs or cost bogeys early.**
3. **Define a pricing strategy that supports your sales strategy.**
4. **Base all cost estimating rationale on the assumption that nothing is new; everything has been done before.**
5. **Prepare or tailor written estimating guidelines for each competition.**
6. **Minimize negotiated price decrements by using the most credible rationale.**
7. **Consider not bidding if the primary focus of your sales team is on cutting the price.**
8. **Disclose your price in the executive summary, unless prohibited.**

1 Differentiate value and price.

To win a bid and maximize your profits from a contract, differentiate price and value.

- Price is what you charge for a product or service.
- Value is your prospect's perception of what the product or service is worth.

Value is both tangible and intangible. Tangible value is the quantified improvement in a prospect's profit or a decreased loss. Intangible value is by definition not quantified and often undervalued.

Even for government procurements, price is rarely the single factor that determines a buying decision. Often other less tangible factors influence the buying decision, all forming a perception of value. This is true even for commodity items; in buying a gallon of fuel a driver will put a value on the safety, cleanliness, and courtesy of one service station over another to justify or rationalize a higher or lower fuel price.

Prospects must attach a value to one offer that is higher than the price to justify a purchase. In mathematical terms, buying requires the following to be true:

Value > Price

An offer has to be affordable, so the price must meet this requirement:

Budget > Price

Smart prospects always have alternatives. The selection process among vendors requires choosing the offer with the best value for the price:

(Value - Price) Winning Offer >
(Value - Price) All Competing Offers

These equations are visualized in figure 1.

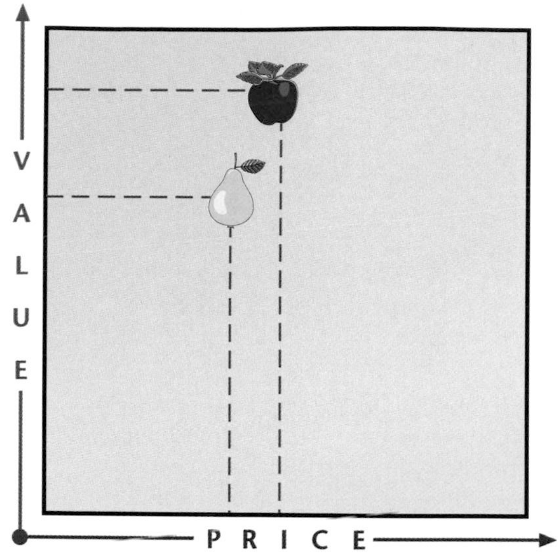

Figure 1. Comparing Apples with Pears. *Using the concept of value and price, high-priced objects may be preferred to low-priced objects as long as extra value compensates. The apple offers added value but at a higher price. Whether the added value justifies the higher price is purely a judgment made by the prospect.*

NOTE: While this example is clear but possibly trivial, many of the most disciplined selling organizations use a similar approach. Sales teams from these organizations develop formal, quantified value propositions containing the following elements:

- Specific—States what products and services are to be purchased, and who will purchase them.
- Measurable—Tells how much is to be purchased.
- Timed —Cites when the purchase will be made.
- Result—States, quantitatively if possible, the result or process change the client anticipates.

See **Value Propositions**.

Consider an example of the concept:

Assume that you live in Dallas and want a vacation in London. You have three ticket choices.

OPTION	DESCRIPTION	PRICE
1	Economy seat with Delta to London Gatwick	$450
2	Club seat with British Airways to London Heathrow	$1200
3	Economy seat with a charter carrier to London Heathrow with an 8-hour stop in Greenland	$200

The option you choose depends on the value you attach to the different features of each choice. Your ideas on this will be unique and may embrace unfair perceptions. Assume that getting to London is worth $800 to you. So which one is the best deal?

OPTION	ISSUE		VALUE - PRICE
1	Getting to London	$800	
	Gatwick less convenient than Heathrow	-$50	
	You like Delta's food	+$20	
	Option Value	**+$770**	**– $450 price = +$330**

OPTION	ISSUE		VALUE - PRICE
2	Getting to London	+$800	
	Great wine and food	+$50	
	Lots of leg room	+$50	
	Option Value	**+$900**	**– $1,200 price = –$300**

OPTION	ISSUE		VALUE - PRICE
3	Getting to London	+$800	
	Could be unsafe	-$100	
	Lose a day of vacation	-$200	
	Save money on London Hotel	+$150	
	Airport meal in Greenland	-$50	
	Option Value	**+$600**	**– $200 price = +$400**

So the third option is the best deal. Had option 2 been the only ticket you could get, you would have stayed at home as the worth is negative.

2

Develop should-costs or cost bogeys early.

NOTE: When your government audits your cost, as is done in the U.S., should you disclose cost bogeys to the proposal team? Best practices vary. Depending on the local Defense Contract Audit Agency office, cost bogeys that are disclosed to team members may be considered cost and pricing data and must be disclosed. For this reason, some proposal managers use cost bogeys to sanity-test estimates but do not disclose them to the team.

Most sales professionals like to avoid any early discussion of price because it leads to objections from the prospect. Instead, they leave price discussions to the end when the prospect requests a lower price. Then they talk about added value, or say, "We cost more but we're worth it." Citing this price-performance justification at the end is too late because it does not relate to the value derived by the prospect. If the prospect does not see the added value, you will not overcome the price objection.

Instead, in the early meetings with a prospect, discuss the contribution your organization can make to profitability. Once you have both determined the potential contribution, the prospect can better establish and justify a purchasing budget, and you can establish your should-cost target or cost bogey.

A common and poor approach to pricing and costing is to give the design team a description of the prospect's needs and ask your team to create a best solution or at least a good solution.

Usually, about halfway through the proposal process, the first cost roll-up reveals your solution far exceeds the prospect's budget.

A best-practice approach to pricing and costing is to use both top-down and bottom-up costing approaches until they converge.

- **Top-down costing** begins with each prospect's perception of value, the prospect's budget, and comparisons with other similar projects, adjusted as appropriate. The overall price is broken into target cost or bogeys by task, service, and hardware.

  Early development of should-costs that sets cost bogeys for estimators reduces the number of cost and design iterations. Accurate top-down estimates require similar methods, materials, and processes.

- **Bottom-up costing** is simply a cost roll-up of time and material estimates with appropriate overheads added.

  Because bottom-up estimators are criticized for undercosting and are often commended for overcosting, bottom-up estimates tend to incorporate various safety factors at each cost level that result in high estimates.

3

Define a pricing strategy that supports your sales strategy.

See **Strategy.**

A sales strategy that emphasizes leading-edge performance is inconsistent with a pricing strategy that emphasizes selecting the lowest cost component, method, supplier, or subcontractor. Similarly, a sales strategy that emphasizes the efficiency and productivity of the seller is inconsistent with a high price.

When your technical and cost teams are physically separate without an agreed pricing strategy, you usually arrive at a technically superior, high-cost solution. First, influence, or at least determine, whether the prospect is driven by total added value, maximum technical performance, market image, acquisition cost, or total cost of ownership. Next, determine the probable approach of your competitors. Finally, adopt a discriminating position that best matches the prospect's needs.

See **Service Proposals,** *guideline 7.*

Early in the competition, use your knowledge of the prospect's issues to estimate the value the prospect attaches to your offer. Then adjust your features to improve your profit. The strategy is simple:

- Add features that cost you little and the prospect perceives as delivering benefits of high value.
- Drop features that cost you a lot but the prospect perceives as offering little value.

Try to persuade the prospect to require a solution that is better matched to your capabilities than to your competitors'. The key is influencing the bid request early. Your aim is to establish requirements that are expensive for competitors to meet.

If you are late in the game and trying to find a solution for a bid request influenced by a competitor, you must try to reengineer the prospect's vision. Specifically, you must persuade the prospect to highly value your discriminators to the detriment of the competitors' discriminators. The success of this strategy hinges on whether the prospect has the latitude to change the requirements or to select a noncompliant solution.

Do all you can to favorably influence the requirements and define your solution, then brainstorm ways to improve your solution. For example, when competing for a cost-driven services contract, brainstorming ways to improve the solution might generate the following list of questions:

- How can you reduce management layers?
- Can management's span of control be increased?
- Where should people be placed within grades?

NOTE: Incumbents often have less latitude to suggest changes in how services are delivered. Prospects wonder why the incumbent's cost-saving proposals have not already been implemented.

- Can you redefine grades, cross-train, change work hours, or change work locations?
- How can headcount be reduced?
- Can the cost of fringe benefits be reduced, or can anticipated increases of these costs be reduced?
- What incentive programs could increase productivity?
- Are all current overhead allocations appropriate?
- Could some services be outsourced?
- Can outsourced services be reduced or be delivered by a lower-cost vendor?

Whatever your strategy, brainstorm ways to increase your competitiveness, then select the most valid ideas and implement them in your proposal.

4 Base all cost estimating rationale on the assumption that nothing is new; everything has been done before.

Cost analysts in the government sector assume everything has been done before. Base your estimating rationale on the same assumption.

Given this advice, a medical researcher asked, "How do I know what it will cost to cure cancer?" The reply, "That is not what you are proposing to do. That's the prospect's goal. You are proposing to do a literature search, conduct certain tests, analyze the results, and prepare draft and final reports." All of these tasks were ones they had done before.

In the commercial sector, few prospects want to purchase serial #001. The risk of being the first is often too great. Similarly, base all estimates on the most similar historic tasks. Breakdown the project until you can identify subtasks that are similar to subtasks from previous projects.

5 Prepare or tailor written estimating guidelines for each competition.

Unique, complex programs require new estimating guidelines for each competition. For services or products that are similar from bid to bid, consider whether your current guidelines warrant tailoring.

Estimating guidelines cover the following types of assumptions:

- Program schedule and milestones to determine when costs occur
- Work Breakdown Structure (WBS) to indicate what work will be done by which cost centers
- A make versus buy subcontracting determination
- A Statement of Work (SOW) and WBS dictionary to define the services and products to be delivered
- A deliverables list, including all hardware, services, and data
- Relevant financial ground rules regarding escalation, facility capitalization, facilities and locations of work, direct labor and overhead rates, preapproved rates, etc.
- The level at which costs will be estimated, disclosed, and reported, if required

Estimating ground rules should be written for the following reasons:

- Only written ground rules are auditable and defensible, both externally and internally.
- Estimators working in teams must be consistent.
- When costs must be disclosed, include the ground rules in the cost volume introduction to increase your credibility.
- Partners, vendors, and subcontractors need ground rules to give accurate and competitive estimates.
- Written ground rules reduce both schedule and cost risk.

6 Minimize negotiated price decrements by using the most credible rationale.

Government procurement officials typically require full disclosure of all task descriptions, cost estimates, and rationale. The soundness of the rationale determines their subsequent price negotiating position. A poor rationale leads to larger price decrements during negotiations.

Government auditors rank estimating rationale in the following order, from most to least reliable:

1. Firm, negotiated, forward price agreement
2. Actual historic cost with appropriate escalation
3. Quotation from vendor (internal or external)
4. Engineering estimate

7

Consider not bidding if the primary focus of your sales team is on cutting the price.

See **Bid Decisions.**

As the deadline nears to submit a proposal, some account teams spend most of their time seeking a further price cut and little time on any aspect of the proposal. Their time allocation suggests they think only the price is important and often reflects their sales strategy.

Anyone can sell the low price—that is done in catalogs and by computer. Sales professionals sell value early and throughout the sale. If the entire focus is on price, reconsider your positive bid decision.

8

Disclose your price in the executive summary, unless prohibited.

While price is seldom the primary determining factor in a complex sale, price is always in the top four. Every executive summary should address the prospect's top issues, including price.

See **Executive Summary.**

Of all the guidelines in this *Proposal Guide*, the overriding one at the proposal submittal stage is: ***Do what the prospect asks***. If the rules of the procurement prohibit pricing data outside the cost proposal, follow the prospect's rules.

The other reason cited for not including the price in the executive summary is as follows:

> *Our price could turn them off if they see it before they read our proposal. We put it in the back in a separate pricing section so they will have to read our proposal first.*

Evaluators read proposals any way they want to. When they want to see the price, they will find it. The decision maker and the most important influencers often only read the executive summary. Give them the information they need and want.

A successful account executive related this story:

> *In our market, I always try to personally deliver our proposal and walk the prospect through the key points. They usually give me about 5 minutes before they tune-out and look for the price. Now I always put the price on the first or second page so I can keep their attention.*

As noted in guideline 1, prospects seldom exceed their budget. The early look at the price is an easy screening method.

Conceptually, prospects often mentally construct a diagram similar to the one in figure 2. Assume five bidders, A through E, with the prospect's budget shown between the dotted lines. Bidder A would be rejected as unrealistically low, probably indicating poor understanding of the requirements. Bidder E would be rejected as overspecified, complicated, or not cost competitive and similarly rejected.

Bidders B, C, and D are all in the competitive range. The winner will be the one perceived to offer the greatest added value. Bidder D, very slightly over the budget, could stay in competition on two conditions: (1) the prospect has some budget flexibility, (2) D is perceived to offer greater added value than B or C.

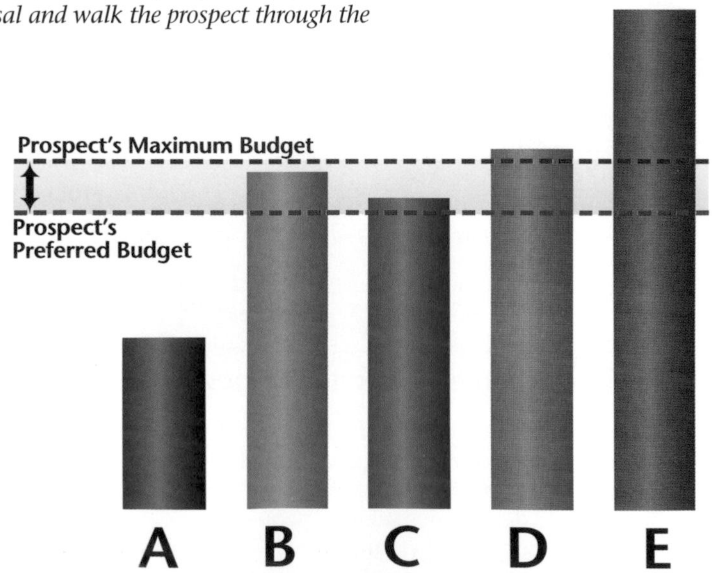

Figure 2. Establishing the Competitive Range. *Prospects look for ways or reasons to eliminate uncompetitive bidders to simplify their selection decision. The selection of B, C, or D will depend on whether the budget is fixed and the perceived added value of each offer.*

Process is defined as a systematic series of actions or steps directed toward a specific end. Effective business development processes consist of systematic actions that result in new business. Organizations exhibiting business development best practices systematically repeat the same steps across the entire organization.

Organizations with effective business development processes enjoy the following benefits:

- Enhanced business capture effectiveness
  - —Costs decrease
  - —Cycle time shortens
  - —Productivity increases
  - —Improved forecasting
  - —Improved management control

Defining, building, and sustaining an effective business development process requires management focus and continuous effort. Barriers include corporate inertia, individual resistance to change, and constantly changing priorities that blur focus and erode commitment. Managers of organizations that capture numerous orders tend to shift their focus from capturing orders to delivering orders profitably.

The impetus to reengineer an organization's business development process often stems from one of the following events:

- Newly formed organization with no established process
- Newly merged or reorganized organizations with multiple processes
- Changes in senior management or sales management
- Failure to meet sales goals or win-rate goals
- Large increases or decreases in staff

To develop a best-practice business development process, implement the first six guidelines in order. The additional guidelines support implementation and improvement and can be implemented in parallel or any convenient order.

Process

1. **Commit to a single, flexible, scalable business development process based on industry best practices and championed at the executive level.**
2. **Align your business development process with your prospects' buying cycles.**
3. **Define process phases broadly, delineated by clear, mandatory milestones with verifiable inputs and outputs.**
4. **Use document-based reviews at each milestone to control and add value to the process.**
5. **Efficiently adapt your process to individual opportunities by using flexible support tools.**
6. **Define business development roles, responsibilities, and levels of authority, including thresholds by types of opportunities.**
7. **Align your business development process with corporate policies, strategies, practices, and other processes.**
8. **Document your process to make it consistent and repeatable.**
9. **Train participants to give them the understanding and skills to follow the process.**
10. **Support business development professionals with tools, automation technology, and professional support.**
11. **Designate a process owner to collect metrics, to foster continuous improvement, to maintain tools, and to maintain support infrastructure.**

1 Commit to a single, flexible, scalable business development process based on industry best practices and championed at the executive level.

Organizations with a single process can team more effectively. Individuals assigned to capture and proposal teams can immediately focus on the opportunity rather than determining or justifying what needs to be done.

Individuals who do not realize their processes differ from the team's can be problematic. When these individuals' expectations are not met, their commitment is lost and team spirit suffers.

A flexible process can be adapted to different types of opportunities, different markets, different prospects' requirements, and different proposal requirements. A scalable process can be adapted to differing sizes of opportunities, proposal delivery deadlines, and available resources.

You can determine industry best practice by regularly comparing your process to other organizations, by participating in industry forums and professional associations, and by engaging professionals that specialize in business development best practice reviews and business development process re-engineering.

A promising product of best practice reviews has been the development of a business development capability maturity model. Structured similarly to the capability maturity model used to measure the maturity of software development organizations, the objective is to predict an organization's ability to capture business by directly linking results to measured clusters of related activities. Figure 1 summarizes five maturity levels and some of the activities characteristic of each level.

LEVEL	FOCUS	CHARACTERISTIC ACTIVITIES
5. OPTIMIZING PERFORMANCE	Continuously and predictably improving business development performance within the enterprise	Continuous process improvement is enabled by quantitative feedback from the process and by piloting innovative ideas and technology.
4. MANAGED SYSTEM	Managing, controlling, and measuring a business development system integrated with enterprise operations and processes	Detailed measures of the process and product quality are collected. Both the process and products are quantitatively understood and controlled.
3. STANDARDIZED PROCESS	Following a standard, defined process across the organization	Process for both management and engineering activities is documented, standardized, and integrated into a standard process for the organization. All projects use an approved, tailored version of the organization's standard process.
2. REPEATABLE ACTIVITIES	Addressing individual opportunities by reusing past project management and business development practices	Basic project management processes are established to track cost, schedule, and functionality. The necessary process discipline is in place to repeat earlier successes on projects with similar applications.
1. AD HOC	Pursue "interesting" opportunities, depends on individual heroics	Process is characterized as ad hoc and ocassionally even chaotic. Few processes are defined and success depends on individual effort and heroics. Management visibility only at beginning and end.

Figure 1. Measure the Maturity and Capability of Your Business Development Organization. *When clusters of related activities are performed collectively, key goal-sets are achieved. These activities and the process discipline to consistently complete these activities indicate the maturity of an organization.*

The benefits of committing to a single, flexible, scalable business development process will be lost without a champion at the executive level. Reorganizations, corporate inertia, individual resistance to change, and constantly changing priorities will blur focus and erode commitment. Two examples illustrate the point:

After sitting through 4 days of business development training, the managing director of a large organization was asked to approve an executive summary. He returned the executive summary with the following note: *You have attended the training. This is no longer acceptable.* Word of the incident spread quickly and everyone adopted the new standards and approach.

The executive vice president of business development wanted to establish a single process and global standards for business development to improve business capture effectiveness. After actively participating in the development and documentation of a single business development process, he commissioned custom training for all process participants. He attended the entire first workshop with all of his direct reports. In the next 10 workshops, he personally introduced the workshop, reviewed participants' work, and concluded the workshop. All subsequent workshops were introduced and concluded by one of his direct reports. Within 3 years, this organization improved from second to first in global market share.

2 Align your business development process with your prospects' buying cycles.

Prospects care about their needs, not yours. Prospects have different needs at different phases of the buying cycle. Design your process to address prospects' needs as their needs change.

The process outlined in figure 2 meets the single, flexible, and scalable criteria of guideline 1. The fixed milestones required for every opportunity establish the framework of a single process. Flexibility and scalability come from intelligently tailoring the steps between milestones.

The top two bars depict prospects' buying phases and milestones. The bottom two bars show the alignment with the selling phases and milestones.

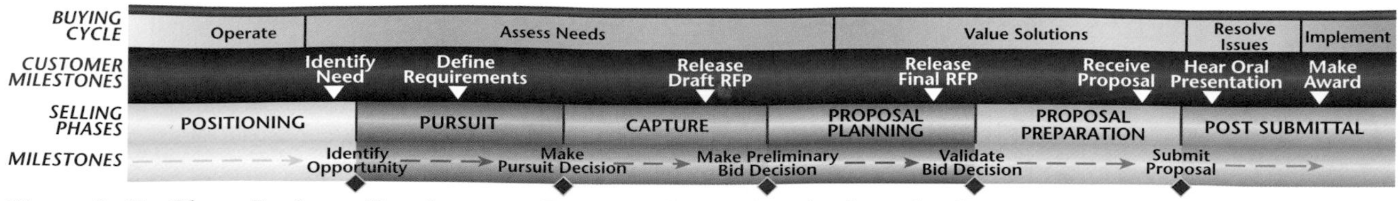

Figure 2. Six-Phase Business Development Process. *The six-phase business development process is shown aligned with buying phases. Readily identifiable customer and selling milestones are shown. Customer milestones mark key customer/prospect decisions. Selling milestones separate the selling phases.*

NOTE: "Customer Milestones" may seem inconsistent. In this *Proposal Guide,* "prospect" applies to pre-sales activities and "customer" applies to post-sales activities.

As prospects *Operate*, they are not thinking about buying. Prospects' needs are latent. Yet products wear, personnel change, and prospects' needs change. During the Operate phase, sellers increase their understanding of prospects' needs, position their organizations as capable of meeting those needs, and identify discrete opportunities.

During the *Assess Needs* phase, prospects' latent needs become explicit as prospects determine if each need merits satisfying. Sellers need a process that helps prospects assess the pro's and con's of satisfying each need and solving or reducing their problems. Value-added selling begins here, with prospects and sellers collaboratively quantifying the impacts to prospects' organizations.

See **Compliance and Responsiveness, Customer Focus, Executive Summary, Outlining, Page and Document Design,** *and* **Strategy.**

During the *Value Solutions* phase, prospects initially identify potential solutions, then assess the relative value of those solutions to their organizations. Thus alternative solutions are potentially more acceptable to prospects early rather than later in this phase.

During the *Resolve Issues* phase, prospects have tentatively selected a solution and are trying to determine what could go wrong. Risk avoidance is paramount, so sellers need to emphasize risk management, the value of the solution to prospects, and the value lost through further delay.

During the post award *Implement* phase, prospects are primarily focused on attaining the anticipated benefits. Sellers need to continue to reinforce the value delivered and highlight the additional value of further enhancements. Too many sellers become so focused on completing their delivery that they are blind to additional opportunities.

The principle of aligning your business development process with prospects' buying cycles can be applied at a deeper level. Intended to be representative rather than comprehensive, the following recommendations reflect process alignment. The relevant sections in this Proposal Guide are shown in parentheses after each item.

- Stay customer-focused. Talk about the prospects' needs, not about your needs. (COMPLIANCE AND RESPONSIVENESS)
- Link every aspect of your solution to a prospect-owned need. (EXECUTIVE SUMMARY)
- Avoid prospect dissonance and mistrust by aligning your message throughout the sales process. Politicians call it, "Staying on message. (CUSTOMER FOCUS)
- Tell prospects why they should select you. Do not make them dig for the answer. (STRATEGY)
- Influence prospects' needs early in the sales process. As the sales process concludes, submit a 100 percent compliant proposal to make it easy to evaluate. (COMPLIANCE AND RESPONSIVENESS)
- Allocate proposal pages according to the relative importance of the topic to the prospect. (OUTLINING)
- Use a page design that emphasizes your compliance. (PAGE AND DOCUMENT DESIGN)
- Always include an executive summary to satisfy the needs of individuals who lack the time to read your proposal. (EXECUTIVE SUMMARY)
- Include pricing in the executive summary unless prohibited by the prospect's purchasing requirements. (EXECUTIVE SUMMARY)
- Submit at least one copy of your proposal for each evaluator. (COMPLIANCE AND RESPONSIVENESS)

3 Define process phases broadly, delineated by clear, mandatory milestones with verifiable inputs and outputs.

Define phases broadly to include the wide variety of opportunities pursued by your organization. Narrow definitions encourage participants to work outside the process.

The framework business development process introduced in figure 2 is expanded in figure 3. Selling phases are clearly separated by management decision points or milestones: lead identification; the pursuit, bid, and bid validation decisions; and proposal submittal. Clusters of potential activities are listed under each phase. Documents generated in those activities verify the output of a phase and are input for a subsequent phase.

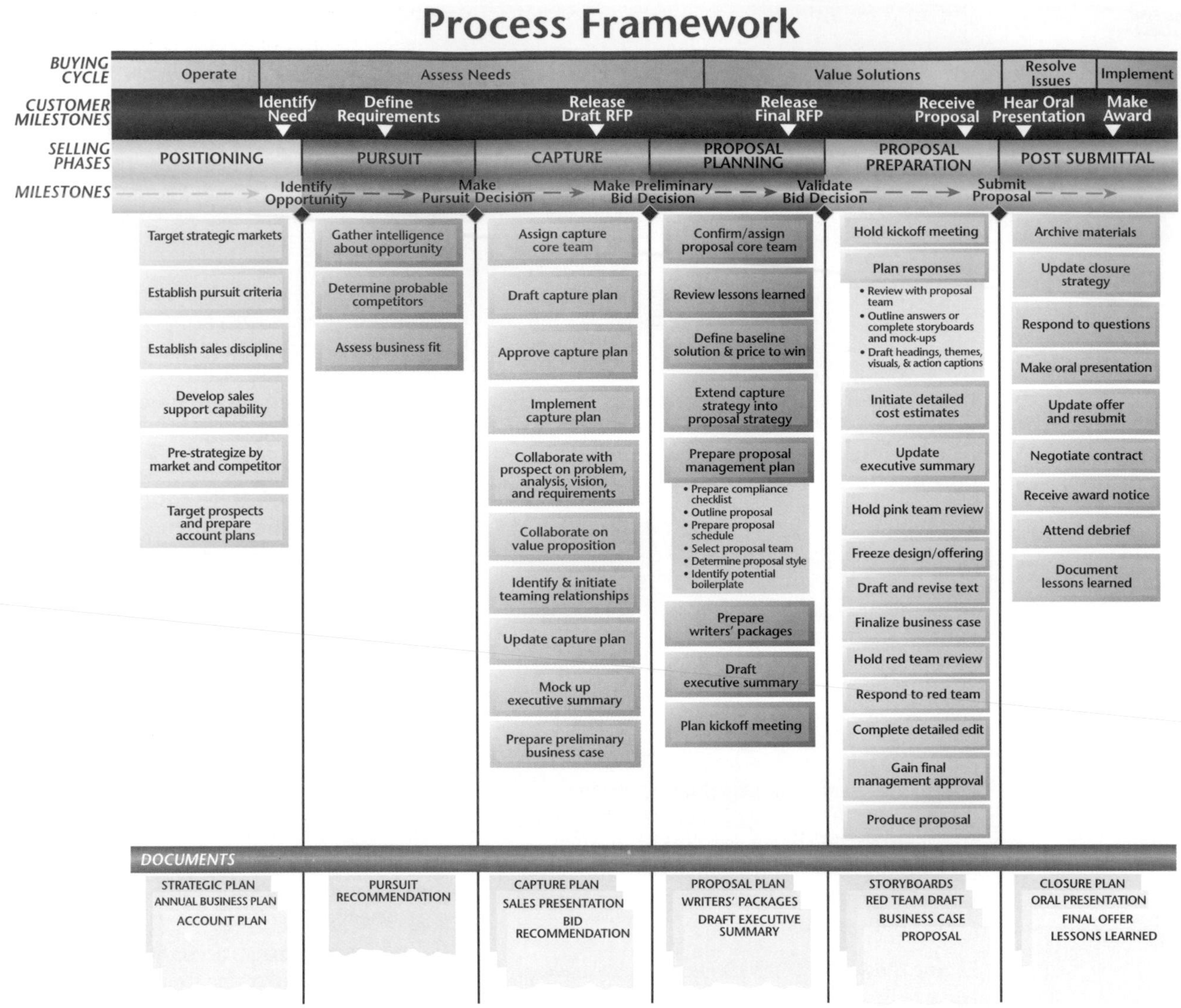

Figure 3. Broad-Based Process Framework for New Business Capture. *This framework process is aligned with the prospect's buying cycle. Management milestones apply to every opportunity. The business development process is divided into six phases for both sales and sales-support functions. Proposal milestones apply to all but the smallest opportunities. Since documents are the only solid evidence that certain steps have been done and are the only way to assess the quality of the work, key documents are shown along the bottom of the chart. While the milestones are firm, this process must be tailored extensively for different organizations in different markets.*

This framework process is divided into six phases:

1. **Positioning**—Marketing activities establish your organization's presence and capabilities, all aimed at identifying leads.
2. **Pursuit**—Newly identified leads are assessed to determine your organization's interest and whether they are winnable.
3. **Capture**—Individuals in prospects' organizations are positioned to prefer your solution and organization.
4. **Proposal Planning**—The proposal effort is planned while sales efforts continue.
5. **Proposal Preparation**—The proposal is prepared, approved, and submitted.
6. **Post Submittal**—Prospects' questions are answered, leading to contract negotiation and award.

Defining clear, mandatory milestones with verifiable inputs and outputs establishes a solid framework for all opportunities, large or small. Thorough, predefined quality checks at each milestone minimize wasted effort and increase capture effectiveness.

All opportunities benefit from a few, well-conceived management milestone reviews. Each milestone is described below:

Pursuit Decision—The goal is to make an informed decision about your ability to pursue effectively and to allocate appropriate resources for capture planning. The authority to decide to pursue may vary by size of opportunity.

See **Capture Planning, Bid Decisions,** *and* **Reviews.**

Preliminary Bid Decision—When you cannot get the order without a proposal, management must decide whether the opportunity warrants allocating resources to begin planning the proposal and your solution before receiving the final bid request. Have your capture activities put you in a favored position with the prospect?

Bid Validation Decision—With 60 percent of the typical capture cost spent between the bid decision and final management review, can you afford to allocate the resources to win? Has any prospect requirement changed, creating unacceptable risk? Have competitive conditions changed?

Final Management Review—Risking 0.5 to 4.0 percent of the value of the job in business development cost is one risk. The greater risk is your potential financial liability if you win with a poorly designed, high-risk, or underpriced offer.

Final Proposal Review—Before submitting your final, revised offer, you ask much the same questions as in the final management review. What can you afford to change? Is the risk acceptable?

While the degree of effort varies with the size of the opportunity, management has a vital role in each management milestone review.

4 Use document-based reviews at each milestone to control and add value to the process.

See **Reviews.**

Documents are the only evidence you have that an intellectual task has been completed. Without a document, you cannot control and manage intellectual work.

The quality of the document reflects the quality of the thinking and the quality of the work. Establish quality standards for each required document. Manage to your standards. Do not omit reviews or compromise your standards.

5 Efficiently adapt your process to individual opportunities by using flexible support tools.

Defining your process at a higher level makes it simpler to understand and remember. Embedding complexity in the support tools makes following established process easier.

Tools need to support knowledge management and collaboration. Knowledge management includes boilerplate development, retrieval, and maintenance as well as process management. Process management tools direct the user, save time, and improve effectiveness.

Consider the following example.

An account executive needs to generate an executive summary for a proposal. The usual practice is to pull a prior executive summary, "Search and Replace" prospect and product names, customize a few sentences, and submit to sales support for refinement or submit directly to the prospect.

As a best practice, the account executive has been trained to use an executive summary template that contains prompts and descriptions of appropriate content. For example, when prompted to draft a theme statement, a second prompt will cause definitions, standards, and examples to be displayed. The template might be linked to a database containing potential graphics and descriptions of products and services. The database is easily searchable by topic. The graphics are further linked to multiple potential action captions. Further, underlying software can check the draft for key components much like a word-processing spell and style checker.

Potential tools come in many forms, from paper templates and forms to fully integrated web-based, electronic systems. To be broadly accepted, your process must do more than give direction—it must give help to users. Tools that save time and improve effectiveness help users.

Not all tools are created equal. Some tools speed the activity cycle, permitting a user to produce more proposals. But if the effectiveness of the proposal is unchanged, the cost of the tool may exceed the benefits.

A software proposal preparation tool can speed boilerplate retrieval and proposal assembly. While the printed proposal may be attractive, it will fail if the proposal is poorly organized, lacks customer focus, fails to directly address the prospect's needs, and demonstrates little understanding of the prospect's business.

6 Define business development roles, responsibilities, and levels of authority, including thresholds by types of opportunities.

Roles are customary functions of a person in business development. Functions such as capture manager, proposal manager, proposal specialist, writer, and estimator are roles. A single person can be assigned and can fill multiple roles. In some organizations, a person in the account manager position might assume sales, proposal manager, proposal writer, estimator, and reviewer roles.

Responsibilities are tasks that a person is accountable for, whether they complete the task themselves or assign the task to another person. In business development, people in roles are assigned specific responsibilities. Traditionally, an individual in the proposal manager role is responsible for the preparation of the proposal document to a defined standard and time.

See **Proposal Management Plan** *and* **Team Selection and Management.**

Levels of authority delimit the power of a person to command, direct, or decide. Levels of authority establish both whether the person can make a decision and the limits of the decision. For example, the level of authority to make pursuit, bid, and bid submittal decisions should vary with the size and risk of the opportunity.

Business development processes are more flexible and scalable when roles, responsibilities, and levels of authority are clearly defined. Decisions are clearer, easier, and faster. A person who understands multiple roles is more versatile. Managers can keep projects on track by verifying that roles are assigned and responsibilities understood.

7 Align your business development process with corporate policies, strategies, practices, and other processes.

Alignment is critical in all areas. A corporate policy of openness and honesty is incompatible with bait-and-switch sales tactics. A corporate strategy to be the technology leader is more compatible with a sales approach that emphasizes added value than one that stresses low price. Performance metrics must be aligned with incentive programs and practices.

Business development process effectiveness is significantly enhanced when aligned with other organizational processes. Review the following standard practices:

- A short sales and proposal delivery cycle requires a short review process.
- Reviewers rewarded for preventing risk may cause greater revenue loss than the potential cost of the risk.
- Aligned capture and project delivery processes reduce transition cost and risk, and improve profitability.
- Field sales processes that capture information required to prepare the proposal reduce proposal preparation cost and enhance capture effectiveness.
- Proposal preparation teams that align their process with the sales contact management system reduce productivity-robbing demands on field sales.

8 Document your process to make it consistent and repeatable.

In practice, defining a process and documenting a process are difficult to separate. Defining a process begins with diagrams, descriptions, and definitions. The process required to attain consensus and approval will prompt further documentation. In fact, the need to document a process is essential to clearly define a process.

Documentation can assume many forms. Keeping in mind that your process must both guide and help users, ask yourself the following questions:

- Where and when will users refer to the documentation?
- Do users work in a central office or in remote locations?
- Will users always have laptops available when traveling?
- How will the form and format affect availability, acceptance, and repeated use?
- How easy will it be to update and keep users' copies current?

Many organizations develop small, compact process guides ranging from 3" x 5" to 5" x 7" bound formats. Distributing your process in a traditional, large-format ring binder virtually assures users will not find it useful. Users can reference a compact paper copy virtually anywhere.

Consider distributing electronic copies in PDF format on compact disc as a supplement or a replacement for the compact printed process guides. Add electronic tools and templates to the compact disc, hyperlinked to process descriptions and definitions. Make all documentation, tools, and templates available on-line to authorized personnel.

Remember to give copies of your process guide to new and reassigned employees and to collect the copies of those who leave. However, security can be overdone. Most business development processes are not that unique or confidential. Broad distribution and availability are usually the best choices. Ultimately, your competitive advantage will be the discipline of users to follow the process rather than the process itself.

9

Train participants to give them the understanding and skills to follow the process.

Users must not only understand and accept the process but also need the skills to execute and adapt it appropriately. The same applies to supporting tools. Users must be able to locate the appropriate tool, use it properly, and explain its use to others when required.

An initial and ongoing investment in training is critical. To achieve maximum return, training must be process specific rather than generic. Participants must practice the expected skills in the training and receive immediate feedback to improve their performance. Without practice, participants usually return to their pre-training approach.

10

NOTE: Corporate champion and process owner are both roles. The same person seldom fills both roles. The corporate champion, a senior executive, seldom has the time to fill the process owner role.

Support business development professionals with tools, automation technology, and professional support.

The corporate champion and process owner must provide an infrastructure or environment that supports success. Infrastructure includes three major categories:

- Aligned incentive programs
- Enabling technologies that support knowledge management and collaboration
- Empowered professionals who guide process implementation, support users, and assure quality and renewal

11

Designate a process owner to collect metrics, to foster continuous improvement, to maintain tools, and to maintain support infrastructure.

Process owners collect metrics to quantify the business development process. Quantification makes knowledge more open, understandable, and uniform within an organization with a single process. Quantitative comparisons between groups with different processes, whether in the same or different organizations, are interesting but less useful.

Processes erode quickly without an owner. Consider these examples:

- A simple template with the wrong logo is no longer used.
- An electronic template incompatible with an upgraded operating system is abandoned.
- Boilerplate graphics and text describing obsolete products and services might prompt a prospect to select another source or increase your risk if a purchase leads to a dispute.
- Metrics are collected but not analyzed. Subsequently, those metrics are not recorded, are recorded only when convenient or advantageous, or are not recorded accurately.

Metrics are the basis for continuous improvement—we manage what we measure. Using good metrics, you can demonstrate reduced sales support costs, shrinking cycle times, and improved proposal quality. All usually reflect higher win rates.

Metrics also help process owners understand what elements of their processes work well and what elements need to be changed. Accurate and credible metrics are the only valid way to justify requests for additional resources, to resist reductions in current resources, or to measure the value of enabling technologies and tools.

Consider the following questions when determining what metrics to collect:

- **How will you use this metric?**

  If you cannot anticipate its use, do not track it. For example, tracking turnaround time from different outside printing vendors could help you decide which printer has earned more of your business. The same statistic from an internal department that is giving good service is less useful.

- **Can the metric be collected with minimum impact to staff and clients?**

  Try to capture metrics as by-products of your normal process. For example, collect labor hours from time sheets. Determine page counts from printing records.

- **Does the potential value of the data exceed the cost of collection?**

  A relatively expensive program to obtain prospects' feedback on wins and loses is often justified. Conversely, one process owner noted that they did not compute a cost per page even though it could be calculated from available data. Their central expenses were minimal, proposal teams worked virtually from home offices, travel costs were eliminated, and internal printing costs were annually allocated to business units on a revenue basis. Neither the process owner nor the responsible mangers were interested in a cost-per-page metric.

- **Does the metric broaden your potential understanding of the processes that you own or can influence?**

  Keeping metrics on organizations or individuals outside your control and influence may only lead to conflict. If you have no control over your field sales force, why track data on account executives? Leave it to sales management. Avoid tracking metrics that overlap unless you are trying to determine which metric is most representative.

  For example, overlapping metrics might be kept on desktop publishing (DTP). You could track pages per day of combined graphics and text, or separate measures of pages per day of text and graphics per day. The appropriate measure might depend on whether your DTP professional also does the graphics and whether the ratio of graphics per page is expected to change.

Figure 4 lists potential business development process metrics.

Commonly Collected Business Development Metrics	
Proposal quality	
Duration (start to finish)	
Staff hours or days expended	
Hours or days by resource	
Win/loss	
$ Won/lost	
Sales contact	
Prospect name	
Prospect feedback	
Number of copies	
Page count	
Word count (vs. page count)	
Number of graphics	
% New vs. existing graphics	

Figure 4. Potential Business Development Process and Proposal Metrics. *Business development and proposal process owners track many of the listed metrics but never track all of them. Try to limit the number of different metrics collected without compromising the amount of data collected. Balance your collection cost against the potential value of the metric.*

Establish a set interval to review every tool. Make sure the tool is accurate, adds value, and is being used. Review the accuracy of your boilerplate two to four times per year. Set an expiration date on each piece of boilerplate. Remove expired boilerplate, clearly warn users, or place it in a separate expired file.

Many organizations have invested in tools that were promised to save time but did not improve effectiveness. Evaluate the effectiveness of your tools broadly, as illustrated in these examples:

> A process owner developed boilerplate databases and retrieval systems and measures writers' productivity in pages per day. As a result, the writers insert more boilerplate, appearing to increase productivity. Consider adding measures of quality, customer focus, compliance, win rates, or direct prospect feedback.

> A process owner measures the number of proposals issued to gauge sales force and proposal center productivity. The organization purchased proposal preparation software to improve the productivity of both groups. Subsequently, the number of proposals written and submitted doubled, but sales revenue remained flat as win rates drop. While the software may be effective, also review the organization's pursuit and bid decision discipline.

Process owners normally manage business capture centers and any directly assigned support people. Business capture centers may include proposal preparation and production facilities and individuals supporting business development activities. Proposal managers, proposal specialists, graphic artists, writers, editors, and desktop publishers are often based in the business capture center and assigned to specific proposal projects.

The ideal process owners are viewed as mentors who offer support as well as assistance. Encourage sales and sales support people to see themselves as professionals and to adopt a professional attitude. Encourage membership and participation in professional associations. Reimburse the nominal membership fees.

Encourage exchange visits with other organizations. Regularly schedule sessions to share process metrics, exchange ideas, and discuss continuous improvement ideas. Empower employees to make appropriate decisions, and reward those that demonstrate proactive initiative.

Say *Thank you* often and in imaginative ways. Professionals need and value personal recognition and acknowledgment as well as monetary compensation.

Production is the step that turns all of your hard work into the product that represents the quality of your products and services. Prospects assume that if you cannot organize a team well enough to produce a quality document then you probably cannot deliver quality products and services.

Make the quality of your proposal consistent. Poorly prepared or differently presented or appended materials suggest uneven quality.

Decide early how the proposal will be produced as the process will affect schedules, timelines, and how the proposal is written. Decisions on layout, software, graphics, and color can significantly affect production.

Production personnel frequently are under-appreciated, misunderstood, involved too late in the process, and repeatedly abused. However, some production managers forget that they manage a service organization.

Excellent production support throughout the proposal preparation process is essential to consistently win competitive business. While having a dedicated proposal production support group is ideal, two extremes are common:

1. Production is done by the sales support staff or the proposal team. Both may lack the time, skills, and resources required.
2. Production is done by a company organization that also supports product manuals, newsletters, brochures, technical reports, and marketing presentations.

Publications groups may have conflicting, prior commitments; limited familiarity with customer-directed documents; and a "First In First Out" approach. Carefully plan all aspects of production and delivery.

Production

1. **Establish a clear vision of what the prospect expects to be delivered.**
2. **Identify and assign the production management role and include that person in your core team planning.**
3. **Set clear ground rules in a written proposal production plan to minimize rework.**
4. **Determine precisely what will be produced for each milestone review.**
5. **Test all systems prior to production.**
6. **Determine how the proposal will be "packaged" and delivered while section writers are planning and preparing initial drafts.**
7. **Maintain a secure master book of hard-copy files backed by electronic files.**
8. **Ruthlessly enforce version control on a section-by-section basis.**
9. **Increase your quality checks and production time if proposal production is remote.**

1 Establish a clear vision of what the prospect expects to be delivered.

See **Compliance/ Responsiveness** *and* **Outlining.**

You must understand the prospect's expectations before you can meet them. Imagine getting a 1,000-page proposal when you expected 100 pages. Imagine the opposite.

When the prospect establishes clear document preparation and delivery requirements in the bid request, follow them. When these requirements are unclear or unstated in the bid request, or when preparing an unsolicited proposal, always explicitly discuss proposal requirements with the prospect.

Guide the prospect toward a proposal that is both easier to evaluate and easier to prepare, usually a shorter proposal. Be careful about what you suggest; you may get it, as these examples illustrate:

An account executive asked if the prospect would like to see a video submitted with the proposal. When the prospect said, "Yes," the account executive's organization had limited time and resources to produce anything that looked better than an amateur, home movie.

An account executive asked the prospect if they would like to see a concise proposal that simply focused on what they planned to do on the immediate project. The prospect agreed. Unfortunately, the account executive's support group was only equipped to do a Search and Replace for the prospect's name and print 250 pages of boilerplate.

A multimillion dollar, multiple-volume proposal was completed by an aircraft manufacturer for a large Federal bid. The plane was waiting at the local airport to deliver the proposal. Unfortunately, the small aircraft could not take off when they discovered the packaged documents weighed more than 3,000 pounds.

2 Identify and assign the production management role and include that person in your core team planning.

The production management lead supervises the publication process, including word processing and graphic support, desktop publishing to integrate text and graphics, overall document design, and printing.

The complexity of the proposal influences whether this is a role assigned to the proposal coordinator, the proposal manager, or to a separate full-time position. Early involvement reduces the cost of proposal rework far more than the cost of their time.

Involve the production lead early to foster a commitment to do what is needed to win. Ideally, the production lead, graphic artists, and editors are directly assigned to support individual proposal teams.

Proposal managers on larger proposals do not have to be production experts, but they do need to know what to discuss with the person who is assigned the production management role. The proposal manager, the proposal coordinator, or the production manager should prepare the following items:

- **Presubmission Checklist:** Lists all items required by the prospect
- **Printing and Delivery Checklist:** Lists all items that must be selected or prepared, and all tasks that must be completed that are relevant to printing, document assembly, packaging, and shipment
- **Print Mock-up:** Tells the printer how to correctly assemble the proposal

A sample presubmission checklist, a printing and delivery checklist, and a print mock-up are shown in figures 1, 2, and 3, respectively. When you show these examples to most production managers, they will nearly always understand and complete the checklists for your proposal.

Presubmission Checklist

Item	Notes
❑ Cover	
❑ Cover Letter	
❑ Proprietary/Nondisclosure Notice	
❑ Signature Papers	
❑ Bid Bond	
❑ Performance Bond	
❑ Small or Disadvantaged Business Qualification	
❑ All Certifications of Compliance	
❑ Table of Contents	
❑ Compliance Matrix/Cross-Reference Matrix	
❑ List of Figures	
❑ Acronyms/Glossary/Definitions	
❑ Executive Summary	
❑ Technical Volume	
❑ Management Volume	
❑ Support Volume	
❑ Relevant Experience/Past Performance Volume	
❑ Cost Volume	
❑ WBS/WBS Dictionary	
❑ Index	
❑ Appendices	
❑ Exceptions	
❑ Brochures, Data Sheets, Reports	
❑ List of Sources of Supporting Materials	
❑ Supplementary Technical Data or Reports	

Figure 1. Prepare a Presubmission Checklist. *Prepare a presubmission checklist to help you identify, prepare, and assemble all required materials. Limit submissions to only the materials requested by the prospect. Inclusion of an item in this figure does not mean that item should be included in your proposal.*

Printing and Delivery Checklist

Item	Notes
❑ Printer selected	
❑ Delivery method determined	
❑ Back-up delivery determined (if needed)	
❑ Cover sent to printer	
❑ Tabs identified, named, and sent to printer	
❑ Paper for cover, tabs, text identified and ordered	
❑ Paper received by printer	
❑ One- or two-sided printing	
❑ Binder determined and ordered	
❑ Final art complete	
❑ Final text complete	
❑ All inserts to printer	
❑ Art and text integrated	
❑ Final print mock-up prepared	
❑ Electronic files to printer	
❑ Electronic submittal prepared (usually burned on CD-ROM)	
❑ Printing complete	
❑ Documents assembled with all inserts	
❑ Final turn-through (all copies)	
❑ Materials packaged for shipment	
❑ Shipment	
❑ Delivery verified	

Figure 2. Prepare a Printing and Delivery Checklist. *Using this checklist as an example, ask your production lead to prepare a specific list for your proposal. Checklist items will vary with proposal complexity. Portions of this list will be repeated for each internal review cycle. Experienced managers of large proposal efforts often plan on three production passes or cycles before Red Team and three more production passes from Red Team to submittal.*

The thumbnail print mock-up, or print dummy, is used to show the printer the number of pages in each section, where to insert tabs, photos, foldouts, or any other nonstandard items. The print mock-up is particularly important when you print double-sided and assembly is done by an organization separated from the proposal team.

PRODUCTION REQUEST FORM

Proposal Name: Robo Warrior **Date Submitted:** 3-25-20XX **Date Required:** 4-7-20XX

Contact Name: Paula Duncan **Contact Numbers:** 322-007 (office) 277-3476 (cell)

Instructions: **Print:** ☒ **Two-sided** Tabs and body
☒ **One-sided** Covers

Binding: corporate binder

Inks:
Proposal body: 2/2 (Black & PMS 540)
Tabs: 1/1 (PMS 540)
Cover 4/0

Paper:
Size: 8.5x11
Drilled: ❑ **no**
☒ **yes, #:** 3-hole drill
Stock: house 28# for body; tab stock; Cover 80# Matte Coat

Show Page Layout below:

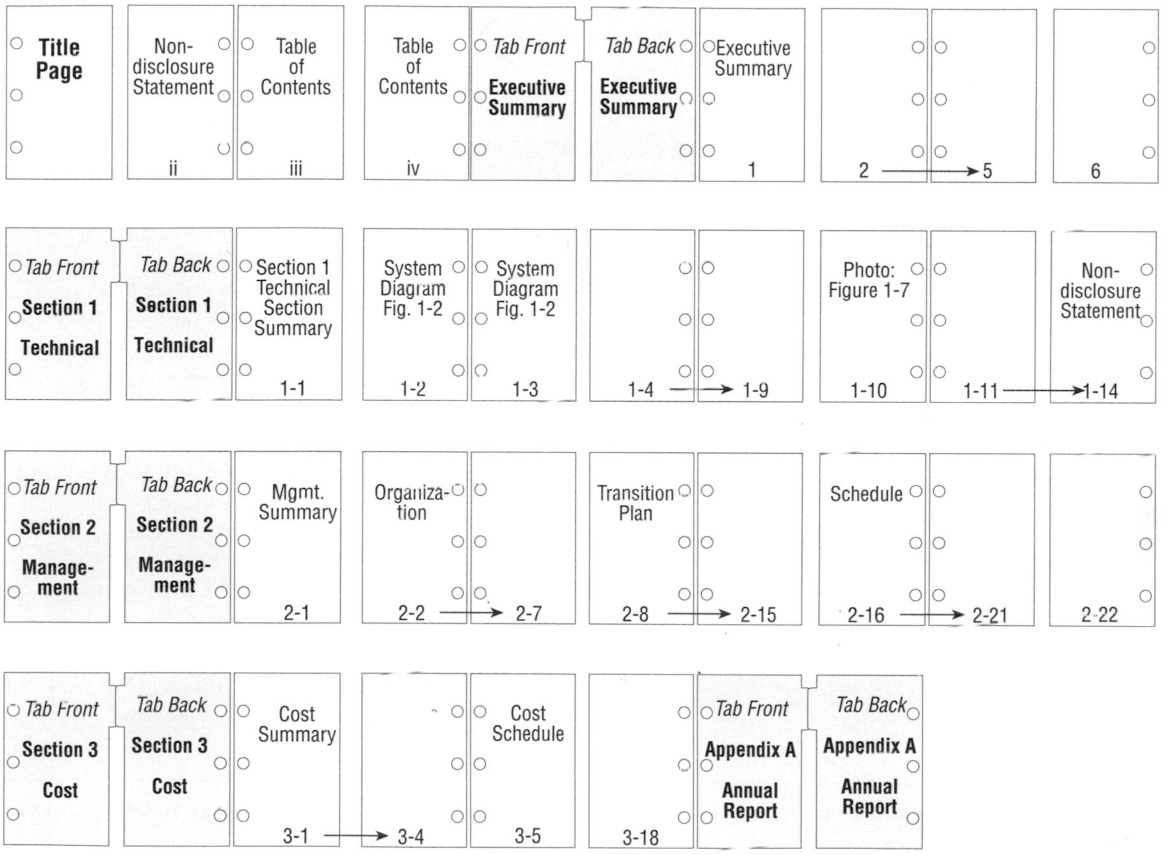

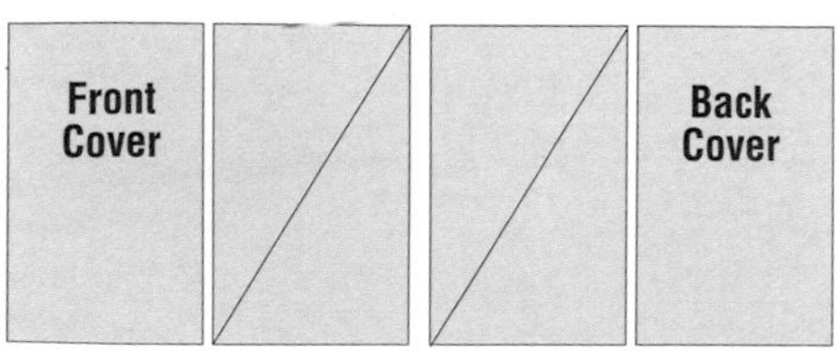

PAGE COUNT SUMMARY

Section	Page total
Lead Pages:	4
Executive Summary:	6
Technical Section:	14
Management Section:	22
Cost Section	18
Tabs	5
Covers (front & back)	2

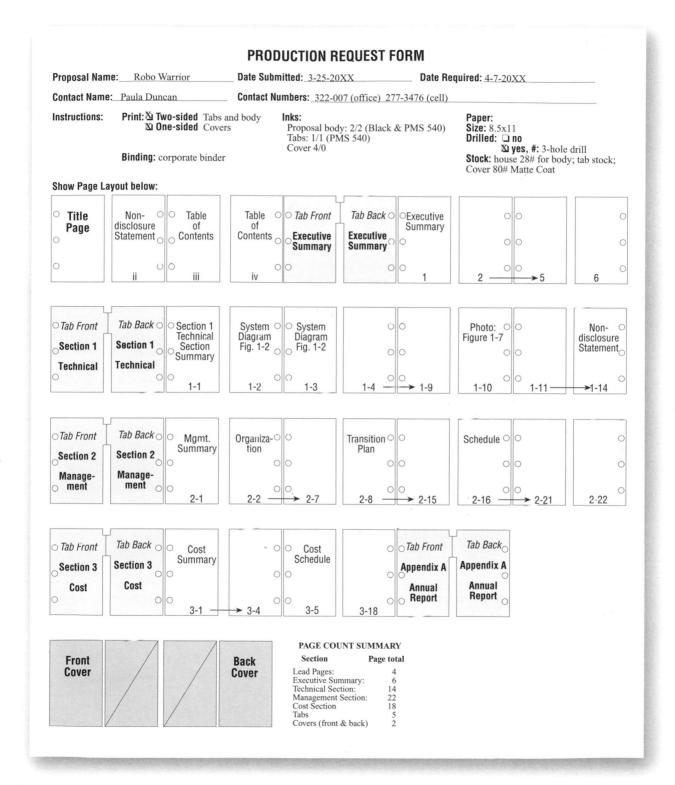

Figure 3. Reduce Production Errors by Preparing a Print Mock-up. *Print mock-ups tell the printer where major sections begin and end. Indicate all tabs and major graphic items, especially those placed as low-resolution or FPOs (For Placement Only) that will need to be manually inserted or replaced with the high-resolution scan or image by the printer.*

3

Set clear ground rules in a written proposal production plan to minimize rework.

Set ground rules to control how the proposal is processed through each draft. Include ground rules in the writers' packages distributed at the kickoff meeting.

Also see **Proposal Management Plan.**

Set ground rules to manage the flow and style (such as spacing, boxing, or shading) for the following items:

- Storyboards
- Mock-ups
- Graphics
- Section drafts
- Time and material estimates

Flow procedures define how the drafts are processed and usually include deadlines. Style procedures set standards for each document, both form and content.

Style procedures for writers should be kept as simple as possible to both save writers' time and to simplify production. Extra formatting by writers must be removed by production before imposing a standard style sheet. Eliminate this wasted effort.

Configuration control ensures the most current version of each proposal section is safely stored and available on an as-needed basis to other members of the proposal team.

Insist on a written production plan, which is the only clear proof that you have that the plan is complete and correct.

Your written proposal production plan should address both process and production issues.

Process issues

- How documents are prepared, reviewed, and printed
- How hard and soft files are managed, named, stored, and backed up
- How various proposal tools, templates, and forms are obtained, used, submitted, displayed, and reviewed
- Who will be given access to files and materials, and the degree of access permitted

Production issues

- How the proposal will appear, including a detailed electronic style sheet that establishes both interim and final page layout, headers, footers, font choice and size, etc.
- What materials will be used, including paper, tabs, and binders
- What types of headings, captions, jargon, acronyms, titles, and naming conventions will be used
- What, how, and who will prepare other required items such as the cover letter, table of contents, compliance or cross reference matrix, lists of figures, acronym list, glossary or index, transmittal letter, tabs, and special forms or certifications
- How the proposal will be produced, including the number of copies and volumes; printing schedule; printer, backup printer; special print needs such as oversize documents, pockets, or tabs; and color photographs or pages
- How security will be maintained on all materials from the kickoff through final production and archiving

4

Determine precisely what will be produced for each milestone review.

See **Reviews**.

Interim reviews create a production dilemma. Senior reviewers give a more thorough review to material that looks more professional. Yet more professional looking material increases production support costs.

Compromise by reviewing for the right things at the right time.

At the Blue Team, perform a strategy and solution review. Prepare copies of the first draft of the executive summary, the Bidder Comparison Matrix, the Integrated Prospect Solution Worksheet, strategy statements assembled into a strategy white paper, and prospective win themes. None require extensive production assistance.

Make reference materials available for each evaluator, such as a draft or final bid request and relevant marketing intelligence.

Limit the **Pink Team** review to the storyboards and mock-ups. Some organizations include the first draft of the proposal, and others have multiple Pink Teams, reviewing each additional draft.

Few organizations pursuing non-Federal business have time for more than one Pink Team, if any. Assuming storyboards and mock-ups are reviewed on the walls or displayed on tables, then production assistance is limited to preparing reference materials and comment forms for each reviewer.

Most reviewers expect a near-final document for the **Red Team**. You can reduce your production cost and perhaps facilitate revisions if management will agree to the following simplifications:

- Print all review copies on paper with pre-punched holes and insert them in ring binders. Copying on one side simplifies production moderately, but reviewers will not see opposing pages.
- Start each section on a new page to facilitate dividing the proposal for different reviewers and distributing pages with reviewers' comments to the people making revisions.
- Consider not integrating the graphics into the text prior to the review if you anticipate major changes. Instead, insert each graphic on a separate page immediately after its reference in the text. Present graphics in their finished size.
- Integrate the graphics and text prior to the final review if you believe the proposal will require few revisions and if your production approach makes changes relatively easy.

Although less expensive initially, proposals produced by word processor are 40 percent more expensive to modify than desktop published proposals because every change affects pagination.

Identify production support needs early. Estimate how many times each page will be produced both before and after the Red Team. For large, complex, U.S. Federal-type proposals, assume three production passes prior to Red Team and three production passes after Red Team. Figure 4 offers some production time estimates that you can use until you develop more accurate estimates for your organization.

See **Scheduling.**

Task	Time
Simple graphic	1-2 hours each
Complex graphic	2-4 hours each
Retouch photo	1-2 hours
Complex illustration	1+ days
Desktop publishing (DTP) with clean text import	30-60 pages/day
DTP with graphics development	5-10 pages/day

Figure 4. Estimate and Identify Production Support. *Obtain the necessary production support. Without adequate support, writers with limited production skills are forced to prepare their own graphics and design pages. Proposal quality drops, and the total cost increases.*

5

Test all systems prior to production.

If systems are not checked, something will go wrong. Proposal managers frequently see one of the following problems:

- Screened or shaded effects will fade out on one copier and increase in intensity on another, obscuring the text.
- Word-processed proposals will print differently depending on the printer, the printer driver, and the precise supplier of the selected font. Fonts with the same name from different vendors might print differently.
- When sending electronic proposals, the only way to ensure the document will print exactly as intended is to send it in PDF format.
- Contributors are likely to be using different software or different releases of the same software, especially if they develop their own graphics.
- If contributors submit electronic files with embedded graphics, some are likely to be embedded incorrectly. Request text and graphic submittals in separate files.
- When files are sent via e-mail, files can be corrupted by different ISPs (Internet Service Providers), firewalls, and mail encoders and decoders (plug-ins).

See **Electronic Submittal.**

Check everything, especially when you have remote contributors or teaming partners.

6

Determine how the proposal will be "packaged" and delivered while section writers are planning and preparing initial drafts.

See **International Proposals** *and* **Page and Document Design.**

Packaging includes determining the binding method, the size and number of binders required, and cover art. More than a few proposal managers have been surprised by proposals that outgrew the binders that were ordered.

Cover art can get your proposal read in a commercial competition. Good covers both attract readers and project the bidder's win strategy. If you develop custom covers, develop and approve the art early as color printing on custom stock will take more time.

On smaller proposals, prepare a custom cover in one of the following inexpensive ways:

- Cut a page from one of your marketing brochures, then overprint the proposal title text.
- If the above material is not suitable for printing, print the text on a transparency and place it over the graphic. If the print might be marred in handling, create a reverse image electronically, then print it on the back of the transparency.
- Consider using some of the prospect's materials for the cover, especially if you can directly connect those materials to your offer.
- Create your own cover, print on heavier stock, then laminate.

Use quality binders. Economizing on binders is false economy and high risk.

Consider how proposals with multiple volumes will be packaged for shipment. Consider individually wrapping each binder to reduce damage and to prevent binders from opening during shipment.

If being late means automatic disqualification, plan a backup delivery system. International proposals increase delivery problems. While reducing delivery problems, in-country production can lead to other potentially greater problems:

- Skilled editors and proofers may not be available.
- Content can be altered.
- Expenses increase if final reviewers must work in-country.
- Security may be compromised.

7

Maintain a secure master book of hard-copy files backed by electronic files.

Maintain a master book containing copies of all material in the latest, approved version. All contributors must accept that none of their work is complete until it is inserted in the master book.

The master book can take several forms. Most are kept in ring binders by the proposal specialist, production manager, or proposal manager. When material is revised, the new material is inserted in the binder; the previous version is placed in a backup file ordered by section and date.

Insist on getting electronic files with all hard copy submittals. Store them on a server that is frequently backed up. Ensure that all contributors insert their name, section number and name, date, time, and page number in the footer of every page.

The master book is also used to check the printed copies. Turn through each printed page to confirm pages are not missing or printed blank.

8 Ruthlessly enforce version control on a section-by-section basis.

Version control is needed to prevent more than one person from making changes on the same material in different files. All writers have inadvertently lost track of files on computers. The potential for problems with multiple versions of files seems to increase with the square of the number of contributors on the proposal team.

Version control is held by only one person on a section-by-section basis. Normally, writers will have version control through the initial reviews of their content. Once version control is passed to the proposal coordinator or production, insist that all suggested changes be made on hard copy, or on hard copy backed by electronic insertions.

9 Increase your quality checks and production time if proposal production is remote.

See **International Proposals.**

Remote production could mean in another building, another city, or another country. Each presents different challenges.

Always have one person from the proposal team present at the print location during heavy production to answer questions and detect errors early.

Front load production by printing components or sections early. Components that can be printed early include covers, tabs, inserts, foldouts, and appended materials.

Print individual sections as they are approved. Early print options include resumes, past performance, management, and the executive summary.

International production invites special problems:

- Software, hardware, printers, keyboards, spell checkers, and paper quality may vary.
- Paper size may be A4 versus 8.5 x 11 inches.
- Ring binders change in number and size.
- Translation can create further delays and the need for an additional review.
- Language dialects vary.

Printers do have equipment breakdowns, so identify a backup printer.

Electronic submittals invite additional production problems, far more than are discussed here, so be forewarned.

Proposal Management Plans (PMP) document the roles, responsibilities, tasks, and deadlines before writers start developing proposal sections, volumes, and ultimately the complete proposal.

Establish direction, then velocity. Too many proposal managers start holding too many meetings with writers and managers before planning is complete. The result is wasted effort, conflicts, and loss of commitment to a quality effort.

Save time by extracting and adapting content from the capture plan and account plan with direction from the account executive. Insert boilerplate PMP descriptions of roles and procedures.

Proposal Management Plan

1. **Always prepare a Proposal Management Plan.**
2. **Complete and review the PMP prior to the kickoff meeting.**
3. **Distribute the PMP at the kickoff meeting.**
4. **Keep the PMP current, but manage to the plan.**
5. **Develop a PMP template for your organization.**

1 Always prepare a Proposal Management Plan.

Preparing a Proposal Management Plan (PMP) is a proven best practice that leads to improved win rates and higher quality proposals produced with less frustration and cost. When you do not have time to prepare multiple drafts, always prepare a PMP.

Many commercial sector proposal plans begin in a conference call termed the proposal kickoff, which is at best a loosely organized planning meeting. At a minimum, develop a strawman PMP before the conference call.

2 Complete and review the PMP prior to the kickoff meeting.

See **Executive Summary, Kickoff Meeting,** *and* **Process** *for a discussion of the other tools, events, and milestones.*

Core team preparation, the planning activity between the Bid and Proposal Kickoff milestones, requires developing three documents:

1. Proposal Management Plan
2. Draft Executive Summary
3. Proposal Kickoff Package

Review the PMP with management to get their buy-in and endorsement. If they are not willing to support the effort as outlined, you must change the plan or review your bid decision.

If you must call a kickoff meeting prior to completing the PMP, advise contributors that they will be given clear assignments later. Set the date for the meeting and ask contributors to clear their schedules.

3 Distribute the PMP at the kickoff meeting.

The PMP is your plan for the entire effort. Distributing the PMP clarifies everyone's tasks and engenders confidence that their efforts are well managed and supported by management. A well conceived PMP suggests that you are not wasting contributors' time.

Your complete kickoff meeting package includes five items:

- PMP
- Storyboard forms
- Writing template
- Cross-reference matrix
- Draft executive summary

4 Keep the PMP current, but manage to the plan.

Reflect changes in the RFP, dates, and contributors by updating the PMP. Absent external changes, avoid sliding completion dates. Manage to the plan.

5 Develop a PMP template for your organization.

The format and contents of a PMP should vary with the complexity of the proposal, the size of the proposal team, the value of the proposal, and the experience and skills of the managers and contributors.

The contents of a PMP are summarized in figure 1. A template for a PMP is presented in thumbnail form beginning on this page and continuing on the following three pages, figures 2 through 12.

PMP CONTENTS	ATTACHMENTS
1. Proposal Project Summary	A. Proposal Schedule
2. Customer Profile	B. Proposal Outline
3. Competitive Analysis	C. Writers' Information
4. Proposal Strategies and Themes	D. Proposal Strategy
5. Staffing Roles and Responsibilities	E. Executive Summary
6. Proposal Operations	F. Work Breakdown Structure (WBS) and WBS Dictionary

Figure 1. PMP Contents. *Include these topics in your PMP in the detail appropriate to each proposal effort.*

1.0 PROPOSAL PROJECT SUMMARY

General Information

- Customer
- Contract Name
- Solicitation Identification
- Type of Contract
- Terms of Contract
- Estimated Contract Value
- Duration of Contract
- RFP Release Date
- Proposal Due Date
- Customer Procurement Office

PMP-1

1.0 PROPOSAL PROJECT SUMMARY

Project Focal Points

- Program Manager
- Marketing Manager
- Teammates
- Capture Plan
- Capture Team Head

Project Scope and Deliverables

- Scope of Work
- Primary Tasks
- Deliverables
- Proposal Organization

PMP-2

Figure 2. PMP Proposal Project Summary. *Written primarily for upper management, reviewers, and the proposal team, this section of the PMP summarizes the prospect's program needs, key program information, key program personnel, overall scope, and deliverables.*

See **Strategy.**

2.0 CUSTOMER PROFILE

Intelligence on Customer Organization

- Mailing Address
- Program Manager
- Contracting Officer
- Selection Members

Selection Process

Customer Needs, Issues, and Hot Buttons

Customer Perception of Our Company

PMP-3

Figure 3. PMP Customer Profile. *This section identifies key members of the prospect organization, then summarizes the selection process and the prospect's perception of your organization.*

3.0 COMPETITOR ANALYSIS

Our Approach and Perceived Strengths/ Weaknesses

Program Approach

- Key Technical Element
- Key Management Element
- Capture Plan
- Capture Team Head

Perceived Strengths	Perceived Weaknesses
1.	1.
2.	2.
3.	3.

Bidder Comparision Matrix

Issues	Weight	Us Score	Company 1 Score	Company 2 Score
Total Score	100			

PMP-4

Figure 4. PMP Competitive Analysis. *This section summarizes the key elements of your approach and the prospect's perceptions of your competitive position.*

See **Discriminators, Strategy, Team Selection and Management,** *and* **Theme Statements.**

4.0 PROPOSAL STRATEGIES AND THEMES

Proposal Strategy Statements

- We will emphasize: ______________________

  ____

  by: ______________________

  ____

  ____

- We will emphasize: ______________________

  ____

  by: ______________________

  ____

  ____

Pricing Strategy

Relevant Experience and Past Performance

Proposal Theme Statements

Text linking benefit to a discriminator (feature of your offer).

PMP-5

Figure 5. PMP Proposal Strategies and Themes. *The strategy statements indicate what you* ***plan*** *to include in your proposal to support your major claims. Themes are actual statements that will be printed in your proposal.*

5.0 STAFFING, ROLES, AND RESPONSIBILITIES

Name	Company/ Division	Role	Proposal Responsibility	Telephone/Fax	e-mail
		Capture Team Manager			
		Selected Capture Team Members			
		Program Manager			
		Proposal Manager			
		Proposal Development Specialist			
		Volume Managers			
		Director of Business Development			
		Chief Technical Innovator			
		Product Marketing Manager			
		Field Office Representative			
		Proposal Critical Areas			
		Teaming Division/Companies			
		Consultants			

PMP-6

Figure 6. PMP Staffing, Roles, and Responsibilities. *This section is used primarily to improve teamwork and understanding among individuals assigned to the proposal team. Extend the matrix to include additional information as needed. Descriptions of roles and responsibilities can be taken from earlier PMPs.*

6.0 PROPOSAL OPERATIONS

Facilities

Support

Procedures

Development Aids or Tools

See Scheduling and Outlining.

PMP-7

Figure 7. PMP Proposal Operations. *This section indicates the resources available, procedures, and development tools that will be used. Much of this section can be extracted from earlier PMPs.*

PMP ATTACHMENT A: PROPOSAL SCHEDULE

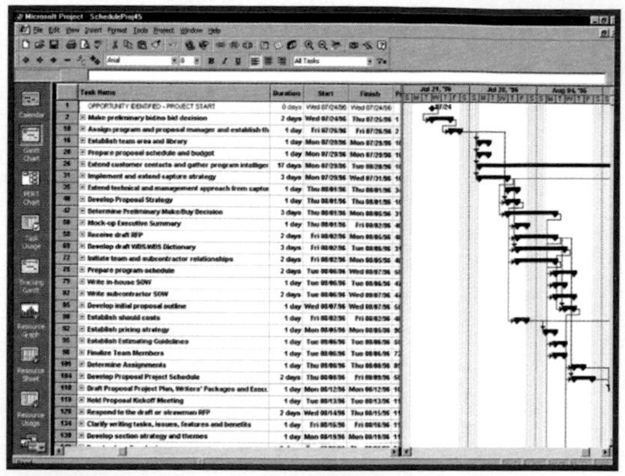

PMP-8

Figure 8. PMP Proposal Schedule. *Issue a milestone schedule at the kickoff meeting, then follow up with an "inch-stone" schedule.*

PMP ATTACHMENT B: PROPOSAL OUTLINE

Writing Assignments

Proposal Par #	Proposal Section Title	Relevant RFP Par #'s	Author	Page Limit Target	Storyboard Assigned	1st Review Date	Final Review Date	Mock-up Review Date	Pink Team Date	Graphics Due Date	1st Draft Date	Red Team Date
None	Exec Sum	M	S. Ross	4	3-19-00	3-25-00	3-28-00	3-31-00	4-2-00	4-10-00	4-15-00	4-28-00
1.0	Tech Ov	L.2.1	W. Lou	2	3-21-00	3-26-00	3-28-00	3-31-00	4-2-00	4-10-00	4-15-00	4-28-00

See Scheduling and Storyboards and Mock-ups.

PMP-9

Figure 9. PMP Proposal Outline and Writing Assignments. *Assign a single person with the primary responsibility for each proposal section. Consider integrating the outline, assignments, and completion dates into the same matrix.*

PMP ATTACHMENT C: WRITERS' INFORMATION

Storyboard Forms

Website References

Boilerplate Files

Writing Templates

Style Guidelines

PMP-10

Figure 10. PMP Writers' Information. *Include any information, tools, form, or references to resources that will help writers complete their assignments correctly and efficiently.*

See **Executive Summary**.

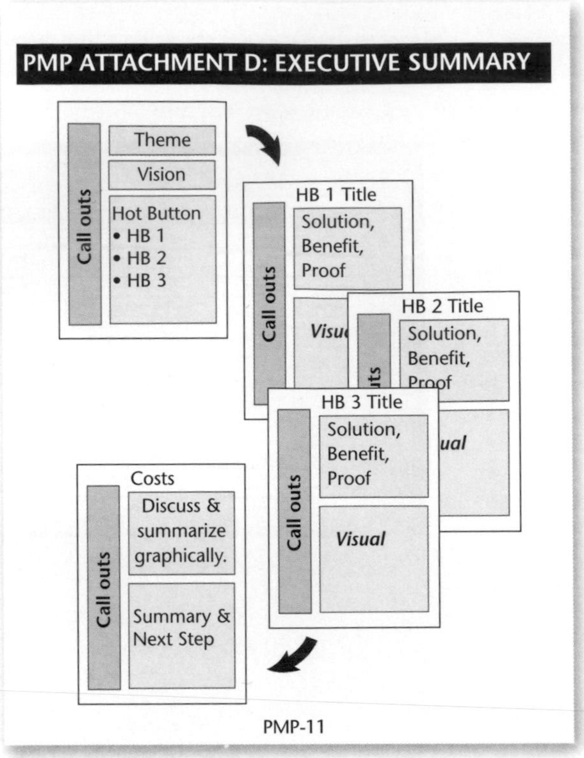

Figure 11. PMP Executive Summary. *Include the most recent version of the proposal executive summary.*

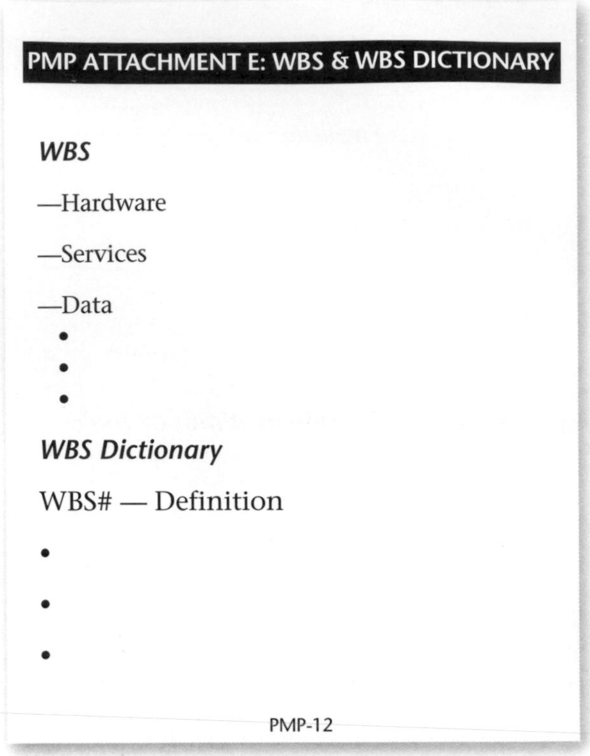

PMP ATTACHMENT E: WBS & WBS DICTIONARY
WBS
—Hardware
—Services
—Data
•
•
•
WBS Dictionary
WBS# — Definition
•
•
•
PMP-12

Figure 12. PMP WBS and WBS Dictionary. *This section both defines and separates the seller's proposed work into hardware, services, and data elements. The WBS is essential to describe and cost your proposal tasks.*

Question/response proposals result from bid requests that consist of a series of questions. Bidders are asked to answer the questions in order.

Bid requests largely composed of questions are common in telecommunications, professional services, health care management, and many international sectors. Question/response proposals are rare in government proposals.

See **Executive Summary**.

NOTE: An excerpt from a question/response proposal is included in **Model Documents**, p. 257.

Many question/response bid requests are created by consultants hired by prospects' organizations because they lack the internal expertise or time to prepare the bid request themselves. Consultants compete for this business by selling a more thorough approach, often resulting in more questions, longer responses, and more evaluation time.

Increase your win rate by concentrating on two activities:

1. Place additional emphasis on your executive summary, the only part of your proposal the prospect is likely to read.
2. Develop a response strategy to enable you to concentrate your effort on the most important questions.

The second activity requires taking a modified storyboard-like approach. Allocate your time, plan your response, review your planned response, then draft your response.

Question/Response Proposals

1. **Review all questions and identify critical ones.**
2. **Allocate more time to investigate and space to answer critical questions.**
3. **Use more boilerplate on less-critical questions.**
4. **Quickly outline each response and review with management before drafting.**
5. **Identify where graphics can be used to cut text.**
6. **Answer the question.**
7. **Insert section summaries to provide perspective and to gain a competitive advantage.**

1 Review all questions and identify critical ones.

Review all the questions on an 80-20 basis. Identify the 20 percent that are of equal or greater importance than the remaining 80 percent. Look for questions with the following characteristics:

- Involve the prospect's major issues
- Offer an opportunity to discriminate your offer
- Create a gap between the requirement and your immediately available solution

Depending on the size of the proposal and the time available, the proposal manager, the writer, or both can review the questions.

2 Allocate more time to investigate and space to answer critical questions.

Giving each person the same number of questions to answer usually results in an uneven work load. Ask writers to split their time between the two groups of questions but to devote more time to the 20 percent that are critical.

3 Use more boilerplate on less-critical questions.

See **Organization**.

Offer short, concise answers to the simpler, less-critical questions. If a more extensive answer is needed, draft a short introduction; then support your answer with boilerplate.

4 Quickly outline each response and review with management before drafting.

Ask writers to outline their answers to the critical questions first, brainstorm their response to the most difficult ones, then review their answers with the core team. If more research is needed to answer a question, decide who will do it and move on to the next question.

Your goal is to be 100 percent compliant and 80 to 90 percent correct with your first answer to all questions.

Answer every question in the first sentence of your answer. Use the remaining text and graphics to support your answer.

5 Identify where graphics can be used to cut text.

See **Action Captions** *and* **Graphics.**

Think "graphics first."

Most question/answer proposals are deadly boring. Given the same answer to the same question, the question answered with a graphic and minimal text will nearly always outscore a competitor's response answered with text alone.

If you insert a graphic with an action caption, you will have much less text to write. If the graphic lacks a caption, add one. If it has a caption, tailor it to the proposal.

6 Answer the question.

Proposal writers can err by failing to answer a question and by overanswering a question.

As noted in guideline 4, answer each question in the first sentence, then support your answer with boilerplate. Writers tend to insert the boilerplate first, then answer the question.

Overly elaborate answers can create more questions. Lawyers coach witnesses to limit their answers. Follow the same "keep it simple" approach.

In the following example, the poor response offers a lot of information without directly answering the question. The last two sentences seem to conflict with the first sentences. The better response directly answers the questions in the order asked, omits potentially confusing details, and does not mingle the discussion of maintenance costs and upgrade costs.

Poor response

Is software maintenance available? If yes, is the price included in the price of the software?

Operating system (OS) and database management software (DMS) maintenance is regularly applied at no additional cost. Also FLOORS software, database access software, utilities, and all other system software utilized by the Master Control system will require no maintenance fees. Any maintenance or upgrade can be done by your technicians or ours. Our maintenance is supplied on a time-and-materials basis at $600/day.

Better response

Is software maintenance available?

Yes. ISI provides regular software maintenance on all system software used by the Master Control System.

If yes, is the price included in the price of the software?

Yes. Software maintenance is included in the price of the software. You would incur NO additional costs for software maintenance.

7 Insert section summaries to provide perspective and to gain a competitive advantage.

See **Organization.**

NOTE: Do not insert section summaries or graphics if doing so violates bid request instructions.

With question/response proposals, evaluators may read your answers but still have no clear perspective or general understanding of your approach.

Insert a short section summary before answering individual questions on a common topic. Enhance it with a summary graphic when appropriate. Evaluators will appreciate the added perspective and often give higher scores as long as the summary is concise. The helpful tone of your approach suggests that your organization is easy to work with.

Few organizations submitting question/response proposals bother to include summaries other than the executive summary, so a series of concise major topic summaries gives you a competitive advantage. Make each summary more persuasive by stressing the overall benefits to the prospect at the beginning. End the summary by noting that each question from the prospect's bid request is answered in the order listed in the bid request.

Good example of a proposal section summary.

> ***4.0 SOFTWARE MAINTENANCE***
>
> ***ISI offers Acme comprehensive, trouble-free software maintenance at no additional cost for 10 years following software installation.***
>
> All of Acme's needs for convenient, low-cost, system availability are met by our software maintenance plan. Our Client Services Organization was commended by Software Research, Inc. as, ". . . one of the premier service organizations in the information services industry." We deliver 24-hour-a-day, 7-day-a-week support, and are able to resolve 99 percent of all problems within 1.57 hours.
>
> Below are our responses to the specific questions in your bid request regarding software maintenance.

Relevant experience and past performance are directly solicited sections in many bid requests and are vital content for all proposals. Both are frequently evaluation criteria in government bid requests. Both are also redundant words, but the customer is always right.

Relevant experience and past performance are quite different but directly related.

Relevant experience includes past, similar experience of the offeror. Relevant experience applies to the organization as a whole, the specific actions being performed, or the experience of the individuals contributing to the services proposed.

Past performance indicates how well you did similar work: the results, impact, or process changes resulting from performing the work. However, some bid requests may exclude similar work performed by proposed individuals when they were not part of your organization.

Without proof of experience and performance, proposals are a collection of "trust me" claims. The fatal error for many proposals is to relegate all experience and performance data to a separate section or attachment.

Integrate relevant experience and performance data into the body of the proposal adjacent to your claims.

Even when separate relevant experience and performance sections are requested, you still need to include both within other proposal sections to support your claims. Different evaluators reviewing different sections seldom connect your proposed approach with proof offered in a separate section.

Relevant Experience and Past Performance

1. **Include all relevant experience and past performance data in your proposal in the exact location the bid request requires.**
2. **Integrate examples as support wherever you make claims of experience and performance.**
3. **Emphasize experience and performance graphically.**
4. **Use a "success story" template to tell a consistent, complete story.**
5. **Address all weaknesses known or potentially known by the prospect.**
6. **Emphasize personal lessons learned over lessons learned from others.**

1 Include all relevant experience and past performance data in your proposal in the exact location the bid request requires.

Directions in the RFP can be quite detailed. Follow them explicitly.

See **Compliance and Responsiveness** *and* **Outlining.**

Prospects view past performance as one of the best indicators of future performance. As proof, U.S. acquisition regulations require past performance as one of two *mandatory* evaluation factors, along with price or cost.

The Office of Federal Procurement Policy indicates the following areas to be considered:

- Quality of product or services
- Timeliness of performance
- Cost control
- Business practices
- Customer (end user) satisfaction
- Key personnel past performance

2 Integrate examples as support wherever you make claims of experience and performance.

Much like the guidelines for introducing and integrating graphics with text, integrate your support of claims on the same or a facing page. Evaluators should not have to turn the page to find support.

Support and scientific proof are not the same. If a prospect is concerned about completing a task on schedule, one example of completing a task on schedule *supports* your claim. Proof might be completing the same task on schedule 99 percent of the time.

Too many proposal writers, concerned about poor past performance, offer no support of their claims. Cite the following as proof of performance:

- Bonuses or awards paid
- Complimentary customer statements, letters, or client newsletter excerpts
- Performance ratings
- Exceptional aspects or quantifiable benefits

3 Emphasize experience and performance graphically.

See **Graphics** *and* **Photographs.**

Graphics draw evaluators' attention and persuade emotionally as well as logically. Seeing a photograph of a task being performed adds credibility.

Visualize and emphasize the benefit whenever possible over raw data. A table of Mean Time Between Failures (MTBF) data is not nearly as interesting or as emotionally charged as seeing people enjoying the service.

Consider combining the graphic and the data. Cover either half of figure 1 to see the difference.

With acceptance in 234 countries, our SmarT™Card makes your travel more convenient and safe.

#	*Accepted*	*Refused*	*Percent*
23	22	1	95.6
25	25	0	100.0
		⋮	
500	*495*	*5*	*99.0*

Independent surveys show a 99 percent acceptance rate in 234 countries.

Figure 1. Visualize Benefits Over Features. *While many writers can build tables, numbers presented on their own are not as effective as a visual alone or a visual with the numbers. Note the difference by covering either half of figure 1.*

4 Use a "success story" template to tell a consistent, complete story.

Templates help proposal writers support claims consistently and credibly. Follow the steps listed below and illustrated in figure 2:

1. Select and insert a graphic. The graphic does not have to prove the claim. Rather it enhances credibility and commands attention.
2. Indicate the prospect's need.
3. Indicate the basis or reason for selecting your organization.
4. Indicate the solution you delivered and the resulting benefit, quantified when possible.

NOTE: Examples cited to support the seller's claims are often referred to as "success stories." Look for relevant success stories in your organization's marketing materials, news releases, employee news-letters, and web pages.

See **Action Captions.**

Early Completion Earns $200,000 Award Bonus. *Global Manufacturing needed to complete a critical plant expansion on a fast-track basis under difficult winter conditions. After a careful evaluation of six design-build contractors, Global awarded the contract to Shipley Constructors. We completed the expansion 23 days ahead of schedule, on budget, and earned a $200,000 bonus.*

Figure 2. Use Graphics to Support Claims. *Write your caption in a prospect-focused style. Include the prospect need, the reason you were selected, and the result. Make the caption long enough to tell the complete story.*

5 Address all weaknesses known or potentially known by the prospect.

Also see **Strategy.**

If you lack directly relevant experience, try to break the proposed tasks into subtasks, each of which you have done.

A company with no PC manufacturing experience might emphasize its ability to design similar electronic components, source standard subassemblies and components, test their design, and assemble components reliably.

A laboratory researching a cure for cancer might emphasize its ability to review existing literature, attract experienced cancer researchers, conduct specific tests, and produce clear reports.

If performance was not as good as you would like, you must address it in at least one of the following ways:

- Cite the lessons learned.
- Cite the changes you have already made in your approach, and emphasize the positive results attained, if any.
- Cite your decision to team with another organization or hire a proven individual with a record of performance in the area.

When poor performance or unfavorable ratings are explained well, you introduce a risk mitigation and avoidance strategy. Never over apologize. Admit the facts and move on. Relevant experience and performance all relate to the prospect's risk, so emphasize the benefits of lower risk.

A common way to emphasize either the experience of individuals or the task experience of your organization is with a "meatball chart" like the one in figure 3.

NOTE: List the tasks required on one axis. On the other axis, list either the experience, technologies, regulations, organizations, or licenses that are needed to perform the tasks requested.

EXPERIENCE
● Remedial Action
▲ Treatability/Pilot Study
■ Both
★ Key Personnel

	REMEDIAL ACTION TECHNOLOGIES																				REGULATORS							AGENCIES		
	Neutralization process	Metals precipitation	Chemical stabilization	Covering/capping contaminated soil	Installing leachate drain	Transporting/disposing haz. waste offsite	Bioremediation (insitu & above ground)	Thermal Desorption	Incineration on/offsite	Soil washing before disposal	Soil venting, soil vapor extraction	Pumping/treating contaminated ground water	Installation of slurry walls	POL recovery systems	Airstripping	Carbon absorption	Groundwater monitoring	Solvent extraction	Chemical decomposition & solidification	Others, specify USTs drums	CERCLA	RCRA	TSCA	CWA	CAA	OSHA	SDWA	U.S. EPA Region 9	Guam EPA	Hawaii Dept of Health
PROGRAM MANAGER																														
★ Mark Wadsworth	●	■	●	●	●	●	●		●	▲	●	●	●	●	●	●	●	▲		▲	●	●	●	●	●	●	●			
SR. PROJECT ENGINEER																														
★ Ramona Lyons			■	■	■	■			●	●		■	■	●	●	●	■	●	■	●	■	■	■			■	■	■		
Feng Tze Hsu				●	●	●						●				●			●	●				●		●		●	●	●
Scott Parker	●	■	■	■	■	●	●	■	■	▲		■	●	●	●	■	●		■		●	●	●	●	●	●		●		●
PROJECT MANAGERS																														
★ Eric Weiss	●	●	▲	●	●	●	■	■	●	▲	■	■			●	●	●	●	▲	■	●	●	●	●	●	●		●		
Paul Cardis				●	●	●					■	■		■			●				●	■	●	●		●	●		●	
Sydnie Marchant		▲	▲			●	■	■			■	■		●		■	■				■	■				●		■		■
SR. PROJECT SCIENTIST																														
★ Artie Bokko	▲	▲		●	●	●	▲	▲		▲	▲	■			■	■	●				●	●	●	●				●		
James Thompson	■	■	■	■	■	●	■	■	▲	▲	■	■		■	▲	■	■			■	■	■				●				
Kathryn Moore	▲	▲	●	■	●	●	▲		▲		▲	■	■	■	▲	■	●		▲		■	■		●		●	●	■		
STAFF SCIENTIST																														
★ Danielle LeMond				●	●	●				●		●	●				●	▲			●	●						●		
Andrew McBride				■	■							■	■	■	■		■	■			■	■				■		■		■
Jihyun Park		●		●	●	●			●			■	■		■	■	●				■	■				■		■		
Wayne Stuart	●	●	●	●	●	■	●	●	■		●	■		●		■	●		■	●	●	●	●	●	●	■				
Lynn Arcaris	■	■	▲	■	●	●	■	▲	■	▲	■	■			■	■	■	●	▲	■		●	●	●	●		●	●	●	
STAFF ENGINEER																														
★ David Jamison	■	■	■	■	■	●	■		●	●	●	■	▲	●	●	■	■	●			●	●	●		▲	■	■	●	●	●
Padmala Aramyan	■	■	▲	■	■	■	■	▲	●	▲	▲	■	●	■	■	■	■	●	▲	■		●	●	●	●		●	●	●	
S. Arceneaux	●		■	●	●	●		▲			●	■	■	●	■	■	●	▲				●				●				
Richard Head				●		●						●			●	●	●			●	●	●	●			●	●			
Koji Arai			▲	■	▲	■	▲		▲		●	■		■			■	▲	▲		●	●	●	●	●	●	●	●		
QC OFFICER																														
★ Carolyn Olson			●	●	●	●	●			■		●	●	●	●	●	●	●	●	●			■	■	●		●	●	●	●

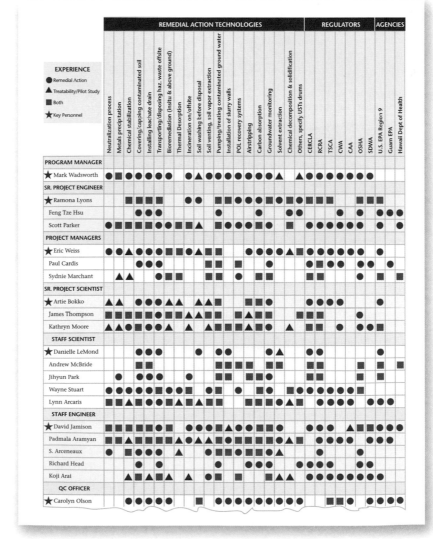

Figure 3. Use Meatball Charts to Emphasize Experience. *While often complex, the complexity supports the message that, "We have ample experience and capability." Use smaller versions to support discussions of an individual's experience.*

Another method is to develop a matrix that relates the tasks anticipated, relevant experience, technologies required, potential problems, and your proposed solution. Shown in figure 4, this type of graphic is a powerful way to demonstrate your technical understanding.

While violating recommendations to keep graphics simple and uncluttered, casual readers are impressed that everything seems to be covered. Detailed readers like these charts because they reduce the time needed to review resumes, relevant experience, and past performance charts.

TASKS ANTICIPATED	TEAM EXPERIENCE EXAMPLES	REMEDIAL TECHNOLOGIES APPLIED	PROBLEM AREAS	RESOLUTION COST SCHEDULE IMPACT
Leaking fuel tanks and pipelines	Confidential Client (#14)	• Ex situ bioremediation • Tank demolition	• Site characterization underestimated amount of contaminated soil by factor of 4 • Limited space for bioremediation	• Bioremediation in sequential lifts allowed original schedule to be met • Used remediated soil for backfill. (Over 2 million yd^3)
	Mystic River Petroleum Storage Area (#33)	• Groundwater treatment • Soil venting • Covering/capping of contaminated soils	• POL recovery • POL contaminated soil • PCB contaminated soil • Metal contaminated soil • UST removal	• Removed 9,000 gals. liquid hazardous waste • Met budget and schedule • Closed six USTs • Closed RCRA disposal facility • Removed over 3,600 chemical drums
Lined and unlined landfills	Moab Superfund Site (#22)	• Groundwater monitoring • Soil vapor extraction • Pump and treat	• Unlined quarry used as hazardous waste disposal site • Groundwater contamination under residential area	• Groundwater monitoring • Soil vapor extraction • Pump and treat
	Red Sands Superfund Site (#29)	• Neutralization • Chemical stabilization • Cap & cover • Leachate drains • Incineration • Groundwater monitoring: pump & treat • Carbon absorption	• Acidic tarry waste in floodplain • Benzene emissions	• Solidified material, placed in new landfill out of floodplain • Reduced cost by more than 50 percent over incineration alternative

Relevant Experience Reduces Risk. *The ECO Team's experience is directly relevant to environmental issues in your bid request, significantly reducing performance risk.*

Figure 4. Use Matrices to Relate Experience to Technical Understanding. *When examples of experience must be placed in another section, matrices like this one tie relevant experience directly to your technical discussion in the body of the proposal. Even if evaluators do not check each one, they get the strong impression that you have relevant experience.*

6 Emphasize personal lessons learned over lessons learned from others.

Too many incumbents with performance problems fail to understand and present their lessons learned as strongly as they could. Reading how to juggle does not make a person a juggler.

Reading all of the studies about how and why a component failed or a service was inadequate is always inferior to having done the study. Some items or facts, often intangible, are omitted.

The following example illustrates how an incumbent used direct, personal experience to win a 5-year contract renewal:

A company that operated a government facility under contract for three consecutive, 5-year terms was competing for another 5-year renewal. To avoid the appearance of favoritism, the government intentionally limited the size of the solicited proposals to negate the incumbent's advantage.

The incumbent's overall strategy was to stress the complexity of the tasks it performed to frighten the evaluators from changing contractors. The proposal strategy was to present the proposed tasks and lessons learned in a detailed series of tables, charts, diagrams, and lists to emphasize the complexity of those tasks.

The incumbent won. A comment in the debrief was, *"We did not realize that the support you provided was so complex."*

Resumes in a proposal are critical to selling what is often your most important discriminator—the individuals whom you propose.

See **Organization.**

Resumes, like other documents, should be organized according to the readers' needs. However, resumes are evaluated differently when individuals are being hired versus when teams are being hired from a proposal.

People filling individual positions screen resumes to eliminate unsuitable applicants before reading in depth to determine who to invite for interviews. Individuals' resumes usually begin with an employment objective, then present a logical progression in their experience, skills, and training.

Evaluators who screen resumes in proposals face a more complicated task; multiple positions and tasks are involved and the subsequent personal interviews, if any, are limited. Proposal resume evaluators are trying to assess four aspects of each team:

1. Understanding of the prospect's needs
2. Degree of commitment
3. Match between position requirements and the individuals proposed
4. Team coverage of all requirements

Sellers lose when they only demonstrate adequate resources. Resumes in best-in-class proposals address all four aspects:

1. Clearly define the requirements of each key position
2. Name and commit individuals for all key positions
3. Include tailored resumes to precisely match position requirements and individuals' specific experience
4. Use matrices to demonstrate all requirements are covered

Resumes

1. **Always name the individuals recommended in your proposal.**
2. **Tailor the resumes for key positions in every proposal.**
3. **Identify who will be proposed and prepare their resumes before the heavy writing and production effort begins.**
4. **Arrange your tailored resumes in a functional requirement and/or accomplishment format.**
5. **Include abbreviated or summary resumes of individuals proposed for key positions in the body of your proposal.**
6. **Assemble a resume database that is searchable, current, and easily tailored.**
7. **Keep resumes brief, clear, and error free.**
8. **Use capability and skill matrices to emphasize the total capabilities of large teams.**
9. **Avoid adding photos of the people proposed unless it supports your strategy.**

1 Always name the individuals recommended in your proposal.

If you want to win, get over any resistance to naming people in your proposal. A clear, best practice when selling services is to name specific individuals who will do the work.

Resistance to using specific names is usually because the bidding organization cannot be certain that the individuals recommended in the proposal will be available when the project is awarded.

Do your best to be realistic. Do not intentionally propose a "bait and switch." In the long run, you lose your credibility. If you fear a competitor might propose its most experienced people with no intention of using them, ghost them as shown in the following examples:

> We could follow common practice and propose using only our most experienced people to provide this service. Instead, we have done our best to identify and propose the most experienced people we expect to be available at the anticipated start date. Should any individual proposed not be available, we will give you the right to review and approve all changes.

If you doubt the importance of naming individuals, consider how some service bid requests read:

> Indicate by name the individuals who will provide services. Indicate whether they will serve a primary or secondary role. All individuals with primary roles must be full time. For individuals with secondary roles, indicate the percentage of their time already committed to other projects, name those projects, and indicate the percentage of time that will be available for this project.

2 Tailor the resumes for key positions in every proposal.

If you do not have time to tailor the resume for key positions, you should not be bidding. Tailor each resume to emphasize the fit between the requirements of the position and the experience of the individual proposed.

Clearly identify all key positions. In one debrief, a losing bidder was told:

Your failure to recognize the Software Development Manager as a key position indicated your lack of understanding of the requirements.

Your identification and justification of the key positions should be part of your strategy.

3 Identify who will be proposed and prepare their resumes before the heavy writing and production effort begins.

Teams that wait to name individuals for key positions until the end run out of time to tailor resumes. Force an early decision and get the resumes tailored.

If necessary, tailor the resumes of several individuals for the same position. Then insert the correct one at the end.

4 Arrange your tailored resumes in a functional requirement and/or accomplishment format.

Resumes are usually ordered in one of the following ways:

- Reverse chronology
- Functional requirement
- Accomplishment
- Narrative

The **reverse-chronology resume** lists experience and education from latest to earliest.

The **functional-requirement resume** organizes work experience by job function, disregarding chronology.

The **accomplishment resume** features positive achievements and emphasizes results over chronology.

The **narrative resume** is written in first or second person, telling a story about the person, presenting data in complete sentences.

Functional and accomplishment resumes are best for proposals. Evaluators try to minimize risk, hence their concern that the bidder understands the requirements of the position, and the named individual has performed the same task well in the past.

The easiest proposal resumes to evaluate are the ones that directly match the functional position requirements to the accomplishments, like the one shown in figure 1. Resumes like this can be quite compact, permitting two or three to be placed on a single page. Develop this type of resume in the following manner:

1. List the name of the person and the position you are proposing them to fill at the top.
2. Develop a list of the primary functional requirements of the position. List them on the left side, most important ones first.
3. Directly adjacent, list where the person has performed the same duties, stating their accomplishments or results achieved.
4. List the years they performed the job, if appropriate, making it easy to total their years of similar experience.
5. List any other relevant data about the person in the column to the right.

The width of the columns can vary, depending on the amount of information required. This type of resume can be rapidly assembled from standard, searchable resumes kept in a resume database.

Name, Position

Responsibilities	*Years*	*Relevant Experience*	*Professional*
• Major responsibility	3	Describe what they accomplished.	List degrees, additional training, licenses, patents, certifications, professional associations, awards, etc. List the most important ones first, as space permits.
	2	Describe what they accomplished.	
• Major responsibility	1	Describe what they accomplished.	
	2	Describe what they accomplished.	
• Major responsibility	3	Describe what they accomplished.	
	4	Describe what they accomplished.	
	15	**Years**	

Figure 1. Develop a Functional Requirement /Accomplishment Resume Template for Your Proposals. *This design visually emphasizes the direct relationship between responsibilities and relevant experience.*

5 Include abbreviated or summary resumes of individuals proposed for key positions in the body of your proposal.

Abbreviated resumes inserted in the body text are an easy way to answer the questions in the bid request and to make evaluation easy.

Several examples are shown in figure 2, with a slightly different design.

NOTE: This type of resume conserves space in page-limited proposals. Full, inclusive resumes can still be appended.

COSMOS PROGRAM	Aye C. Klearly
Manager Requirements	*Qualifications*
• Licensed Professional Engineer • 6 years' experience with space imaging projects • 4 years' experience as senior project engineer	• Professional Mechanical Engineer, B.S. Mechanical Engineering • Business Management Certificate • 8 years' experience with NASA projects • 13 years as a project manager; 8 years as a senior project engineer

COSMOS PROGRAM	Izzy D. Bosse
Superintendent Requirements	*Qualifications*
• 5 years' construction management experience • 1 year of experience on NASA construction projects	• 18 years' construction management, including 5 years on Mt. Olympus observatory update • 4 years managing NASA construction projects

Figure 2. Insert Summary Resumes Within Body Text. *The two examples, designed for a balanced, two-column proposal page design, directly match the requirements. Position requirements are either established in the bid request or by the proposing organization as it develops its management approach.*

6 Assemble a resume database that is searchable, current, and easily tailored.

Develop a standard, searchable resume database. Numerous database software products are available.

Consider some of the proposal preparation software products. While many of these products are of questionable value for preparing prospect-focused proposals, some offer excellent ways to retrieve and match position requirements to personnel capabilities using internet-like search engines.

Assign a person to regularly update resumes, not just to build the initial set. Many organizations routinely insert long resumes that are more than 5 years old and that contain obviously irrelevant information.

Place an expiration date on each resume, just like your boilerplate. Automatically flag expired resumes for updates at set intervals. If no update is received within 3 months, then remove the resume from your database.

7 Keep resumes brief, clear, and error free.

All of the resumes included in your proposal must meet the clear and brief criteria. Keeping them error free is critical when evaluators are looking for reasons to eliminate bidders. Mistakes imply poor quality and are valid grounds for elimination.

Do not expect to hear poor quality cited as a reason for elimination in debriefs, but it is cited in private.

Some bid requests include forms that must be completed for named positions. However, the forms are often poorly designed, difficult to read, and waste space.

When faced with a typed, lined form, recreate the form in the exact order given, as shown in figure 3. Group the information and summarize it to make the resume easier to read. While some might consider this risky, evaluators have given positive feedback to this effort. Seek the prospect's approval if possible.

Place the following note at the beginning of the resume section:

All the following resumes are arranged in the order requested and contain all information in the order requested on the forms in your bid request. To make them easier to read, we have reentered them to facilitate your evaluation and to maintain a consistent appearance.

Bid request excerpt:

All personnel proposed for key positions must meet the following minimum requirements:

- ***Project Manager***—*Two years of management experience and five years of applications development*
- ***Application Development, Lead Programmer/ Analyst***—*five years of programming experience*
- ***Common Code Development***—*. . . (text omitted)*

For each position, also complete the Resume Data Forms.

RESUME DATA FORM

Position ______________ Name ______________

Education ______________

____

Hardware ______________

Software ______________

Experience ______________

____

PROJECT MANAGER

Noah Lott

EDUCATION	HARDWARE	EXPERIENCE
M.S. Computer Science, University of Iowa, 1987 MBA, UCLA, 1992	IBM 3400 & 370, Digital Alpha servers, Cisco Systems routers, PC and Apple networks **SOFTWARE** OS/MVS, DOS/VSE, VM/CMS, ISPF, COBAL, C++, NOVELL, DR DOS, MAC OS 4 through 9.0.4, Microsoft Windows NT	***YEARS*** / ***ASSIGNMENT*** 1 Managed major application development project for IS under a contract awarded by General Motors. Supervised a team that grew from 5 to 30 professionals during 3 months. Completed project 2 weeks ahead of schedule and within budget. 1 Project leader for Y2K update for major petrochemical producer. Tested, re-coded, debugged, and replaced major legacy systems. Supervised a team of 12. Project completed on schedule. Achieved a 20 percent annual cost reduction and experienced no Y2K service interruptions. **2 Total Management Experience** 4 Developed numerous utilities programs for a major consulting engineering company. Applications included security, CAD/CAM, general ledger reporting, estimating, and project management. Based on the savings generated, the client awarded two one-year contract extensions for additional work. 3 Developed applications software for the US Census Bureau to operate on IBM 370 series computers. Involved structuring, storage, and retrieval of large data bases. 1 Developed and maintained home delivery contract and data collection systems for large publishing company on Windows NT network. **8 Total Years of Applications Development**

Figure 3. Design Resumes that Do Not Have to be Read. *Given the bid request requirements, evaluators can easily see if the person meets their requirements without having to read the resume. Many evaluators check a few, then accept the rest as accurate.*

8 Use capability and skill matrices to emphasize the total capabilities of large teams.

Reviewing resumes has to be one of the dullest tasks for an evaluator. Simplify this review by offering capability and skill matrices like the one shown in figure 4.

See **Graphics.**

The graphic works on two levels, although it violates the guideline to keep graphics simple and uncluttered. For the senior evaluator, the graphic gives the impression that the requirements for people with a wide range of skills are both covered and backed up.

For the detailed resume evaluator, the matrix offers a way to summarize capabilities, yet perhaps not read all the resumes. The detailed evaluator will likely check a few for accuracy, then accept the matrix as accurate. Make sure that it is accurate.

EXPERIENCE
● Remedial Action
▲ Treatability/Pilot Study
■ Both
★ Key Personnel

	REMEDIAL ACTION TECHNOLOGIES																				REGULATORS							AGENCIES		
	Neutralization process	Metals precipitation	Chemical stabilization	Covering/capping contaminated soil	Installing leachate drain	Transporting/disposing haz. waste offsite	Bioremediation (insitu & above ground)	Thermal Desorption	Incineration on/offsite	Soil washing before disposal	Soil venting, soil vapor extraction	Pumping/treating contaminated ground water	Installation of slurry walls	POL recovery systems	Airstripping	Carbon absorption	Groundwater monitoring	Solvent extraction	Chemical decomposition & solidification	Others, specifically USTs, drums	CERCLA	RCRA	TSCA	CWA	CAA	OSHA	SDWA	US EPA Region 9	Guam EPA	Hawaii Dept of Health
PROGRAM MANAGER																														
★ Mark Wadsworth	●	■	●	●	●	●	●		●	▲	●	●	●	●	●	●	●	▲		▲	●	●	●	●	●	●	●			
SR. PROJECT ENGINEER																														
★ Ramona Lyons			■	■	■	■			●	●		■	■	●	●	●	■	●	■	●	■	■	■			■	■	■		
Feng Tze Hsu				●	●	●						●				●			●	●				●		●		●	●	●
Scott Parker	●	■	■	■	■	●	●	■	■	▲		■	●	●	●	■	●		■		●	●	●	●	●	●		●		●
PROJECT MANAGERS																														
★ Eric Weiss	●	●	▲	●	●	●	■	■	●	▲	■	■			●	●	●	●	▲	■	●	●	●	●	●	●		●		
Paul Cardis				●	●	●					■	■		■			●				●	■	●	●		●	●		●	
Sydnie Marchant		▲	▲			●	■	■			■	■		●		■	■				■	■				●		■		■
SR. PROJECT SCIENTIST																														

Figure 4. Use Capability and Skill Matrices to Emphasize Your Total Team's Capability. *List the positions and people on one axis and some combination of their skills and experience on the other axis. The example uses shapes to differentiate the types of experience and the role of each individual. While complex, it does serve both senior evaluators and detailed evaluators.*

9 Avoid adding photos of the people proposed unless it supports your strategy.

In general, more things can go wrong when inserting photos with resumes than can go right:

- Is the photo current? Outdated photos get the same reaction from evaluators as you have when looking at old school yearbooks.
- Do all the photos look alike? Dissimilar appearance, backgrounds, dress, or lighting detract from your claims of having an integrated team.
- Are you positive that all evaluators are free of prejudice? Appearance has no bearing on a person's ability to perform. What if someone objects to a person's gender, age, youth, race, hair color, hair length, facial hair, height, or weight?
- Do you have the time to take photos? Are the people available? Do you have the systems to incorporate and print quality photos?

See **Photographs.**

Use photos if they support your strategy. For example, if the prospect organization knows and likes the people proposed, the photo reinforces that relationship. If you have been building the relationship between the people proposed and the prospect during the capture process, use photos.

The most effective use of photos in a proposal is to emphasize teaming experience with group photos and to emphasize applications experience with site photos.

Reviews, done correctly, are the most cost-effective way to improve a proposal. Every review has three phases: preparation, the review, and implementation, with clear objectives for each phase.

The essential quality principle driving each review is to review for the right things at the right time.

For perspective, compare a proposal review to using a map, road signs, and your odometer to check your course on a car trip. A poor approach on a 200 mile trip would be to check your position when the odometer hits 200 miles, much like conducting your first and only proposal review shortly before it is due. In both instances, when on course, you are fortunate. When off course, you have little time to make corrections.

See **Process.**

Just as most drivers check their position at major cross roads, proposal professionals check progress at major decision points.

As a result, best-in-class organizations have a clearly defined business development process characterized by established process milestones and review points. They also require their review and proposal teams to be trained in their process. Each review must meet two goals:

1. **Comprehensive**: They cover the strategy, your solution, compliance, responsiveness, reasonableness, best value, schedule, management approach, and consistency.
2. **Constructive**: They maintain a positive, collaborative tone; improve the proposal; improve your win probability; and improve the ability of individuals and the team to capture future business. Require constructive recommendations; eliminate vague, negative comments.

Reviews

1. **Define your organization's process milestones and review points.**
2. **Conduct a Blue Team to review your capture plan and validate your win strategy.**
3. **Conduct a Black Hat Team to review competitors' likely strategies and solutions and update your win strategy.**
4. **Conduct a Pink Team to validate the deployment of your strategy and verify compliance.**
5. **Conduct a Red Team to evaluate the proposal for customer focus, completeness, and clear communication of your win strategy and solution.**
6. **Conduct a Gold Team to confirm the offer in the proposal entails acceptable profit and risk.**
7. **Conduct a Lessons Learned Review to determine how your processes, strategies, and people can be improved.**
8. **Follow a consistent process for each review.**
9. **Make clear review assignments and balance each reviewer's work load.**
10. **Review for consistency and compatibility between volumes and sections.**
11. **Assign a "gadfly" reviewer to skim all sections.**
12. **Select appropriate reviewers for each team and review task.**

1 Define your organization's process milestones and review points.

Best-in-class organizations believe they are successful because they have the best processes. Other organizations believe they are successful in spite of their processes.

Defining critical, value-added milestones establishes a solid framework that enables individuals to innovate while maintaining an effective, collaborative approach.

While the number of milestones varies with the size of your business and the opportunities pursued, every organization must establish its management decision milestones and the number, type, and quality standards for its reviews.

The management decision milestones and their relationship to team reviews are shown in figure 1. Add or delete milestones as appropriate. Consider the length of your business cycle, the number of people involved, the size and risk of the opportunities, and your commitment to actually follow your own process.

Briefly, the "identify opportunity" decision says that you are interested in the opportunity and it fits your strategic direction. The **Pursuit Decision** says that you have learned enough to warrant developing a capture plan. The **Bid Decision** recognizes that you cannot win without preparing a proposal, so you decide to authorize proposal development. The **Submit Decision** indicates your acceptance of the profit and risk profiles offered in the finished proposal.

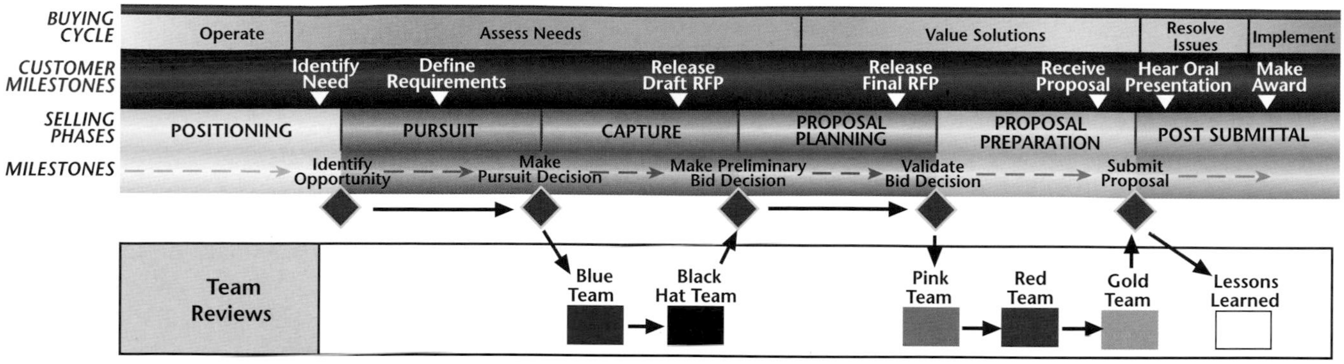

Figure 1. Relationship Between Selling Phase Milestones and Team Reviews. *Senior managers participate in the decision milestones. They decide which reviews are conducted, who participates, and how they are conducted. The arrows indicate when they occur. This framework needs to be tailored and the timeline fixed for each organization. The authority to make the "identify opportunity" decision is usually delegated to sales and not reviewed by management.*

2 Conduct a Blue Team to review your capture plan and validate your win strategy.

See **Strategy.**

Blue Team members are independent of the proposal team and knowledgeable about the prospect, your offerings and capabilities, and your competitors' offerings and capabilities.

They primarily review your capture plan, validating your win strategy and solution. The emphasis is broader than the proposal, focusing on what actions your organization can take to position your organization as the prospect's preferred choice and ideally getting the contract without a competitive proposal.

When conducting a Blue Team, keep the following checklist in mind:

- ✔ Validate thoroughness and completeness of win strategy.
- ✔ Test strategy against prospect needs and requirements.
- ✔ Validate that the strategy provides a clear advantage over competitors and their approaches.

3 Conduct a Black Hat Team to review competitors' likely strategies and solutions and update your win strategy.

Black Hat Team members are independent of the proposal team and are experts on the customer and competitors. They try to anticipate the competitors' strategies and solutions, letting you test the soundness of your strategy.

Black Hat Teams may be conducted multiple times in major competitions. Simplified versions are helpful for smaller competitions.

When conducting a Black Hat Team, keep the following checklist in mind:

- ✔ How do you shape the game?
- ✔ What are the competitors' likely strategies?
- ✔ How do you stack up against the competition in technical, price, risk, and past performance?
- ✔ What are the competitors' strengths and weaknesses?
- ✔ What issues do you ghost?
- ✔ Who does the customer prefer?
- ✔ How do you unseat the incumbent?
- ✔ How do you remain the incumbent?
- ✔ How do you become the competitor to beat?
- ✔ How can you counteract competitors' promotion and advertising campaigns?

4

Conduct a Pink Team to validate the deployment of your strategy and verify compliance.

See **Daily Team Management** *and* **Storyboards and Mock-ups.**

The Pink Team is a review of the storyboards, mock-ups, or writing plans done before beginning to draft text. Ideally, Pink Team members are independent of the proposal team. However, members are often associated with the team but must not review portions they have managed or prepared.

Team members must thoroughly understand the prospect's requirements, the bid request, your win or capture strategy, and the essential elements of preparing compliance checklists, outlines, and response matrices.

Pink Team members generally review wall mounted storyboards and mock-ups or the equivalent.

When conducting a Pink Team, keep the following checklist in mind:

- ✔ Provide information packets to reviewers well in advance.
- ✔ Provide reviewers with tables, adequate space to move around, and ample wall/ white board space.
- ✔ Organize the review team, defining responsibilities for each member.
- ✔ Display proposal section materials in the sequence that matches the flow of the proposal.
- ✔ Hold a review in-briefing to orient reviewers, to answer questions, and to ensure clear assignments.
- ✔ Document all comments and recommendations.
- ✔ Copy review outcomes and debrief the proposal team.

5

Conduct a Red Team to evaluate the proposal for customer focus, completeness, and clear communication of your win strategy and solution.

Red Team members are similar to members of the Blue and Black Hat teams. They are independent of the proposal team and offer different perspectives. The most effective teams include experts on the prospect; the prospect's industry; competitors; your organization, technology, and approach; and on preparing and presenting winning proposals.

Ideally, you have overlapping members from all the review teams to prevent conflicting direction from different review teams. All reviewers must combine their findings into one set of recommendations. **Avoid either separate or serial reviews.**

Aim to schedule the Red Team about two-thirds through the proposal development phase to give you time to respond to the recommendations. Get the most from the review by giving reviewers your entire proposal.

Depending on the discipline and formality of the Red Team, reviewers either write on copies of the proposal or use special forms. Writing on the proposal is the easiest but usually the poorest review tool.

The complicated reviews of larger proposals need to be controlled by using a formal Red Team review form. The structure will depend on the market sector and reviewers. A sample is shown in figure 2. Common elements are a log number (for tracking), section number and page, qualitative and/or quantitative score, comment or question, recommendation, reviewer name, and date.

When conducting a Red Team, keep the following checklist in mind:

- ✔ Plan the Red Team Review thoroughly.
- ✔ Appoint a single person to lead and manage the Red Team.
- ✔ Select Red Team members early, have them attend the proposal kickoff meeting, and have some serve on the Pink Team.
- ✔ Prepare a documentation set for the Red Team and provide it to members at least 3 days ahead of the review.
- ✔ Organize the Red Team to mirror the customer evaluation structure, guidelines, operation, etc.
- ✔ Conduct the Red Team based on the bid request, using a structured evaluation plan.
- ✔ Use both qualitative evaluation and quantitative scoring.
- ✔ Require a formal presentation of findings to the proposal team.
- ✔ Organize and control responses, ensuring accountability.

As soon as possible after the Red Team, assign most of the authors to other tasks. At this stage, you need a small, focused group to implement the Red Team's recommendations. A one-person rewrite is better than a team rewrite at this stage. Most authors are tired, the Red Team recommendations are hard to accept dispassionately, and excellent writing skills are often needed more than content expertise.

RED TEAM REVIEW FORM

Date: ______ Proposal: ______________________________ # ______

Reviewer: ______________ Section Title/No: ______________

EVALUATION REQUIREMENTS

Factor (Title & Description)	
Sub-Factor (Title & Description)	
Element (Title & Description)	

RFP REQUIREMENTS

Section L:	
SOW:	
CDRL:	

PROPOSAL REFERENCES

Volume Tab: ______________

Paragraph #: ______________ **Page #:** ______________

INSTRUCTION TO EVALUATOR: *Make comments and identify strengths and weaknesses on the entire section. Score at lowest level, as indicated on the Evaluation Score Sheet.*

COMMENTS/STRENGTHS/WEAKNESSES

RECOMMENDATIONS

© Shipley Associates.

RED TEAM EVALUATION SCORE SHEET

Proposal: ______________________________ # ______

Factor: ______________________________

Total Factor Weight (percent): ______________

Maximum Total Score (points): ______________

Sub-Factor/Element/ Sub-Element	WEIGHT			SCORE	
	Sub-Factor	Element	Sub-Element	Raw	Weighted
TOTAL					

© Shipley Associates.

Figure 2. Use a Red Team Review Form to Improve Consistency and Constructiveness. *While the structure will vary by market sector and organization, the forms shown are representative. Included elements permit comments to be tracked and encourage reviewers to be constructive. The form at left would be used by individual reviewers. The form at right would be used to compile the scores of all reviewers.*

6 Conduct a Gold Team to confirm the offer in the proposal entails acceptable profit and risk.

Gold Team members are senior managers in the bidding organization who are directly responsible for the offer and its execution. Gold Team members are primarily concerned about the profitability and risk of the offer in the proposal and much less about the proposal as a selling document.

Proposal contributors are often disappointed when senior management hardly look at the proposal.

One managing director explained his proposal review approach as follows:

> *At the pursuit decision, I am committing a few tenths of a percent of the value of the contract for selling. At the bid decision, I am committing up to one percent of the value of the contract to prepare the proposal. But at the Gold Team, I am looking at what we could lose, perhaps up to 25 percent of the contract value. I am responsible to the shareholders to make a profit and prevent losses.*

Conduct the Gold Team 1 to 2 weeks prior to submittal, completing the following tasks:

- ✔ Validate your understanding of prospect issues and requirements.
- ✔ Critically assess the "robustness" of the proposed technical solution.
- ✔ Verify that the proposed cost/price conforms to the price-to-win strategy.
- ✔ Assure the viability of the program management concept and approach.
- ✔ Test the final articulation of proposal discriminators.

7

Conduct a Lessons Learned Review to determine how your processes, strategies, and people can be improved.

Participants in the Lessons Learned Review are from the capture and proposal teams. The ideal would be to have the prospect's debrief at the same time, but you will probably have to incorporate it later.

Conduct the Lessons Learned Review shortly after submittal while memories are fresh. One way to keep it positive is to combine it with your victory party to thank contributors for their hard work.

When conducting a Lessons Learned Review, keep the following checklist in mind:

- ✔ How "correct" was our strategy?
- ✔ Did we have accurate, useful market intelligence? Did our cost bogey match the actual customer budget?
- ✔ Did we get high-level management support early?
- ✔ How effective was our proposal management process?
- ✔ How well did team members work together?
- ✔ Was the proposal consistent within/ between volumes? Did it conform to all bid request instructions?
- ✔ Did we produce the proposal at a reasonable cost in reasonable time?
- ✔ How did the proposal contribute to winning or losing?

8

Follow a consistent process for each review.

No matter the color of the review, use the same process to prepare for, conduct, and respond to each review.

Prepare by training both the reviewers and the proposal team in how to conduct the review and what to expect. Discuss how to keep the tone of the review positive and constructive.

Project a single operative directive for all reviews: *Tell us how we can make this a better proposal*. The review directive is not: *Tell us what is wrong with this proposal.*

After giving a summary report, give one-on-one debriefs as needed. Track both recommendations and corrections.

All review recommendations are just that, **recommendations**. The core group responsible for the win need to determine if recommendations are valid and the nature of your organization's response. Document your decisions.

9

Make clear review assignments and balance each reviewer's work load.

Without specific assignments, reviewers will gravitate to the following portions of a proposal in the order indicated:

1. Executive summary
2. Technical volume summary
3. Cost summary (not the details)
4. Personal area of expertise or interest

Some portions are overreviewed; some are not reviewed at all.

To get a first-class review, target 40 pages per reviewer per day. This is a best-in-class target in the Federal proposal sector where proposals are 90 percent unique to each competition. When more boilerplate can be tailored for each proposal, you can double this to 80 pages. The primary factor is the percentage of new material versus tailored material.

Give reviewers primary and secondary assignments. The primary assignment is mandatory. The secondary assignment is optional, depending on the time available.

Assign two people to every section. If you must compromise, focus on the most important parts first.

Reviewers must do more than read and react. They must read and analyze the bid request and your strategy (ideally before coming to the Red Team); check the outline for compliance; check their assigned sections for compliance and responsiveness; review for themes, benefits, features, discriminators, ghosts, graphics, action captions, and consistency; and complete review forms.

Address showstoppers early. By early afternoon of the first day, reviewers will have identified the showstoppers or critical deficiencies. Schedule an early meeting with the proposal core team to address each one and begin immediate corrective action.

10

See **Themes, Graphics, Action Captions, Headings,** *and* **Organization.**

Review for consistency and compatibility between volumes and sections.

The two most difficult and yet important aspects of a proposal to make consistent are costs and schedules.

Cost volumes are no longer evaluated in a vacuum. While most government competitions require a separate technical and cost evaluation, they also request some of the technical evaluators to review the cost portions after completing their technical evaluation. These evaluators check what was proposed against what was actually costed.

Of course, commercial and many international government evaluators can look at all parts simultaneously.

Schedules are abundant in government proposals and in the better nongovernment proposals because bidders must define project milestones and delivery dates. Assign at least one reviewer to identify inconsistencies in all schedules in all sections and volumes.

11

NOTE: The gadfly performs a macro review for consistent themes and content rather than a micro review for common writing style. Editing a proposal until all style differences are elminated is a laudable but usually an expensive, time-consuming, and often unrealistic goal. Do, however, eliminate obvious style shifts that distract evaluators from your message.

Assign a "gadfly" reviewer to skim all sections.

A single reviewer seldom gets to edit the entire proposal to confirm a consistent message and look. Appoint a gadfly to review the entire proposal to ensure it sells, is comprehensive, and tells a consistent story.

The gadfly lets others focus on compliance and responsiveness. The gadfly checks compliance with your quality standards for themes, format, graphics, action captions, style, headings, summaries, and introductions.

One difficulty in performing the gadfly role is that you are easily distracted by something; you follow the distraction and miss other items.

Improve your gadfly review by using the Horizontal and Vertical Review technique, summarized in figure 3 on the following page. Each review entails a complete pass through the proposal to check a single item.

Visualize your entire proposal mounted on the wall. Each section is displayed left to right in sequence from beginning to end. Individual sections are posted in page sequence, top to bottom, vertically.

In the first horizontal review, examine all themes sequentially to ensure they meet the criteria for effective themes. In the second horizontal review, check graphics with their action captions. In the third horizontal review, check headings, then check callouts in a fourth horizontal review. Check all aspects of section organization in a vertical review.

Because the theme statements, callouts, headings, graphics, action captions, summaries, introductions, and other aspects of organization are the primary style elements to project your strategy, improving their quality and consistency is one of the most economical ways to improve a proposal's win potential.

12

Select appropriate reviewers for each team and review task.

Reviewers on each review team need to have the expertise to contribute to the particular team. Increase the breadth of each review by increasing the diversity of the reviewers. Select reviewers with expertise about the following topics:

- The prospect's business and immediate needs
- The prospect's industry or business sector
- Your products and services
- Your competitors' products and services
- Your management approach and experience
- Your competitors' management approach and experience
- Your costs and your competitors' costs
- Proposal preparation and communication
- Presentation preparation and coaching, when required

Reviewers should never double as contributors because they cannot maintain a clear perspective. However, reviewers can often make constructive contributions after completing the review.

Maintain a core group of reviewers across the different review teams to avoid or at least reduce conflicting recommendations.

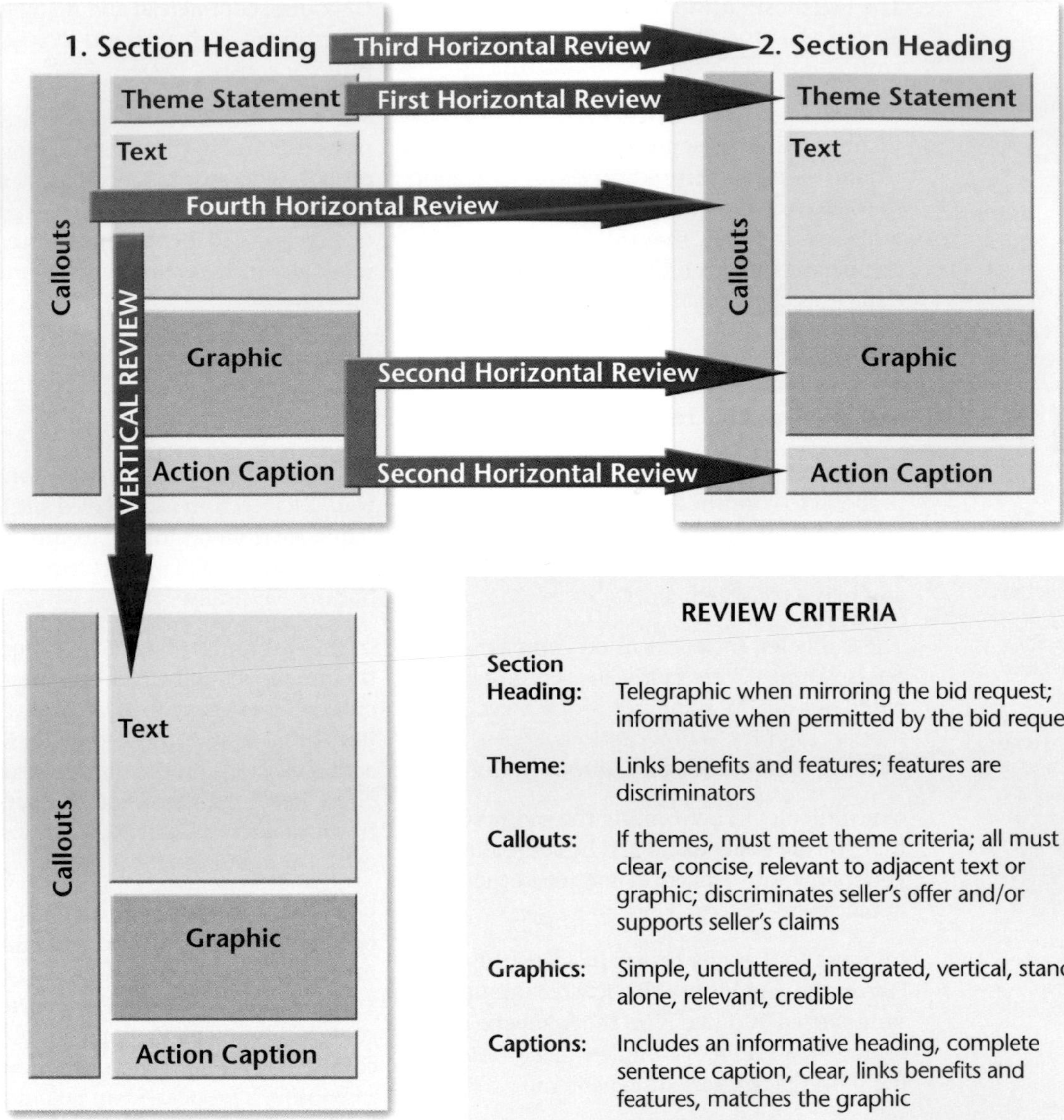

REVIEW CRITERIA

Section Heading:	Telegraphic when mirroring the bid request; informative when permitted by the bid request
Theme:	Links benefits and features; features are discriminators
Callouts:	If themes, must meet theme criteria; all must be clear, concise, relevant to adjacent text or graphic; discriminates seller's offer and/or supports seller's claims
Graphics:	Simple, uncluttered, integrated, vertical, stand alone, relevant, credible
Captions:	Includes an informative heading, complete sentence caption, clear, links benefits and features, matches the graphic
Text:	Discusses things most important to evaluator: summarizes, directly answers bid request questions, establishes order for reader, follows order introduced, sets up or disguises boilerplate, clear, concise, correct

Figure 3. Improve Review Consistency with Horizontal and Vertical Reviews. *Visualize your proposal mounted on the wall. Imagine having separate horizontal review teams reviewing themes, headings, callouts, graphics and captions sequentially. Have a vertical review team review section organization. Each review by each team or individual reviewer entails a complete pass through the entire proposal while examining a single element.*

Risk management is the seller's strategy for managing or containing the risks inherent in a proposed approach or offer. The underlying assumptions are that every offer entails risk and that risk can be contained or reduced with appropriate management.

NOTE: *Company risks* are internal concers or gaps and are not relevant unless they affect *proposal* or *performance* risk.

Some sellers prefer to avoid any discussion of risk. They correctly see risk as negative but incorrectly avoid discussing risk because it is a negative topic.

Prospects know every offer entails risk; the best practice is to explicitly discuss how the risk in your offer will be managed. Government buyers of complicated systems are well aware of risk and require risk management plans in proposals. As a result, risk management practices, including formal discussions of risk in proposals, are more advanced in government market sectors than the nongovernment sectors.

Risk is normally associated with cost and schedule, but risk permeates every aspect of a program, including program management, technical performance, quality, service support, and security. Proposal teams often struggle to demonstrate that their solution offers the least risk. However, most prospects recognize that superior value justifies increased risk. The key is to understand what degree of risk is acceptable to each prospect.

Risk Management

1. **Recognize all aspects of risk.**
2. **Develop a risk management strategy.**
3. **Consider placing a risk management paragraph in your executive summary.**
4. **Analyze and discuss risk and risk management similarly in each proposal section.**

1 Recognize all aspects of risk.

Evaluators normally focus on risk in two evaluation criteria items: proposal risk and performance risk.

Risk assessment addresses both risk *magnitude* and the *probability* of occurance.

Proposal risk is the risk associated with a seller's proposed approach to meeting the bid request requirements. Proposal risk includes both your technical and management approach.

Performance risk involves evaluating the seller's ability to perform based on relevant present and past performance. Evaluators consider the data included in your proposal and data gathered independently. Evaluators assess several factors:

1. Is the experience you cite relevant?
2. What was the result?
3. What did you learn that reduces risk on this contract?

Risk is not limited to the prime contractor. Performance evaluations include all proposed members of your team, including partners, other corporate divisions, subcontractors, and vendors.

In the U.S., the Office of Federal Procurement Policy (OFPP) has increasingly emphasized performance risk. Other sophisticated buyers are doing the same.

Buyers realize that minor savings in the purchase price are often lost when they select a higher risk contractor. To better identify positive or negative patterns in contractors' performance records, OFPP has taken several initiatives to standardize the evaluation of performance risk:

1. Evaluate corporate performance rather than just experience. (What if the result of the experience was poor?)
2. Check references of past customers.
3. Develop standard questionnaires to improve both quality and comparability.
4. Encourage contractors to complete customer satisfaction surveys every 6 months.

Seeing what sophisticated buyers are evaluating begins to suggest what should be in your proposal.

2 Develop a risk management strategy.

Risks are both *managed* and *mitigated*, but rarely eliminated.

Assume prospects will learn about your past performance, either on their own or through your competitors. Most prospects develop a pretty good information network within their industry.

Developing a risk management strategy is a key part of your overall strategy development. Use the same strategic approach:

See **Strategy**.

1. **Emphasize** your strengths.
2. **Mitigate** your weaknesses.
3. **Neutralize** your competitors' strengths.
4. **Highlight** your competitors' weaknesses.

And do all this without mentioning your competitors by name.

Where you have demonstrated strong performance, tell the prospect why you are the low risk choice. Include testimonials, quotations from performance reviews, award fee ratings, published data, and data that you have collected to support your claims. What others say about you is more credible than what you say about yourself.

Where your performance was weak, emphasize what you learned and what changes you have made. If you try to hide your weaknesses, prospects assume nothing has changed.

Neutralize competitors' strengths by discussing the lessons learned from studying industry best practices or by hiring people with similar performance experience.

Highlight competitors' weaknesses by citing trade-off analyses of different approaches. Or cite your early failures or known industry failures, then contrast them with your recent successful performance.

3 Consider placing a risk management paragraph in your executive summary.

Risk is often a discriminator and can be an effective way to ghost competitors. Decision makers and senior influencers are more likely to worry about risk, what could go wrong, than about relatively minor price or technical differences.

See **Executive Summary**.

Identify the top two or three areas of greatest risk, then briefly discuss your risk management approach in the executive summary. If competitors do not discuss risk, evaluators may assume they do not understand the problem. Your discussion must be credible and real, or it could backfire.

Discuss risk management in one or two short paragraphs as shown in the following example:

> Software development projects have been notoriously difficult to estimate correctly and to deliver on schedule. Acme Software has developed sophisticated and detailed metrics from all of our software development projects since 1989, enabling us to significantly reduce performance risk. Our specific management approach is discussed in detail in the section 3.2 Software Project Management.

Another best practice is to support your risk management with a chart similar to the example in figure 1.

Risk area:	*Risk assessment:*	*Impact with our proposed management approach:*	*Summary of our approach:*	*Discussed in proposal section:*
Key personnel not available	Medium	Low	All positions filled & backups identified	4.5
Limited construction area on site	High	Low	Use modular design, construct modules offsite, then assemble on site	2.3

Figure 2-3. Major Risks Mitigated. *The two biggest risks to on-time completion have been addressed in our risk management plan.*

Figure 1. Place a Risk Management Matrix in the Executive Summary. *Consider supporting a short risk management discussion with a matrix that summarizes the major risks and assesses the risk both without and with your mitigation approach. If space permits, add columns like the two on the right that summarize your approach and indicate where your approach is discussed in the proposal.*

4 Analyze and discuss risk and risk management similarly in each proposal section.

Top-level discussions of risk must be supported where relevant in each proposal section. Evaluators look for an established, proven risk management process to identify, assess, track, manage/mitigate risk.

Increase the credibility of risk discussions and cut writing time by following a consistent process to both analyze risk and draft your response.

See **Organization** *and* **Theme Statements**.

Risk Analysis Procedure

1. Identify all risk areas.
2. Assess the risks (low, moderate, or high), on a defined scale.
3. Prioritize each risk according to its potential impact on the solution, schedule, or cost.
4. Determine and analyze the causes, not the symptoms, of the risks.
5. Develop alternative, backup, or parallel procedures to track, manage, reduce, or eliminate the risks.
6. Assess the modified risk with your proposed risk management approach, considering how the changes could impact other aspects of your solution.

Draft your risk management story in a similar style in each major proposal section.

Writing Procedure

1. Introduce each risk management section with a theme statement, a section summary, and a preview or introduction.
2. Consider including a more detailed form of the risk management matrix illustrated in figure 1.
3. Identify and define all relevant risks. Be complete and honest but not alarmist.
4. Follow each defined risk with an explanation of how the risk will be managed. Cite clear decision points tied to your proposed alternative, backup, or parallel approach. Demonstrate your ability to manage this risk by citing experience, independent research, or trade studies.

Sales letters include any document sent to a prospect that is designed to advance a potential sale. Effective sales letters are customer focused, clear, concise, and well organized.

See **Customer Focus** *and* **Organization**.

See **Executive Summaries** *and* **Letter Proposals**.

The purpose of each sales letter is to advance the sale to the next realistically achievable objective, clearly supported by the benefits to the prospect. Writers of sales letters must be able to answer two questions:

1. What is my purpose in writing this letter?
2. What would I like the reader to agree to do next?

When sales letters fail, the writer often failed to answer the previous two questions. Clear and correct writing is an effective way to help readers understand you and accept your ideas. Poor writing causes confusion, potential distrust, and possible rejection of your ideas.

The process described for strategizing, organizing, drafting, and revising effective sales letters is similar to the approach recommended to prepare executive summaries and letter proposals. Both are specialized forms of sales letters.

Many types of sales letters are written during a typical sales cycle, as shown in figure 1. Note how the objective of each letter changes as the sale advances.

Sales Letters

1. **Follow a disciplined, four-step writing process to quickly and consistently write effective sales letters.**
2. **Use the Strategy Template to strategize your sales letters.**
3. **Follow the Four-Box organizational structure.**
4. **Draft quickly and uncritically, following your Four-Box Organizer.**
5. **Revise to add value, clarity, and brevity.**

NOTE: Five model sales letters are included in **Model Documents,** pp. 230–235

Figure 1. Effective Sales Letters Have Clear Objectives. *Sales professionals prepare a wide variety of letters. For each type of sales letter a typical sales objective is suggested, specifically, what the seller would like the prospect to agree to do next. Note how the objective of each sales letter changes as the sale advances.*

1

Follow a disciplined, four-step writing process to quickly and consistently write effective sales letters.

The best sales professionals plan carefully and make every client contact count. Sometimes writing a sales letter is easy; everything flows. Other times writers struggle and dislike the result.

The only way to quickly prepare effective sales letters every time is to follow a disciplined process, one that you both understand and have practiced. Prepare effective sales letters by following the four steps listed below and summarized in figure 2:

1. **Strategize**—Determine what you want your prospect to agree to do next and why the prospect should agree to do it.
2. **Organize**—Present a persuasive argument from the prospect's perspective. Organize your presentation around the prospect's interests and subordinate the details about your organization, services, and products.
3. **Draft**—Draft quickly and expect imperfection. You will save time and reduce your frustration.
4. **Revise**—Allow time between drafting and revising. Then efficiently revise in three stages, fixing major items before minor items. First, check your major points for clarity. Second, rework paragraphs and sentences to make them more concise. Third, check and correct your grammar, punctuation, and spelling.

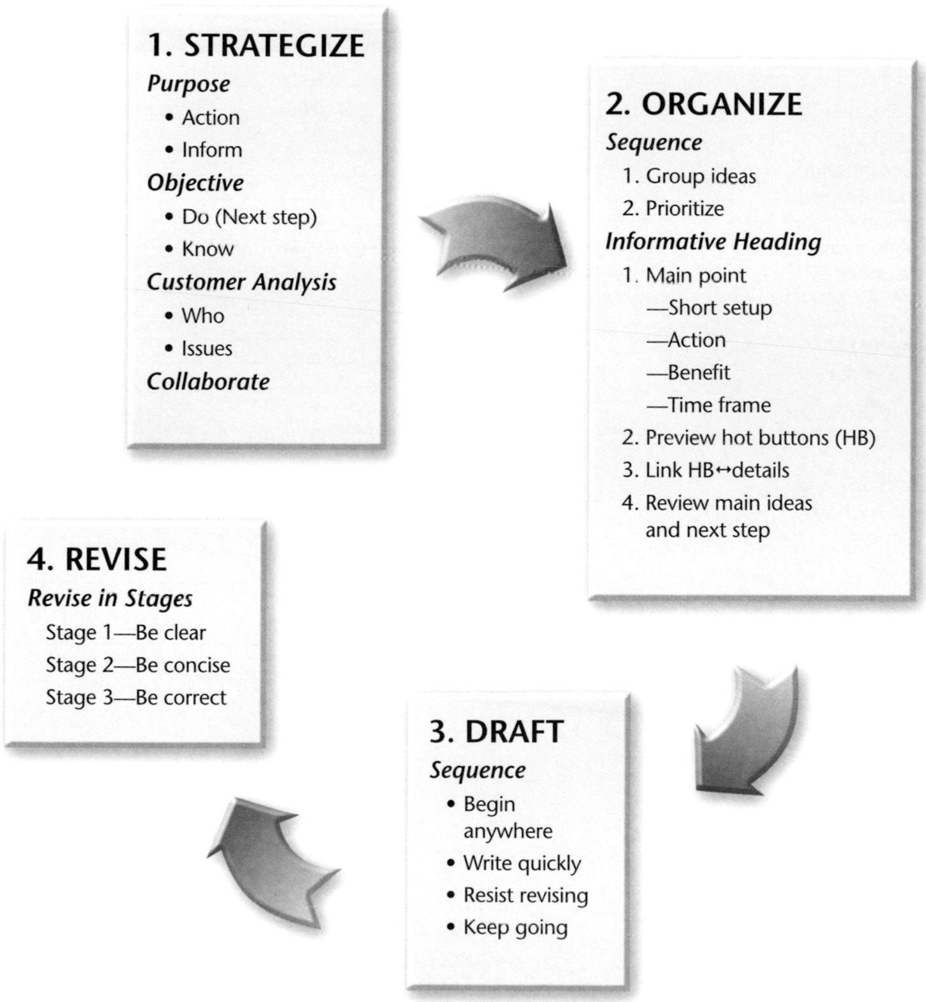

Figure 2. The Customer-Focused Writing Process. *Write persuasive sales letters every time by following a proven, repeatable process. Details of this four-step process are outlined here, discussed in the following rules, and illustrated in the model documents section of the* Proposal Guide.

2 Use the Strategy Template to strategize your sales letters.

NOTE: Purpose is best defined as what the writer wants the reader to do and to know.

Prepare your strategy by completing the Strategy Template shown in figure 3. Use the Strategy Template every time until you are thoroughly comfortable with this process.

Many sales documents fail because they are vague and unclear, accurately reflecting the fuzzy thinking and minimal planning of the author. Ask two questions to test the strategy of any sales document:

- What was the writer's purpose?
- What does the writer want the reader to agree to do next? *(action)*

The first question is broad. The second is focused. The purpose of most sales documents is to obtain action or to inform. Action is required to advance the sale, the preferred purpose. To inform is a relatively weak purpose.

An effective sales letter motivates the prospect to the desired action because of the persuasive information in the letter.

What does the prospect need to know that would persuade the prospect to take that action? A prospect-focused strategy is based on the assumption that people act in their own best interest. If you are looking for a Win-Win situation, then your prospect's objectives and your objectives must align.

In complex sales, sales documents often have multiple readers, including the decision maker and others who influence the decision maker. List the various prospects or readers, then list their issues. Whenever possible, develop issues collaboratively with prospects.

NOTE: The Strategy Template is most useful when developing a new document. Experienced and skilled writers can skip this template under two conditions:

1. You are revising an existing document.
2. You are confident your strategy is correct.

As your skills improve, go directly to the Four-Box Organizer found in guideline 5.

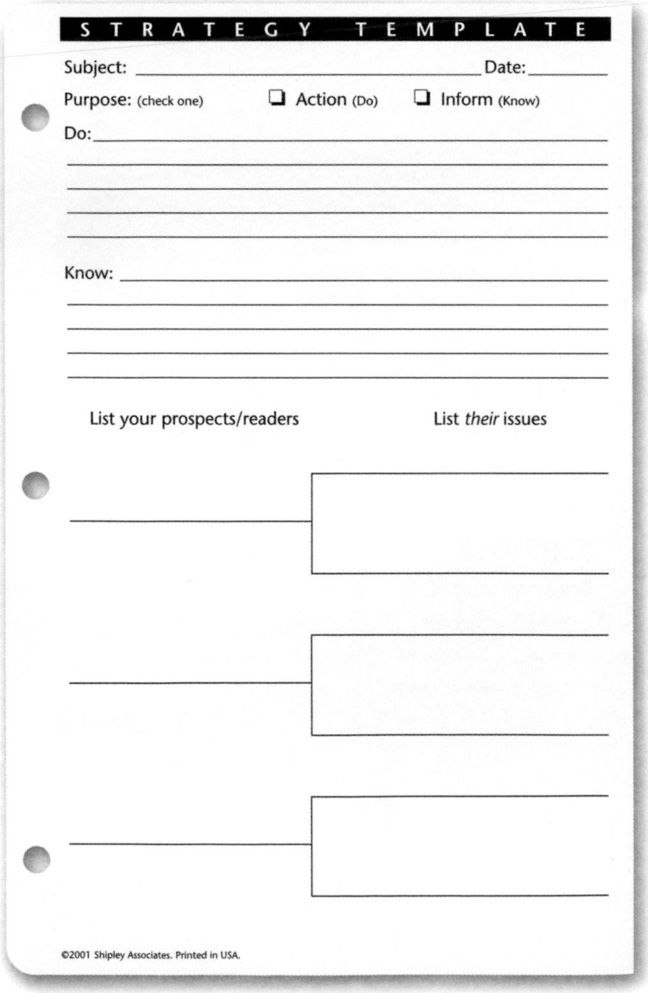

STRATEGY TEMPLATE

Subject: ______ Date: ______

Purpose: (check one) ❏ Action (Do) ❏ Inform (Know)

Do: ______

Know: ______

List your prospects/readers | List *their* issues

©2001 Shipley Associates. Printed in USA.

Figure 3. Use the Strategy Template to Develop Your Strategy. *Using the Strategy Template will help you develop a more persuasive strategy. Avoid two errors: (1) dismissing the Strategy Template as too obvious, and (2) filling it with empty jargon.*

3

Follow the Four-Box organizational structure.

Use the Four-Box Organizer shown in figure 4 to present your argument in a customer-focused, persuasive style. Use the annotations in the margin and within the template as a guide. Your ideas will evolve as you move from the Strategy Template to the Four-Box Organizer. Expect imperfection.

See **Choosing Correct Words, Customer Focus,** *and* **Lists.**

Draft an informative subject line. Summarize your most significant *Do/Know* statements. Try to include benefits and features. Make it as short as you can while still being fully informative. The ideal subject line length is about 6 to 12 words. Shorter is less likely to be informative; longer is more likely to reduce impact and readership.

Begin with a signal word to immediately announce the action desired and to signal the content to the reader. Typical signal words vary with your purpose:

ACTION PURPOSE	INFORMATION PURPOSE
DO:	**KNOW:**
Proposal	Agenda
Recommendation	Notice
Request	Announcement
Invitation	Response

Good example

SIGNAL WORD

Summary of most significant Do/Know statements

BENEFITS *(Optional)*

Invitation to meet with Silicon Glen's Exec to discuss how outsourcing can reduce office support costs.

In Box 1, use setups if needed to connect to a previous event. Most readers are initially trying to place your sales letter in context. Keep your setups short. Often a short phrase will suffice:

Good examples

- In our September 15 phone conversation, you said coping with rapid change and reducing cost were driving your fiscal year planning by . . .
- As you requested in our January 15 meeting, . . .

Then summarize the prospect's overall need in a customer-focused manner. Prospect ownership of the need must be explicit.

In Box 2, establish the prospect's issues, tying them to the overall need and making ownership explicit. For emphasis, introduce issues in a display list. List them as the prospect did or in decreasing order of importance to the prospect.

In Box 3, link all of your information to one of the prospect's issues. If you cannot forge the link, your information is irrelevant. Eliminate irrelevant or extraneous information. Address each client issue in the order introduced in Box 2.

In Box 4, restate your main ideas linked to the benefits to the prospect. Indicate the action required, and directly state the next step. Be proactive. Avoid ending with stale jargon or cliches.

4

Draft quickly and uncritically, following your Four-Box Organizer.

Most sales professionals find that after completing the Strategy Template and Four-Box Organizer, their letters practically write themselves.

Draft quickly, expecting imperfection. Writing is creative; revising is critical. If you try to do both at the same time, you will do neither well, and you will take much longer.

Frequently refer to the Strategy Template and Four-Box Organizer to stay focused.

5 Revise to add value, clarity, and brevity.

Revise in three stages to save time. Fix the major items before the minor items. View revision as an opportunity to make your sales letter better. This is a realistic goal if you have followed the first three steps. If not, you often feel the urge to start over.

Follow the three-step revision process outlined in figure 6.

Few of us can see our own mistakes. Always ask someone else to review your sales letters.

The Peer Review Template, shown in figure 5, is a tool designed to help peers and managers constructively review sales letters.

FOUR-BOX ORGANIZER

SUBJECT LINE (signal word, summary of significant *Do and Know*)

1. PURPOSE (Do/Know)

2. PREVIEW
-
-
-

3. DETAILS

4. REVIEW

©Shipley Associates. Printed in USA.

Figure 4. The Four-Box Organizer. *Use this template to convert your strategy from the Strategy Template into a customer-focused, clearly organized, and persuasive sales document. Follow the suggestions in the template. Use this template to organize every sales letter.*

PEER REVIEW TEMPLATE

What was the writer's purpose?

What did the writer want the reader to agree to do/know next?

Would the requested action be the next realistically achievable step most likely to advance this sale? ❑ Yes ❑ No

If not, what do you recommend?

List the prospect's/reader's hot buttons:

©2001 Shipley Associates. Printed in USA.

Figure 5. Peer Review Template. *Managers and peers can improve their coaching of writers by (1) comparing the results of the Peer Review Template with the information found in the Strategy Template and the Four-Box Organizer and (2) evaluating sales documents using only the Peer Review Template. If this template is difficult to complete, the document is unlikely to be successful.*

REVISE IN THREE STAGES

FIRST STAGE REVISION (BE CLEAR)

Subject Line
- Begin with a *signal* word.
- State what the reader should *Do* or *Know.*
- Include *Benefit* (optional).

Objective
- State up front.
- Be specific and clear.

Setups
- Use if necessary.
- Keep short.

Customer Focus
- Name prospect before yourself.
- State benefits before features.
- Make hot button ownership explicit.
- Tie hot buttons to your solution.

Content and Organization
- Summarize; then preview your content.
- Organize around prospect's hot buttons.

Key Information Highlighted
- Use informative headings and subheadings.
- Use lists.
- Use white space for emphasis.
- Use **boldface**, underlining, *italics*, CAPITALS, color.
- Use clear graphics with action captions.

SECOND STAGE REVISION (BE CONCISE)

Paragraphs
- Use six lines maximum.
- Use one major idea per paragraph.

Sentences (15-20 word maximum)
- Use active voice, *Who does what?*
- Use strong verbs.
- Cut false subjects: *it, there.*

Words
- Cut gobbledygook.
- Cut wordy phrases.
- Solve word problems.
- Cut the fat.

THIRD STAGE REVISION (BE CORRECT)

Proofread Thoroughly
- Check grammar, punctuation, spelling, word choice, and number usage.

Know Where to Find the Rules
- Franklin Covey *Style Guide.*
- Current dictionary.
- Specialized references.

Figure 6. Revise in Three Stages. *In the first stage, address content. Make sure you present the right message about the prospect's issues and offer real value. In the second stage, make your message as concise as possible. In the third stage, correct spelling, punctuation, and grammar. Careless errors suggest potential poor quality elsewhere.*

Scheduling your proposal is essential to visualize the task ahead and monitor progress. Even a one-person, single-day proposal benefits from having a schedule.

Common scheduling principles apply equally to proposals. Preparing a realistic schedule requires a clear understanding of each task and the capability of the individuals assigned. The task of developing a schedule clarifies your understanding of the proposal preparation project.

The complexity of the schedule depends on the size of the proposal and the number, expertise, and location of contributors.

One of the most common mistakes in proposal management is poor scheduling. Tasks originally regarded as optional become mandatory. The time lost to nonproposal preparation activities at the beginning and end leaves surprisingly little time for writing.

Something goes wrong on every proposal. Expect and prepare to cope with changes. The following broad guidelines will improve your overall scheduling effectiveness:

1. Consider the total time available, then deduct 10 percent for a reserve to handle unanticipated tasks and problems. Use the remaining 90 percent to schedule all proposal activities.
2. Build a list of events that have to be scheduled. A generic list of potential proposal preparation tasks is given in figure 1. Schedule the major events first, then add the finer details or granularity later.
3. Complete the major milestone schedule prior to the kickoff meeting. After the kickoff meeting, build an "inch-stone" schedule, planning events to the day and hour (see guideline 6).

Scheduling

1. **Develop a proposal schedule backwards from the drop-dead date.**
2. **Schedule a proposal as you would any other project, using the same scheduling tools.**
3. **Minimize sequential tasks. Maximize parallel tasks.**
4. **Realistically estimate the time required for specific tasks based on your own standards.**
5. **Assign a person to each task with start and end dates. Avoid assigning people indefinitely to the proposal.**
6. **Divide major tasks into smaller, discrete tasks.**
7. **Avoid scheduling weekends and holidays.**
8. **Know and plan proposal production time.**
9. **Schedule time for all planned reviews, allowing time to implement valid recommendations.**
10. **Lock down the project scope early to enable contributors to work efficiently in parallel.**
11. **Schedule the time to prepare the essentials of the Proposal Management Plan (requirements checklist, outline, strategy, response matrix, and style sheet).**
12. **Maintain a continuous focus on meeting every schedule date.**

1 Develop a proposal schedule backwards from the drop-dead date.

Begin at the drop-dead or due date because late proposals are usually eliminated.

Schedule time to deliver the proposal. Electronic delivery may be faster but can increase production time.

Then consider print time. Outside printing often takes longer than in-house because printers try to keep their facilities producing at capacity. Your job deadline may be affected by the printing vendor's entire workload. Allow time for a page-turn after printing to check each copy.

Consider time for the final senior management buy-off, perhaps a final Gold Team. Then schedule time to prepare for the Gold Team.

When you begin to lose perspective, examine the proposal events or tasks from the beginning. How much time was lost getting the bid request to the proposal manager? In a 28-day schedule, time lost at the beginning waiting for the bid request and at the end for reviewing and production leaves perhaps 14 days to actually develop the proposal.

ACTIVITY	START DATE	END DATE
Set budget and scope	____	____
Receive approval to start	____	____
Determine review cycles	____	____
Develop baseline solution	____	____
Draft Proposal Management Plan (PMP)	____	____
Mock up executive summary	____	____
Train proposal contributors	____	____
Bid request release	____	____
Receive bid request in-house	____	____
Analyze bid request	____	____
Prepare compliance matrix	____	____
Update strategy & PMP	____	____
Review solution, strategy, and PMP	____	____
Prepare & conduct kickoff meeting	____	____
Freeze design	____	____
Initiate detailed costing	____	____
Develop storyboards	____	____
Pink Team review (of storyboards)	____	____
Create first draft	____	____
Final graphics cutoff	____	____
Receive & review costs	____	____
Prepare & conduct Red Team	____	____
Revise draft	____	____
Finalize costs	____	____
Final review of draft	____	____
Final executive summary to production	____	____
Final text revisions & editing	____	____
Desktop publishing	____	____
Gold Team	____	____
Final production & assembly	____	____
Page turn	____	____
Packaging	____	____
Delivery time	____	____
Due date	____	____

Figure 1. Prepare the Proposal Schedule Backwards. *Add or delete items as appropriate, then develop your proposal schedule backwards from the delivery date. Tasks are listed in an approximate chronological order. Start dates and end dates will overlap with parallel task scheduling.*

2 Schedule a proposal as you would any other project, using the same scheduling tools.

Simple timeline charts are adequate for simple proposals. Full critical path software tools are more appropriate for complex proposals.

Using the scheduling software tool that you know is often more critical than trying to select the best package.

3 Minimize sequential tasks. Maximize parallel tasks.

Clear task descriptions, quality standards, and start and end dates enable contributors to work in parallel without conflicts. Fast-track construction managers plan parallel tasks to radically shorten total construction time. Do the same on your proposal.

If you hear contributors saying that they are waiting on someone else to finish his or her task before they start, you have sequential tasks and are probably in trouble.

4

Realistically estimate the time required for specific tasks based on your own standards.

Too few organizations have developed time standards or metrics for specific proposal tasks. They simply do what they can in the time available.

However, many organizations have been estimating document production time for years. Begin by adopting similar standards for similar proposal development tasks until you develop your own standards.

Meaningful productivity standards must be accompanied by complexity and quality standards. Standards are most useful to show trends in your organization and much less useful to compare different organizations.

For example, bidders on complex, custom systems will have more design costs incorporated in their proposal writing standards than bidders of relatively similar products and services. A one-page-per-day standard for proposal preparation in one organization may be superior to an eight-page-per-day standard in another.

Also see **Production.**

Extensive use of proposal boilerplate and search and retrieval software can radically increase the pages per day a writer can produce, but what is the effect on the quality and win rate? Without a clearly implemented strategy and a clearly organized document, you may simply be rearranging the deck chairs on the Titanic; you are still going to lose.

Figure 2 offers some metrics to estimate writing time per page depending on the availability, relevance, and quality of boilerplate available.

TASK	TIME
Writing—new material	4 pages/day
Writing—extensive revision	8-10 pages/day
Writing—minimal revision	20-25 pages/day
Simple graphic	1-2 hours each
Complex graphic	2-4 hours
Retouch photo	1-2 hours
Complex illustration	1 + days
Red Teaming (new)	40 pages/day
Red Teaming (with extensive boilerplate)	80 pages/day
DTP (clean input)	30-60 pages/day
DTP with graphics development	5-10 pages/day

Figure 2. Estimate Time Standards by Task. *Use these time standards as a start until you develop more appropriate standards for your organization. Requiring less time in your organization is not necessarily excellent performance nor is taking more time a sign of poor performance.*

5

Assign a person to each task with start and end dates. Avoid assigning people indefinitely to the proposal.

While once common, too many organizations continue to assign people to participate on proposal teams from the kickoff to submittal. Get them on the team; then get them off. While your scheduling is more detailed and complex, you will have fewer individuals to manage at any single time and will cut preparation costs.

Assign one person primary responsibility, even if multiple people contribute. In some cases that person might not be the primary writer or content expert.

Consider the time to complete each task, determine the time available per day, then set the start and end date. Pay for the task, not show-up time.

6

Divide major tasks into smaller, discrete tasks.

Assigning major tasks with relatively long completion times increases your risk. If the contributor stalls early, you find out too late to respond.

Contrast the following two approaches to section writing assignments. Assume that the assignment is made on the first Monday, and the completed section is due on the second Friday.

Approach 1 (General and poor)

Take the bid request, identify and answer all of the implementation and management questions, and complete a responsive management section in 2 weeks. (Actual elapsed time is 10 days, excluding the weekend, or 12 days, including the weekend.)

Approach 2 (Specific and recommended)

You have 10 days to complete a reviewed and approved management section. Weekends are not scheduled. Each task is due at the date and time indicated on the following table.

Schedule *due times* rather than *due dates* to smooth work flow, as shown in figure 3. Setting *due times* may also convey a more disciplined tone for proposal development tasks.

See **Daily Team Management.**

DAY	TIME	TASK
1	2 pm	Review bid request response requirements and complete section outline. Identify potential omitted or misaligned tasks and recommend appropriate reassignments.
2	9 am	Draft all section themes to follow first- and second-level headings. Write on transparencies and come prepared to review them with the team.
3+	time	(Additional tasks not listed here)
⋮	⋮	⋮
10	2 pm	Submit completed draft as both electronic file and hard copy, reviewed and approved by your volume manager.

Figure 3. Schedule *Due Times* for Tasks. *Smooth work flow by setting both due dates and due times for proposal development tasks.*

7

Avoid scheduling weekends and holidays.

You may have to work on weekends and holidays, but do not plan to. Contributors find it negative from the beginning and lose commitment to a winning effort. Many feel abused. Contributors feel that if management considers winning competitive new business important, they should assign additional resources.

When you do ask contributors to work weekends, management must be visible, both as a morale booster and to encourage continued commitment to quality work.

When contributors routinely work more than 10 hours per day and 6 days per week, productivity tends to drop to little better than what could be done in a 40-hour work week.

8

Know and plan proposal production time.

See **Production.**

Production people tend to be the most routinely abused individuals on a proposal team. They inherit the consequences of all the scheduling and management mistakes. After they work extended days and weekends to complete a proposal on time, management tends to view that performance as standard.

Consider adding 50 percent to your production estimate to cope with potential time delays. Use any extra time to polish the proposal, do a thorough page-turn to identify small errors, and increase the overall quality of the production.

9

Schedule time for all planned reviews, allowing time to implement valid recommendations.

See **Reviews.**

Delaying scheduled reviews results in the following common problems:

- Individuals completing their sections on time are delayed.
- Reviewers have conflicts, forcing a change of reviewer who has less time to prepare.
- Reviewers are rushed, reducing the quality of the review.
- You lose time to respond to reviewers' recommendations.

One reviewer can do a quality review on approximately 40 pages per day. If the proposal uses extensive boilerplate and has had previous reviews by the assigned and other evaluators, you can increase this to 80 pages per day but the quality will drop.

10

Lock down the project scope early to enable contributors to work efficiently in parallel.

The project schedule should be distributed at the kickoff meeting. Avoid schedule changes except those prompted by external events, such as changes in the bid request.

Major changes indicate poor management. Frequent minor changes, 99 percent of them delays, suggest a lack of discipline or that proposal managers are not honest with their teams. Contributors begin to expect delays and are less disciplined about completing tasks on time.

11 Schedule the time to prepare the essentials of the Proposal Management Plan (requirements checklist, outline, strategy, response matrix, and style sheet).

See **Proposal Management Plan.**

Pressure from management or impending deadlines prompts proposal managers to schedule kickoff meetings before the essential elements of the PMP are complete. Contributors then commence work that is loosely defined, requiring more extensive revisions or even starting over.

Avoid rework by doing things right the first time. Clearly define each task assignment, including clear quality standards. Contributors seldom meet a proposal manager's expectations when they do not understand their tasks.

While planning seems to delay initial work, planning actually saves more time than it takes.

12 Maintain a continuous focus on meeting every schedule date.

See **Daily Team Management.**

Holding a daily stand-up meeting is one of the best ways to keep contributors focused on meeting every schedule date. Remind them what must be accomplished and the impact of slipped dates.

Planning smaller, discrete tasks also helps maintain schedule focus. Improve schedule focus by using one of the following approaches:

- Send short, concise, daily e-mails to each contributor, especially if the team is dispersed.
- Post an enlarged schedule on the proposal room wall. Contributors see it daily. Refer to the schedule in every morning stand-up.

Some proposal managers schedule two stand-up meeetings each working day. They quickly review progress and expectations for the day in a morning meeting. They use a mid- to late-afternoon meeting to review inch-stone progress and unresolved issues.

Service proposals and product proposals are more alike than many writers think, especially when used in complex sales. In complex sales, few buyers select products or services because of their appearance. Winners are selected based on the benefits that the buyer believes will be delivered.

Certainly products are tangible and services are intangible. However, thinking products are easier to sell than services reflects an immature or incomplete view of the sales process.

Successful sellers of both products and services help their prospects build a vivid vision of how prospects' processes will improve after selecting their solution.

While prospects may feel more comfortable paying for a physical product than an intangible service, the product only promises to deliver something that is intangible, just like the service.

Prospects have the difficult task of selecting services without knowing the quality of the services to be delivered, so they rely on indicators:

- Experience with the seller
- Promptness, clarity, and courtesy of responses to inquiries
- Relationship with the sales team
- Quality of presentations and demonstrations made
- Relevant experience and performance of the selling organization and the individuals proposed
- Customer testimonials
- Quality of the proposal submitted
- Price, whether high or low

Your success with these indicators will help demonstrate your understanding of the services needed.

Service Proposals

1. **Create a vision for the prospect of what life will be like after you deliver your solution.**
2. **Visualize your solution with graphics and good writing.**
3. **Discriminate services using people.**
4. **Discriminate services with clear descriptions of what will be done.**
5. **Present service processes graphically.**
6. **Exploit or attack incumbency, as relevant.**
7. **Cut costs, not margins.**

1

Create a vision for the prospect of what life will be like after you deliver your solution.

Every sale of a service or product impacts the buyer's processes:

- Reduces operating or capital cost
- Improves quality
- Improves service level
- Reduces cycle time
- Improves profitability

The vision you create for your prospect must cover three areas:

1. What and how services and products will be delivered
2. How people and processes in the prospect's organization will be impacted
3. How individuals and the prospect's organization will benefit, both tangibly and intangibly

2

Visualize your solution with graphics and good writing.

See **Graphics** *and* **Photographs.**

Both graphics and text are essential for visualizing your solution and making it memorable.

Consider how images are used in advertizing to indicate customer satisfaction. Advertisers present images of happy people using the product or experiencing or recalling the service to convey feelings of satisfaction.

Novelists use words to evoke such vivid personal images of events, places, and emotions that many people are disappointed when they see the movie. Or recall how people viewing images of an event often remark, "You had to be there."

To improve your proposals, consider the following methods to convey a service or product vision in each of the three areas listed under guideline 1:

1. **What and how services and products will be delivered**

   Use graphics such as sequential sketches, photos, or icons with short subcaptions.

   Use text to present lists of sequential tasks or actions that will be taken.

2. **How people and processes in the prospect's organization will be impacted**

   Use graphics such as sequential sketches or photos to show what their employees will do or see.

   Use screen prints of the images operators will see on their operations console.

   Use photos of other customers using the same products or experiencing the same or similar services.

   Use text to describe the impact of a product or service, as in the following emotional proposal excerpt for a cancer detection device:

   Imagine, doctors operating on a patient can point a RxT laser at live tissue, analyze the reflected light through a spectroscope and PC, and immediately determine if the tissue is malignant or benign. Further imagine that this can be real within 16 months if you fund this program.

   The following example was used to sell a design contract:

   A proposal for a traffic management system for a major northern European city used 2-1/2 pages to describe how the system would cope with a typical winter morning commute. The scenario described minute by minute how traffic was rerouted to cope with snowfall, accidents, and temporary tie-ups.

3. **How individuals and the prospect's organization will benefit, both tangibly and intangibly**

   Use graphics such as individuals appearing relaxed, happy, satisfied, and more energetic, whether using the product or experiencing the service.

   Combine before-and-after images. An architectural firm took photos of a proposed site, then superimposed images of the proposed or a similar facility.

   Use familiar icons such as images of stacks of coins, bills, or gold bars to represent monetary benefits or smaller trash bins or fewer trash bins to represent reduced waste.

   Use text to help evaluators visualize the impact of *not* having an item or service, like the cancer detection device discussed earlier in item 2:

   Imagine the consequences when a surgeon removes too little tissue. Further imagine the impact when a surgeon removes too much tissue.

   Contrast real-time cancer detection with the alternative biopsy method. Doctors send patients through recovery while waiting for test results. Patients and their loved ones are subjected to a painful, higher-risk, and anxiety-filled recovery, perhaps followed by further surgery.

3

Discriminate services using people.

See **Discriminators** *and* **Resumes**.

People are potentially the most powerful discriminator when selling services. To be a discriminator, two conditions must be met:

1. The feature cited must be unique; clearly, no two people's abilities are identical.
2. The prospect must care about the uniqueness of the person or people, a condition often created during the sales process.

Use the following methods to discriminate your people:

- Always name the people you propose to fill key positions. Correctly identifying which positions are key also demonstrates your understanding of the tasks required.
- Consider naming the people proposed for additional positions.
- Indicate the percentage of their time to be devoted to this project and the percentage of time already committed to other projects.
- Introduce the key people to the prospect organization's influencers and decision maker during the capture process, prior to submitting your proposal.
- Consider ghosting typical bait-and-switch tactics to emphasize your honest, realistic approach.
- Tailor all resumes. Place abbreviated resumes in the body of your proposal.
- Include individual photos of the people proposed only if you have previously introduced them to the prospect organization.
- Include photos of groups or teams containing individuals proposed if they show previous teaming experience or specific performance experience.
- Use matrices to summarize the directly relevant skills and experience of individuals on your team.

4

Discriminate services with clear descriptions of what will be done.

Take a hint from some of the most experienced and sophisticated purchasers of complex services. U.S. government agencies often require an Integrated Master Plan (IMP) and an Integrated Master Schedule (IMS). Prepare and include task descriptions with clearly defined and measurable completion criteria, directly tied to your project schedule.

Generalized, boilerplate descriptions of tasks and generic schedules will win only if your competition is equally incompetent or lazy.

5

Present service processes graphically.

See **Graphics** *for examples. See also* **Relevant Experience/ Past Performance** *and* **Resumes.**

When described in text, most service processes appear hopelessly complex. When presented graphically, they appear clear and straight forward, increasing an evaluator's confidence in the seller.

Consider some of the following ideas for service graphics:

- Include a series of small icon-like sketches to illustrate each service step.
- Present an excerpt of a service procedure from your service manual.
- Insert a sequenced, numbered checklist.
- Insert actual screen shots or graphics from your on-line service manual.
- Show a flow chart.
- Use a collage of photos or sketches to illustrate the variety of services available.
- Emphasize quality results by inserting a service report, service rating, or positive quotes from customers.
- Insert summary resumes that emphasize relevant experience.
- Insert photos showing the proposed people performing identical or similar tasks.

6

Exploit or attack incumbency, as relevant.

Incumbents win approximately 80 percent of all re-competes. Surveys of why incumbents lose cite poor service as the overwhelming reason.

Exploit incumbency by fixing all service problems before the bid. If you are too late, stress the specific corrections planned and the complexity of the required service. Fear of change is a powerful incentive to retain the incumbent.

When attacking incumbents, stress the specific steps you will take to improve service. While incumbents can be replaced on price, many winners regret the losses resulting from a low-ball win.

7

Cut costs, not margins.

The cost differences between the top bidders in service competitions is often a fraction of a percent. Develop a more competitive price by focusing on cutting costs out of your bid rather than simply reducing margins.

See **Pricing.**

Bidders that uniformly pare time and materials estimates by a uniform amount over the entire bid are effectively reducing margins. A cost evaluator with more than 30 years of experience called this the "peanut butter approach." If you must resort to this method of cost cutting, he recommended simply reducing the total cost, calling it a management contribution.

Make your bid more competitive by looking for ways to improve delivery efficiency. To improve your cost competitiveness, consider the following methods:

- Increase the span of control of managers, effectively reducing head-count in your most costly labor categories.
- Reduce the levels of management.
- Adjust the placement of individuals in required labor categories. When prospects mandate labor categories and rates, they typically cite midpoints in each category. You may not have to propose at the midpoint.
- Establish a new cost center for each major bid to prevent including overhead allocations irrelevant to that bid.
- Identify and incorporate physical assets within your organization that have been fully depreciated. This reduces corporate overhead allocations based on assets.

See **Teaming**.

- Subcontract tasks which can be delivered more economically by others.
- Recalculate all existing cost standards. Existing standards may not be based on the same assumptions. For example, a military depot had been repairing aircraft landing gear. The practice was to upgrade all landing gear to the latest standards whenever any maintenance was performed. The result was that relatively minor repairs had historically high standard costs.

  This depot's practice was similar to requesting a tune-up and getting a complete engine rebuild and upgrade to the latest standards. By developing new standards for each required maintenance action, the depot won a major contract.
- Review all task descriptions to prevent tasks from being overspecified. Identify which tasks could be performed by a lower cost labor category.
- Review delivery processes for potential productivity improvements through skill improvement, tooling improvement, or additional technology.
- Reduce reporting cost by proposing at the minimal level required in the bid request.
- Search for opportunities to cut overhead and increase business through automated order entry, billing, and payment, perhaps using the internet.
- Actively manage the account post sale to identify additional sales that you can deliver cost effectively with the existing or an augmented team.

Customer satisfaction is subjective. Customers must be continuously sold and resold before, during, and after the service is sold. Seamlessly, flawlessly delivered services are often forgotten.

Service deliverers must continuously reinforce the value of their services or risk being replaced or eliminated. The more customized and tailored the service, the harder the incumbent is to replace.

Storyboards and mock-ups are planning tools used to develop and review new content before writing text. Like any tool, they should save time and improve quality to justify their use.

NOTE 1: Storyboards were invented by movie directors, with early use attributed to D. W. Griffith, who directed *Birth of a Nation.* Alfred Hitchcock is reputed to have been the best user of storyboards, while Charlie Chaplin was the worst. Hitchcock planned his shooting to fractions of a second while Chaplin set up the cameras and improvised.

NOTE 2: The Proposal Development Worksheet (PDW) was developed to lessen the initial fear of many writers to storyboards. Writers often completed their PDWs before they knew they had used a storyboard. Most importantly, writers learned how much easier and faster they could draft quality proposal sections when using storyboards.

See **Outlining.**

NOTE3: The word *mock-up (n.),* is hyphenated. When used as a verb *(to mock up)* it is two words.

NOTE 4: A sample storyboard is included in the **Model Documents,** p. 244.

Storyboards and mock-ups are closely related but distinctly different. Both are used to help writers plan, develop, and review key concepts before drafting text.

Storyboards have a one-to-one relationship with major sections of the proposal pertaining to a common topic, while mock-up pages relate directly to proposal pages. For example, a single storyboard may apply to a 10-page proposal section. The mock-up for the same section would contain a full 10 pages.

The motivation to storyboard, whether in movies or proposals, was always the same—to cut costs. In early movie making, silver-coated film was the most expensive element. Now film is inexpensive and the actors, sets, and support crews are expensive. Proposal professionals use storyboards to reduce preparation time and costs.

In the broadest sense, storyboards use words and graphics to outline a concept. When someone builds a house, the storyboard equivalent is a plan book that shows a sketch of the home accompanied by a short description, as shown in figure 1.

Extending the house analogy, the mock-up is equivalent to the floor plan, showing the allocation of space and the relationship of key elements to scale, also shown in figure 1.

One problem among proposal managers and writers is inconsistent definitions. Keep the following definitions in mind:

Outlines are a sequential list of topics to be discussed.

Annotated outlines are outlines with annotations or comments about the contents of the topics. For proposals, annotated outlines may include references to the source of requirements, the author assigned, section length or page allocation, approximate number of visuals desired, and various dates materials are due. When annotated to this degree, the annotated outline becomes the proposal responsibility matrix.

Storyboards are conceptual planning tools used to help writers plan each section before drafting text. They contain assignments, bid request requirements, strategies, preliminary visuals, and content.

Storyboards are frequently misunderstood, misused, and have poor reputations with many proposal writers. Shipley Associates' storyboard form, the Proposal Development Worksheet (PDW), is shown in figure 3.

Mock-ups are page-for-page representations of the actual pages in the finished proposal. Mock-ups contain the same elements as the draft, namely, headings, themes, visuals, action captions, and text. Mock-ups transition writers from the storyboard to drafting.

Like eating the elephant one bite at a time, mock-ups permit writers to draft any section in any order while maintaining the planned organization. Mock-ups help writers appropriately allocate the space devoted to each point.

Anyone who has worked with advertising agencies on brochures has probably encountered mock-ups. Mock-ups are similar in function to prototypes, scale models, floor plans, and general arrangement drawings.

Storyboards and mock-ups aid managers as well as writers. Proposal managers use them to review and improve the writer's plan before wasting time and money on text that cannot be used.

Storyboards and Mock-ups

1. **Use storyboards to develop and review new material.**
2. **Focus on the storyboarding process more than the tool selected.**
3. **Use the core team to prepare the assignment; use the writers to develop the content.**
4. **Make the storyboard a key management tool.**
5. **Use mock-ups to allocate space and simplify the writing task.**
6. **Storyboard sequentially; mock up interactively.**
7. **Train writers to storyboard and mock up.**
8. **Manage the difficult transition from storyboarding to the first draft.**

STORYBOARD

VENEZIA SPECIFICATIONS

Announcing the "Venezia", our newest 2-story design with 4 bedrooms, 2.5 bathrooms and 4,664 total square feet (3,025 finished.) This spacious design features a large family room, laundry room, den and 9 ft. ceilings on the main level. The upstairs has 3 bedrooms and a large master suite with walk-in closet and grand bath. The basement can be finished to include up to 3 more bedrooms and 1 bathroom.

Total Sq. Ft.: 4,664
Finished Sq. Ft.: 3,025
Unfinished Sq. Ft.: 1,639
Width: 52'-9"
Depth: 51'-0"
Bedrooms: 4
Bathrooms: 2 1/2

MOCK-UP

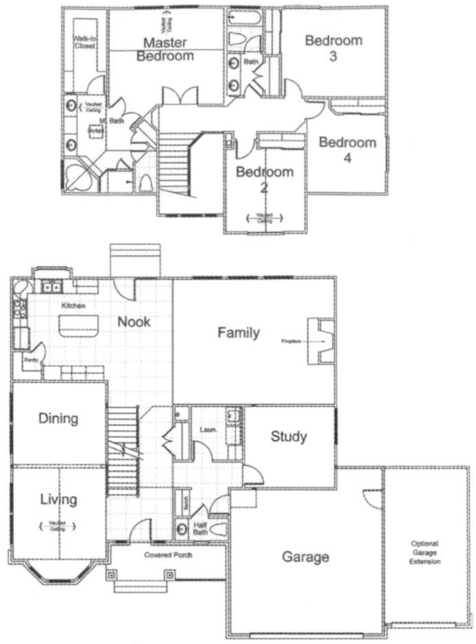

©2001 Ivory Homes

Figure 1. Home Builders Use Storyboards and Mock-ups. *The combination of text and graphics on the left is like a storyboard. Yet few people would proceed on the basis of the graphic and text without first seeing the floor plan. Like a mock-up, the floor plan allocates space and shows the relationships of major design elements. Of course, if money and time were not limited, you could build the house first, then make changes. Early paper changes are both easier and less expensive. The planning takes time and delays the start, but later changes take even more time.* (Images courtesy of Ivory Homes, Salt Lake City, Utah.)

---

1 Use storyboards to develop and review new material.

See **Question/Response Proposals**

Storyboards and mock-ups are most valuable when developing new material. They are less valuable and often should not be used when proposing essentially the same products and services to similar prospects. When you have previously written material (boilerplate) available, focus on tailoring your sales message, adjusting the details and length.

Many proposal efforts do not warrant using storyboards and mock-ups for every section. Storyboards should save more time than they take. For similar informally solicited proposals, use a single storyboard to plan the entire proposal. Then mock up the executive summary, which should be written for every proposal.

For Question/Response bid requests, use a modified storyboard approach to outline and review your responses before drafting. Identify the more important or more difficult questions, then plan and review your response before drafting text.

---

2 Focus on the storyboarding process more than the tool selected.

The overall process of making clear assignments, then planning, reviewing, and approving each writer's approach before drafting is more important than what information is selected to be on the storyboard form.

While some practitioners say their storyboards are proprietary and give them special names, most are not that different. Adapting the storyboard form to fit the effort warranted and the time available is more important than the form's detailed design.

Most storyboards have been developed for large, competitive systems proposals to Federal government. These detailed storyboards are often not directly applicable to small, 2-week, commercial responses.

For example, the topics contained in a detailed Shipley PDW are listed in figure 2 beside a shortened version that might be used for a rapid, commercial response.

Shipley Associates' Sales Proposal Planner is a storyboard-like tool used to plan an entire small proposal. The contents of the Planner are also listed in figure 2.

PROPOSAL DEVELOPMENT WORKSHEET	SHORTENED STORYBOARD	SALES PROPOSAL PLANNER
1. Understanding the Task: Relevant Proposal Information Relevant Bid Request Location **2. Analyzing the Bid Request:** Compliance Section Detailed Section Outline **3. Defining Your Offer:** Major Issues SWOT Analysis Approach (Technical/Management/Other) Features & Benefits Risk Management Relevant Experience Past Performance **4. Developing Your Strategy:** Section Discriminators Relevant Proposal/Volume Strategy Section Strategy Section Theme Statement **5. Creating Key Visuals:** Figure Number Figure Title Action Caption	**1. Understanding the Task:** Section Assignment **2. Analyzing the Bid Request:** Compliance Requirements **3. Defining Your Offer:** Major Issues Approach (Technical/ Management) Features & Benefits Support of Claims **4. Developing Your Strategy:** Section Discriminators Section Theme Statement **5. Creating Key Visuals:** Figure Number Figure Title Action Caption	**1. Positioning the Proposal** Identify Decision Makers, Influencers, and their Issues Build a Bidder Comparison Matrix Draft Proposal Strategy **2. Planning the Proposal:** Allocate Your Time Define Your Baseline Solution Define Your Price-to-Win Develop a Proposal Outline and Requirements Checklist Extend Sales Strategy into Proposal Strategy Design Your Proposal—Develop a Style Sheet **3. Writing the Proposal:** Implement Your Proposal Strategy What's Next?

Figure 2. Tailor Storyboards to the Opportunity. *The first column lists the contents of a detailed Proposal Development Worksheet (PDW) appropriate for large, competitive efforts. The second column lists the contents for a shortened version. The third lists contents of the Commercial Proposal Planner, used to plan rapid response commercial proposals where the services and products being sold are similar for different competitions. Note that this figure merely lists potential contents and is not an actual storyboard.*

3 Use the core team to prepare the assignment; use the writers to develop the content.

On larger efforts, the core team consisting of the proposal manager, volume managers or content leads, and the proposal specialist should develop clear, concise assignments for each contributor prior to the proposal kickoff. At the kickoff meeting, contributors are given their assignments.

A generic storyboard, called a PDW, is shown in figure 3. PDWs are used to prepare both major Federal and commercial proposals.

The portions on "Understanding the Task" and "Analyzing the Bid Request" should be completed by the proposal manager or core team and given to the writers at the kickoff meeting.

If writers develop their own compliance checklists, you will have "orphans" (unanswered items) and repeats (items answered by more than one writer). With repeats, answers often vary and may be costed twice.

Writers need to develop the content in the storyboard to prepare them to write. If their thinking is unclear, their writing will be unclear.

Some proposal professionals advocate using a small, select, trained group to prepare the storyboards completely, then giving storyboards to the writers to save time. This approach usually backfires. Writers tend to ignore storyboards done by others, and they draft text with little forethought.

Most writers can write well if they can develop a clear concept prior to writing. The process of storyboarding leads to a clearer concept, reducing the rework for everyone involved, and improving document quality and win probability.

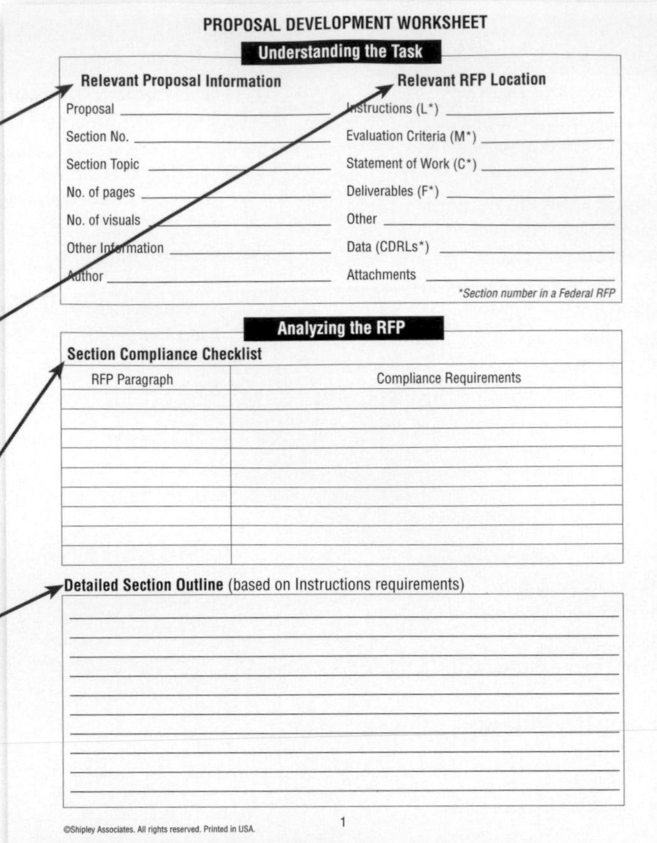

PROPOSAL DEVELOPMENT WORKSHEET

Understanding the Task

Relevant Proposal Information	Relevant RFP Location
Proposal	Instructions (L*)
Section No.	Evaluation Criteria (M*)
Section Topic	Statement of Work (C*)
No. of pages	Deliverables (F*)
No. of visuals	Other
Other Information	Data (CDRLs*)
Author	Attachments

*Section number in a Federal RFP

Analyzing the RFP

Section Compliance Checklist

RFP Paragraph	Compliance Requirements

Detailed Section Outline (based on Instructions requirements)

©Shipley Associates. All rights reserved. Printed in USA. 1

❶ Given to writers by the Proposal Manager or the Volume Manager. If not, ask for it, particularly the number of pages and the number of visuals.

❷ Given to writers by the Proposal Manager or the Volume Manager citing the relevant bid request pages and paragraph numbers.

❸ Should be completed by Proposal or Volume Manager by "stripping" the requirements from appropriate bid request sections. Use the compliance checklist to assure responsiveness and compliance. It is the basis for your outline and response matrix (or cross-reference matrix).

❹ Completed by writers following the outline format specified in the RFP and integrating any other applicable bid request sections as necessary. This is based on the proposal preparation instructions in the bid request.

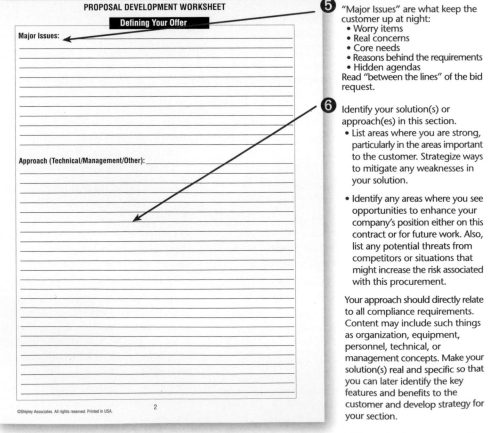

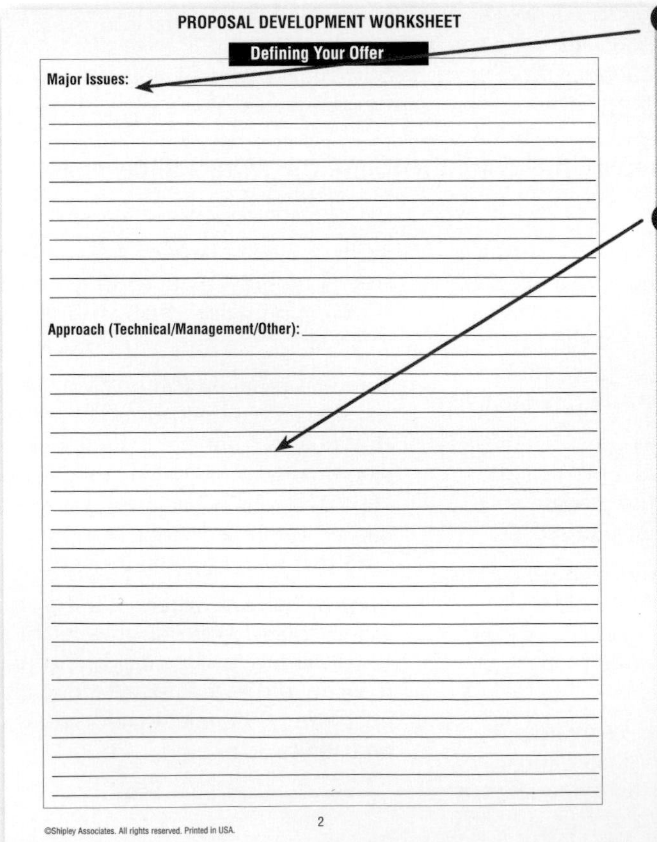

PROPOSAL DEVELOPMENT WORKSHEET

Defining Your Offer

Major Issues:

Approach (Technical/Management/Other):

©Shipley Associates. All rights reserved. Printed in USA. 2

❺ "Major Issues" are what keep the customer up at night:

- Worry items
- Real concerns
- Core needs
- Reasons behind the requirements
- Hidden agendas

Read "between the lines" of the bid request.

❻ Identify your solution(s) or approach(es) in this section.

- List areas where you are strong, particularly in the areas important to the customer. Strategize ways to mitigate any weaknesses in your solution.
- Identify any areas where you see opportunities to enhance your company's position either on this contract or for future work. Also, list any potential threats from competitors or situations that might increase the risk associated with this procurement.

Your approach should directly relate to all compliance requirements. Content may include such things as organization, equipment, personnel, technical, or management concepts. Make your solution(s) real and specific so that you can later identify the key features and benefits to the customer and develop strategy for your section.

Figure 3. Completing the Proposal Development Worksheet (PDW). *Follow the instructions for each portion of the PDW. When space is required, add separate sheets.*

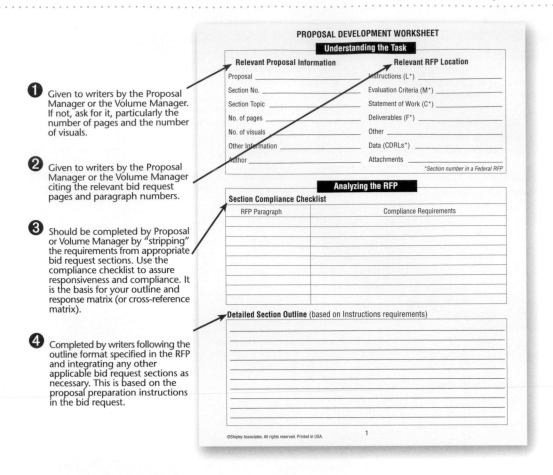

7 Develop the features and corresponding benefits of your offering or solution for this section. Determine which benefits address this customer's issues.

8 Enter areas of risk in technical, cost, schedule, technology, or other areas that are appropriate. These are the risks to your ***customer***, not to your company. How will you mitigate them? Identify the most likely risks, not every possible risk.

9 Identify your company's relevant experience and past performance that support the claims and benefits in your section. *Relevant experience* is **what you did**; *past performance* is **how well you did it**. Tie past performance to the benefits to ***this*** customer on ***this*** program. Try to quantify.

10 Discriminators are features of your offer that are both important to the customer and that differentiate you from the competition.

- Review your offering:
  - —What things are different and/or stronger than your competition?
  - —What things are weaker?
  - —Can you develop "ghosts"?
  - —How will you overcome your weaknesses?
- Assess your competitors' offering:
  - —What are their discriminators?
  - —How will you downplay or neutralize them?

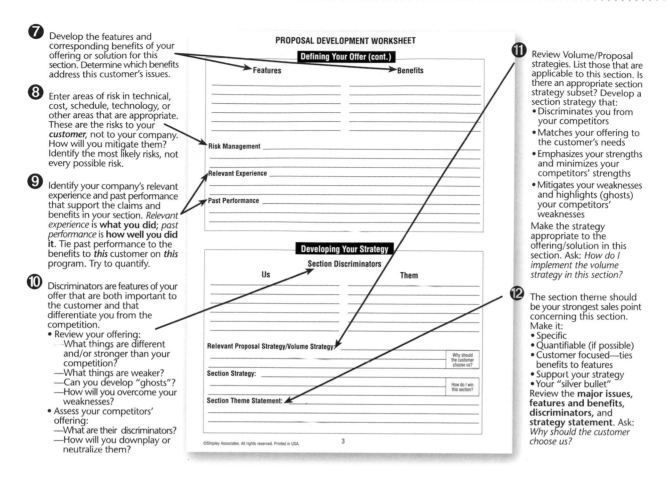

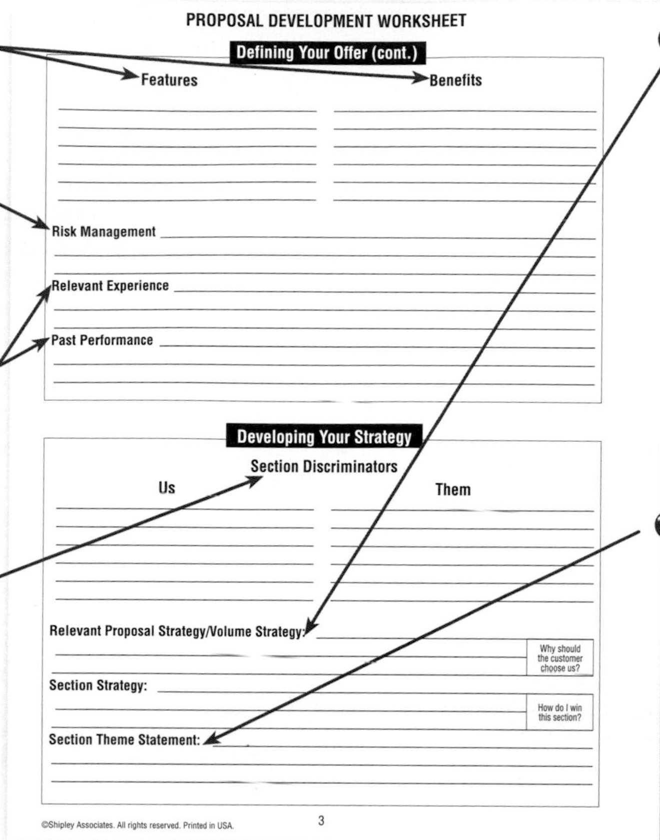

PROPOSAL DEVELOPMENT WORKSHEET

Defining Your Offer (cont.)

Features | Benefits

Risk Management

Relevant Experience

Past Performance

Developing Your Strategy

Section Discriminators

Us | Them

Relevant Proposal Strategy/Volume Strategy:

Why should the customer choose us?

Section Strategy:

How do I win this section?

Section Theme Statement:

©Shipley Associates. All rights reserved. Printed in USA. 3

11 Review Volume/Proposal strategies. List those that are applicable to this section. Is there an appropriate section strategy subset? Develop a section strategy that:

- Discriminates you from your competitors
- Matches your offering to the customer's needs
- Emphasizes your strengths and minimizes your competitors' strengths
- Mitigates your weaknesses and highlights (ghosts) your competitors' weaknesses

Make the strategy appropriate to the offering/solution in this section. Ask: *How do I implement the volume strategy in this section?*

12 The section theme should be your strongest sales point concerning this section. Make it:

- Specific
- Quantifiable (if possible)
- Customer focused—ties benefits to features
- Support your strategy
- Your "silver bullet"

Review the **major issues, features and benefits, discriminators,** and **strategy statement**. Ask: *Why should the customer choose us?*

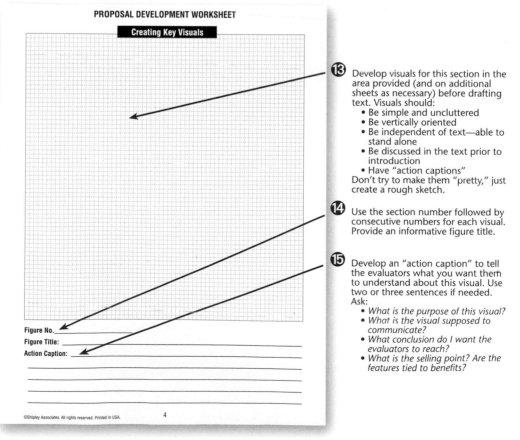

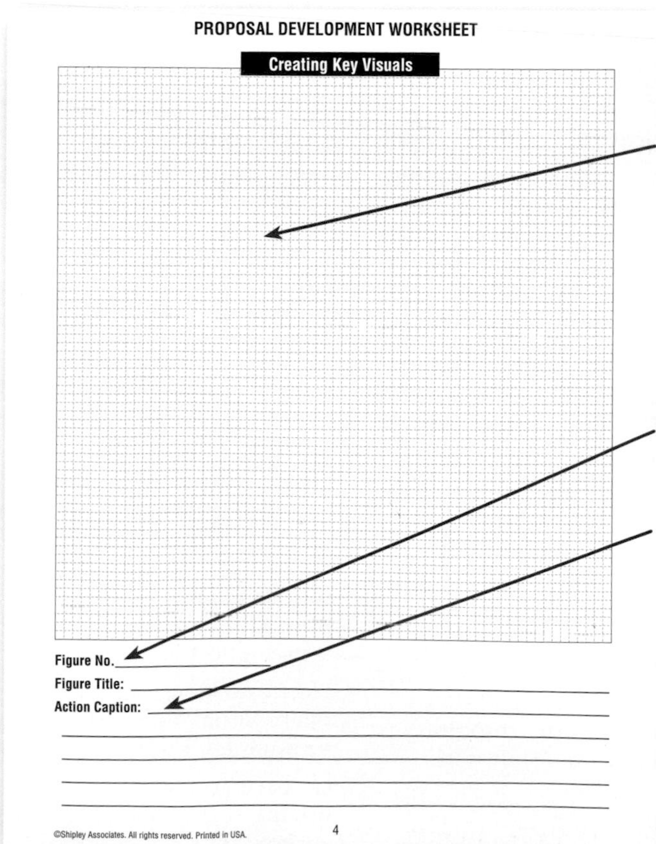

PROPOSAL DEVELOPMENT WORKSHEET

Creating Key Visuals

Figure No.

Figure Title:

Action Caption:

©Shipley Associates. All rights reserved. Printed in USA. 4

13 Develop visuals for this section in the area provided (and on additional sheets as necessary) before drafting text. Visuals should:

- Be simple and uncluttered
- Be vertically oriented
- Be independent of text—able to stand alone
- Be discussed in the text prior to introduction
- Have "action captions"

Don't try to make them "pretty," just create a rough sketch.

14 Use the section number followed by consecutive numbers for each visual. Provide an informative figure title.

15 Develop an "action caption" to tell the evaluators what you want them to understand about this visual. Use two or three sentences if needed. Ask:

- *What is the purpose of this visual?*
- *What is the visual supposed to communicate?*
- *What conclusion do I want the evaluators to reach?*
- *What is the selling point? Are the features tied to benefits?*

4 Make the storyboard a key management tool.

NOTE: Electronic storyboards offer advantages when used and managed properly. Major advantages are (1) storyboard material can evolve into a draft and (2) managers can more easily manage a geographically dispersed team.

Resist the impulse to cut and paste boilerplate into electronic storyboards.

See **Daily Team Management.**

With storyboards, managers can see what writers are thinking before they write, thus reducing expensive rewriting. To ensure that writers treat storyboards seriously, managers must review all storyboards thoroughly and frequently.

Do not wait to review storyboards until they are complete. Review sections incrementally to get writers on track faster.

One way to speed storyboard preparation is to facilitate the work in a workshop-like manner. Follow these steps:

1. Explain each task, establishing clear quality standards.
2. Ask each writer to complete that task in a relatively short time.
3. Circulate, answering any questions.
4. Review individual storyboard sections as a group, encouraging collaborative, constructive information sharing and suggestions for improvement. Repeat as warranted.
5. Advance to the next storyboard section.

Keep a copy of the latest version of each storyboard mounted on the wall in the proposal war room or its equivalent. Walk the walls daily, and encourage team members to do the same.

Post all suggestions for improvement on the storyboards with the reviewer's name and phone number.

Remove unsigned comments. Remove comments that are vague and require further discussion. Anonymous comments are often negative and hurt the team environment. If a comment is valid, sign it and assume ownership.

Comment on storyboard progress in a daily stand-up meeting. Praise the better examples.

Maintain either the original or a first copy in the proposal master book in case any storyboards are lost.

Storyboards can be done by hand or electronically. Both have advantages and disadvantages. For example:

> A proposal manager asked an untrained organization to complete storyboards. The group met and decided that they would have to draft their sections to complete the storyboards. They worked all weekend on their drafts, primarily by pasting in boilerplate. Then they electronically pasted text from their drafts into the storyboard forms. After all, they wanted them to be legible.
>
> The result was terrible. The proposal manager required all subsequent storyboards to be handwritten to encourage thinking before writing.

Their process was essentially the same as constructing the building or apparatus, then preparing the as-built drawings.

5 Use mock-ups to allocate space and simplify the writing task.

Mock-ups are an intermediate step between the storyboard and drafting the text. The act of constructing a mock-up forces writers to consider the relative importance of topics to the prospect and to the offer. After mock-ups are complete, writers can work on any section without losing direction or momentum.

Mock-ups should be done quickly. Neatness does not count. A 5-page section should be mocked up in less than 2 hours; a 20-page section in less than one-half day. Experienced writers can mock-up a 10- to 15-page executive summary in about an hour.

Many writers construct thumbnail mock-ups first. Using thumbnails, they can see the entire document at once, making it easier to allocate topics and content over the available pages. Then they sketch full-scale mock-ups if they need greater detail before drafting. The entire mock-up development process is shown in figure 4 in thumbnail sketches.

Mock-ups should be hand sketched. Constructing pretty mock-ups on the computer wastes time and interferes with the creative process.

Construct a mock-up in the following steps:

1. Establish the overall page layout from the proposal style sheet, such as single- or double-column.
2. Estimate the number of pages for the entire section, including text and integrated graphics.
3. Allocate the pages available to the topics to be discussed according to their importance to evaluators, tempered by their complexity. Then place section subheadings to reserve the space allocated. In formally solicited proposals, top-level topics reflect compliance requirements.
4. Place and label boxes to reserve space for major visual elements like themes, summaries and introductions, and visuals.
5. Go back and begin to flesh out the mock-up. Insert the following items, in the approximate order listed:

- Insert the top-level theme statement from the storyboard.
- Identify each graphic and identify it in the reserved space.
- List the key points to be made.
- Draft complete three-part action captions for each visual.
- Draft every planned theme statement.
- Draft the section summary and introduction.
- Begin drafting text. Start where you feel most prepared or comfortable.

Do not worry about how many iterations are required to do a mock-up.

STEPS

❶ Establish the overall page layout.

❷ Obtain or estimate the number of formatted blank pages available for your section.

Example at right is a page bogey of three pages using double columns.

❸ Overlay your section outline (located on the bottom of page 1 of the PDW) on the pages, drawing boxes for the assigned space for each topic. Base the allocation of space on your best judgment of how much space will be required for each outline topic. Identify adequate space for your section introduction and summary, as shown at right.

❹ Draw boxes to show the location for the graphics you developed on page 4 of the PDW in the locations within the space you designated for each outline item. Describe or sketch the graphic in those boxes, and enter the appropriate figure number, title, and action caption. Identify the location for themes by drawing boxes and entering your section theme(s) from the bottom of page 3 of the PDW.

❺ In each outline space, identify the content that will be discussed under that topic by using key words. Show the estimated space that will be devoted to that topic by the juxtaposition of the key words.

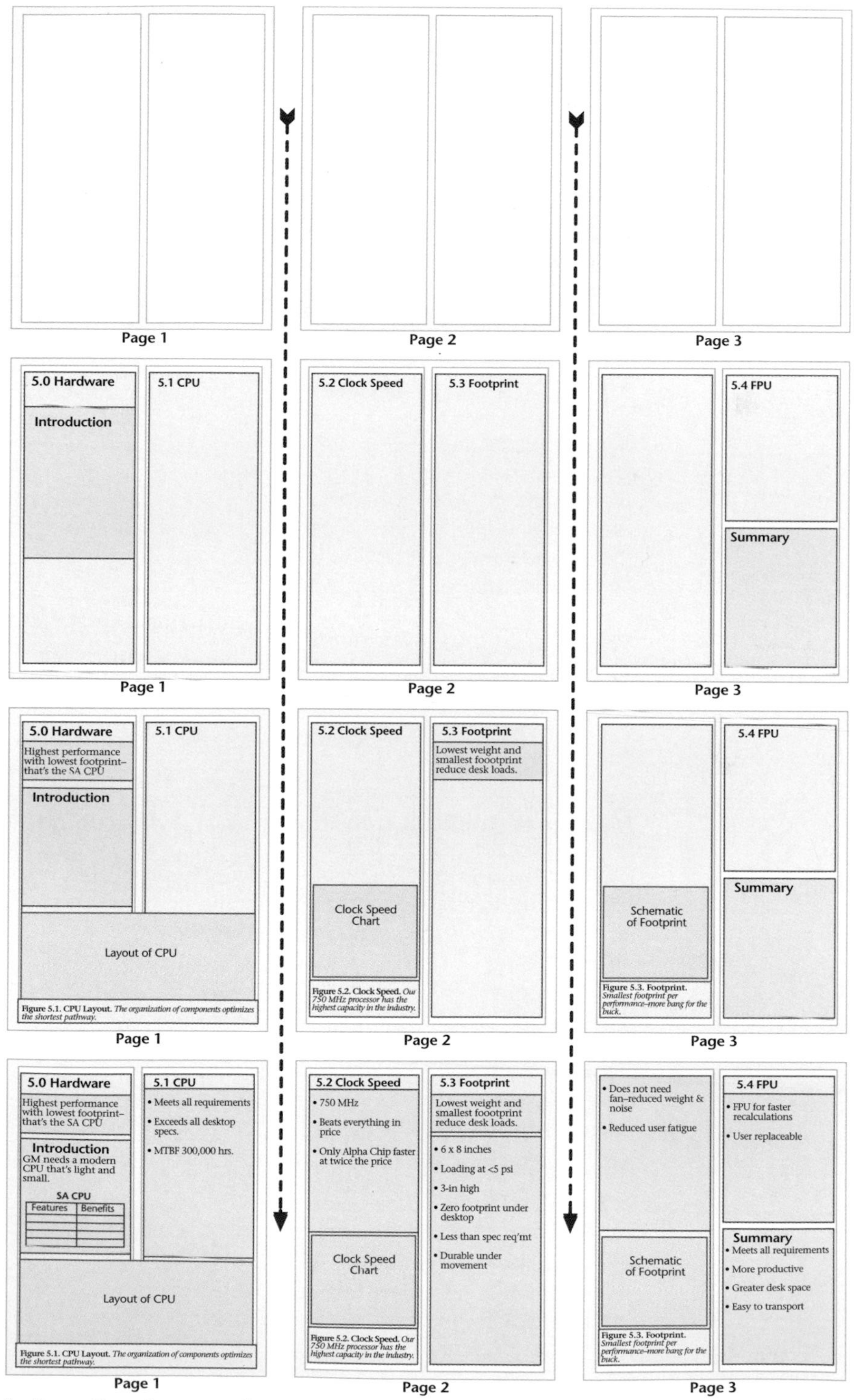

Figure 4. Mock-up Development Process. *Mock-ups evolve from top-level concepts to specific details. After constructing the reduced-size "thumbnail" pages shown, most writers proceed to a first draft. Construct a full-scale mock-up only if the document is particularly important or expensive to produce. While shown here in print form for clarity, most mock-ups are and should be handwritten.*

6 Storyboard sequentially; mock up interactively.

When you prepare storyboards, each portion builds on previous portions, so they must be constructed sequentially. For example, a writer must know a prospect's requirements and major issues before determining benefits.

When you develop mock-ups, use a top-down process, from the general to the specific. Mock-ups constructed sequentially usually cram so much into a small space that they are unrealistic. After review, visuals and tables are often the size of a postage stamp and the space for text is inadequate.

7 Train writers to storyboard and mock up.

Developing storyboards and preparing mock-ups is not intuitive to many writers. Writers need training and must experience how these tools save more time than they take.

When writers are told they will be developing storyboards and mock-ups, they often make comments like the following:

Why waste time filling out forms? I could be writing.

Boy, am I glad that storyboard is done because I have my section already written. Translation: I've already done a "search and replace" on the available boilerplate.

So you want us to draw pretty pictures.

You are turning the proposal into a comic book.

Few writers are convinced storyboards and mock-ups work until they build them. Then they see how much easier it is to draft their section. Here are some of the comments from the converted:

Having everyone throw rocks at my themes and captions in all of their iterations was brutal. But I learned how others were thinking and the improvement was huge.

After you finally let us write our drafts, the section practically wrote itself.

I was asked to join a proposal team that had been working for 2 solid weeks. I remembered what I was taught in the workshop. We had 5 days until the first Red Team. Despite the proposal manager's pressure to see my draft, I completed my storyboard, reviewed it with the volume manager, constructed a thumbnail mock-up, and drafted my section. My section was the only one to pass the Red Team. I went home while the others started over.

8 Manage the difficult transition from storyboarding to the first draft.

Many writers have difficultly transitioning from storyboards, to mock-ups, then to their first draft. They seem to forget everything they went through, sit down at a blank screen, and start writing about themselves, their products and services, and their organization.

To ease your writers' transition from storyboards and mock-ups to their first draft, consider the following techniques:

1. Take the writers' storyboards, in electronic form, and sequentially paste them into a word processing file for the writers.
2. Personally check with each writer within 1 day of when the writer will begin drafting the text. Waiting longer allows their frustration level to get too high.
3. Demonstrate how to move text from a storyboard into a first draft in a group training session; then check with each writer.
4. Ask experienced writers to mentor less-experienced writers.
5. Tape the completed storyboard to a flip chart page or white board. Then draw arrows to show where each item can be moved onto a mock-up page.
6. Remind writers to leave labeled boxes to reserve space for content not yet available.

Strategy is a plan or method for achieving a goal. Strategy and tactics are often confused. In the purest sense, strategy is your preengagement position; tactics are the actions you take to implement your strategy, to convey it persuasively. Both are required to win.

The guidelines for strategy include preconditioning, targeting, and analyzing, then determining and packaging your solution.

See **Process.**

Best practice reviews indicate that organizations that are most effective at winning business have aligned their strategies and processes throughout, including their approach to business development. Their business, market, capture, sales, and proposal strategies and tactics are aligned, coordinated, and consistent.

Misaligned strategies at any level result in inconsistent messages being communicated to the prospect's organization. This dissonance prompts prospects to doubt your message.

To create and present an aligned message, all members of the selling team must agree to a common process and common definitions:

- A business strategy is an organization's plan to achieve overall business objectives.
- A market strategy is an organization's plan to achieve specific market objectives, typically involving multiple sales.
- A capture strategy is the plan to win a specific, definable opportunity.
- A sales strategy should be identical to a capture strategy, i.e., opportunity specific, but sales strategy has been used so generically that the term was not used in this *Proposal Guide*.
- A proposal strategy is a plan to write a persuasive, winning proposal. The proposal strategy is a subset of the capture strategy. Only the tactical aspects of implementation differ.

If the following example describes your organization, you can improve your business capture effectiveness:

> Account executives position prospects based on their uniquely successful previous approaches. Individuals write proposals with little direction from sales, using extensive boilerplate due to limited response time and numerous requests to bid. When asked to make a finals presentation, senior executives deliver standard presentations.

In sum, messages to the prospect tend to be seller-focused and the content changes from message to message. As a result, the prospects doubt both your understanding of their needs and your commitment.

Strategy

1. **Analyze your current position using standard, universally understood, and accepted tools.**
2. **Define and agree to use common definitions of terms.**
3. **Define a specific sales objective after your pursuit decision to better focus on each unique opportunity.**
4. **Identify the economic buyer, the users, and the technical buyers; then list their issues.**
5. **Use an Integrated Prospect Solution Worksheet to arrive at a competitive solution that is aligned with the prospect's issues and requirements.**
6. **Prepare a Bidder Comparison Matrix to discern how the prospect organization perceives your solution versus competitive solutions.**
7. **Select the best solution and develop a specific value proposition for each prospect.**
8. **Draft specific strategy statements that define both what you will do and how you will implement them.**
9. **Use trade-offs to validate your approach and ghost the competition.**
10. **Implement your action plan.**

1 Analyze your current position using standard, universally understood, and accepted tools.

Strategy drives tactics. You always have a position in any sales situation, whether you understand it or not. Developing an effective strategy requires both determining your current position and then improving it versus your competitors' positions.

Using standard tools to develop your strategy improves the quality of the strategy, saves time, and improves the quality of implementation. When strategy development is improvised, implementation is haphazard, uncoordinated, and inconsistent.

Organizations that use common tools to develop strategy spend less time clarifying terms and process and have more time to focus on substance and implementation.

No single tool is ideal. Select tools that are useful and acceptable to most participants. If you are following a particular sales discipline, extend the approach. Use the established templates. Avoid using similar but different tools between sales, sales support, management, engineering, and product management.

2 Define and agree to use common definitions of terms.

NOTE: Concerns that the seller has about a solution or approach are called gaps, the difference between what the prospect wants and what the seller can offer. Issues are owned by the prospect, not the seller. Avoid the confusion caused by mingling prospect gaps and seller issues.

Common understanding requires common terms. Three of the most universally used and misunderstood terms relating to strategy are *issues, motivators*, and *hot buttons*. The relationship of these three terms is illustrated in figure 1 and defined as follows:

Issues are the prospect's concerns. Issues are the worry items that keep the prospect awake at night.

Motivators are the objectives that the prospect is trying to achieve:

- Improve profits
- Increase sales
- Reduce costs
- Improve safety
- Reduce risk
- Improve quality

Hot buttons are a consolidated set of issues and motivators, preferably two to five items. State hot buttons using the prospect's words. Then organize your executive summary around the prospect's hot buttons.

All motivators are issues, but not all issues are motivators:

Example: Training could be an example of a hot button that is an issue but not a motivator. Few prospects are motivated to buy because they get to attend training. However, if users were poorly trained on a previous similar purchase, and problems ensued, then training could be a prospect's hot button.

Figure 1. The Relationship Between Issues, Motivators, and Hot Buttons. *Hot buttons are mostly motivators but could also include a small number of issues that are not motivators.*

3 Define a specific sales objective after your pursuit decision to better focus on each unique opportunity.

Shortly after your pursuit decision, draft a brief, precise sales objective that meets the following criteria:

- **Specific**—States what products and services are to be purchased and who will purchase them.
- **Measurable**—Tells how much is to be purchased.
- **Timed**—Cites when the purchase will be made.
- **Result**—States, quantitatively if possible, the result or process change the prospect anticipates.

Poor Sales Objective

Capture $5 million worth of product and service revenue from Bank-4-U during fiscal year 20XX.

Better Sales Objective

Win 3-year contract extension to supply and support all copy and fax equipment at Bank-4-U's Reno headquarters. The $3.5 million contract renewal will be awarded on or before June 15, 20XX. Bank-4-U's total cost will remain flat, equaling the current annual cost for identical services.

You often pursue multiple purchases from the same organization. But if you find yourself trying to describe multiple buyers or purchase times, you are likely facing multiple opportunities that are better addressed individually. Each opportunity is unique and is best addressed uniquely.

4 Identify the economic buyer, the users, and the technical buyers; then list their issues.

NOTE 1: Roles may overlap. For example, the president of a small technical company might be both the economic and technical buyer.

NOTE 2: Some sales professionals say that there is only one buyer, the individual empowered to make the final purchase decision. All other types of buyers, such as users or technical buyers, are called "influencers."

Economic buyers are the individuals who give final approval to purchase. They sign the check and retain veto power. Economic buyers tend to be concerned about the trade-off between price and performance. They focus on bottom line impact. While many people may offer input and recommendations, only economic buyers can give final approval.

Users are the people who judge the potential impact on their job performance. Their personal success is impacted by the sale, so their concerns are often emotional and subjective. Users' issues are reliability, support, ease of operation, maintenance, safety, potential impact on morale, and potential impact on their personal success. Because they use or supervise the use of your product or service, they can ruin a good sale.

Technical buyers are gatekeepers. They cannot give final approval, but they can give a final "No." Technical buyers often determine the short list. They tend to focus on the features of a product or service as measured against objective specifications established to screen offers.

Technical buyers may not be technical in the scientific sense. Purchasing agents, lawyers, contracts people, and licensing or regulatory authorities are technical buyers. Since technical buyers are primarily focused on how well you meet their screening tests, the better you understand their criteria, the better your chances of getting their recommendations.

Another way to examine buyers is according to their source of power. Power could be economic, control (typically users), or technical. Or power could be by level of management, such as executive management, middle management, and operations.

After identifying all the different types of buyers, list the issues of each individual buyer. The most important issues of the entire organization are usually associated with a majority of the buyers.

5 Use an Integrated Prospect Solution Worksheet to arrive at a competitive solution that is aligned with the prospect's issues and requirements.

See **Capture Planning** *and* **Executive Summary**.

The Integrated Prospect Solution Worksheet (IPSW) is a powerful analysis tool throughout the capture process. The IPSW is first developed as part of the capture plan. The IPSW is shown in figure 2.

Use the IPSW to collaborate with the prospect early in the process to define the issues and influence requirements. The first seller to do this is established as the preferred provider.

If the prospect already has a solution in mind, the IPSW helps define the underlying issues driving the prospect's requirements. Analyze your competitive position, then work to favorably influence the requirements. Aim to become the prospect's preferred provider.

Next, extend your analysis to outline your solution, to outline your competition's solution, and to identify discriminators. Then define the strategies and actions required to better position your solution with the prospect, discussed in guideline 8.

INTEGRATED PROSPECT SOLUTION WORKSHEET

Item #	Prospect Issues	Prospect Requirement	Available Solution	Gap	Competitor Solution	Discriminators	Strategy	Action Required

Figure 2. Integrated Prospect Solution Worksheet. *Begin by filling the "Issues" column when you are early in the process. If the prospect has identified requirements, fill the "Requirements" column. Then complete each row, relating each item in the row.*

6

Prepare a Bidder Comparison Matrix to discern how the prospect organization perceives your solution versus competitive solutions.

See **Capture Planning** *and* **Executive Summary**.

Use the Bidder Comparison Matrix, shown in figure 3, to analyze the prospect's current perception of how your solution compares to various competitors. Use it repeatedly throughout the capture process to measure the effectiveness of your positioning.

The Bidder Comparison Matrix, like the IPSW, is potentially an excellent collaborative tool for the seller and the prospect.

Issues	Weight	Us Score	Company 1 Score	Company 2 Score
Specific Experience				
Low Price				
Familiarity with Manager Named				
Ability to Meet Schedule				
Total Score				

Figure 3. Bidder Comparison Matrix. *First list the prospect's issues, then the relative weight of each issue as perceived by the prospect. Establish the relative weight of each issue in one of three ways: (1) Use the prospect's evaluation criteria, (2) Assign a weight, forcing the total score to equal 100, (3) Assign an arbitrary weight (such as 1-to-5). Then assign a score (perhaps 1-to-10). Complete each row horizontally, indicating your estimate of the prospect's perception of each competitor's ability to satisfy that issue. Compare the products of the weight times the score. The absolute value of the numbers assigned is not important. Only the comparative value matters.*

7 Select the best solution and approach and develop a specific value proposition for each prospect.

After targeting an opportunity and analyzing your position, freezing your solution may seem obvious. Even so, too many sellers either delay selecting a solution, continue to modify their solution, or carry too many solutions, alternates, or options through the sales cycle. The result hurts in several ways:

- Members of the selling team present generic, vague, and unconvincing solutions to the prospect in both presentations and proposals.
- Product and service specialists are compelled to prepare multiple solutions, so the quality of each solution declines.
- Prospects are confused by the options, made uncomfortable with the seller's vacillation, and are generally not persuaded to select you.

See **Value Propositions**.

Value propositions are a fundamental aspect of how your solution is packaged and presented to the prospect. The relatively judgmental and softer concept of best value is cited as an evaluation factor in many U.S. Federal and commercial bid requirements. Rather than being forced to adhere to specific and potentially incomplete quantitative criteria, best value preserves room for judgment.

NOTE: Total added value is the summation of the benefits minus the purchase cost and implementation cost of the seller's solution.

Value propositions are a more disciplined and quantitative way to present your solution, used by many organizations in commercial market sectors. Sales presentations and proposals have always stressed linking the features of your solution to the benefits to the prospect. Fundamentally, a value proposition is the summation of the benefits of your solution.

Value proposition = Σ Benefits of seller's solution

Having determined your solution, prepare value propositions for each type of buyer: the economic buyer, the users, and the technical buyers. Value propositions flow directly from the sales objective but the better ones are detailed, specific, and quantified.

Value propositions establish the value basis for the business relationship. They describe how your solution will improve the prospect's business and how that improvement will be measured. Tailor value proposition(s) to each type of buying influence.

Value propositions include the following elements:

- Quantified business improvement
- Timing
- Solution
- Investment cost
- Payback
- Results measurement and tracking

The best value propositions are developed collaboratively with the prospect. Collaboration increases the probability that the prospect's organization will accept your quantitative analysis.

Ideally, authorized representatives of both the prospect and the seller organizations sign the written value proposition, and they mutually agree to proceed without competitive proposals. Prospect signatures are unlikely without participating in developing the value proposition.

A sample value proposition targeting the economic buyer follows:

> Global Corporation will realize a $3,500,000 reduction in information technology support costs over the next 5 years, commencing May 1, 20XX, by contracting with Computer Heroes, Ltd., at a cost of $2,000,000 per year. Global Corporation will be paid $500,000 for all of Global's IT assets, and Computer Heroes will provide all IT support. Global Corporation will enjoy a 30 percent annual reduction in IT costs, assuming the agreed prices and the same services currently required continue to be delivered. All costs will be available to you on-line and documented in monthly invoices.

8 Draft specific strategy statements that define both *what* you will do and *how* you will implement them.

Strategy can be implemented in four fundamental ways:

- **Emphasize** your strengths
- **Mitigate** your weaknesses
- **Highlight** your competitors' weaknesses
- **Downplay** your competitors' strengths

Effective strategy statements incorporate both strategic and tactical aspects. The strategic portion establishes your position. The tactical portion defines how you will implement the strategy, the action steps. Use the template in figure 4 to develop more effective strategy statements. Think of the strategic part as "what you will do," and the tactical part as "how you will do it."

STRATEGY STATEMENT TEMPLATE

- We will emphasize our strengths in: ______________

  by: ______________

- We will mitigate our weaknesses in: ______________

  by: ______________

- We will highlight our competitors' weaknesses in: ______________

  by: ______________

- We will downplay our competitors' strengths in: ______________

  by: ______________

©Shipley Associates

Figure 4. Strategy Statement Template. *Using either the Integrated Prospect Solution Worksheet (figure 2) or the Bidder Comparison Matrix (figure 3), identify your relative position versus each of your competitors. Then draft one strategy statement for each issue or requirement. Treat the "How" portion as possibilities, implementing those that you can support with facts or resources. Collect all of your strategy statements and distribute them to the entire capture team and proposal team.*

NOTE: Strategy statements are planning statements. They cite what you or a writer will do. They are not actual text or graphics that will appear in the proposal.

Strategy statements apply at the capture, proposal, and proposal section level. Capture strategy statements are global. They apply to all aspects of the sales cycle.

Capture strategy example

What:

We will emphasize our ability to complete the design-build of a distribution center on time

By:

- Taking the prospect on a plant tour of the XYZ distribution center in Orlando, FL
- Citing three other distribution centers completed on schedule during the past 5 years
- Providing contact names, phone numbers, and quotes verifying our on-time completion of three similar projects

Proposal strategy example

What:

We will emphasize our ability to complete the design-build of a distribution center on time

By:

- Including in our proposal photos of the XYZ distribution center in Orlando, FL
- Citing three other distribution centers in a table in our proposal, all listing the center, place, owner, promised completion date, and actual completion date
- Listing in our proposal the contact names, phone numbers, and quotes verifying our on-time completion of three similar projects

Section strategy statements, while more limited in scope, are essentially the same as proposal strategy statements in form, content, and implementation.

A well-written proposal strategy statement enables the reader to visualize how the strategy will appear on the page. For example:

- *Describe* or *Discuss* implies text.
- *Show* implies a graphic.
- *Include* a sketch, drawing, photo, table, flow chart, or graph.
- *Cite* or *Quote* implies text set off or emphasized by different formatting or white space.

If you cannot visualize the page, refine the strategy statement.

In terms of implementation, the way you emphasize your strength may be identical to how you highlight a competitor's weakness. Similarly, how you mitigate your weakness may be identical to how you neutralize a competitor's strength, as demonstrated in the following examples:

Proposal strategy example

Your competitor has a reasonable reputation for completing projects within budget. Your organization had a recent cost overrun on the similar ABC project. The strategy statement to mitigate your weakness and downplay the competitor's strength might be the same.

Proposal strategy statement example

We will mitigate our weakness in completing similar projects within budget by:

- Citing the lessons learned from the recent ABC project
- Including a table listing all materials and subcontract tasks that have been pre-negotiated prior to submittal.

We will downplay our competitor's strength in completing similar projects within budget by:

- Citing the lessons learned from the recent ABC project
- Including a table listing all materials and subcontract tasks that have been pre-negotiated prior to submittal.

9 Use trade-offs to validate your approach and ghost the competition.

Trade-offs show you have considered alternatives and have selected the best solution for the prospect. Instead of just selecting the first item available or your usual approach, you considered the prospect's needs, risks, and budget, and offered the solution that maximizes benefits and minimizes risks.

Ghosting is simply offering a trade-off when one of the alternatives you rejected is being offered by the competition. You ghost the competition when you raise the specter of some weakness of theirs.

The primary way to downplay competitors' strengths and highlight their weaknesses is through ghosting. Never mention competitors by name. Instead, reject their approaches.

One of the advantages of ghosting is that you do not have to fully justify your position. You only create doubt, as shown in the following examples:

We first thought a full design-build approach would be ideal, as it could shorten the time to completion by 3 months. However, with the lack of reliable data on the stability of the soil at the site and the potential for hazardous materials, we have proposed a full site characterization and analysis prior to design. Our conservative approach reduces the risk of construction interruptions and potentially more costly site remediation.

We considered using the recently developed new glue to assemble the supersonic aircraft at a reduced cost, but rejected glue as being potentially higher risk in long-term use versus the long-proven rivet approach.

Figure 5 offers some additional ghosting approaches. Use ghosting judiciously. Overuse can turn off the prospect.

COMPETITOR'S WEAKNESS	YOU STRESS
Safety problems	Cite your strong safety record. Offer industry averages for comparison.
Labor unrest	Emphasize the importance of a reliable workforce. Note that avoiding the cost of a strike justifies higher hourly wages.
High design cost	Emphasize low overheads and specific industry focus.
Poor reliability	Stress redundant design costs less than lost revenues from poor availability.
Extended downtime	Emphasize your local service center and built-in diagnostics.
Cost overruns	Cite the extra care taken in estimating, material selection, and purchasing.

Figure 5. Use Ghosting to Validate Your Approach. *Plan your ghosts carefully at the capture or proposal manager level. Determine what ghosts will be introduced and where they will be inserted in your proposal. Trade-off analyses are appropriate in every proposal section where realistic alternatives are available.*

10 Implement your action plan.

A limited strategy that is implemented is superior to an excellent, unimplemented strategy. Like all other planning tasks, maintain a balance between strategy development and implementation.

Action is required to persuade the prospect to select your solution. Figure 6 lists some of the reasons strategies are not implemented and suggests improved approaches.

WHY STRATEGIES ARE NOT IMPLEMENTED	IMPROVED APPROACHES
Capture actions are not assigned to a single, responsible individual	Assign one person with resources and completion dates.
No consequence for failure to complete	Establish regular capture plan reviews.
Strategy regarded as confidential	Communicate to all team members.
Strategy developed late	Develop and review the capture strategy after the pursuit decision. Extend the capture strategy to a proposal strategy and distribute at proposal kickoff.
Proposal strategy not evident in drafts	Use storyboards to flow strategy into sections. Always review drafts with the approved storyboards present.
Writers include unsupported claims	Insist that all claims must be substantiated.

Figure 6. Improve Strategy Implementation. *Follow these recommendations to better implement your strategy throughout the sales cycle. Balance the time spent planning versus implementing.*

Team selection and management is a matter of roles rather than positions. Proposal efforts range from a single person to dedicated teams comprising hundreds. Selecting team members and managing them varies widely by organization, market sector, and even culture. Most aspects of project team management apply equally to proposal teams.

Team Selection and Management

1. **Establish a proposal management structure with defined roles and responsibilities.**
2. **Tailor your approach to each proposal by adjusting role assignments.**
3. **Document your approach in a proposal management plan.**
4. **Select the right types of people for each role.**
5. **Differentiate process and content responsibilities.**
6. **Scope all tasks based on a clear vision of the document to be delivered and realistic time standards.**
7. **Manage the proposal like all other corporate strategic projects.**
8. **Reward good performance.**

1 Establish a proposal management structure with defined roles and responsibilities.

Certain roles must be filled on every proposal team. If you vary the role to suit the people available, proposal quality will suffer.

The following roles are required on all proposal teams of all sizes.

The **capture manager** must win the order and is responsible for all prospect contact before, during, and after the proposal is submitted, conforming to the prospect's rules. The capture manager owns the capture strategy.

The **proposal manager** leads the team and is responsible for resources, planning, scheduling, development, and production. The primary focus of proposal management must be to produce a winning proposal document. The proposal manager owns the proposal strategy, derived from the capture strategy.

The **project manager** develops a winning solution that complies with the organization's objectives. Generally the project manager is responsible to the strategic business unit manager for profitability and risk management.

See **Process**.

The **volume leader** develops a specific volume for the proposal manager. Volume managers are directly responsible for all input into their volume.

The **proposal coordinator** or specialist helps the proposal manager control the proposal development process. Typical tasks include helping develop and update all plans, schedules, materials, and files; coordinating with other process specialists; and helping with all reviews.

The **production lead** supervises all aspects of production, including word processing, graphics, desktop publishing, and production.

The **editor** ensures that all materials, both text and graphics, meet the organization's style standards.

The **proposal writers** obtain whatever information is required to draft and deliver a compliant, responsive, clear, and persuasive proposal section to proposal management when scheduled.

The **time and materials estimators** prepare supportable task descriptions, time and material estimates, and estimating rationale when required that precisely match the tasks described by the corresponding writers.

The **pricing staff** roll time and material estimates into a final price that meets all prospect and seller standards.

The focus of each of these roles changes as you progress through the six-phase business development cycle: (1) Positioning, (2) Pursuit, (3) Capture, (4) Proposal Planning, (5) Proposal Development and Production, (6) Post Submittal Negotiation and Closure.

2 Tailor your approach to each proposal by adjusting role assignments.

All of the roles described in guideline 1 must be assumed on all proposals. Ignore any of them and the quality of your proposal will drop.

On small proposals, combine roles in a single individual. On large proposals, several people may share a single role. Worry more about having the role covered than about how you assign the roles among the individuals available.

3 Document your approach in a proposal management plan.

See **Proposal Management Plan.**

Any plan worth doing must be written. Even on a one-person effort, develop and document a minimum plan, then work to the plan.

Define the structure and content required in your organization's proposal management plans as part of your business development process definition and documentation. If you happen to be assigned the proposal manager's role in one of the many organizations that lack a defined process, tailor your organization's project management process to the proposal project.

4 Select the right types of people for each role.

Different skills are required for the different roles. Some people are suited to multiple roles, some are not. Figure 1 summarizes some of the skills that help individuals fill specific roles more effectively.

ROLES	SKILLS AND EXPERIENCE
CAPTURE MANAGER	Big picture; prospect focused; marketing savvy; has senior management access and respect; understands proposal development; guides solution development, teaming, price to win, and strategy development; knows competitors' products, services, people, and reputation
PROPOSAL MANAGER	Disciplined project manger; leads as well as manages, knows, and drives the process; has senior management access, respect, and a sponsor; generalist that can focus on details; can delegate content issues to focus on process
VOLUME MANAGER	Can maintain the respect of writers (content specialists) while managing the process to standards and schedules; disciplinarian; excellent trainer, coach, and communicator; content generalist with some detailed knowledge; allergic to jargon, platitudes, unsupported claims, and fluff
PROPOSAL SPECIALIST	Believes the process works; understands and often prepares compliance checklists, outlines, cross-references matrices, WBS, WBS dictionaries, and schedules; can help writers with hardware, software, and storyboards; knows where to find relevant reuse materials; pleasant, professional nag; knows where to go or who to talk to for information and action; obsessed with meeting the details of schedule, compliance, and quality; functions well without sleep; thrives on adrenaline; works well with all members of production staff
SECTION WRITER	Technically knowledgeable; knows where to get needed information and willing to do it; clear, logical thinker; can see prospect's view; understands pros and cons of alternative approaches; computer literate and competent writer; can follow directions and listen.

Figure 1. Select the Best Person for the Role. *Consider the skills and experience listed as desirable for the role listed.*

5 Differentiate process and content responsibilities.

Proposal managers, proposal specialists, and production leads tend to have process responsibilities. When in a process role, remember that many contributors are primarily concerned about content. People in content roles will only concern themselves with process if they are convinced that the process will save them time and embarrassment while letting them focus on content.

Those in capture management, sales, program or product management, estimating, and pricing are primarily interested in content. When their content interests conflict, they all see process issues as an irritant that forces them to compromise the content.

Volume managers tend to have split roles: they have been selected to manage a process, producing a winning volume, but they usually have a content background relevant to their assigned volume. They often find the content issues more interesting and fail to manage the process to the schedule.

6 Scope all tasks based on a clear vision of the document to be delivered and realistic time standards.

See Scheduling.

Any person using a parametric approach to estimating knows that accurate estimates rely on the assumption that the content and process must remain the same. Similarly, a 1,000-page proposal will require more writing time than a 100-page proposal, assuming similar tasks and processes. Develop a clear vision of the product you will deliver, then specify the tasks required to produce that product.

If you have a consistent process and clearly defined tasks, you can accurately scope your proposal based on standards collected from earlier proposals. The obvious flaw is that few organizations collect the data required to develop proposal management standards.

Proposal professionals tend to look to someone else to suggest the correct standard, but with inconsistent processes, products, management, resources, and skills between organizations, standards transfer poorly. Develop your own.

7 Manage the proposal like all other corporate strategic projects.

Best practice reviews show that organizations that are most effective at winning business view winning new business in a competitive environment to be one of their most strategic and important activities. Organizations that effectively capture new business possess many of the following characteristics:

- They assign their best people to proposals, not whoever is available.
- Management requires individuals seeking to advance to senior management to demonstrate an ability to contribute to and manage teams that capture new business.
- They define and document their business development process.
- They train the participants and provide the resources required.
- They regularly review capture and proposal projects like all other strategic projects.

8 Reward good performance.

Good performers must be rewarded and encouraged at all phases of a proposal project. Commend good performance in the daily meetings. Recognition is often more effective than prizes or monetary rewards.

Sell your approach and process. People who understand why they are doing something are more willing to exceed your expectations.

Hold a victory party immediately after submittal, win or lose. Too many participants never hear if you have won or lost.

Many contributors to proposals are temporarily assigned, pulled from their regular position. Their managers tend to be inconvenienced by the loss and may remember it negatively at the next performance review. Thank good performers in writing, sending a written note to their managers. Some proposal managers ask the best performers to tell them when their salary review is due, then they personally talk to these performers' managers to support a better review.

The best proposal managers seem to be able to make the effort fun in some way. Most proposal managers will be managing another proposal development project and would like the best individuals to be willing to help again.

Teaming is a strategy where two organizations agree to jointly pursue an opportunity either to improve their chances of winning or to decrease their chances of losing. In a broad sense, teaming can range from informal prime-subcontractor relationships to the creation of a new joint-venture organization.

Organizations approach teaming from different perspectives. The most common perspective is to pursue a teaming arrangement if the resulting competitive advantage justifies the additional management burden and potential loss of work share. Others may pursue teaming to eliminate a competitor; lock up a subcontractor; obtain access to a particular market; meet prospect work share requirements; attempt to win more favorable terms from a partner; obtain information about a competitor through the teaming partner; share the financial risk and development cost; or obtain access to new processes, methods, facilities, or business confidential information. The General Motors-Toyota Tumi joint venture auto assembly operation in California is an example of teaming to obtain access to new processes, methods, facilities, and business confidential information.

Teaming

1. **Use the Bidder Comparison Matrix to analyze potential teaming combinations.**
2. **Negotiate a common vision as the basis for teaming and agree to a written teaming agreement.**
3. **Establish a management structure with clear lines of authority.**
4. **Consult with prospects and consider their roles in team formation.**
5. **Define each teaming partner's work share in advance in a Work Breakdown Structure (WBS).**
6. **Separate decisions about work share and team management.**
7. **Address issues like intellectual property, licensing, bid costs, bid process and management, program development costs, allocation of financial risk, and legal issues early before they destroy the team.**

1 Use the Bidder Comparison Matrix to analyze potential teaming combinations.

See **Strategy**.

The Bidder Comparison Matrix is an excellent tool to examine the strength of various teaming combinations from the prospect's perspective. As illustrated in figure 1, primary prospect issues and requirements are listed in the left column. All requirements are assumed equal with a maximum possible score of five. List potential teaming combinations, then rate or score each team on each factor **from the prospect's perspective**. The Integrated Prospect Solution Worksheet tool can be used similarly to analyze the various solutions possible with different teaming partners. Using these tools can make your teaming analysis more objective.

The example in figure 1 shows how to use the Bidder Comparision Matrix to analyze different teaming combinations.

2 Negotiate a common vision as the basis for teaming and agree to a written teaming agreement.

The best teaming relationships exist when team members share a common vision and values. An organization driven to be the low cost producer is likely to conflict with an organization focused on customer service or technical leadership.

Contrasting management focus breeds conflict, requiring greater management attention. All team members must recognize the need for each member and respect their contribution in order to resolve intermediate conflicts.

Teaming arrangements need to be written, negotiated, and signed early. In one major competition, the lawyers representing two joint-venture partners were still arguing about the joint venture agreement at the time of the final Red Team. The strained relationships among team members, reluctance to share information, and poor coordination were clear to the Red Team.

Plan team-building activities early to improve cooperation and reduce risk.

The competition is to research and test the feasibility of using composites in bridges. Both Fiberdyne and Sterling are similar research organizations with no clear edge over the other bidders. RH is primarily a fiber and resin materials producer, while FF is primarily a large, composite component manufacturer. American Bridge, as a bridge builder, seems to be in a hopeless situation, but they have strengths where all others are weak. The best combinations seem to be AB with F or S. From AB's view, F or S might be preferable to others since this is primarily a research contract.

PROGRAM REQUIREMENTS	FIBERDYNE (F)	STERLING (S)	RH	FF	AMERICAN BRIDGE (AB)	CONSULTING ENGINEERS (CES)	AB & F or S	AB & RH	AB & FF	AB & CES
Evaluate economic feasibility	2	2	3	2	5	5	5	5	5	5
Evaluate technical feasiblity	4	4	4	3	3	4	4	4	4	4
Evaluate materials	5	5	4	3	1	3	5	4	3	3
Analyze design impact	5	2	3	2	4	3	5	4	3	3
Survey relevant applications of components	5	5	4	3	1	3	5	4	3	3
Evaluate production methods	4	4	4	5	3	2	4	4	5	3
Develop component designs	4	4	4	5	3	2	4	4	5	3
Prepare final report	4	4	4	5	3	3	4	4	5	3
Publish findings	3	3	3	2	4	3	4	4	4	4
Present at industry forums	3	3	3	2	2	4	3	3	2	4
TOTAL	36	36	36	33	30	35	42	40	41	38

Figure 1. Use Bidder Comparison Matrix to Analyze Teaming Combinations. *This tool lets you compare the relative strengths and weaknesses of individual bidders and various teaming combinations.*

3

Establish a management structure with clear lines of authority.

Shared team management does not work. Some teams rotate the managing responsibilities on longer-term contracts, but customers are often uncomfortable with potential lapses when management rotates. The best teams see themselves as distinct strategic business units where the primary loyalty of individuals on the team is to the team rather than the parent organization.

The teaming relationship must be more robust than an arms-length subcontract. Teaming requires more cooperation and trust to avoid increasing risk.

Lines of authority must be clear, especially if individuals from different parent organizations are collocated. Customers want to know which individuals have what level of authority so they know who can resolve potential problems.

A former four-star general on the Red Team for a joint venture made the following comment:

In all my years as a source selection authority, we never made a single award to a joint venture. It wasn't that we had anything against joint ventures. The proposal simply wasn't clear about precisely who was in charge of what activities, and what were their preapproved levels of authority.

Apply that observation to any type of teaming arrangement, from joint ventures to groups within the same organization:

- Insert management organization charts in the proposal.
- Name all key managers and other positions, if possible.
- Indicate team members' responsibilities, level of authority by type of decision, preapproved spending limits, and whether they have hiring/firing authority.

4

Consult with prospects and consider their roles in team formation.

Prospects have a stake in recommending teaming and their preferred team members. Whether encouraged by the prospect or not, you must persuasively justify why you have teamed, the role of each team partner, and why that partner was selected.

Forced teaming arrangements increase risk. Consider whether forced teaming is worth the increased risk.

5 Define each teaming partner's work share in advance in a Work Breakdown Structure (WBS).

Even at the proposal stage, teams never jell until the work share is defined through a written WBS. Two things can happen if the workshare is not defined; both are bad:

- Tasks are omitted because, "Someone else has it." Omitted tasks are not described or priced, increasing financial and performance risk and decreasing your chances of winning.
- Tasks are included in multiple places, increasing the cost and making you less competitive. Citing different approaches to the same task suggests that you cannot work well as a team.

Appoint a small subgroup representing all team partners to develop the WBS. Frequently, work shares must match the funding percentages of the purchasing organizations, specific work locations, and specific subcontractors selected. Typical examples are NATO weapons procurements and export sales that include coproduction or offset requirements.

6 Separate decisions about work share and team management.

The organization with the largest work share does not have to be the prime management partner. Select the management partner based on the partner with the best ability to manage or on the prospect's preference. Consider the following example:

> In one teaming arrangement, Partner A, with 80 percent of the workshare, was to be the prime or managing partner. Partner A was recognized by the prospect for excellence in research and development (R&D) but they had no record of managing a large production contract. Worse yet, Partner A was typically delivered late and had frequent cost overruns on R&D contracts.
>
> Partner B, with only 20 percent of the work share, had an excellent record of production contract management experience. Nearly half of the 90-day bid preparation period passed before Partner A would agree to let Partner B become the managing partner.

7 Address issues like intellectual property, licensing, bid costs, bid process and management, program development costs, allocation of financial risk, and legal issues early before they destroy the team.

No organization wants to lose its intellectual property and establish a competitor. Establish what must be disclosed for smooth contract performance. Licensing under a royalty agreement is an alternative.

Bidders that have common, compatible approaches to business development and proposal preparation have an edge. The proposal is a mini-project that leads to the major project. Both must have clear management structures with clear lines of authority.

Collocation of proposal teams is ideal, but virtual teaming is increasing. Few individuals have common visions of what is meant by a virtual team. Managers of virtual teams must deal with four issues:

- **Hardware**—Contributors often work on different platforms with different capacities and different printers.
- **Software**—Different operating systems, programs, releases or versions of programs, fonts, print drivers, networks, gateways, and communication protocols usually mean that the teaming partner's input seldom arrives as you thought it would.
- **Process**—When the process and terms used differ, individuals cannot communicate clearly. Worse, they often do not know it. Teams with a common process and a capable proposal manager will prepare a superior proposal in one-half the time.
- **Culture**—Teams in different time zones create obvious challenges. However, organizational culture variations are often larger than national culture variations. Do not underestimate the problems from different organizational cultures and the impact on hardware, software, and process. Individuals who know one platform, one software package, and one process will resist change to the bitter end.

Most of the current focus in virtual proposals is around hardware and software. The tougher and lingering issues involve process and cultural differences.

THEME STATEMENTS

Theme statements in proposals link a prospect benefit to the discriminating features of your offer. Themes tell readers why they should select you. The most powerful themes contain the most unique discriminators, something the prospect wants that no one else offers.

See **Strategies**.

Win themes or major themes apply at top levels. They usually tie a single, unique discriminator to a critical prospect need:

> Development risk and cost are eliminated by selecting the only transport aircraft in this class that is in current production.

Theme statements are not sales slogans, like the catchy phrases most commonly seen in consumer marketing:

Have it your way™
Where's the beef?™
Just do it™
It's the economy, stupid.
Be all you can be™
We try harder™
When it absolutely, positively has to be there overnight™

Section, topic, or paragraph themes are specific statements that appear in a consistent place and style within a proposal. Section themes are the primary focus of this section.

Business capture teams sometimes confuse strategies and theme statements. Strategies = things to do. Themes = things to say. Effective strategies have two parts:

- Strategic—the position you will take
- Tactical—the specific actions you will take to attain the desired position

Inserting theme statements in a proposal is one tactical way to implement a strategy.

Experienced business development professionals often use the terms *theme* and *strategy* interchangeably, confusing both their prospects and their sales support teams.

Theme Statements

1. **Use a logical process to brainstorm theme statements.**
2. **Use theme statements consistently.**
3. **Link benefits to features, trying to state benefits first.**
4. **Quantify benefits if possible.**
5. **Draft concise theme statements, preferably in a single complete sentence.**
6. **Differentiate section theme statements and section summaries.**
7. **Ensure benefits go beyond advantages.**
8. **Tailor your theme structure and approach to the evaluation process.**
9. **Use the Theme Litmus Test to enhance the impact of your theme statements.**

---

1 Use a logical process to brainstorm theme statements.

See **Discriminators** *and* **Features, Advantages, and Benefits.**

Following a logical process enables you to develop meaningful theme statements more consistently and quickly. Use the following theme statement brainstorming checklist to help you determine the key point you want the prospect to remember:

- What is the point of this section?
- Why should the prospect be impressed with what you're proposing?
- What aspect of your offer or approach makes it worth buying?
- What do you offer that is different from competitors' approaches?
- What makes your offer unique, desirable, or beneficial?
- What does your offer do for the prospect?
- Why should the prospect prefer you over the competition?
- Does your offer answer the question, *So what?*

Brainstorming sparks creative input from the entire team.

You may prefer to develop theme statements more logically. Proposal theme statements should flow from the capture and proposal strategy. If you have neither, follow the process outlined below:

1. List the prospect's issues.
2. List a feature of your solution that addresses each issue.
3. Define the issue as specifically and uniquely as possible.
4. Identify a similar success story. Try to quantify the benefit.
5. Draft a theme statement linking the feature and the quantified benefit to a customer issue and substantiate the claim in the proposal.

NOTE: While helpful, you do not need to substantiate your claim in the theme statement, but you must substantiate your claim in the proposal.

Review the following examples to see how these five steps would work:

1. A prospect in the travel clothing and accessory business is concerned about increasing telemarketing sales revenue.
2. You sell IT support services, including supplying and supporting Point-of-Sale software and terminals for e-commerce and catalog sales.
3. Individual sales clerks often do not know the customer's purchase history, interests, or which related items they could recommend.
4. You helped a client achieve a 35 percent increase in dollars per order in a similar situation with a bicycle component and accessory telemarketing retailer.
5. Incorporate the previous information into a theme statement: If Expedition Clothing sees gains similar to Saddle Sores Bike Company, your typical $100 per order sale would increase to $135, for a total annual revenue increase of $3.5 million, after installing Sales Aide™ software and terminals.

2 Use theme statements consistently.

Place theme statements consistently throughout the proposal at the beginning of every major section, subsection, or summary. If you use theme statements in the first- and second-level sections, (section 3 and section 3.1, for instance), use them for all first- and second-level sections. If you insert theme statements at other points in the proposal, do it consistently.

Give theme statements an identical appearance. Most theme statements are visually emphasized to differentiate them from body text, as illustrated in figure 1. The amount of emphasis can vary from the minimal emphasis of a single-sentence opening paragraph in standard body text font to a large, bold, colored font surrounded by white space, borders, shading, or other emphasis devices.

One style is to place theme statements at the top of every page of a proposal. However, theme statements that appear in a predictable position, like a page header, tend to be ignored.

Writers forced to create theme statements to fill the space assigned when they have no discriminating features will often draft poor, ineffective theme statements. When too many theme statements are included, no matter where they are placed, evaluators have said, "We knew that was the marketing hype, so we ignored them."

3 Link benefits to features, trying to state benefits first.

NOTE: Do not "fall on your sword" over whether benefits appear before features. If benefits and features are clearly linked and the features are discriminators, then you have an effective theme statement.

See **Customer Focus**.

Evaluators must see a clear, logical link between the benefit and the feature included in each theme statement. While every benefit could plausibly be linked to lower cost, you do not have to take them all that far.

The following story illustrates the "plausible trail" concept:

> An account executive had been traveling for 3 weeks. Immediately after takeoff, he pulled a crumpled pile of receipts from his briefcase, placed them next to his expense form on the seat tray, and said, "And now to create a plausible trail."

The prospect must see the link between the feature and the benefit.

Poor example

> Our Easy Link™ software will reduce your cost.

Better example

> The intuitive, graphical user interface of our Easy Link™ software can reduce your training time from 4 hours to 1 hour.

Prospects buy benefits, not features. Improve the customer focus of your theme statements by stating the benefit before the feature. The impact is subtle but makes the theme statement more persuasive.

Best example

> Reduce your training time from four hours to one hour due to the intuitive, graphical user interface of our Easy Link™ software.

4 Quantify benefits if possible.

Theme statements that include quantified benefits tend to be more credible.

Theme statement—benefit not quantified

> Reduce order entry cost by installing **e**-Entry™ order entry software.

Theme statement—benefit quantified

> Reduce order handling cost 30 percent by installing **e**-Entry™ order entry software.

Quantified benefits must be supportable. If you cannot support your claims, change your theme statement. Support your claims in the proposal shortly after making the claim.

Whenever possible, quantify the benefits collaboratively with the prospect. Prospects who help determine the potential benefits of your solution are more likely to continue to believe the calculation is correct.

1. Shaded with drop cap and contrasting font

2.0 TITLE

Our team of 47 software engineers has a combined total of over 600 years of experience designing, testing, and installing conversion software on time and within budget.

2. Larger contrasting font

2.0 TITLE

Our team of 47 software engineers has a combined total of over 600 years of experience designing, testing, and installing conversion software on time and within budget.

3. Top and bottom rules

2.0 TITLE

Our team of 47 software engineers has a combined total of over 600 years of experience designing, testing, and installing conversion software on time and within budget.

4. Second color contrasting font

2.0 TITLE

Our team of 47 software engineers has a combined total of over 600 years of experience designing, testing, and installing conversion software on time and within budget.

5. Shaded box, second color, two-column format

2.0 TITLE

Our team of 47 software engineers has a combined total of over 600 years of experience designing, testing, and installing conversion software on time and within budget.

Unified Network Management provides integrated end-to-end control of all your physical network resources. The result is direct, dedicated, quality service . . .

Figure 1. Give Theme Statements a Consistent, Appropriate Emphasis. *Different styles are appropriate for different prospects and markets. Select a tasteful, appropriate style and use it consistently throughout each proposal.*

State the quantified benefit realistically and precisely. Broad generalizations are perceived broadly; overly precise numbers will not be believed. For example, the 30 percent savings in the previous theme statement will be interpreted as plus or minus 5 to 10 percent:

Theme statement—benefit more precisely quantified

Reduce order handling cost 33 percent by installing **e**-Entry™ order entry software.

Depending on how the calculations were completed, the following theme statement borders on being too precise:

Theme statement—benefit more precisely quantified

Reduce order handling cost 33.4 percent by installing **e**-Entry™ order entry software.

The following theme statement is too precise to be credible:

Theme statement—benefit too precisely quantified

Reduce order handling cost 33.37 percent by installing **e**-Entry™ order entry software.

5 Draft concise theme statements, preferably in a single complete sentence.

The longer the theme statement, the more likely the evaluator will not read it. Writing short, concise, discriminating theme statements is difficult.

If you can remove any words in your theme statements without changing the meaning, do it. If you can use a shorter but still accurate word, do it. If you can use a short, active verb instead of jargon, do it.

Note how following these recommendations improve the following theme statement:

Poor example

Our integrated design process, incorporating the lessons learned on all earlier generation aircraft engines, has resulted in an engine that uses four common fastening systems for engine assembly, offering maximum maintainability.

Too many features confuse the reader. Which ones are most unique? Most sellers would claim to have an integrated design process and to incorporate lessons learned.

Better example

Our engine uses four common fastening systems for maximum maintainability.

Now cut the jargon. Fastening systems are bolts; maximum maintainability means easy to fix.

Better example

With only four common bolts used for assembly, our engine is easy to fix.

Then put the benefit first.

Our engine is easy to fix because only four common bolts are used for assembly.

Save the proof for the section graphics and text. Do not try to incorporate complete proof in the theme statement.

Evaluators tire from reading long theme statements. High-impact theme statements resemble sound bites. If evaluators had to justify why you should be selected, what should they say? Draft selection justification statements for the evaluators in your theme statements.

Many adults recall an English teacher who said, "A complete sentence reflects a complete thought." With theme statements, a complete sentence is more likely to contain both features and benefits. Theme statements that are incomplete sentences too frequently contain only features or only benefits. Good theme statements enable the reader to answer both questions: "So what?" and "How so?"

One way to test your theme statements is to read them aloud. Most theme statements that sound good are good. We can actually tolerate reading longer theme statements than we can tolerate hearing them. If you have to take a breath when reading your theme statement, it is too long. Focus your thoughts and shorten your theme statements.

6 Differentiate section theme statements and section summaries.

Writers often create long theme statements that incorporate all of the key features and benefits discussed in the section. These long theme statements make better section summaries. Use them as the first paragraph in the section, then write a concise, focused theme statement.

Note how the following section summary is converted into a concise, specific, and focused theme statement.

Section Summary

All environmental waste cleanup services will be conducted by our 75-person team, centrally located in Omaha, Nebraska. Ima Green has successfully managed this team for 3 years, completing 22 cleanup actions on schedule and at or under budget. Team members are licensed to perform all action requested in the bid request.

Section Theme Statement

Ima Green's team has completed 22 cleanup actions for your organization during the past 3 years. All cleanup actions were on schedule and at or under budget

To illustrate the difference between a section theme and a section summary, try the following two-part exercise:

1. Consider the place where you live. When you were looking for your current apartment or house, you probably saw several places at the same price. Jot down the specific feature that prompted you to select the one where you live. Typical answers are "location," "space," 'the fireplace," "large garage," "fenced yard," "it was bright and airy," or "it just felt good."
2. Now write a one- or two-sentence description of the place where you live. Typical descriptions read like a real estate agent's description:

The home is a 2,000 sq. ft. brick rambler with 3 bedrooms, 2 full baths, a full basement, located on a .25-acre lot near neighborhood schools.

Form a theme statement by linking discriminating features identified in part one to a benefit. The second statement is a summary. Emulate this in section themes.

7 Ensure benefits go beyond advantages.

Benefits are something that prospects have acknowledged they want and value. Benefits are owned by prospects. Advantages are potential benefits. Advantages sound good, but prospects may not actually want them. In some instances, prospects may value the advantage, turning it into a benefit, once they understand how it helps them.

Proposal writers cannot draft effective themes if they do not know what prospects value. Consider the following examples:

You can economically commute to work with this new hybrid gasoline-electric auto, rated at 65 miles per gallon.

What if a prospect is looking for an auto to race in weekend road rallies?

Your fitness will improve rapidly when you use the Pro Star programmable treadmill for only 20 minutes, 4 days per week.

See **Features, Advantages, Benefits.**

What if a prospect detests walking or running, lacks space to place a treadmill, lacks the initiative to workout alone, or simply does not care about personal fitness? Then the treadmill offers this prospect no benefit.

Organizations that use boilerplate extensively often have ineffective themes in their proposals. The benefits, while desirable, are often generic rather than specific and are not in the prospect's terms.

Consider a proposal to provide a telephone system to a business. A typical proposal includes a list of 50 features of the phone system linked to the benefit of each feature. Many prospects see no need for 80 percent of the features, so the system appears over specified, complex, and more expensive than necessary. Many of the remaining 20 percent of the features are linked to benefits that are not particularly interesting to the prospect.

In an attempt to cover all aspects of their system, sellers unintentionally turn off prospects.

8 Tailor your theme structure and approach to the evaluation process.

Proposal professionals advocate distinctly different standards for theme statements, usually because a particular approach has worked well in a specific market. All of the following approaches are used:

1. Place a single theme statement only at the beginning of sections, typically at a uniform indenture level.
2. Place a theme statement anywhere a significant discriminator is discussed.
3. Place a series of theme statements at the beginning of major sections in a single box.
4. Place a single theme statement at the top of every page.

Each approach has potential advantages and disadvantages, depending on how the proposal will be evaluated. Remember that having focused, persuasive content is much more important than the number of theme statements and the placement of those theme statements in your proposal.

The **first two approaches** are more effective in the less-disciplined, more-casual approach to evaluation common in many nongovernment market sectors. Short, concise theme statements are more likely to be read and remembered when the winner is being selected in a group discussion. The telling comment from an evaluator is likely to be something like the following: "I think we should go with Company A because they were the only one that . . . " The evaluator's justification usually mirrors a particularly effective, persuasive theme statement.

The **first three approaches** effectively capture the attention of "skimmers." Skimmers are usually senior managers who play a major role in the selection decision but are not assigned a formal evaluation role. Skimmers read only the parts that capture their interest.

Placing a single theme statement at the beginning of the section requires a writer to identify the single most important discriminator in the section and incorporate it into the theme statement. The concept is correct, but the implementation is more difficult.

Placing theme statements anywhere a significant discriminator is discussed suggests the seller has numerous discriminators. If a theme statement directly answers a specific bid request question or requirement, the highly visible theme statement makes evaluation easy.

The risk in requiring theme statements at set points in a proposal is that writers might lack a discriminating feature, writers must draft more theme statements, and often these theme statements are not as focused and persuasive. Evaluators reading numerous theme statements are less likely to remember your major discriminators.

The **third approach**, placing a collection of themes in a single box at the beginning of a section, has advantages in complex, formally solicited proposals with a detailed, disciplined evaluation process. The example in figure 2 demonstrates this process.

Summarizing your response to the compliance requirements in a single place makes evaluation easy, potentially increasing your score. However individual evaluators at the item level have minimal influence over the final selection. Evaluators with decision making power tend to skim proposals and are less likely to remember anything said in a collection of themes. They are more likely to remember a single, concise statement.

The **fourth approach**, placing themes at the top of every page, is the least-effective choice. Evaluators tend to perceive themes at the top of the page as headers and ignore them. Writers forced to draft a theme for every page tend to draft ineffective, general, and less-persuasive theme statements.

NOTE: The only difference between *pull quotes* and *margin themes* is whether the statement is identical to what is said in body text.

Theme statements are things you say in the proposal to support your strategy. Writers have alternative devices to theme statements to emphasize their strategy in a proposal, specifically, informative headings, action captions, pull quotes, and margin theme statements. Each emphasis device is explained below:

- *Informative headings* are similar to themes, even if they do not incorporate both features and benefits.
- *Action captions* include features and benefits, but they can be longer than themes. The graphic seems to prompt people to eagerly read long captions when they refuse to read long themes.
- *Pull quotes*, often found in magazine articles, resemble themes. Pull quotes are literally quotes pulled from the text and displayed in a larger point size, often in the margin or with body text wrapped around them. Readers tend to remember items that are repeated and emphasized.
- *Margin theme statements* are often placed in page margins adjacent to where the point is supported, anywhere in a proposal section. Margin quotes are effective. Consider using them in all proposals.

See **Action Captions; Features, Advantages, Benefits;** *and* **Headings.**

Compliance requirement	***Theme statement***
INDICATE YOUR APPROACH TO SITE REMEDIATION	**THE KLEAN TEAM WILL REMEDIATE EACH SITE IN A RAPID, COST EFFECTIVE MANNER BY:**
Discuss cost-effective practices, ...	•Eliminating double handling of material
job site safety, ...	•Loading trucks with identical material to eliminate decontamination
team structure, ...	•Limiting team size by assigning individuals qualified to handle several jobs
and how you will use subcontractors, if relevant.	•Using specialized subcontractors wherever they are available, qualified, and cost competitive

Figure 2. Limit Grouped Themes to Formally Evaluated and Solicited Proposals. *Grouped themes reflect individual section compliance requirements. In this example, compliance requirements are listed on the left. The corresponding group theme is shown on the right. Grouped themes are typically placed at the beginning of a proposal section. A similar alternative is to place a benefit-feature matrix at the beginning of each proposal section that reflects the compliance requirements.*

9 Use the Theme Litmus Test to enhance the impact of your theme statements.

Chemists use litmus paper to quickly discriminate acidic and basic solutions. Writers can use the theme litmus test to quickly discriminate effective and ineffective theme statements.

Can you honestly answer "No," then "Yes" to both of the following questions?

1. Could the competition plausibly make the same claim?
2. Could an evaluator cut-and-paste this theme statement into an evaluation form to justify giving you the highest rating for a factor or subfactor?

If not, then refine your theme statement. Try to make your feature more specific until it is unique. Then try to make the benefits more precise. Try to quantify the benefits.

While not foolproof, these questions can help you detect themes that require improvement. Eliminate jargon, slogans, and platitudes from your theme statements. Consider the following examples:

Poor

Elbonia Telephone has committed to partnering with the Elbonian Navy to assure success.

Improved

The Elbonian Navy can eliminate the cost of purchasing their own communications satellite by leasing encrypted and secure channels from the Elbonia Telephone satellite network.

Poor

Master Constructors is uniquely qualified to manage your project.

Improved

As the only company to ever construct a bridge of this type and length, we will assign the same project manager and construction superintendent to better ensure completion on time and within budget.

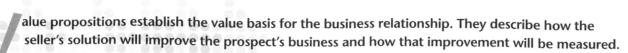

Value propositions establish the value basis for the business relationship. They describe how the seller's solution will improve the prospect's business and how that improvement will be measured.

Value propositions are opportunity and prospect specific and are developed collaboratively with the prospect over the course of the sale.

Value propositions go beyond traditional theme statements by incorporating as many as possible of the following elements:

- Quantifies the anticipated business improvement
- Specifies the timing of the benefits
- Specifies the timing of the costs
- States the payback period
- Specifies how the results will be measured and tracked

Because executives, users, and technical buyers have different issues and values, prepare a different value proposition for each type of buyer. For each distinct opportunity, state the total added value of all value propositions in a single summary value proposition.

Value Propositions

1. **Establish a single sales objective as the first step in developing a value proposition.**
2. **Exploit value propositions as a collaborative selling tool.**
3. **Use a template to develop value propositions.**
4. **Develop unique value propositions for each type of buyer.**
5. **Organize your executive summary around your value propositions.**
6. **Address common obstacles to using value propositions.**

1 Establish a single sales objective as the first step in developing a value proposition.

Shortly after your pursuit decision, draft a brief, precise sales objective that meets the following criteria:

- **Specific**—States what products and services are to be purchased and who will purchase them.
- **Measurable**—Tells how much is to be purchased.
- **Timed**—Cites when the purchase will be made.
- **Result**—States, quantitatively if possible, the result or process change the prospect anticipates.

Sample sales objective

Our sales objective is to persuade Global Corporation to outsource information technology (IT) support, currently costing them $2,850,000 annually. Global is seeking an annual cost reduction of 30 percent, commencing May 1, 20XX, and would like the provider to purchase the existing IT assets.

Like most initial sales objectives, not all criteria are met. The purchasing organization is named but not the purchasing individual. Current costs are named, but not the cost of the seller's solution or the cost of the prospect's assets. Drafting a sales objective is a good way to determine what additional information you need.

Sellers often pursue multiple purchases from the same organization. If you find yourself using "and" to describe multiple buyers and multiple purchase times, you might be facing multiple opportunities that are better addressed by multiple sales objectives.

2 Exploit value propositions as a collaborative selling tool.

The objective of collaborating with the prospect to develop a value proposition is to convince the prospect to award the contract without competitive proposals. The prospect must be convinced that the opportunity cost of delaying exceeds the potential savings from competing the contract.

Collaboration between the prospect and the seller offers the following potential advantages:

- Both gain a clearer understanding of the prospect's objectives and potential benefits.
- Both better understand the actions required of each party, which reduces risk.
- The prospect becomes the seller's advocate in the prospect's organization.

Value propositions flow directly from the sales objective. The best value propositions are specific. Ideally, authorized representatives of both the prospect's and the seller's organizations sign the formal value proposition, and they mutually agree to proceed without competitive proposals.

3 Use a template to develop value propositions.

Templates help sellers draft better value propositions in less time. When a template is not used, the result is often vague, qualitative, and hard to measure.

Value propositions should include the following elements:

- Quantified business improvement
- Timing
- Solution
- Investment cost
- Payback
- Results measurement and tracking

A template for drafting value propositions is shown in figure 1.

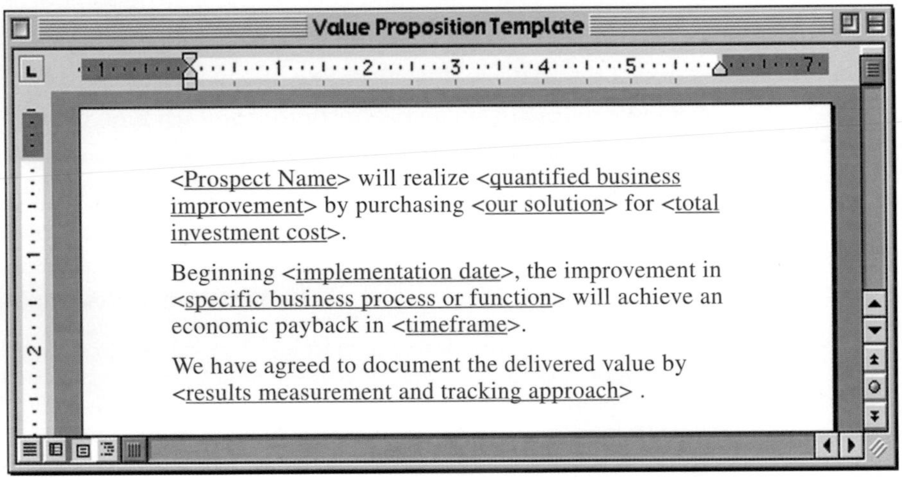
Value Proposition Template

<Prospect Name> will realize <quantified business improvement> by purchasing <our solution> for <total investment cost>.

Beginning <implementation date>, the improvement in <specific business process or function> will achieve an economic payback in <timeframe>.

We have agreed to document the delivered value by <results measurement and tracking approach> .

Figure 1. Use a Template to Develop Value Propositions. *The better value propositions are developed with the prospect and contain the elements listed. Value propositions sound stronger if the benefits are placed at the beginning.*

4 Develop unique value propositions for each type of buyer.

Three broad types of buyers are the economic buyer, the users, and the technical buyers.

The **economic buyer** is the person who gives final approval to purchase. They sign the check and retain veto power. Economic buyers tend to be concerned about the trade-off between price and performance. They focus on bottom line impact. While many people may offer input and recommendations, only the economic buyer can give final approval.

The **users** are the people who judge the potential impact on their job performance. Their personal success is impacted by the sale, so their concerns are often emotional and subjective. Users' issues are reliability, support, ease of operation, maintenance, safety, potential impact on morale, and potential impact on their personal success. Because they use or supervise the use of your product or service, they can ruin a good sale.

The **technical buyers** are gatekeepers. They cannot give final approval, but they can give a final "No." Technical buyers often determine the short list. They tend to focus on the features of a product or service against objective specifications established to screen offers.

Technical buyers may not be technical in the scientific sense. Purchasing agents, lawyers, contracts people, and licensing or regulatory authorities are technical buyers. Since technical buyers are primarily focused on how well you meet their screening tests, the better you understand their criteria, the better your chances of getting their recommendations.

NOTE 1: Roles may overlap. For example, the president of a small, technical company might be both the economic and technical buyer.

NOTE 2: While value propositions targeted at individual buyers may overlap, the summary value proposition targeting the economic buyer incorporates all benefits and costs.

Another way to examine buyers is according to their source of power. Power could be economic, users (control), or technical (knowledge). Alternatively, power could be indicated by level of management, such as executive management, middle management, or operations.

Tailor value proposition(s) to each type of buying influence. The following three value propositions target each type of buyer and are extensions of the earlier example of a single sales objective under guideline 1:

Value Proposition for the economic buyer

Global Corporation will realize a $3,750,000 reduction in information technology support costs over the next 5 years, commencing May 1, 20XX, by contracting with Computer Heroes, Ltd., at a cost of $2,000,000 per year. Global Corporation will be paid $500,000 for all of Global's IT assets, and Computer Heroes will provide all IT support. Global Corporation will enjoy a 30 percent annual reduction in IT costs, assuming the agreed prices and the same levels of services currently required continue to be required and delivered. All costs will be available to you on-line and documented in monthly invoices.

Value Proposition for user

Commencing May 1, 20XX, the department allocations for IT support for the current types and levels of service will be reduced an average of 30 percent. Outdated legacy systems will be transitioned to lower cost, current, commercial off-the-shelf hardware and software. Departmental managers will be free to focus on core management tasks without the distractions of IT issues. All costs will be available and verifiable on-line and documented in monthly invoices tied to Global work order numbers. With Computer Heroes assuming responsibility for all hardware and software (paying Global $500,000 for the current assets), department managers will no longer have to submit and defend IT capital requests.

Value Proposition for technical buyer (IT professionals)

Commencing May 1, 20XX, IT professionals will have extensive and varied opportunities for personal growth and advancement within their profession. Computer Heroes will offer positions to all IT employees and will maintain current pay levels for those positions. As an industry leader, all positions will be reviewed and adjusted to industry standards. Opportunities for training and advancement will be offered to all employees on an equal basis through our Intranet web site, our employee newsletter, regular all-hands e-mails, and job site postings.

Value Proposition for technical buyer (contracts)

Commencing May 1, 20XX, all IT support, both employees and assets, will be seamlessly transitioned to Computer Heroes, saving Global Corporation $750,000, per year over current costs. All cost savings will be calculated on the basis of providing identical levels of service and can be verified on-line by comparing monthly, itemized invoices.

5 Organize your executive summary around your value proposition.

If developing value propositions is an integral part of your business development process, organize your executive summary around your value propositions.

See **Executive Summary.**

Begin the executive summary by stating the summary value proposition that targets the economic buyer, the sole person who can sign the check. Follow the summary value proposition with the underlying value propositions. Then present all aspects of your solution against one of the underlying value propositions, substantiating how your approach delivers the value claimed. Conclude by showing how the underlying value propositions add up to the opening summary value proposition.

Use the Four-Box organizational structure discussed in the Executive Summary section and summarized in figure 2. For organizational purposes, treat each underlying or subvalue proposition as a hot button.

Some aspects of value cannot be quantified. Sometimes, individuals in either prospects' or sellers' organizations cannot agree on the quantitative added value.

Always state the intangible or nonquantified values of your proposed solution. If the quantified added values of competitors' solutions are close to yours, the intangible added values could win the contract. State your quantitative added value before your qualitative added value.

See **Executive Summary** *and* **Sales Letters.**

BOX 1—Present the summary value proposition prepared for the economic buyer. State the collaborative basis for this value proposition, indicating ownership by both the prospect and the seller.

BOX 2—Present two to five subvalue propositions in a bulleted list. The total should equal the total value cited in Box 1.

BOX 3—Present each subvalue proposition in the order introduced. All proposed products and services must be aligned with one of the subvalue propositions. By the completion of Box 3, all aspects of your offer should be covered. Expand or contract the space devoted to each subvalue proposition according to its relative importance to the prospect.

BOX 4—Summarize the total value and total cost, previously cited in Box 1. Close by previewing the next logical step in the sales process, usually how your proposal is organized. If immediate negotiations are possible, suggest a time to begin.

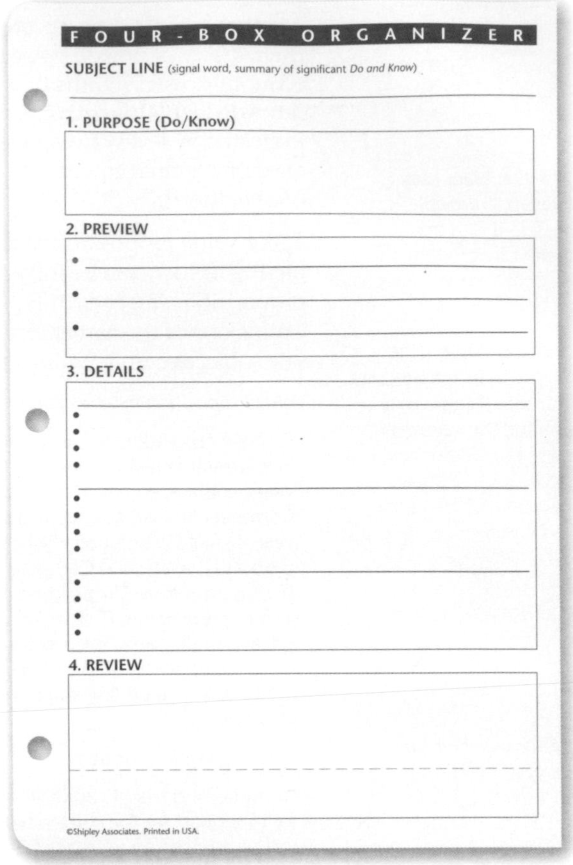
FOUR-BOX ORGANIZER

SUBJECT LINE (signal word, summary of significant *Do and Know*)

1. PURPOSE (Do/Know)

2. PREVIEW

3. DETAILS

4. REVIEW

©Shipley Associates. Printed in USA.

Figure 2. Organize Your Executive Summary Around Your Value Proposition. *Open with your summary value proposition to the economic buyer. Regard each major subvalue proposition as a hot button. Then align all major aspects of your offer against one of the subvalue propositions. Close with a short summary of your total value proposition, and preview how your proposal is organized.*

6

Address common obstacles to using value propositions.

NOTE 1: A relatively common practice in proposals in all markets is to insert theme statements. A best practice is to quantify the benefits in the theme statement, then substantiate the claim in the proposal shortly after the theme statement.

See **Theme Statements.**

NOTE 2: Individuals working in regulated government markets where contacts between the seller and the prospect are limited or prohibited can still benefit from developing value propositions. A quantified value proposition based on reasonable assumptions will be more persuasive than a vague, qualitative claim to offer best value.

Most organizations have difficulty with value propositions. The chart below lists some of the common problems and suggests potential solutions.

The deep understanding of the prospect's business required to develop a value proposition can favorably discriminate your organization. With government purchasers adopting commercial acquisition practices, value propositions might give you an edge.

REASONS VALUE PROPOSITIONS MISUSED	POTENTIAL SOLUTIONS
Legal or contracts people refuse to allow any specific statements to limit potential liability.	Carefully state all assumptions and conditions.
Few people understand value propositions as a disciplined concept.	Train all participants in the process.
Short sales cycles limit prospect-seller collaboration.	Develop "generic" value propositions.
Excessive targeting of multiple opportunities limits prospect-seller collaboration.	Improve Pursuit and Bid/No Bid milestone discipline.
Seller-developed value propositions are summarily rejected by prospects.	Find a friendly collaborator, sell on a basis other than "best value," or no bid.
Prospects' distrust of the seller or purchasing restrictions limit or bar collaboration with sellers.	Develop greater trust, or sell on a basis other than "best value."

Writing for grants is a branch of proposal writing practiced largely by nonprofit organizations seeking funds to maintain or expand their services. Grant writers can win more dollars by following sales proposal guidelines and best practices.

Writing for grants is a branch of proposal writing practiced largely by nonprofit organizations seeking funds to maintain or expand their services. Grant writers can win more dollars by following sales proposal guidelines and best practices.

A grant is a *monetary award* given by a *funder*. Funders are government agencies, foundations, corporations, or even private individuals. Most funders require a grant proposal that describes and justifies how the funds will be used.

Funders support an array of activities—from the **emotional** to the **pragmatic** and **mundane**. For example, an *emotional* grant might support children born with birth defects, a *pragmatic* grant might fund high-temperature proton exchange membrane research, and a *mundane* grant might be used to repair sidewalks.

Superior grant applications are persuasive sales documents.

Funders require grant applications consisting of an application form, a proposal, or both. An application form is exactly that—a form that asks for the applicant's name, address, and other information, including the applicant's reasons for requesting the funding. Formal application forms simplify evaluation, foster the appearance of fairness, and may reduce application time.

A grant proposal, as discussed in this *Proposal Guide*, is usually an original document with a logical structure and a clear argument for funding. For some grants, a full grant application requires both a completed form and a written grant proposal.

A primary difference between a grant proposal and a typical sales proposal is the number of competitors. Most sales proposals have fewer than ten competitors, while hundreds may vie for a single grant or a portion of the funds available.

Grant proposals share common elements with proposals for professional services, such as architectural, engineering, and Research and Development (R&D). Both have numerous competitors, and the evaluations often incorporate peer reviews. Most grant proposal guidelines apply to professional services proposals.

Grant proposals also share common elements with U.S. Federal professional services and R&D proposals, and most *Proposal Guide* guidelines apply. Both respond to varying well-defined criteria but operate under the same "no single right answer" concept that drives grant proposal diversity.

Writing for Grants

1. **Verify your eligibility.**
2. **Identify funder's explicit, implicit, and hidden issues.**
3. **Consider how your proposal will be evaluated.**
4. **Carefully follow all submittal instructions.**
5. **Follow sound document organization principles.**
6. **Lead with a one-page executive summary.**
7. **State your goals as an attractive, positive vision, linked to quantitative objectives.**
8. **Describe the acute needs of your target population vividly and precisely. Appeal emotionally, backed by the most credible facts available.**
9. **Address the program's goals in every section.**
10. **Directly link project objectives, activities, milestones, and costs.**
11. **Link all expenses to required activities.**
12. **Use emphasis devices to engage reviewers, simplify review, shorten the proposal, and raise your score.**
13. **Support all claims.**
14. **Limit appendices to requested material.**

1 Verify your eligibility.

See **Compliance and Responsiveness.**

Everyone in your organization must both understand eligibility guidelines and agree to comply with those guidelines.

Eligibility rules are complex, so verify your eligibility. Eligibility applies at several levels:

- Minimum standards to apply for the grant
- Preferences or extra points given to bidders with desired characteristics
- Acceptable service approaches

For example, government funders may set cost-effectiveness criteria. Programs exceeding the cost-per-participant criteria are ineligible.

All funders have award guidelines and funding priorities. Save time by scanning funders' profiles in the awards guidelines for the following items:

- *Limitations* describe locations, applicants, or activities they will not fund.
- *Purpose and activities* should reflect your organization's values.
- *Fields of interest* should fit your program activities and target population. Funders might not use your terms or jargon.
- *Types of support* must match how you plan to use the funds. Funders may direct, limit, or exclude support for capital investments, overhead, operating activities, travel, paid staff, or consultants.
- *Previous grants* or *grantees* may be excluded. Conversely, funders might prefer to focus funding in a specific area or to direct funding to specific organizations.
- *Grant amounts* may be limited due to budget constraints or the desire to fund multiple programs. Some funders will not fund more than a set percentage of an applicant's total budget.

Determine the types and sizes of grant awards made by non-profits in the U.S. by reviewing their Internal Revenue Service Form 990, available online. Look for the ***Grants and Contributions Paid*** section. As a new applicant, limit requested amounts to the top 25th percentile. New applicants seldom win the largest grants.

2 Identify funders' explicit, implicit, and hidden issues.

See **Strategy.**

Issues are funders' concerns, not yours. Applicants' concerns are gaps.

Explicit issues are stated and owned by funders. Use funders' terms. Do not paraphrase or switch to your own terms.

Implicit issues are implied, may or may not be understood, and are often not readily apparent to everyone. Implicit issues must be made explicit in the proposal.

Hidden issues are either unknown or intentionally unstated. The most dangerous hidden issues are "unmentionable." For example, public figures may be reluctant to discuss some issues for fear of alienating an important constituency. Address hidden issues positively or avoid them.

The first place to look for funders' issues is in their stated funding goals and objectives. Review funders' other public materials. Discuss funders' issues with individuals from their organizations, when possible, without becoming a pest or violating funders' guidelines.

All proposals, including grant proposals, should focus on funders' issues. The goals, objectives, proposed activities, experience, and performance of the applicant are relevant and interesting to evaluators only if they are linked to funders' issues. Being worthy of receiving the grant seldom discriminates. Many applicants are worthy. You must convince them that you will address their issues and be more than merely worthy.

3 Consider how your proposal will be evaluated.

Influence reviewer selection when possible. Recommend peer reviewers and submit a "conflict of interest" list, when permitted.

Winning proposals are easy to evaluate at every evaluation stage. Easily evaluated proposals receive higher scores. The following evaluation steps are typical:

- Initial screening
- Independent, individual review and scoring
- Identification and resolution of anomalies
- Approval for funding
- Permission to proceed and funding

In the initial screening or pre-review, reviewers screen proposals to reduce their workload and to stay within the law or their own award guidelines. When facing 100 proposals, reviewers have a strong incentive to simplify their work by quickly eliminating unqualified proposals.

Government funders must follow the law or their decisions can be challenged. Nongovernment funders have more latitude, but they generally stay within their organizations' guidelines.

Reviewers use common screening criteria:

✔ Are all required forms included?

✔ Are all forms completed and signed?

✔ Are page limitations and format guidelines met?

✔ Are requested funding levels acceptable?

✔ Are all eligibility guidelines met?

✔ Are all required dates met (submittal, commencement, conclusion, reporting)?

Government agencies, foundations, and corporations set review criteria in the grant guidelines. Using a point-based rating system, your proposal must score a minimum number of points to be recommended for funding.

Staff or peer reviewers independently review and score proposals that meet initial screening criteria. Peer reviewers are selected individuals with expertise in the field. Each reviewer scores each section numerically against a standard and supports their scores with explanatory comments. Most grant proposals are scored on a 100-point scale.

Anomalies between reviewers' scores are identified and resolved, usually in a conference call. Reviewers are asked to discuss and defend their scores when high and low scores vary more than a predetermined amount.

Being recommended for funding does not necessarily mean you are funded. Sufficient funds might not be available or known. Meeting the cutoff score does not ensure funding and the authority to proceed.

In general, the more detailed the evaluation process, the larger the proposal. Corporations and private individuals tend to want short proposals, less than five pages, and have a less-formal evaluation process. Engage them in the first page or forget it.

Governments tend to use more formal evaluation procedures and request larger proposals.

Foundations' evaluation processes vary from formal to informal. Determine each foundation's process and preference before proposing.

---

4 Carefully follow all submittal instructions.

Also see **Customer Focus** *and* **Outlining.**

Follow all submittal instructions. Reviewers are reluctant to search for out-of-place information. An inability to follow instructions suggests that you might not do what you say if funded.

Do not deviate from the submittal instructions because the instructions are illogical. The reviewer probably did not write the submittal instructions, and your more logical approach makes reviewers' tasks more difficult.

When instructions are not clear, explain your approach. Always explain your approach in a customer-focused manner:

Poor explanation

While you did not specifically request the background and history of our organization, we have included it in the "Overview" section to demonstrate our long commitment to improving the reading skills of elementary school students.

Better, customer-focused explanation

To simplify your evaluation, we have summarized our prior elementary school student reading skill enhancement activities in a short sidebar. All subsection topics are discussed in the order requested in your submittal guidelines.

5 Follow sound document organization principles.

See **Organization.**

While the principles of organization vary slightly from document to document, organizational guidelines for grant proposals and sales proposals are similar.

The required contents for grant proposals varies by government agency and foundation. Figure 1 summarizes and contrasts the contents for both.

Proposal Guide ORGANIZATION section guidelines for grant proposals are adapted and summarized below in order of importance.

Carefully follow all submittal instructions, as noted in guideline 4.

Organize information to simplify evaluation. Use graphics, tables, informative headings, and callouts to help reviewers both find and relate information.

See **Choosing Correct Words.**

Group similar ideas. A scattered, disorganized response suggests you cannot organize and manage proposed activities.

Order points in decreasing order of importance to the reader. Reviewers quit reading when they find the answer to their question or when they lose interest. State your most important point first. Saving the best for last often means reviewers do not read it or implies that it is not very important. Always stay within the funder's required structure.

Summarize at all levels. Assume reviewers quit reading after the first sentence of each section. Have you summarized your key message?

Assume reviewers quit reading after the first paragraph. Have you stated your key messages?

Follow or close each summary with an introduction or preview of what follows. Assuming reviewers understood your key message in the summary, an introduction tells them where can they find support, elaboration, or clarification.

Adjust your writing style to the reviewers. Use the correct terms, but do not overuse jargon and acronyms. While reviewers may be familiar with certain jargon and acronyms, these terms are dull, less vibrant, and have less emotional appeal. Remember that persuasion requires both emotion and logic. Too many grant writers mistakenly assume that reviewers have similar backgrounds and love to read jargon, big sentences, and big words.

GOVERNMENT AGENCY	*FOUNDATION*
1. Application cover form 2. Executive summary or abstract 3. Table of contents 4. Program narrative 5. Budget 6. Certifications, forms 7. Attachments	1. Cover letter (Introduction, purpose, amount requested, closing) 2. Cover sheet (Requesting organization, key contact, mission statement, finances, summary of grant request) 3. Narrative (Executive summary, description of the program and proposed impacts) 4. Attachments (Limited to requested items)

Figure 1. Contents Lists for Grant Proposals. *Required contents vary, so these are general. Corporations tend to want even shorter, simpler proposals than foundations. For example, target 30 pages for government agencies, 7-to-10 for foundations, and 3-to-5 for corporations, excluding required attachments.*

6

Lead with a one-page executive summary.

Also see **Executive Summary, Graphics, Service Proposals,** *and* **Theme Statements.**

The executive summary is the most important page in a grant proposal. It sets the tone for individual reviewers and is often the only portion read by the decision-maker.

Call your executive summary whatever the funder calls it in the application guidelines. "Abstract" is acceptable, if that is the funder's term.

If funders request an executive summary, submit one. If they do not request an executive summary, give them a one-page, maximum, executive summary anyway. This falls under the *summarize at all levels* guideline.

Grant executive summaries should meet the following criteria:

- Connect the funder's goals and objectives to the goals and objectives of this grant.
- Summarize the need or problem you are addressing.
- State your goals and measurable objectives.
- Summarize your initiative, linked to the funder's objectives, and discriminate "Why you?"
- Summarize the impact (benefit), cost, timing, and funding required.
- Incorporate visual, emotional support of your claims.

7

State your goals as an attractive, positive vision, linked to quantitative objectives.

Goals are ends, outcomes, the state that you will attain. Goals are rooted in the vision of what you will attain when the grant is completed. Goals are not measurable or timed. Funders always have a goal. To win, funders' goals must be your goals.

Objectives are measurable, timed milestones. Each goal has a supporting series of measurable objectives or benchmarks that lead to the goal. The objectives in the grant announcement must be the objectives for your program. Address every objective in your needs or problem statement and link every activity to an objective.

Outcome objectives are more powerful, persuasive, and ultimately more successful than process objectives.

See Guideline 10.

You can write outcome or process objectives. Outcome objectives are stronger and more convincing because they imply a measurable improvement. Outcome objectives tend to begin with words like *expand, increase, reduce,* or *collect.*

Process objectives are not quantifiable or measurable; they are either complete or not complete. Process objectives tend to begin with words like *provide, establish, develop, initiate,* or *create* and link project deliverables/activities to outcome objectives.

Write process objectives only if required. Since funders prefer measurable outcomes for their funding, not just activity, outcome objectives are more powerful and persuasive.

State goals and objectives in a single sentence. If you cannot, simplify.

Superior objectives incorporate three parts:

- What quantified change will occur?
- Who will be impacted?
- How will they be impacted?

Review the following goal and sub-objectives:

Good example

> **Goal 1**: Improve the reading skills of American children
>
> **Outcome objective 1a:** Improve the reading ability of 25 grade 1-4 children in the Gallatin Valley by two grade levels.
>
> **Outcome objective 1b:** Dedicate 100 Pet Partner® hours per week to practice reading with individual, grade 1-4 children in the Gallatin Valley at participating public libraries and elementary schools.

Notice how the following process objective is weaker and less persuasive than outcome objective 1b.

Less effective process objective

> **Process objective 1c:** Provide the opportunity for grade 1-4 children in the Gallatin Valley to practice their reading skills by reading to Pet Partner teams at participating public libraries and elementary schools.

What if none of the children participate? How many libraries, schools, and children must participate for the program to be successful?

While the target group is clear, the number of children, practice hours, and service locations should be cited or identified.

8

Describe the acute needs of your target population vividly and precisely. Appeal emotionally, backed by the most credible facts available.

Federal grants must contribute to the benefit of the public as a whole, not just the benefit of an individual public agency.

Clearly differentiate public needs, the funder's needs, your target population's needs, and your own needs for funding.

Vividly emphasize the acute problem that you will address if your grant is funded. Funders want the greatest benefit for the money spent. They also want to fund where needs are greatest. Adopt a strategy that needs are dire and immediate, and that their funding will relieve the suffering.

Write about all aspects of the problem. Be specific. Cite credible facts and statistics. The most-to-least credible sources of statistics about the needs, your services, and your organization are listed in order:

- What this potential funder says
- What other, similar funders say
- What truly independent sources say
- What you say

Less successful proposals tend to emphasize the last of these—applicants' opinions about the needs, their services, and their organizations. All applicants stress their worthiness. Making identical assertions will not discriminate your request.

Keep all facts current, with nothing older than five years. Demonstrate your expertise but do not exaggerate. Precisely address every program objective in the grant application, describing each service lacking in your area.

Addressing the need as dire can be difficult when seeking a renewal, extension, or supplementary funding. Funders might question your effectiveness. Instead, emphasize the need to expand a proven but limited program; show that the needs of people *outside* your program are still dire; or explain that the people being served have additional needs.

Poor example

Numerous politicians, educators, and media articles have bemoaned the poor reading skills of young children. A significant minority that begin their education with poor reading skills remain poor achievers in all areas. Those that begin behind stay behind. You can help Gotham City elementary and preschool children succeed by supporting the R.E.A.D.® Program.

Better example

In 2002, in our highest poverty schools, 68 percent of fourth graders could not read at the basic level, according to the U.S. Department of Education. Over the last 15 years, 15 million students have graduated from high school without the ability to read at the basic level. First Lady Laura Bush noted in her *Ready to Read-Ready to Learn* initiative:

> We know that children who have poor beginning reading skills are less likely to develop better reading skills throughout their school careers. Children, who start school behind, often stay behind. We can reverse that trend.

Your own report, *Gotham City Education Statistics for 2002,* cited 3000 students in this at-risk category. Your own statistics noted that in 2001, R.E.A.D. participants improved their reading skills two to four grade levels. At a cost of less than $200 per child, the Gotham City School District should not only renew the R.E.A.D. Program, but also support its expansion to serve 500 at-risk children during the 2003–2004 term.

Note how the poor example was based on the applicant's opinion and lacked statistics. In contrast, the better example cited facts from the U.S. Department of Education, the First Lady, and the potential funder's own study. Also note that the dire continuing need focuses on the population not yet being served.

9

Address the program's goals in every section.

See **Customer Focus** *and* **Theme Statements.**

The typical contents of a grant were listed in guideline 5. Address the program's goals in every section. Remember that the funder's goals in the grant application are your goals for this program.

Much like drafting customer-focused theme statements, begin the first sentence of each section by restating a funder's goal linked to the topic that you are discussing. Consider these examples:

Executive Summary Theme Statement

Your goal of reducing the auto traffic congestion in the Gotham City central business district by 10 percent can be met by funding the Loaner Bike Program at $5,000 per month.

Program Narrative Theme Statement

Gotham City's 10 percent auto traffic reduction goal can be met if 15 percent of the sub-one mile trips within the core area are via a maintained, free, convenient fleet of Golden Gotham loner bikes positioned in 80 convenient bike racks.

Budget Theme Statement

The 10 percent auto traffic reduction goal is achieved with a low initial cost because the bikes come from unclaimed property.

Note that all three theme statements link the auto traffic reduction goal to a specific feature of the applicant's program.

10

Directly link project objectives, activities, milestones, and costs.

See **Relevant Experience/ Past Performance,** *figure 4 for a related example matrix.*

Linking proposed activities to at least one objective suggests that the activity is necessary. Linking milestones to an objective suggests you know how to manage the activities and measure progress. Linking all costs to objectives suggests that all costs are necessary.

When grant writers fail to link objectives, activities, milestones, and costs, reviewers question their necessity. Linking them all suggests that you understand exactly what you will do when funded.

The best way to link objectives, activities, milestones, and costs is in a matrix. Constructing this matrix will test and improve your understanding of your program. Since few grant writers link objectives, activities, milestones, and costs, your program appears clearer, better managed, lower risk, and more cost effective.

11

Link all expenses to required activities.

Linking expenses to required activities is an extension of guideline 10. Presenting a total budget is easier for the writer than for reviewers, who cannot easily determine if all items are necessary.

Prepare your standard budget, but then allocate all items against the activities. Split categories among activities. Present your allocated budget, not the combined budget.

Emphasize added value in your budget. For example, an organization seeks $20,000 to train, supervise, and motivate 100 volunteers that each donate 2 hours weekly over 1 year (a total of 10,000 service hours following training). The grant writer could argue that professional administration would cost $40,000, not $20,000, and volunteers' time at $15/hour is worth $150,000. Thus, the value proposition for the funder is to spend $20,000 for $190,000 worth of services.

No one wants to pay for anything that appears unnecessary, especially the individuals charged with selecting programs to be funded and monitoring their performance. A program manager for a government agency, corporation, or foundation would feel pretty good about spending $20,000 for $190,000 worth of services.

Do not feel that what you are proposing to do is so deserving that you must be funded. Good grant writers present all programs as deserving. Give reviewers a quantitative as well as an emotional justification to fund your program.

12

Use emphasis devices to engage reviewers, simplify review, shorten the proposal, and raise your score.

See **Action Captions, Graphics, Headings, Lists, Page and Document Design, Photographs, Presenting Cost and Price Data, Relevant Experience/ Past Performance,** *and* **Theme Statements** *for explanations and examples.*

The best grant proposals are about the service, not the provider of the service. Use all of the emphasis devices discussed in this *Proposal Guide* to emphasize your services.

Photos and graphics may have many interpretations. Do not put in a photo just because it is a great photo. The photo must be directly relevant to the services proposed. Figure 2 shows six photographs and notes why they should or should not be used in a particular proposal.

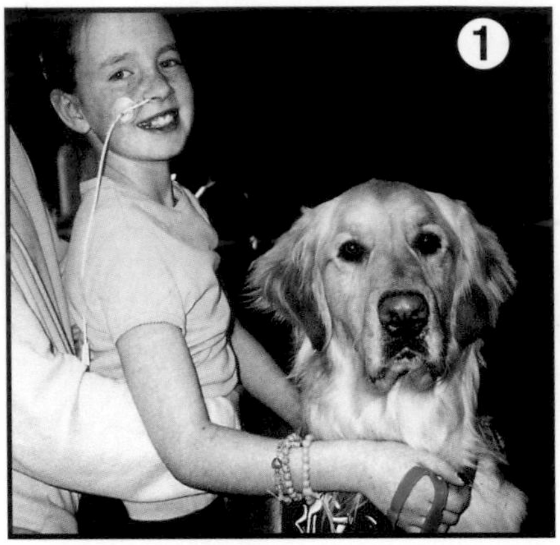

1. This photo emphasizes a patient with a therapy dog, but this is not a R.E.A.D.® program service. Emphasize photos that show the proposed service, not other services of the organization, however worthy.

2. It's hard to resist this photo, but the emphasis is on the dog. A reviewer primarily concerned with improving children's reading skills could easily question, *Why should I be funding someone's pet?* Even if the reviewer understands the concept, how might it appear to their employer? Emphasize the person receiving the service.

3. This photo is ideal. Both volunteers are focused on the reader. Reading is clearly the primary activity and the entire Pet Partner team is shown delivering the service.

4. While this child is not reading, no one can miss his pleasure. The volunteer is appropriately present but de-emphasized in the background. Note how this actual caption made a powerful point: *Children who participate report that they know the dogs are listening to them. We all value good listeners; children are no exception.*

5. The emphasis is clearly on the service, but the volunteer is not shown. Could someone think the dog is unsuper-vised? While a good photo, it is not as effective as photos 3,4, and 6.

6. The success of this photo depends on the "spin" in the caption. A careful reviewer might note that the adult is reading, not the child. The following caption makes the photo effective: *While children spend most therapy time reading in a relaxed, supportive environment, the adult partner will occasionally assist with difficult words or passages.*

Figure 2. Selecting Appropriate Photos. *A favorite, grant-worthy, and innovative program is Reading Education Assistance Dogs (R.E.A.D.), by Intermountain Therapy Animals (ITA). R.E.A.D. is just one of several ITA programs. The goal of the R.E.A.D. program is improving the literacy skills of children through the assistance of registered Pet Partner therapy teams. While the R.E.A.D. program has been featured in the Wall Street Journal, ABC World News with Peter Jennings (10/27/00), and NBC Nightly News with Tom Brokaw (4/19/02), the R.E.A.D. program could be confused with other ITA programs that a potential funder would not support. Do not lose funding by discussing worthy but unrelated programs.* (Images and excerpts courtesy of Intermountain Therapy Animals, Salt Lake City, Utah.)

13 Support all claims.

Emphasize your claims and support them. Preserve your credibility with reviewers by removing all unsupported claims.

Note that support and proof differ. Support requires at least one example. Proof is much stronger and more difficult to substantiate.

For example, delivering a service one time is support that you can do it again. Proving that you can deliver a service every time requires a 100 percent successful track record.

14 Limit appendices to requested material.

If the materials are not requested or required, do not include them. Do not place materials in an appendix because you think they are interesting, because you always include them, or because you think the grant application should have asked for them. Instead, focus your attention on the most important pages, the body of the proposal.

Appendices are used to streamline documents. Incorporate materials of interest to all reviewers in the proposal. Place materials of interest to only a few readers in an appendix.

See **Appendices.** *All aspects apply to grant proposals.*

Grant writers often append complimentary news clippings, citations, awards, thank-you letters, service photos, facility photos, and quotes from local officials and organizations. While well received, the approach with the most impact is to incorporate excerpts in the proposal to directly support your claims. Do both when space and time permit.

Refer to all appended materials in the body of the proposal. Include short informative summaries of each appended item.

Order appendices in the following order:

- As requested in the grant application
- As referenced in the proposal

To clearly distinguish the proposal and the appendix, number proposal pages and letter appendix pages, *A-1, A-2, . . ., B-1,* etc.

Grant applicants often do not meet directly with funders. Instead of stuffing an appendix with additional and costly materials, list the materials, services, and presentations that are available upon request. If they bite, you get an audience that others might not get. This proven sales tactic can give you a significant advantage.

The model documents in this section illustrate best practices in business development and current business English.

All documents follow the guidelines discussed in the *Proposal Guide* as closely as possible, subject to the unique aspect of the specific competition.

Most of the model documents were slightly altered from the original to disguise the seller and the customer. Some documents were written specifically for this *Proposal Guide.*

To reduce the space required, some of the longer documents have been shortened. vertical dots indicate document breaks. The initial summary and introductory portions of all major sections are included.

The following suggestions will help you use these models to improve your own sales documents.

1. Rely on the overall organization and design rather than exact words and phrases. Most of the time the circumstances of each competition differ.
2. Chose words and phrases that sound like you. Words taken from other documents often appear unnatural to the reader and prompt them to doubt your message.
3. Read the notes at the side and bottom of the documents carefully and refer to the reference sections. Remember that guidelines are not rules. Use sound judgment to tailor your documents for each competition.
4. Begin your own collection of model documents. Collect documents and excerpts from documents that seem appropriate for your industry and organization but also consider outside documents to identify new best practices.
5. Refine and polish every new document that you prepare, regardless of the source. Win more business and improve your persuasiveness by following the principles discussed and illustrated in this *Proposal Guide.*

Model Documents Table of Contents

#	ITEM	TYPE	PAGE
1.	Sales Letter	Prospecting	230
2.	Sales Letter	Follow-up to a Phone Call	231
3.	Sales Letter	Follow-up to a Meeting	232
4.	Sales Letter	Invitation to a Sales Event	233
5.	Sales Letter	Request for RFP Modification	234
6.	Executive Summary	Informally Solicited Commercial Proposal	236
7.	Executive Summary	Incumbent's Informally Solicited Services Proposal	238
8.	Executive Summary	Formally Solicited Government Proposal	240
9.	Cover Letter	To Decision Maker with Buying Criteria	241
10.	Cover Letter	To Decision Maker without Buying Criteria	242
11.	Cover Letter	To Buyer for Formally Solicited Government Bid	243
12.	Storyboard	Formally Solicited Government Bid	244
13.	Proposal Section	Formally Solicited Government Bid	246
14.	Proposal Section	Casually Solicited Commercial Bid	252
15.	Proposal Section	Question and Response Proposal	257
16.	Capture Plan	Major Program, Text Format	258
17.	Capture Plan	Major Program, Presentation Format	274

1–PROSPECTING LETTER

❶ Attention line targets a group of individuals.

❷ The informative subject heading begins with a benefit to entice the reader.

See **Features, Advantages, and Benefits; Headings;** *and* **Themes.**

❸ Opens with a potential issue or pain to gain interest, then states the benefit the seller hopes to deliver. Identifies the writer and requests a defined but limited meeting.

See **Sales Letters.**

❹ Indicates the writer's basis for the prospect's issues without being arrogant.

See **Customer Focus.**

❺ Bullet lists of potential benefits for emphasis while previewing the organization of the rest of the letter.

See **Lists** *and* **Organization.**

❻ Headings precisely reflect the previewed topics and are bold for increased emphasis.

See **Lists** *and* **Organization.**

❼ Summarizes the opening issue and requests the meeting.

See **Organization** *and* **Sales Letters.**

❽ Vividly describes the requested meeting and links it to the benefits.

See **Sales Letters.**

❾ Marketing research suggests 95 out of 100 people read a "P.S." first. The "P.S." is read when other parts are skipped. Proactively states the next step in the same, precise tone used to visualize the requested meeting.

CPA$-R-U$ 1040 A Street, Centerville UT 84010 801.333.7000
www.cpas-r-us.com

8 May 15, 20XX

❶ **Attention: Executive Committee** (Joe Best, Walt Rosen, Kevin Davidson)

ACME Corporation
P. O. Box 30
Fort Worth, TX 76137

❷ **Subject: Save Taxes with Tailored Solutions from CPAs-R-Us**

❸ Organizations and individuals often pay unnecessary taxes. As one of the owners of CPAs-R-Us, I am writing to you to determine who is the most appropriate person in Acme to meet with me for 45 minutes on January 11 or 12 when I am in Fort Worth. By tailoring your tax planning, both ACME and your executives can gain the most favorable tax posture and ensure that you pay only the tax required by law.

❹ If your organization is like many others that we advise, you could significantly reduce the annual tax bill of both your organization and senior executives with tax planning assistance from CPAs-R-Us:

❺
- **Save taxes through proper planning**
- **Enhance executive income with individually tailored tax planning**
- **Save time and cost with tailored international, national, and local tax solutions**

❻

Save taxes through proper planning

You can minimize international, federal and local taxes on business transactions with CPAs-R-Us's continuous tax planning. You get regular advice for maximizing credit (research activity and other areas), anticipating problems, and planning for opportunities rather than just reacting to past events.

As you expand, you'll need the timely, efficient tax planning we can give you as a result of our size and extensive practical experience with a large clientele.

Enhance executive income with individually tailored tax planning

Your executives can enhance their income and benefits with a tailored program to help them build capital through income tax savings, while Acme benefits from favorable funding arrangements and improved executive retention.

Save time and cost with tailored international, national, and local tax solutions

You'll benefit from our frequent contact with national and district IRS offices as we obtain early answers to tax questions and rulings on tax aspects of proposed transactions. You'll avoid tax controversy and cut time and costs because of our expertise in resolving tax disputes efficiently and informally.

❼ If you feel you might be spending more on taxes than required, we should meet. I won't waste your time, we won't discuss the tax code, and you will not be subjected to "sales tactics."

❽ What you will experience is a direct, concise presentation that may open up new opportunities for ACME and ACME executives to minimize cost, improve cash flow, and enhance your executive's personal income.

Sincerely,

G.R Eyeshade

G.R. Eyeshade, CPA
800-333-3333

❾ P.S. I will personally follow up this letter with a phone call on Friday, January 5, between 3:00 and 5:00 p.m. Please let your executive assistant know your answer so I may schedule the meeting when I call if appropriate.

NOTE: Sales prospecting letters are usually designed to persuade the prospect to agree to hear more or take minor action. The more action requested of the prospect, the less likely the letter will be successful. Effective sales letters must persuade without offending. The "pitch" must be positive, informative, sincere, factual, and credible. This letter opens and closes with the pitch. The features of the seller's offer in the middle are emphasized by boldface headings.

❶ The informative subject line begins with a signal word, "Invitation," that signals the writer's objective, then states "what" and "why." The "why" is an anticipated benefit to the prospect.

❷ Capitalizing only the first word in a title is an acceptable and increasingly common practice. Select a style and use it consistently in the same document.

See **Headings.**

❸ The short setup refers to and summarizes a previous conversation.

See **Sales Letters.**

❹ The prospect's issues are stated and ownership is explicit.

See **Customer Focus** *and* **Sales Letters.**

❺ Both subheadings mirror the issues in the introduction.

See **Sales Letters.**

❻ Note how most paragraphs begin by referring to the prospect, improving the overall customer focus of the letter. Benefits are stated before features.

See **Customer Focus** *and* **Features, Advantages, and Benefits.**

❼ The seller proactively sets a follow-up time, justifies the timing as being in the best interest of the prospect, and restates potential benefits.

February 16, 20XX

Tom Tidy
Vice President, Administration
Silicon Glen Manufacturing
75 Research Park Drive
San Jose, CA 95321

❶ ❷ **Subject: Invitation to meet with Silicon Glen's Executive Committee to discuss how outsourcing can reduce office support costs**

Dear Tom:

❸ In our February 15 phone conversation, you said coping with rapid change and reducing costs were driving your FY20XX planning and were vital to Silicon Glen's survival. You said that if cost reductions of up to 30 percent were possible, you would set up a meeting with Silicon Glen's Executive Committee.

❹ You indicated two issues concerned all Silicon Glen executives:

- **Accelerating new product development**
- **Driving down costs at Silicon Glen**

❺ **Accelerating new product development**

❻ Executives are frequently distracted by routine support issues. When the agreed office services are provided by Office Imaging (OI), executives can focus on product development.

Your executives can monitor the status of any support task on-line using our ISO 9000 certified Customer Care® management software. An on-site manager uses the same package to select and manage all outside vendors as required. You can also use the latest, most cost-effective imaging products, a big help to time-constrained managers and designers.

Driving down costs at Silicon Glen

❻ Silicon Glen's office support costs will decline or OI will not offer a contract. We will collaborate with you on a detailed cost analysis with the results committed contractually.

Your cost reduction is partially based on OI's greater buying power on equipment and supplies. We further reduce your cost by sharing the site management load with other current contracts in your immediate area.

Shipping costs of your extensive training and support manuals can be cut by 80 percent because we can print and ship locally, including your international locations.

While not yet discussed, most of our new clients are concerned about the future of transferred employees. Actually, OI can offer real advancement opportunities in their career fields that are often not available in highly technical organizations like Silicon Glen.

❼ Due to the urgency of your planning cycle, I will call you next Monday to confirm the date and time of our meeting to further discuss how OI can help you accelerate product development while reducing costs. You may call me at 800-555-5555 if I can answer any questions.

Sincerely,

Sarah R Williamson

Sarah R. Williamson

Office Imaging
1000 Hollister Parkway
San Andreas, CA 94301
415.322.0001
www.officeimaging.com

3–FOLLOW-UP TO A MEETING

❶ The signal word is really two words. The heading includes both a feature and a benefit.

See **Features, Advantages, and Benefits** *and* **Sales Letters.**

❷ The short setup refers to the prior meeting and restates the prospect's request. The paragraph summarizes the prospect's needs and establishes perspective.

See **Sales Letters.**

❸ The prospect's goals are stated and ownership is explicit.

See **Customer Focus.**

❹ Subheadings mirror the stated goals from the prior introduction.

See **Sales Letters** *and* **Organization.**

❺ Details are subordinate to the goals in the paragraphs. Benefits continue to be emphasized and tied to features of the seller's offer.

See **Organization** *and* **Sales Letters.**

❻ The writer's goal is to gain the prospect's agreement on how the proposed consulting services will be evaluated. The "recommended approach" of the subject line is detailed in an attached evaluation plan.

❼ The next step is to review and ideally agree to accept the plan to evaluate the effectiveness of and scope of services proposed.

See **Sales Letters.**

Shipley Associates 653 North Main Street • Farmington, Utah 84025 • 801.451.2323 • 888.772.WINS • FAX: 801.451.4660 • www.shipleywins.com

Helping the World Win Business™

November 15, 20XX

Ann Archer
Marketing Director
Global Aerospace
Goddard Street
St. Louis, MO

❶ **Subject: Recommended Approach to Evaluate How Proposal Assistance Can Increase Global's Sales**

Dear Ann:

❷ In our November 14 meeting, you and Jane Smith asked me to outline how Global Aerospace could benefit from proposal consulting assistance during the next 12 to 18 months. Given the 46 proposals Global is currently preparing, the 26 additional opportunities qualified, and your lack of additional trained employees available, a prompt decision is critical.

❸ **You cited three goals for the next 12 to 18 months:**

- Maximize backlog during the current market upturn
- Improve your business capture effectiveness ratio
- Use existing resources most effectively

❹

Maximize backlog during the current market upturn

You can increase your win rate and total backlog capture by carefully applying our professional assistance to all bids, based on our 82 percent win rate. With all of Global's available resources assigned to 46 bid teams, pursuing many of the 26 additional qualified opportunities without assistance will likely reduce your win rate and possible total sales revenue.

Improve your business capture effectiveness ratio

By reducing or eliminating the rework in proposal preparation, we can document that total preparation costs are reduced 30 to 50 percent. And proposal quality improves, contributing to a higher win rate. While outside consulting is more expensive on a daily basis, Global avoids the cost and distraction of recruiting, training, and layoffs. ❺

Use existing resources most effectively

Global's experts can contribute to more bids more efficiently with efficient proposal management and support from Shipley Associates. You employ only the experts you need, when you need them.

❻ I am confident that by following the attached evaluation plan, we can both evaluate and scope what type of proposal consulting assistance would best help Global Aerospace capture the most business cost effectively.

❼ I will call you next Monday after you and Jane Smith have had a chance to look it over. Please call me at 888-772-9467 if you have any questions in the meantime.

Sincerely,

Paula Dunn

Paula Dunn
Account Manager

Attachment

NOTE: Many professional sales methodologies recommend the approach used in this sales letter. The seller's aim is to gain control or at least influence the evaluation process without being manipulative. If the prospect feels manipulated, the sale is lost. Prospects will accept this approach only if it seems to be in their best interests.

❶ The subject line immediately signals that this is a personal invitation. The desired action is in the subject line.

See **Headings.**

❷ The invitation is repeated in the first sentence. The setup is placed at the end of the sentence, tied to the prospect's issues. A setup needs to be short and early but does not have to be placed at the beginning of the first sentence.

See **Organization** *and* **Sales Letters.**

❸ The issues are explicitly owned by the prospect.

See **Customer Focus.**

❹ The subtitles mirror the prospect's issues and are introduced as run-in headings. The boldface type adds less emphasis than headings on a separate line.

See **Page and Document Design.**

❺ All of the seller's supporting details are placed against the relevant issue. Each supporting paragraph names the prospect first, increasing the degree of customer focus.

See **Customer Focus.**

❻ The opening sentence summarizes the seller's request. The second sentence states the next step the prospect can expect from the selling organization and leaves a phone number if the prospect wants to call earlier.

See **Sales Letters.**

Chemical Partners
20001 West Huntsville Highway
P.O. Drawer 304
Huntsville, TX 77336-0304
409/762-3000
www.chempartners.com

March 20, 20XX

Mr. James Bond
Laboratory Manager
Secret Clinical Laboratories
Hidden Boulevard
Thinville, CA 00700

❶ **Subject: Your invitation to observe a demonstration of our Triglyceride Separation Center (TSC)**

Dear James:

❷ Attend a demonstration of our Triglyceride Separation Center (TSC) to see how this system will address the concerns and needs that you expressed in our meeting last week.

You expressed a need for:

❸
- **Quicker turnaround on test results**
- **Greater automation to handle the increased work load**
- **Minimal rebaselining after system change**

❹ **Quicker turnaround on test results.** You will experience quicker turnaround on test results because the TSC has an extended curve range of 500 mg/ml. The extended curve range reduces the number of dilutions required, and thus shortens the reporting time on test results.

Since implementing the TSC system, we have increased throughput by 15 percent, reduced labor costs 20 percent due to increased automation, and cut downtime for rebaselining by 23 percent . . .

—Ms. Nancy Rosedauge, CEO, LabTech, Ltd.

❺ **Greater automation to handle the increased work load.** Your lab can enjoy a totally automated procedure with 24 results in 45 minutes, using this TSC system.

Minimal rebaselining after system change. As you will see in the enclosed comparative study, converting your system to the TSC will require only minimal rebaselining. The study shows excellent agreement between your Polyglobal One-Step assay and our TSC, although the TSC produces slightly lower values.

❻ You could see a demonstration at the local Triglyceride Center in Thinville. Jane, our local representative, will call to schedule a demonstration for you. If you have additional questions, please consult the enclosed product overview and call us at 800-700-0007.

Best regards,

Ima Starr

Ima Starr
Chemical Partners, Inc.

cc: S. M. Body

5–REQUEST FOR RFP MODIFICATION

❶ The informative subject line begins with the signal word labeling the letter as a "request." A feature is linked to two benefits.

See **Features, Advantages, and Benefits** *and* **Headings.**

❷ The request begins with the benefit to the prospect, the only reason for the prospect to agree to the request. The setup, a reference to the prospect's RFP, is delayed until after the benefit. Every request in every sentence is linked to a benefit.

See **Features, Advantages, and Benefits.**

❸ This sentence introduces the structure of the letter.

See **Organization.**

❹ Each request for modification begins with the customer benefit, then states the current RFP language. Then the change is justified in detail from the prospect's perspective.

See **Features, Advantages, and Benefits** *and* **Organization.**

❺ The seller has made the change easy for the prospect by including complete text for the change.

❻ Labels in the left margin make the letter easy to follow. The clear page design enables the reader to more easily focus on the content.

See **Page and Document Design.**

IT Partners, Inc.
1000 Derby Road
Chicago, IL 50501
312.333.3000

January 15, 20XX

Art A. Quire
Purchasing Manager
Big Corporation
Winston Street
San Diego, CA

❶ **Subject: Request to modify Big Corporation's IT outsourcing RFP to reduce cost and enhance flexibility**

Dear Art:

❷ To better meet Big Corporation's IT outsourcing objectives of reduced cost and enhanced flexibility, we recommend two changes in your RFP dated December 15, 20XX. Our recommended changes will help Big Corporation meet its objectives while obtaining more competitive bids. To ensure our proposal is fully compliant and responsive, a prompt decision is critical.

❸ For each recommended modification, we have quoted your RFP, explained our reasoning, and offered a draft RFP text replacement. We request two modifications.

1. To reduce your cost and improve flexibility, eliminate the 10-year firm fixed price provision.

❹

Current provision: *All bidders must quote firm fixed prices for each and every year of the 10-year contract.*

Comments: The uncertainty of inflation in out-years will force all bidders to increase prices to cover inflation risk. Any increase or decrease in the type or level of services required will limit Big Corporation's flexibility to adjust. You could be locked into old technologies and unable to quickly respond to your customers.

❺ **Recommended change:** *All bidders must quote firm, fixed prices on each task, with the annual cost being the simple sum of the cost of all tasks. All required tasks and task pricing will be reviewed annually.*

2. To improve flexibility by easing the restriction on any change in "key positions."

❻

Current provision: *All bidders must name all persons proposed for all key positions, and no substitutions are permitted.*

Comments: As written, the provision could be interpreted to apply from the proposal stage through the entire 10-year term of the contract. Big Corporation's requirements likely will change, requiring different skills in key positions. Individuals also may change jobs or even choose to retire. Allowing changes with your approval will permit both organizations to employ the best person available to meet the current need.

Recommended change: *All bidders must name all persons proposed for all key positions. Substitutions are permitted only after review and approval by Big Corporation's designated contract administrator.*

Big Corporation IT RFP
January 15, 20XX
Page 2

❼ The summary restates the benefit and the requested action.

See **Organization.**

❼ I hope you agree that the two RFP changes recommended will help Big Corporation reduce cost and improve flexibility. We look forward to receiving an addendum to your RFP so that we can prepare a fully compliant and responsive proposal.

❽ The seller proactively offers to follow up and leaves a contact number.

See **Sales Letters.**

❽ I will call you on Tuesday to clarify any details, or you can reach me at 801-333-3000.

Sincerely,

Daniel Miller

Daniel Miller
Proposal Manager

❾ The attached electronic file reduces the effort required for the prospect to make the requested changes.

❾ Attachment: 1 PC computer disc with electronic file in MSWord® and text-only formats

6–INFORMALLY SOLICITED COMMERCIAL PROPOSAL

❶ Executive summaries usually carry an unambiguous telegraphic heading for instant recognition.

See **Executive Summary** *and* **Headings.**

❷ This customer-focused theme opens by naming the prospect, stating a benefit, and then linking the benefit to a discriminator. The word "partner" was used because the prospect requested a partner.

See **Customer Focus; Features, Advantages, and Benefits;** *and* **Themes.**

❸ This paragraph demonstrates the seller's understanding of the prospect organization's vision.

See **Executive Summary.**

❹ This "linking statement" demonstrates the alignment between the prospect's organizational vision and the objective of the immediate buying group within the prospect organization.

See **Executive Summary.**

❺ This sentence incorporates both a short setup and a summary of what the prospect has requested in meetings. Setups in executive summaries are occasionally dropped because the reader is assumed to understand, or delayed because other information is more important to the reader.

See **Executive Summary and Organization.**

❻ The needs or issues are clearly "owned" by the prospect, and the list of needs is named immediately before the list. Quote prospects directly, even if the items are not parallel.

See **Customer Focus** *and* **Lists.**

❼ A reference quote substantiates the seller's experience and performance.

See **Relevant Experience/ Past Performance.**

Cascadia Timber

❶ Executive Summary

❷ **Cascadia Timber can reduce the cost of forest management in remote, roadless areas by selecting a partner to supply 20 versatile ultralight aircraft and proven long-term support.**

❸ Cascadia Timber is ranked as the No. 1 company in the world by Forester's Monthly for low cost, innovative forest management. Cascadia Timber Chairman Woody X. Pine set the following strategic direction:

> *We have to do everything better, more efficiently from a cost point of view, more effectively from an impact point of view.*
>
> **—Cascadia Timber Annual Report, 1996**

"In 10 years of flying the Endeavor for Special Forces, we have been impressed with the durability and portability of the aircraft after successive airdrops in difficult terrain.

Jenair's enthusiastic support was superb."

—Major Buck Rogers ❼

Cascadia Timber's Forest Management Division helps improve efficiency and effectiveness by adopting innovative forest management practices. ❹

In support of Cascadia Timber's strategic direction, the Forest Management Division verbally requested proposals for 20 ultralight aircraft to be used as a forest management tool. ❺ In our meetings with Forest Management and purchasing, individuals cited four primary needs: ❻

1. Affordable, portable, and easily transportable
2. All-conditions observation and communication platform
3. Safe and easy to fly
4. Easy to assemble and maintain in the field

❽ Affordable, portable, easily transportable

Cascadia Timber can purchase 20 Endeavor ultralights from Jenair for $9,500 each, less than one-half the cost of 3/4-ton 4-wheel drive trucks. The Endeavor offers a unique combination of features:

- For portability, the wings, tail assembly, fuselage, and down tubes are oriented along a slim axis and secured in a rugged transport case.
- Transportable by three people by design, not modification. Two carry the 196-lb. fuselage crate, one carries the 45-lb. engine crate.

❾

❿ **Figure 1. Proven in Use.** *While no forest management group currently uses any type of ultralight, the Endeavor has been proven in similar operations with Special Forces personnel since 1984.*

Jenair Sports, Inc.
1400 Airport Road
Boulder, CO 80150
970.359.1000
970.359.1431 (FAX)
www.jenair.com

–1–

(8) The four primary prospect needs are addressed in the order introduced. The wording of each is identical to the numbered list to eliminate possible confusion by the reader.

See **Organization.**

(9) The graphic and caption support the seller's claims. The use of a photograph suggests the aircraft is real.

See **Graphics.**

(10) The two-part action engages the reader with the informative heading then seeks to suggest a minimal-risk alternative.

(11) Note how most paragraphs open with benefits, the most important aspect to the prospect.

See **Customer Focus;** *and* **Features, Advantages, and Benefits.**

(12) The Benefit-Feature table also lists benefits first. Most writers tend to think "features" before "benefits."

(13) Here, the seller both summarizes the offer, states they can do the job, and softly asks for the order.

See **Executive Summary.**

(14) The seller restates the most significant discriminator in a single-sentence paragraph.

See **Executive Summary,** *and* **Page and Document Design.**

(15) The high-level proposal outline in the left margin previews how the seller's proposal is organized. If the executive summary has captured readers' interests, they can easily turn to the information that is the most interesting.

See **Organization.**

(16) The final paragraph indicates compliance and flexibility. Note how the tone shifts if "enhancements" becomes "changes."

See **Choosing Correct Words.**

Cascadia Timber

(8) All-conditions observation and communication platform

(11) To ensure accurate and safe observation in all conditions, the Endeavor offers positive stability, the ideal control response. During level flight, the pilot can concentrate on observation, knowing the aircraft tends to fly itself. For stable observation during turns, the aircraft maintains the uniform attitude the pilot commands, instead of seeking to return to a flat attitude.

For versatility, the Endeavor can be equipped to land on land, water, and snow.

Air-to-ground communication is improved by the rear engine which minimizes pilot noise when compared with front engine models.

(8) Safe and easy to fly

> **Jenair Pilot Training Named Industry's Best.**
>
> The Ultralight Pilots' Association selects Jenair's pilot training program as "Best" in their annual competition.
>
> —*Small Aircraft News*, July 10, 1995

Safe and easy operation requires good design and excellent pilot training. Endeavor's design offers clear benefits:

Benefit	Feature
Excellent ground control	Trailing landing gear and control stick steering
Smooth ground ride	Landing gear with built-in shock absorbers
Rugged	Survived 16 airdrops without damage
Safe, effective training	Award-winning training program

(12)

Cascadia foresters can focus on forest management because the Endeavor is easily maintained. Routine checks of cables, snap-lock bolts, fittings, and simple preflight tests are sufficient for safe operation. Weekly checks of engine fluids, landing gear and the prop are required. Annual engine overhauls and in-depth checks of the prop are required and can be done at Cascadia's convenience by Jenair personnel.

Reliable, rugged flight instruments, proven in 10 years of use, require only annual calibration.

(8) Easy to assemble and maintain in the field

To ensure fast, accurate assembly, nondestructible instructions are permanently attached beneath the instrument panel. To ensure assembly tools are always available, they are also connected by a steel cable and attached to the aircraft.

Special Forces tests demonstrated assembly in 10 minutes. Inexperienced personnel complete a first assembly/disassembly in 40 minutes.

(13) Cascadia Timber has kept on the leading edge of innovative forest management techniques. Jenair Sports welcomes the opportunity to supply 20 Endeavor aircraft, flight and maintenance training, and long-term maintenance and inspection support.

(15)

PROPOSAL OUTLINE

1. Executive Summary
2. Aircraft Description
3. Program Overview
4. Management Approach

While many ultralights are used for recreation, the Endeavor's unique 10-year use by Special Forces personnel over similar terrain and more difficult conditions reduces the risk of use in continuous operation. (14)

Our proposal mirrors the issues discussed in our meetings. Should your requirements change, we welcome the opportunity to discuss further enhancements. (16)

–2–

7–INCUMBENT'S INFORMALLY SOLICITED SERVICES PROPOSAL

❶ Theme statement names the prospect first, then cites a benefits linked to the seller's key discriminator.

See **Customer Focus** *and* **Themes.**

❷ The first two paragraphs demonstrate the seller's understanding of the prospect's needs. The prospect is commended for excellent achievement. The seller's role in the prospect's success is subtly implied but deemphasized.

See **Executive Summary.**

❸ This short paragraph states the need or pain.

See **Executive Summary.**

❹ The pain is stated positively and additional immediate needs are linked to the overall organizational need. The unusually long, four-paragraph setup was used to forcefully discriminate the incumbent's deep understanding of the prospect's needs to Western's senior managers.

See **Executive Summary** *and* **Strategy.**

❺ The term "bid management" rather than "proposal management" is used to reflect the prospect's terminology.

❻ The prospect's evaluation criteria are listed precisely as stated in a meeting with the buyer. The list is named immediately prior to the list.

See **Lists.**

❼ The incumbent seller's strongest discriminator is substantiated by proof from the prospect's organization.

See **Relevant Experience/Past Performance.**

❽ This sentence says the seller can meet the prospect's needs. Note that the prospect's spelling has been used.

See **Executive Summary** *and* **International Proposals.**

WESTERN HOVERCRAFT

Executive Summary

❶ **Western Hovercraft can increase its ability to win key contracts by selecting a proven business development partner.**

❷ **Western Hovercraft is at a crucial stage of capturing business—one of opportunity and risk.** Western has invested significant time, energy, and resources in establishing its proposal development process. That investment has had positive results, including the recent MOD Attack Hovercraft win and an improved win rate on export sales bids. Western's £3 billion order book is the envy of larger competitors.

Today, MOD agencies and many Export Sales customers respect the professionalism and quality of Western's proposals. Government contractors on both sides of the Atlantic, both partners and competitors, admire the quality of Western's proposals. The positive customer comments on Western's current proposals are a marked contrast to the comments made less than 4 years ago.

❸ However, backlog does not pay current operating expenses. Western must manage expenditures and cash flow to capture additional orders at a minimum cost.

❹ **Western's managers have identified the need to continue improving their ability to capture business by** ❺ **improving bid management.** Additionally, Western is pursuing several must win export orders where process improvements and expert assistance can increase the win probability and reduce capture cost.

❻ Western has established the following bid management improvement objectives:

- **Reduce bid cost**
- **Improve win rate**
- **Increase awareness of risk**
- **Improve control and monitoring of bids**
- **Start up proposal efforts faster**
- **Improve flexibility, including consultancy assistance**

❼ *7th April 20XX*

Please find enclosed the results of the Western Proposal Training Survey . . .

- *85% have directly contributed to proposals*
- *50% saved time*
- *40% reduced cost*
- *85% improved proposal quality*
- *85% used the skills to prepare other documents...*

. . . we have seen a visible improvement in our proposal quality since we commenced training courses last year.

—Bob Westfield
Regional Business Manager
Western Hovercraft

❽ Shipley Associates welcomes the opportunity to continue the improvements begun in 1999, with the results summarised in Bob Westfield's 7th April 20XX letter.

ShipleyAssociates™

1

⑨ The prospect's spelling conventions are used to avoid appearing foreign.

See **International Proposals.**

⑩ A table rather than a bulleted list is used to both summarize the seller's offer and preview how the proposal is organized.

See **Executive Summary,** *and* **Organization.**

⑪ The action caption on the table restates the seller's primary discriminator.

See **Action Captions** *and* **Discriminators.**

⑫ The prospect's hot buttons are all addressed by the service approach requested, so the approach is discussed separately and not aligned to individual hot buttons.

See **Executive Summary.**

⑬ Note how the adjective used in the heading is substantiated when repeated in the text.

See **Action Captions.**

⑭ The proposal is introduced or previewed in both the text and the visually emphasized table of contents in the left margin.

See **Page and Document Design,** *and* **Organization.**

WESTERN HOVERCRAFT

⑨ Western Hovercraft's objectives can best be met by partnering with Shipley Associates, as summarised in figure 1.

⑩

Western's Objectives	Advantages to Western from Partnering with Shipley
• Reduce bid cost	Western can leverage its previous investment in process improvement and training by refining, not redefining, its bid management process.
• Improve win rate	Western has been winning with a Shipley process tailored to the UK and export markets. Compare market-specific win rates.
• Increase awareness of risk	Western can leverage Shipley's experience with 43 of the top 50 US DoD suppliers, who must manage risk to strict DoD standards.
• Improve control and monitoring of bids	Western can apply Shipley's unique mix of monitoring of bids full-service consulting, training, products, and templates to improve bid management.
• Start up proposal efforts faster	Western can start up proposals faster by having Shipley train and coach others to work as effectively as Linda Hale or by having Shipley supply a proven consultant.
• Improve flexibility, including consultancy assistance	Western will obtain maximum value for money with consultants that do not have to be educated about Western. Both consultants proposed for the Phase 1 study have experience with both Western and numerous aerospace organisations.

⑪ **Figure 1. Complete Consultancy,** *Tailored to Western Hovercraft. Only Shipley Associates can offer a full range of services and 4 years of success with Western and associated Western organisations.*

⑫ **Flexible, two-phased approach**

As requested by Sally Barksdale, we propose a two-phased approach:

Phase 1—Study

Phase 2—Execution

⑬ For maximum flexibility, all phases and recommendations will be independent.

⑭ **PROPOSAL OUTLINE**

Executive Summary

1. Unique Partnering Qualifications
2. Responsive Study Approach
3. Schedule and Price

⑭ **How our proposal is organised**

Our proposal is structured as shown to the left. To facilitate your evaluation, section 1 matches each Western objective to Shipley's qualifications and proof of results with organisations setting similar objectives. Section 2 describes our study approach, while section 3 suggests a schedule and establishes the price.

ShipleyAssociates

2

8–FORMALLY SOLICITED GOVERNMENT PROPOSAL

❶ The theme names the prospect first to increase customer focus. The initial broad benefit is linked to the seller's most unique benefit, the ability to "best respond to ad hoc inquiries." Often discriminators are not obvious to less knowledgeable readers.

See **Discriminators** *and* **Themes.**

❷ The need is extracted from the prospect's RFP.

See **Executive Summary.**

❸ "The challenge" both summarizes the prospect's current position and future need.

See **Executive Summary.**

❹ The list of "capabilities" is extracted word for word from the prospect's RFP. Use the prospect's language when you name the hot button list.

See **Customer Focus, Executive Summary,** *and* **Lists.**

❺ The seller states they can do the job.

See **Executive Summary.**

❻ Because this executive summary exceeds two or three pages, the organization of the executive summary is announced.

See **Organization.**

❼ The heading identically reflects the first hot button. The second hot button would be at the top of the next page.

❽ This three-sentence paragraph summarizes the seller's solution to the first challenge. Expand or contract summaries of your solutions as appropriate.

See **Executive Summary.**

GARDEN OF EDEN Department of Human Services

Garden of Eden Department of Human Services — *Executive Information System*

Executive Summary

❶ **Eden's DHS can craft reform programs that work by selecting the Executive Information System that best responds to ad hoc queries by delivering the right information clearly, concisely, and when you need it.**

❷ **The Need**

The Department needs a system that can analyze data encompassing the broad range of human services to help craft reform programs that work.

—EIS RFP, pg. 2.

❸ **The challenge:** The Department of Human Services (DHS) has effectively managed the delivery of public assistance services in the Garden of Eden by efficient administration and innovative cost-control strategies. With program complexity continuing to increase, the DHS's ability to further improve services requires an improved ability to store, access, and analyze massive amounts of complex data efficiently and effectively.

❹ The DHS has requested proposals for a systems integrator to develop an Executive Information System (EIS) that gives DHS personnel the following capabilities:

- **Easily access information by users with varied backgrounds**
- **Quickly handle simple and complex queries, both predetermined and ad hoc**
- **Maintain on-line processing while routinely adding and purging data**
- **Flexibly accommodate program changes and data exchanges with other State departments and county agencies**
- **Efficiently manage the EIS implementation and seamlessly transition to State operation in two years**

❺ Cosmos Information Systems (Cosmos) welcomes the opportunity to design, implement, and support an EIS tailored to the DHS's current and future needs based on our experience implementing similar systems.

❻ **How Our Executive Summary Is Organized:**

- Capabilities
- Development Approach
- Project Organization
- System Architecture
- Costs by Phase

❻ Our executive summary first summarizes the basis for our system recommendation against the overall DHS capabilities listed above, then summarizes our development approach, project organization, system architecture, and costs by phase as required in your RFP.

❼ **Easily access information by users with varied backgrounds**

❽ Users easily access information from their personal computers on their desktop. All staff can develop ad hoc queries using point-and-click tools without writing program code using a Windows-based Graphical Query Language (GQL) tool. To avoid excessive run times or massive data dumps on their PC, GQL allows users to determine run time and output size.

COSMOS SYSTEMS • 1400 Moab Road, Suite 6, East Canaan, IL 45014 • 303.666.0000 • www.cosmos.com

---

NOTE: The same organization can be expanded to accommodate executive summaries and letter proposals of different lengths. This is only the first page of a 12-page executive summary for a state government proposal comprising several hundred pages.

❶ Address the letter as specifically and directly as possible, following all prospect instructions.

See **Cover Letters.**

❷ The subject line signals this is a response to an RFP by number.

See **Cover Letters.**

❸ The opening line first calls attention to the proposal, then establishes context. While the next sentence may seem long or awkward with the enclosed parenthetical sentence, it suggests a personal style while highlighting a discriminator.

See **Organization.**

❹ The prospect's needs are stated in a way that seems to merge with the seller's offer.

See **Customer Focus.**

❺ To keep the cover letter short, the needs are not addressed in the cover letter, but the writer promises to address them in the proposal. Cover letter to decision makers are expected to emphasize the personal commitment and support of a senior manager. The inclusion of the phone number adds support.

See **Organization.**

❻ The single-sentence closing paragraph is used for emphasis.

See **Page and Document Design.**

❼ The most senior manager of the selling organization that is plausibly aware of the proposal should sign this type of cover letter.

See **Cover Letters.**

Shipley Associates 653 North Main Street • Farmington, Utah 84025 • 801.451.2323 • 888.772.WINS • FAX: 801.451.4660 • www.shipleywins.com

Helping the World Win Business™

September 18, 20XX

❶ Ms. Macey S. King
Global Procurement
Ace Global Services
6000 Rock Ledge Drive
Bethesda, MD 20817

❷ **Subject: Response to RFP # RSD-WEB-001, Proposal Consulting Services**

Dear Ms. King:

❸ Enclosed with this letter is our response to your RFP requesting proposal consulting services for Ace Global Services. With the relationship between our companies off to an excellent start, this procurement is an excellent extension of the relationship between our companies. (We're already serving you with proposal consulting services on three proposals.)

❹ Ace has requested relationships with companies with the following approaches:

- Are willing to operate effectively in the Ace Global Services environment
- Are willing to provide services and rates through the Ace Intranet Web Site
- Have an excellent winning record
- Are flexible in their approach
- Can provide excellent value as demonstrated through competitive rates

❺ As you will see throughout our proposal, Shipley Associates is strong in all areas. As the CEO of Shipley Associates, I offer my personal commitment to providing Ace Global Services the best resources and services available. If you have any need to talk to me at any time, either before or after your selection decision, please call me at my direct number: 801-451-2323.

❻ I am personally committed to helping Ace win business.

Sincerely,

Stephen P. Shipley

Stephen P. Shipley
❼ Chief Executive Officer

SPS:jb

Enclosure

10–TO DECISION MAKER WITHOUT BUYING CRITERIA

❶ Cultural differences may change your approach. Here the writer used the prospect's title taken from the prospect's bid request. Beginning the subject line with the signal word "proposal" would have been awkward, reading: "Proposal for Proposal . . . ."

See **Cover Letters, Headings,** *and* **Sales Letters.**

❷ The setup is in the first line, a reference to the bid request .

See **Cover Letters.**

❸ The prospect's objective opens the second sentence to increase customer focus.

See **Customer Focus** *and* **Cover Letters.**

❹ To ensure the prospect is named immediately before the list, the prospect could not be named prior to the seller. When prospects do not state buying criteria, summarize the most important features of your offer. Use the words that you think your prospect would use.

See **Customer Focus** *and* **Lists.**

❺ The closing paragraph emphasizes the compliant and responsive proposal and offers a contact number. Depending on the prospect's evaluation rules, stating a proactive follow-up time could be inappropriate.

See **Compliance and Responsiveness.**

Shipley

SHIPLEY LIMITED

3 North Street Workshops
Stoke sub Hamdon
Somerset
TA14 6QR

Telephone: +44 (0) 1935 825200
Facsimile: +44 (0) 1935 825965

Web: www.shipleylimited.com

Henry Hoogenboom
Global Consulting
Koningsstraat 445 Rue Royale
1000 Brussels
Belgium

❶ ***Proposal Centre Knowledge Management and Structure***

Dear Henry,

❷ Please find enclosed our response to your bid request for the Proposal Centre Knowledge Management and Structure.

❸ To allow you to fulfill your mission and overcome your challenges, we have outlined a three-phase project in our proposal. In this project, we will provide you with the information and the expertise to allow you to reengineer processes and implement the infrastructure needed to sustain a best-in-class proposal operation. We detail how your challenges will be met and describe a practical approach to implementation.

By selecting Shipley Limited, Global Consulting will gain access to proven capabilities in creating best-in-class proposal environments, including:

- World-standard processes, disciplines, and tools
- ❹ Capability growth without "having to learn the hard way"
- Access to a company that is known for its customer focus, rather than a "do it our way or else" approach
- Affordability—take advantage of the breadth of Shipley resource to the extent that is economically feasible

❺ For ease of evaluation, the structure of our proposal precisely mirrors your bid request from section 2 onwards. If you require any further information or clarification of any of the elements of our proposal, please call me on +44 1935 825200.

Yours sincerely,

Tony Birch

Tony Birch
Managing Director

REGISTERED IN ENGLAND AND WALES NO 3426392 REGISTERED OFFICE: SNAPHAUNT, SNAPANT, LOPEN, SOUTH PETHERTON, SOMERSET, TA13 5JJ
WHEN WINNING IS THE ONLY OPTION

❶ The signal word "proposal" is used in the subject line.

See **Cover Letters** *and* **Sales Letters.**

❷ The formal "reference" line with the buyer's solicitation number and date simplifies sorting by a busy buyer or the buyer's assistant.

See **Cover Letters.**

❸ The opening paragraph is the setup.

See **Cover Letters** *and* **Sales Letters.**

❹ The prospect's evaluation criteria or objectives are stated in the second paragraph to increase the relevance of the third paragraph.

❺ This is the only selling paragraph. The last sentence states the seller's most unique discriminator.

See **Cover Letters** *and* **Discriminators.**

❻ This paragraph emphasizes the compliant and responsive proposal and offers contact numbers for different types of inquiries. Stating a proactive follow-up time could be inappropriate since it is limited by buying regulations.

See **Compliance and Responsiveness.**

❼ This paragraph names the key managers and who to contact for specific types of questions about the proposal.

See **Discriminators**, *and* **Relevant Experience/Past Performance.**

WEAPONS-R-US, INC. ◆ **Aeronautics Division**

95610 South Coast Highway, Newport Beach, CA 92658 ◆ 714.720.9000 ◆ www.weapons.com

August 17, 20XX

Contracts Division V (Code 255)
Naval Weapons Center
China Lake, CA 93555-6001

Attention: Barb Buyer

❶ **Subject:** **Proposal from Weapons-R-Us for the Anti-Radiation Missile Countermeasures Program**

❷ Reference: Solicitation N60550-01-R-0202 dated November 14, 20XX

Dear Ms. Buyer:

❸ In response to the referenced solicitation, Weapons-R-Us, Aeronautics Division, is enclosing our proposal for the Anti-Radiation Missile Countermeasures (ARM/CM) Program.

❹ Your RFP evaluation criteria emphasized the desire to select a source offering the best combination of flexibility, technical performance, and cost effectiveness.

❺ Our proposal reflects an experienced technical team in place at China Lake. This team has extensive experience assisting the Navy with anti-radiation missile development, countermeasures analysis, proof-of-concept development, software simulation development and documentation, and systems simulation analysis. We can provide a uniquely cost-effective ARM/CM because we are the only organization with both an experienced team and existing facilities in place at China Lake.

❻ Our proposal is submitted in three volumes as requested in your solicitation:

Volume I – Technical Proposal

Volume II – Management Proposal

Volume III – Cost Proposal

Contractual and administrative items are included in Volume III.

❼ ARM/CM will be conducted within the Advanced Programs Office of our Aeronautical Division, directed by Dr. Noah Lott, Vice President. Technical or programmatic questions may be addressed to Ms. Ivanna Jobb, our proposal manager, at 619-446-9099. Cost, contractual, or administrative inquiries may be addressed to my attention at 714-720-7535.

Sincerely,

N.O. Bull

N. O. Bull
Contract Administrator
Advanced Programs

12–FORMALLY SOLICITED GOVERNMENT BID

PROPOSAL DEVELOPMENT WORKSHEET

Understanding the Task

❶ Relevant Proposal Information

Proposal: Army Ultralight
Section No.: 2.2
Section Topic: Performance
No. of pages: 6
No. of visuals: 6
Other Information: N/A
Author: Bill Yaunt

❷ Relevant RFP Location

Instructions (L*): Page C-27
Evaluation Criteria (M*): Page C-29
Statement of Work (C*): Page C-7 and C-8
Deliverables (F*): Page C-13
Other: None
Data (CDRLs*): None—Only for Cost Vol.
Attachments: None

*Section number in a Federal RFP

Analyzing the RFP

❸ Section Compliance Checklist

RFP Paragraph	Compliance Requirements
2.1.2.2	• Describe the performance capabilities of our XL1117 on SOW C32
L.2.1.2.2	• Provide verification of performance data from actual flight, fieldtesting wind tunnel or lab studies
L.2.1.2.2	• Discuss performance factors
	~ Flight Control & Handling
	~ Aerodynamic Stability
	~ Glider Capability
	~ Noise Muffling
	~ Adaptability environments & operating conditions

❹ Detailed Section Outline (based on Instructions requirements)

2.2 Performance
2.2.1 Flight Control & Handling
2.2.2 Aerodynamic Stability
2.2.3 Glider Capability
2.2.4 Noise Muffling
2.2.5 Adaptability

 1

PROPOSAL DEVELOPMENT WORKSHEET

Defining Your Offer

❺ Major Issues: Low-level, undetected airborne reconnaissance. Air droppable, easy to fly and easy to learn to fly. Operable in a variety of restrictive terrains and adverse conditions. Stable flight maximizing time and attention to reconnaissance mission

❻ SWOT Analysis

Strengths: Positive stability for self-corrective flying enhancing ease of training and flying. High glide ratio, extended range, quick assembly, superb muffling system, balloon tires, and low stall speed. High payload capability

Weaknesses: Long landing roll, restrictive temperature for operations, pull handle starting may be seen as difficult for restart. Top speed less than other ULA

Opportunities: Utilize our "WhisperMuff™ muffler to accentuate our near "stealth" mode of flying. Use our extensive experience and data collected during testing for the Cascadia Timber bid

Threats: Push-button restart of other ultralights. Our long landing roll may make us vulnerable to ghosting. We must find counter argument unless we want to add costly brakes, which may make us non-cost competitive.

❼ Approach (Technical/Management/Other): Offer off-the-shelf model XL1117 with added WhisperMuff™ noise muffler. Capitalize on our extensive test data and experience in the ultralight marketplace. Counter our weakness with compensating strengths

 2

❶ Given to writers by the Proposal Manager or the Volume Manager. If not, ask for it, particularly the number of pages and the number of visuals.

❷ Given to writers by the Proposal Manager or the Volume Manager citing the relevant RFP pages and paragraph numbers.

❸ Should be completed by Proposal or Volume Manager by "stripping" the requirements from appropriate RFP sections. Use the compliance checklist to assure responsiveness and compliance. It is the basis for your outline and response matrix (or cross-reference matrix).

❹ Completed by writers following the outline format specified in the RFP and integrating any other applicable RFP sections as necessary. This is based on the proposal preparation instructions in the RFP.

❺ Major Issues are what keep the customer up at night:

- Worry items
- Real concerns
- Core needs
- Reasons behind the requirements
- Hidden agendas

Read "between the lines" of the RFP.

❻ The SWOT analysis identifies your strengths and weaknesses from the customer's perspective including gaps, positive and negative issues, and worry items.

- List areas where you are strong, particularly in the areas important to the customer.
- List areas where you are weak.
- Identify any areas where you see opportunities to enhance your company's position either on this contract or for future work.
- Identify areas where you see any threats from the competition or from conditions that might negatively affect or create high risk for this procurement.

❼ Identify solutions or approaches to this section. Your approach should directly relate to all compliance requirements. Content may include such things as organization, equipment, personnel, technical or management concepts. Make your solution(s) real and specific so that you can later identify the key features and benefits to the customer and develop strategy for your section.

❽ Develop the features and corresponding benefits of your offering or solution for this section. Determine which benefits address this customer's issues.

❾ Enter areas of risk in technical, cost, schedule, technology, or other areas that are appropriate. These are the risks to your customer, not to your company. How will you mitigate them? Identify the most likely risks, not every possible risk.

❿ Identify your company's relevant experience and past performance that supports the claims and benefits in your section. Past experience is what you did; past performance is how well you did it. Tie past performance to the benefits to this customer on this program. Quantify where possible.

NOTE: Storyboards can be simplified or can be even more detailed than the one shown here. The use of the tool to plan before writing is more important than the actual layout of the storyboard.

PROPOSAL DEVELOPMENT WORKSHEET

Defining Your Offer (cont.)

8 Features	8 Benefits
Positive stability	Forgiving nature for novice pilots
Noise Muffler [WhisperMuff™]	Low detectability—good communications
Extended Range—125 miles	Greater reconnaissance capability
High glide ratio 8:1	More observation time—better recon
Balloon tires	Greater adaptability in more terrain—greater pilot safety

9 **Risk Management** Risk of long landing roll is moderate. We could put on brakes at extra cost, extra weight. However, compensating balloon tires give more landing options and should provide acceptable risk for Army.

10 **Past Experience** Our extensive testing, both in the field and laboratory, along with continuously increasing sales over 20 years should provide evidence of past experience.

Past Performance Our performance on Cascadia contract for ULA use in timber country was excellent. Our track record should provide convincing evidence of cost.

Developing Your Strategy

11 **Section Discriminators**

Us	Them
120-mile range	Electric start
8:1 glide ratio	Higher altitude (12,000 ft)
Balloon tires	Higher speed (65 mph)
WhisperMuff™ muffler	Shorter landing roll (100 ft)

12 **Relevant Proposal Strategy/Volume Strategy:** Emphasize our proven performance over 20 years, extensive testing, and contract cost and schedule performance. [Why should the customer choose us?]

Section Strategy: Emphasize our proven performance, positive stability, balloon tires, high glide ratio, WhisperMuff™ muffler, and extended range. Ghost vulnerability of competitors' lack of muffler and electric start dependent on battery. [How do I win this section?]

13 **Section Theme Statement:** The performance characteristics of the XL1117 meet or exceed all essential design requirements for an effective and easy-to-operate reconnaissance platform. The performance is substantiated by 20 years of flight, field, wind tunnel, and lab test data.

 3

PROPOSAL DEVELOPMENT WORKSHEET

Creating Key Visuals

14

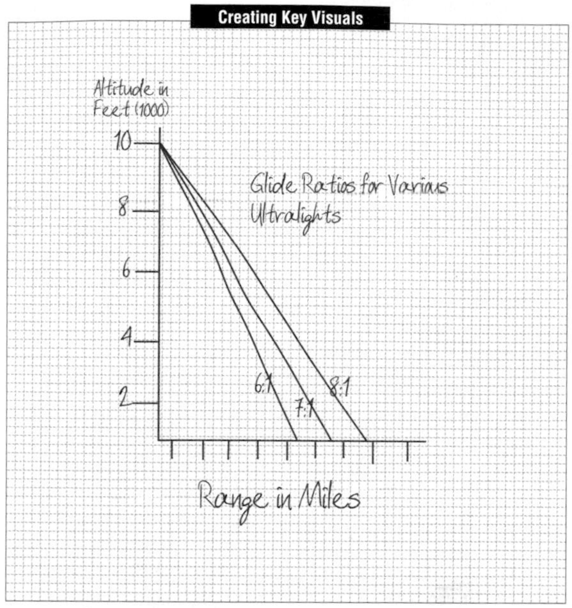

15 **Figure No.** Figure 22-5

Figure Title: Superior Glide Ratio

16 **Action Caption:** A glide ratio of 8:1 allows the LX1117 to have a higher mission versatility with 15% greater range than 7:1 ratio

 4

⓫ Discriminators are features of your offer that are both important to the customer and that differentiate you from the competition.

- Review your offering:
  —What things are different and/or stronger than your competition?
  —What things are weaker?
  —Can you develop "ghosts"?
  —How will you overcome your weaknesses?
- Assess your competitors' offering:
  —What are their discriminators?
  —How will you downplay or neutralize them?

⓬ Review Volume/Proposal strategies. List those that are applicable to this section. Is there an appropriate section strategy subset? Develop a section strategy that:

- Discriminates you from your competitors
- Matches your offering to the customer's needs
- Emphasizes your strengths and minimizes your competitors' strengths
- Mitigates your weaknesses and highlights (ghosts) your competitors' weaknesses

Make the strategy appropriate to the offering/solution in this section. Ask: How do I implement the volume strategy in this section?

⓭ The section theme should be your strongest sales point concerning this section. Make it:

- Specific
- Quantifiable (if possible)
- Customer focused—tie benefits to features
- Support your strategy
- Your "silver bullet"

Review the major issues, features and benefits, discriminators, and strategy statement. Ask: Why should the customer choose us?

⓮ Develop visuals for this section in the area provided (and on additional sheets as necessary) before drafting text. Visuals should:

- Be simple and uncluttered
- Be vertically oriented
- Be independent of text—able to stand alone
- Be discussed in the text prior to introduction
- Have "action captions"

Don't try to make them "pretty," just create a rough sketch.

⓯ Use the section number followed by consecutive numbers for each visual. Provide an informative figure title.

⓰ Develop an "action caption" to tell the evaluators what you want them to understand about this visual. Use two or three sentences if needed. Ask:

- Reasons behind the requirements
- What is the purpose of this visual?
- What is the visual supposed to communicate?
- What conclusion do I want the evaluators to reach?
- What is the selling point? Are the features tied to benefits?

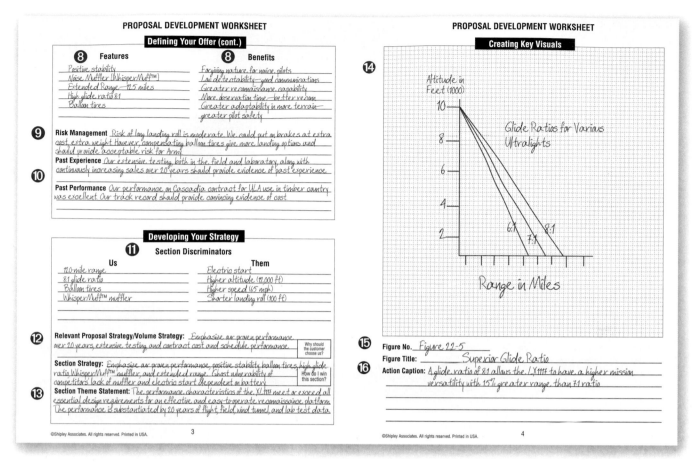

See **Outlining.**

❷ The theme statement links features and benefits in two sentences. Longer themes can be used on larger proposal sections.

See **Themes.**

❸ The prospect's performance needs are summarized.

See **Organization.**

❹ The writer introduces the figure in the text, ahead of the figure.

See **Action Captions.**

❺ Place figures on the same or a facing page so that the reader does not have to turn the page to see the figure. Occasionally, figures must be placed on the following page.

See **Graphics.**

❻ Benefits are introduced before features. The benefit-feature table offers a tempting and easy-to-use summary for the evaluator.

See **Features, Advantages, and Benefits;** *and* **Storyboards.**

❼ The two-part action caption interprets the table for busy evaluators.

See **Action Captions.**

❽ Large proposal sections may include an introduction when space is available in addition to a cross-reference matrix.

See **Organization** *and* **Compliance and Responsiveness.**

❾ The tabular, summary presentation of

Proposal to the U.S. Army — Project Dragonfly

❶ ## 2.2 Performance

❷ **The XL1117 meets or exceeds essential design requirements for an effective, low risk, and easy-to-operate reconnaissance platform. Flight, field, wind-tunnel, and laboratory test data collected over the past 20 years substantiates the XL1117's exceptional performance.**

❸ Effective airborne reconnaissance at the small-unit level requires an aircraft that can be flown virtually undetected at low altitudes by personnel with minimal flight training.

❹ The XL1117 is a versatile as well as reliable ultralight that meets the Army's need for a small-unit, low-level, easy-to-fly reconnaissance aircraft. Figure 2.2-1 summarizes the exceptional benefits of Aerodynamics' ultralight—the Army's best value for mission success. The XL1117 meets or exceeds all essential Army requirements for small unit reconnaissance aircraft.

❺ Figure 2.2-2 on the following page shows the Army requirements along with the XL1117 specifications, and Figure 2.2-3 illustrates the durability of the XL1117's major components.

❻

Benefits	Features
Greater flexibility in photo/radio equipment for increased reconnaissance effectiveness	30 pounds extra payload
Enhanced mission effectiveness because fewer missions can generate necessary information, thus reducing aircraft stress and maintenance	35 miles extra range
Quicker response to mission requirements and less vulnerability for the pilot	20-minute setup time
More forgiving aircraft; less training for pilots	Positive stability
More time for reconnaissance at lower levels	Higher glide ratio
Greater communications capability due to lower detectability; enhanced pilot survivability	Muffled engine noise

❼ **Figure 2.2-1. Overall Best Value.** *Aerodynamics' XL1117 meets or exceeds Army requirements for an ultralight aircraft that maximizes mission effectiveness.*

Through years of experience, we have refined the aircraft design to allow quick, easy assembly by inexperienced users with minimal tools. Current assembly time is 20 minutes or less, depending on experience. The XL1117 also features a payload capacity of 250 pounds, expanding the aircraft's mission versatility and adaptability.

Aerodynamics' XL1117 aircraft is the most thoroughly tested, reliable, and durable aircraft in the ultralight industry. Our aircraft designs stress simplicity and durability, concepts refined by years of flight, wind-tunnel, and laboratory testing.

Major components have a high MTBF, which demonstrates unsurpassed reliability based on actual flight time. Structural components that last twice as long as the industry average attest to our dedication to safety and durability.

The performance characteristics of Aerodynamic's remarkably durable XL1117 closely match the Army's needs for a small-unit reconnaissance platform.

The following major performance factors are discussed in the order requested in the RFP:

❽
- 2.2.1 Flight Control and Handling
- 2.2.2 Aerodynamic Stability
- 2.2.3 Glider Capability
- 2.2.4 Noise Muffling
- 2.2.5 Adaptability

–1–

AERODYNAMICS CORPORATION

performance specifications makes evaluation easy.

See **Graphics.**

10. Subsection themes become more detailed

Proposal to the U.S. Army — Project Dragonfly

❾

Performance Specifications

Paragraph	Design Requirement	XL1117
C.3.2.1	Payload capability 220 lbs	250 lb
C.3.2.2	Top speed ≈ 50 mph	50 mph
C.3.2.3	Cruise speed ≥ 30 mph	40–45 mph
C.3.2.4	Stall speed £ 27 mph	26 mph
C.3.2.5	Sea-level climb rate ≈ 400 fpm	420 fpm
C.3.2.6	Takeoff run £ 150 ft	100 ft
C.3.2.7	Landing roll £ 150 ft	200 ft
C.3.2.8	Ceiling ≈ 10,000 ft	10,000 ft
C.3.2.9	Range ≈ 90 miles	125 miles
C.3.2.10	Sink rate £ 350 fpm	400 fpm
C.3.2.11	Setup time £ 45 min	20 min
C.3.2.12	Operating temperature 0–120° F	0-100°F
C.3.2.13	Operate 0-100% humidity	0-100%
C.3.2.14	Good control response	Very good
C.3.2.15	Good ground handling abilities	Very good
C.3.2.16	Positive or neutral stability	Positive
C.3.2.17	Simple engine start/restart	Yes
C.3.2.18	Sustained glider flight	8:1
C.3.2.19	Engine noise muffling system	Muffled
C.3.2.20	Adaptable	Yes

Figure 2.2-2. Performance Specifications. *Positive stability and high glide ratio provide the XL1117 with the best mix of performance characteristics of any aircraft on the market.*

Component	Construction	Years of Use	MTBF (hours)
Frame	Tubular Aluminum	19	8,200
Engine	Zenob G258	8	1,400
Wings/Tail	Dacron	12	1,200
Controls	100% Mechanical three-axis Joystick	6	3,300
Instruments	Gimble Brothers	2	1,700
Landing Gear	Steel Belted Balloon/Tricycle	16	2,200
Ignition	Mechanical Recoil	19	6, 800
Propeller	Laminated Wood	14	7,900

Figure 2.2-3. High Component Reliability. *XL1117 major components are thoroughly flight tested and offer highly reliable service.*

–2–

AERODYNAMICS CORPORATION

but still link features and benefits.

See **Themes.**

11. Proof of performance must be integrated into the proposal as relevant and not left to a separate, "past performance" section.

See **Relevant Experience/ Past Performance.**

12. The writer offers sufficient background information to both educate an inexperienced evaluator and demonstrate understanding of the requirement. When other offers are equal, this one will appear to be better.

See **Strategy.**

13. Summaries at the end of a section are useful. However, summaries at the beginning are more likely to be read. When time and space are limited, always include summaries at the beginning.

See **Organization.**

14. The graphic on the next page is far more dramatic and emphatic than the text description.

See **Graphics.**

Proposal to the U.S. Army | Project Dragonfly

2.2.1 Flight Control and Handling

⑩ **Proven three-axis, aerodynamic-control steering provides inexperienced Army pilots with an ultralight reconnaissance aircraft that is exceptionally easy to fly.**

The Army requires an ultralight aircraft that can be easily flown by Army personnel for reconnaissance missions into areas not normally accessible by other means of transport.

The XL1117 has a proven design, enabling pilots with limited experience to confidently fly the ultralight aircraft. The easy-to-operate joystick provides three-axis aerodynamic control. The low stall speed and exceptional handling on rough terrain enables the XL1117 to land anywhere.

Figure 2.2-4 shows the XL1117 control systems.

Figure 2.2-4. XL 1117 Flight Control System. *The simplicity of flying the XL1117 is directly tied to the forgiving nature of the control and landing gear systems.*

⑪ Inexperienced pilots often have difficulty making coordinated turns flying aircraft that use weight shift as a primary means of steering. The XL1117 control system eliminates this problem entirely because the control stick operates the rudders on a V-tail and automatically coordinates the wing spoilerons in turns.

⑫ Extensive studies have proven mechanical means of engine control are much more reliable than other electrical starters that depend on batteries. Our engine's recoil starter and toggle make the aircraft easy to switch from powered to glider flight.

The shock-absorbing tricycle landing gear and 10-inch balloon wheels allow safe, smooth landings on rough terrain.

⑬ Flight test data have proven Aerodynamics' control system and landing gear capabilities to be easier to learn and fly than any other aircraft on the market. The XL1117's design will fulfill the Army's need for a dependable reconnaissance aircraft.

2.2.2 Aerodynamic Stability

Aerodynamic's XL1117 spoileron control and positive stability allow novice pilots the complete mobility needed to concentrate on their reconnaissance mission without adversely affecting the aircraft's trajectory.

Two tasks confront inexperienced pilots: they must simultaneously control the aircraft and perform reconnaissance. When pilots have to devote less attention to flying the aircraft, they can focus on their primary task—collecting vital information for the battlefield commander.

⑭ The XL1117 is the world's most easily piloted airplane. Extensive flight testing by the Glider Pilots' Association, an independent industry organization, has revealed no unrecoverable pilot error. Any pilot can release the controls for a complete attitude recovery within seconds. Able to fly itself in a straight line due to its inherent positive stability, the XL1117 requires no positive action by the pilot to recover from an erroneously steep dive or too tightly banked turn. Figure 2.2-5 demonstrates this ease of recovery.

❶ The numbering system and title are dictated by the RFP.

AERODYNAMICS CORPORATION

–3–

⑮ While technically accurate, the poor use of scale actually deemphasizes the glide capability of the aircraft. The benefit of a superior glide capability is minimized. All of the ultralights look like they would "glide like a rock."

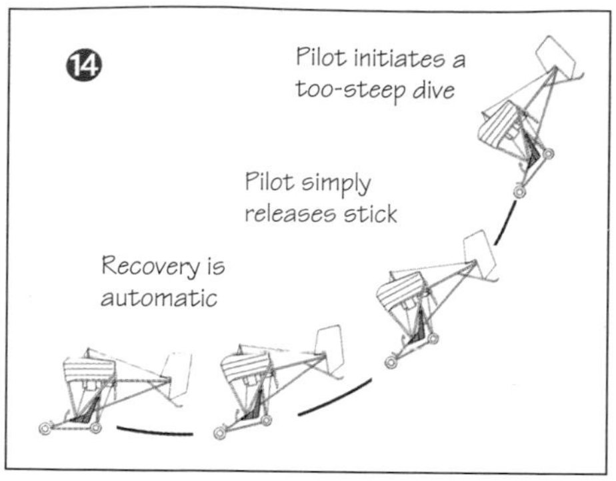

Figure 2.2-5. Positive Stability. *The XL1117's positive stability allows the novice pilot to regain complete control by simply releasing the stick.*

Unlike ultralight aircraft that control bearing through pilot weight shift, spoilerons provide a simple attitude control mechanism that in no way restricts the pilot's freedom of movement. Once pilots are satisfied with their bearing, they have both hands available for taking pictures or accomplishing whatever else the battlefield situation may require.

The XL1117's positive stability and spoileron control gives the Army a mistake-proof reconnaissance craft that doesn't distract a soldier's attention from the mission.

2.2.3 Glider Capability

The XL1117's superior unpowered flight characteristics significantly enhance reconnaissance time by providing the pilot the highest glide ratio and lowest sink rate available on the market today.

The Army needs a reconnaissance platform capable of efficient unpowered and powered flight. In many battlefield situations, engine use may be impractical or even impossible. While powered flight is certainly the primary mode of operation, mission success must not depend on the engine alone.

The XL1117 has the most favorable unpowered flight characteristics available to the Army. An 8:1 glide ratio and a sink rate of 400 feet per minute maximize the pilot's chances of successful mission completion.

Figure 2.2-6 below demonstrates the extended range the 8:1 glide ratio affords the pilot. Another benefit is the absolute stealth mode, in which the pilot kills the engine on purpose for complete silence. The excellent gliding ability of the XL1117 makes this a viable option even for the newly trained pilot.

The XL1117's dual function as a glider and a powered craft will maximize the Army's chances of mission success and greatly expand pilots' in-flight task options.

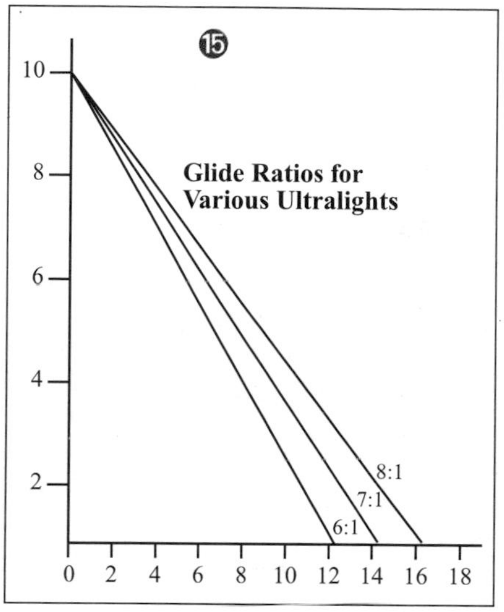

Figure 2.2-6 Superior Glide Ratio. *A glide ratio of 8:1 allows the XL1117 to have higher mission versatility.*

AERODYNAMICS CORPORATION

⓰ The labels in the graphic effectively use familiar, relative noise-level comparisons.

⓱ Substantiation is more credible when taken from independent sources.

See **Relevant Experience/ Past Performance.**

2.2.4 Noise Muffling

Aerodynamics' patented WhisperMuff™ noise suppressor effectively reduces sound emissions to less than 20 decibels, for virtually noise-free reconnaissance.

The Army requires an ultralight aircraft that can fly quietly and safely into enemy territory and effectively gather and communicate reconnaissance information. This requires engine noise muffling that maximizes pilot protection and mission effectiveness.

As figure 2.2-7 demonstrates, the XL1117's noise muffling can greatly decrease the aircraft's vulnerability as an undetectable reconnaissance platform.

Because the WhisperMuff™ reduces sound emissions to less than 20 db, the XL1117 offers radio communications unhindered by engine noise. Rear-mounted engines sometimes allow adequate radio communication, but when unmuffled, compromise the aircraft's function as an undetected reconnaissance vehicle. The muffled XL1117 provides greater pilot and aircraft survivability while making communications simple and clear.

⓱ In a recent test by *Aviation Magazine*, our XL1117 was rated first in minimizing pilot fatigue. Testers cited our WhisperMuff as having the lowest noise emission of any ultralight they had tested.

As a result of Aerodynamics' WhisperMuff noise suppressor, the Army will have unmatched surveillance capabilities and be able to conduct unhindered reconnaissance missions effectively with enhanced pilot safety.

⓰

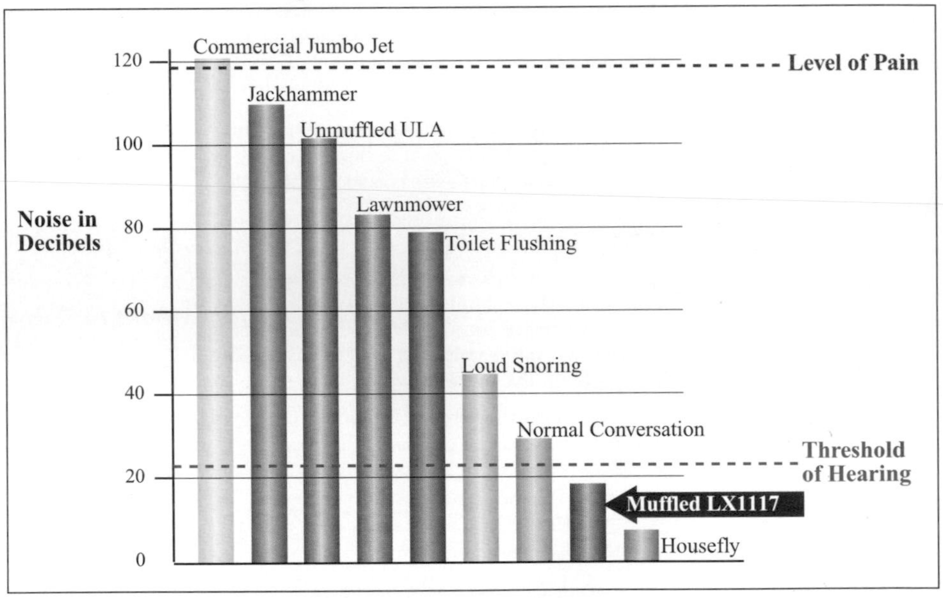

Figure 2.2-7. Muffling Results Comparison. *The XL1117's superior noise suppressing capabilities effectively eliminate engine noise, enhancing reconnaissance effectiveness.*

AERODYNAMICS CORPORATION

⑱ The writer is offsetting a weakness in landing roll against a strength in landing safely over rougher terrain.

See **Strategy.**

⑲ Again, the writer offsets a weakness against a strength.

See **Strategy.**

⑳ The major section closes with a summary of key benefits and features—a best practice. However, closing summaries are relatively less effective in formally evaluated and scored proposals. Evaluators usually stop reading after they find the answer to each question.

See **Organization.**

2.2.5 Adaptability

Shock-absorbing landing gear and tires, short takeoff and landing distances, and a wide range of operating conditions enable the XL1117 to provide reconnaissance capabilities in a variety of battlefield scenarios.

The Army needs a small-unit, low-level, hard-to-detect reconnaissance aircraft adaptable to a variety of restrictive terrains. The aircraft must be reliable, easy to fly, and readily maintained far from support bases.

⑱ The XL1117 is a proven, reliable ultralight aircraft that supports this adaptability requirement. The short takeoff run and landing roll, shock-absorbing tricycle landing gear, and balloon tires ensure exceptional ground-handling capabilities.

Although the 200-foot landing roll exceeds the Army specification of 150 feet, Aerodynamic's investigations indicate that the ability of the XL1117 balloon tires to handle rough terrain means a larger variety of available landing sites.

Figure 2.2-8 shows that the XL1117's range of 125 miles and flight times of over 6 hours can provide Army commanders with more battlefield information than most ultralights with ranges of 80 to 100 miles and flight times of 2 to 3 hours.

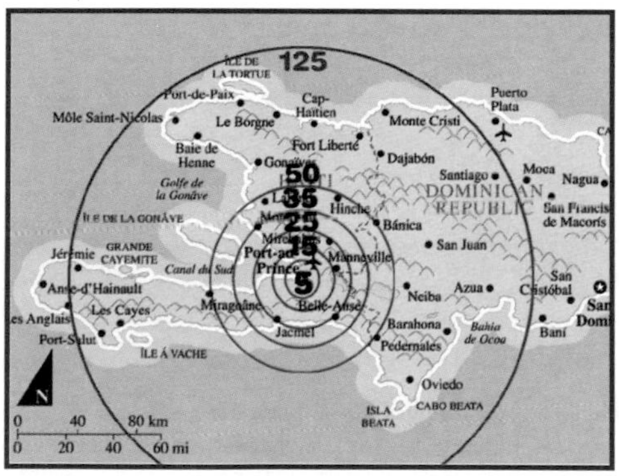

Figure 2.2-8. XL1117 Range. *The XL1117 permits surveillance of more territory due to its extended 125-mile range.*

The Aerodynamic XL1117 has an operational ceiling of 10,000 feet, which is high enough for reconnaissance flights in hilly terrain, but not so high as to endanger the pilot from cold or oxygen deprivation. A humidity range of 0 to 100 percent and an operating temperature range of 0 to 100°F mean the Army can deploy the XL1117 in arctic as well as tropical climates.

⑲ The WhisperMuff™ noise reduction system reduces cooling airflow to the engine. This feature maintains the upper temperature range of 100°F, which falls 20°F short of the Army specification (120°F). A trade study conducted by Aerodynamics' test facility showed that the reduction in detectable noise facilitated by the WhisperMuff provided more operational capability than the additional 20°F operating range, a relatively rare occurrence.

The XL1117 meets or exceeds all essential Army requirements for small unit reconnaissance aircraft. Based on glide ratio, excellent range, quiet muffled operations, and quick assembly time, the Army can count on an aircraft that offers the following combinations of features and benefits:

- Reduces detectability for safer operations
- ⑳ Maximizes time over the reconnaissance target
- Adapts quickly to diverse mission requirements
- Offers a greater range, so fewer missions are required

Other factors, such as control and handling, stability, glider capability, and noise muffling, influence the aircraft's design. Since military operations are global, the aircraft must be readily adaptable to a variety of operating environments.

❶The prospect's logo and colors are placed in the upper-left corner of the page to increase customer focus.

See **Customer Focus,** *and* **Page and Document Design.**

❷The prospect's RFP name is placed in the header of every page.

See **Page and Document Design.**

❸The seller's logo and name are placed in the footer.

See **Customer Focus,** *and* **Page and Document Design.**

❹A high-level win theme or slogan was placed in the footer. The win theme was carefully created to emphasize the seller's primary discriminator and to demonstrate the seller's understanding of the prospect's hot button issue.

See **Strategy** *and* **Themes.**

❺The RFP was a casually written five-page letter. The numbering system could not be matched. Requirements were extracted from the RFP and posted in an italic font in the left margin adjacent to the response. This is the only place where the numbering systems match.

See **Compliance and Responsiveness, Outlining,** *and* **Page and Document Design.**

❻The theme statement links a benefit and a discriminator to the individual proposed.

See **Themes** *and* **Discriminators.**

7. The intentional bolding of key words was designed to attract anyone who scanned the proposal and to make the answer easy to find.

See **Page and Document Design.**

---

❶ BUZZKOLA

❷ PRE-QUALIFICATION OF STRATEGIC ALLIANCE PARTNERS
Request for Proposal

❺ 2. Project Team

2. Scope of Work: Identify single company-wide point of contact for all BuzzKola inquiries

❻ **BuzzKola can streamline project planning by selecting Mr. Lars Nielson of Svensco as your single point of contact for strategic partners with intimate local market knowledge.**

❼ To streamline project planning, Svensco is proposing a single point of contact and a focus on only those countries where we offer unique added value due to our **intimate understanding of the local construction environment.**

Our proposed single point of contact is Mr. Lars Nielson, to be located in Sweden or another location of BuzzKola's choice. Mr. Nielson would provide direct support and coordination through the most knowledgeable local support team, whether it is a Svensco company or another BuzzKola strategic partner.

Propose project teams (organization and named individuals) for:
- *Capacity calculations*
- *Conceptual design, schedule, and cost estimate*
- *Site selection*
- *Basic design package*
- *Capital Project Request*
- *Construction tender package evaluation*
- *Equipment tender package and evaluation*

The Svensco development team follows: ❽

Team Leader ❾	**Lars Nielson, VP Project Management** Civil Engineer, knowledgeable in 5 languages, 16 years' construction process experience—includes Eastern Europe, Middle East, and Russia
Capacity Calculations	**Earl Bouchard, Senior Process Engineer** Chemical Engineer, 20+ years' experience in design and project management—includes the U.S., Puerto Rico, Middle East, Scotland, and South America
Conceptual Design, ❿ **Schedule, Cost Estimate**	**Lars Nielson, Senior Project Manager**
Site Selection	**Nikola Niemi, Project Manager, NIS** *(Newly Independent States)* Civil Engineer M. Sc. (BS-Econ. and M.S. Operation Mgmt.), knowledgeable in 4 languages, 18 years' experience construction—includes Finland, Russia, and the Middle East
Basic Design Package	**Randall W. Pincher, Design Architect** Architect, knowledgeable in new and renovation process plants facilities, 27 years' project experience—includes the U.S., Puerto Rico, and Poland
Capital Project Request	**Dennis MacMahon, Marketing Manager, NIS** Accountant, 17 years' experience in construction business and management reporting, 6 years dedicated to NIS
Construction Tender	**Nikola Niemi, Project Manager, NIS**
Package and Evaluation	**Donald Dahlstrom, Operations Manager** Civil Engineer, 20+ years' experience in construction project management—including Denmark, Algeria, Tanzania, and Sweden; knowledgeable in 3 languages
Equipment Tender	**Chris Cederwold, Purchasing Manager** Package Evaluation Civil engineer; 30+ years' international purchasing experience; Quality Assurance courses & ANSI/ASME certified lead auditor

❸ SVENSCO

❹ *Local simplicity in a complex world*

1

---

⑧ Team roles are listed in the same order as in the RFP.

See **Compliance and Responsiveness.**

⑨ To minimize the space required, only relevant information on each person was included in a table format instead of prose. Because some numbers are 10 or above, all numbers are shown as numerals rather than spelled out.

See **Graphics.**

⑩ When an individual filled more than one role, the information was not repeated.

⑪ The theme statement answers the top-level requirement.

See **Question and Answer Proposals.**

⑫ This is the entire RFP design requirement.

⑬ The informal table of contents roughly matches the RFP excerpt. The subsection headings are previewed along with a short summary sentence.

See **Compliance and Responsiveness.**

⑭ The actual subheading matches the introduction precisely.

See **Organization.**

⑮ Wherever possible, figures were used to shorten proposal preparation time and emphasize compliance. Figures were easier and faster to prepare due to the diverse international background of the contributors. *(Figure 3-1 is not included here.)*

See **Graphics.**

BUZZKOLA

PRE-QUALIFICATION OF STRATEGIC ALLIANCE PARTNERS
Request for Proposal

3. Design Approach

⑪ **An easy-to-use streamlined project planning package will be tailored by Svensco with other strategic partners to develop country-specific estimates within 2 to 5 days.**

⑫ *Based on the workshop and your own expertise, you would be required to develop conceptual design methods and (software) tools to turn around typical project inquiries in 2-5 working days for the following warehouse/ distribution centers and production plant facilities.*

Using the design parameters established in the project orientation workshops and proven conceptual design methods, Svensco will team with the other strategic partners selected by BuzzKola to choose a common design package and tailor it for BuzzKola facilities. We have used and tailored different design packages and think the choice should be based on the best fit for all of BuzzKola's partners.

Our approach to develop the Conceptual Design Package is described in the following order:

⑬ 3.1 **Conceptual Design Methods**—Project planning accuracy depends on a proven design method and is the basis to structure the project planning package.

3.2 **Software and Tools**—A standard package will be tailored for BuzzKola facilities.

3.3 **Schedule**—Describes the tasks anticipated with the minimum and maximum times required to meet the 2- to 5-day target.

3.4 **Design Input and Design Output**—Reviews the level of detail anticipated and how Svensco will compensate if the detail is not available.

⑭ 3.1 Conceptual Design Methods

The accuracy of each design package requires a sound conceptual design process that incorporates the design parameters established in the project orientation workshops. For example, design parameters are used to calculate plant capacity and expansion options from sales volume projections.

⑮ The ***Global Project Delivery Flowchart***, Figure 3-1, the large foldout on the following page, shows the basic process envisioned to estimate and schedule capital projects. To improve estimating accuracy, we pre-define standard steps to adjust for country-specific conditions and variables for each project.

During the ***Programming Phase***, some of the variables in the development process include land rights and leases, taxation issues, laws, custom duties, logistic issues, technical-economical study documentation, local construction regulations, local resources, and other unique requirements.

Following a consistent conceptual design process enables Svensco to produce a credible Conceptual Design Package in the 2- to 5-working day range required. . . .

. . .

. . .

Sections 3.2 through 3.4 were omitted here for brevity.

SVENSCO

1

Local simplicity in a complex world

⑯ This is the entire quoted RFP requirement.

⑰ This preview also summarizes the proposed approach.

See **Organization.**

⑱ The heading matches the introduction.

See **Organization.**

⑲ Success stories are inserted to support claims made in the text.

See **Relevant Experience and Past Performance.**

⑳ Figures are used to provide most of the details.

See **Graphics.**

BUZZKOLA

PRE-QUALIFICATION OF STRATEGIC ALLIANCE PARTNERS
Request for Proposal

⑯ *Based on the successful completion of the basic design package portion of the prequalification exercise, we will ask you to put together the necessary tools and procedures such that you would be in a position to develop a detailed proposal in the form of a fixed price, turnkey contract for the complete supply of the facility to the agreed schedule.*

4. Turnkey Bid Package

BuzzKola's partners will get a detailed turnkey bid package within 4 weeks based on the conceptual design and modifications using our detailed knowledge of local market conditions.

On confirmation from BuzzKola that the conceptual design package has been completed successfully, we will begin developing the turnkey bid package. In this section, we describe the contents of the turnkey bid package and detail our approach to develop a package that meets BuzzKola's requirements to issue the proposal within 4 weeks.

Our approach to develop the turnkey bid package is described in the following order:

⑰ 4.1 Content of the Turnkey Bid Package and Development Tasks
4.2 Additional local input—required to enhance the Conceptual Design Package to meet the local requirements
4.3 Further Value-Added Benefits
4.4 Responsibility and Risk Sharing—will depend on location and completion time required
4.5 Our Approach to Level 2 Countries
4.6 Restrictions and Limitations

⑱ 4.1 Content of the Turnkey Bid Package and Development Tasks

Our planning of the Turnkey Bid Package begins with a clear definition of the end product, defining the output or contents of the package. We will then review the input that we would have for each output item and determine what activities we would have to complete. These activities will become our development tasks.

⑲

Successful Turnkey Project in a Developing Market. *Svensco completed this beverage plant on a turnkey basis, on time and on budget due to careful planning.*

⑳ Outputs, inputs, and activities are shown in figure 4-1. The schedule for the development tasks is shown in figure 4-2.

The goal of the development tasks is to enable BuzzKola's strategic partner to prepare a detailed proposal with a firm fixed level of detail for any selected country and location in the world. We plan to have each relevant Svensco location prepare a start-up plan and materials to enable them to meet your 4-week requirement.

Our approach leverages our local knowledge and then specifically relates it to the BuzzKola facilities requirements to save both time and money to the benefit of all parties. As soon as the details are presented from the Project Orientation Workshop, our local project teams will begin the development tasks required for execution of a BuzzKola facility. The development tasks are identified in figure 4-3.

SVENSCO

Local simplicity in a complex world

1

㉑ RFP text that did not include requirements was not quoted in the proposal.

See **Compliance and Responsiveness.**

㉒ This detailed figure is designed to demonstrate the seller's detailed knowledge and to focus on the proposed project. Too many similar proposals describe generic approaches.

See **Strategy.**

㉓ The action caption explains the figure and also directs the reader to the associated schedule *(Omitted here for brevity).*

See **Action Captions.**

BUZZKOLA

PRE-QUALIFICATION OF STRATEGIC ALLIANCE PARTNERS
Request for Proposal

㉑

Please describe, together with an activity listing and schedule your approach to the . . . development tasks.

㉒

OUTPUT	INPUT	ACTIVITY
Project Description	Scope of Work, estimate and documentation summary	Present proposal
Price	All information mentioned below	Estimate
Conditions of Contract	Scope of Work	Legal input
Project Organization chart	Scope of Work	Produce Project Organization chart and Technical Descriptions
Master Schedule (Gantt chart)	Start-up date by BuzzKola	Planning
Quality Assurance Plan	Quality Plan form	Adjust Plan to project
General		
• Project Data	Basic Design Package	
• Scope of Work	Basic Design Package	Add local specific items
• Technical Specification	Basic Design Package	Add local specific items
• Room Equipment Specification	Basic Design Package	Add local specific items
• Room Finishing List	Basic Design Package	Add local specific items
• Electrical installations	Basic Design Package	Add local specific items
• Mechanical installations	Basic Design Package	Add local specific items
• Water Quality report	Water quality survey form	Measures to analyze the water quality
Beverage Plant		
• Capacity Calculation Report	BuzzKola input	Capacity Calculations
• Plant Specification	Plant Manufacturer input	Proposal from plant mfging
• Equipment list	Plant Manufacturer input	Proposal from plant mfging
• Utility requirements	Plant Manufacturer input	Proposal from plant mfging
Warehouse		
• Sales Volume Report	BuzzKola input	List of Product type
• Material flow/Logistic Report	Sales Volume Report	Logistic analysis
• Equipment list	Logistic report	Market survey

㉓ **Figure 4-1. Contents of the Turnkey Bid Package.** *The content of the Turnkey Bid Package is shown together with required input and the activities required to carry out to be able to reach the final result. A schedule showing the sequence of the activities is shown in figure 4-2.*

•
•
•
•

Sections 4.2 through 4.6 were omitted here for brevity.

SVENSCO

1

Local simplicity in a complex world

(24) The single-sentence summary was designed to tie together the diverse items requested in the RFP.

See **Question and Answer Proposals.**

(25) Generally limit appendices to requested material. The mention of the "tab" suggests a helpful tone.

See **Appendices and Attachments.**

(26) Personnel breakdowns are always difficult. The summary text places a positive spin on overlapping capabilities. The tabular presentation is compact and easy to read.

See **Graphics** *and* **Strategy.**

(27) Success stories are inserted as available and as space permits. Graphics can be placed in either the text or left margin areas. While action captions are placed below most graphics, space restrictions can force alternative placements. Note the structural "success story" organization.

See **Relevant Experience/ Past Performance.**

BUZZKOLA

PRE-QUALIFICATION OF STRATEGIC ALLIANCE PARTNERS
Request for Proposal

5. Backup Data Requirement

(24) The following backup data supplied to BuzzKola is focused on substantiating Svensco's intimate knowledge of specific local markets and our commitment to a long-term BuzzKola—Svensco partnership.

5.1 Svensco Annual Reports

Annual Reports for last 3 years

(25) Svensco annual reports for 1998, 1999, and 2000 are included after the "Corporate Reports" tab.

(26) 5.2 Personnel Breakdown

Personnel breakdown (numbers excluding support staff). Give total and indicate how many have experience with:
i. manufacturing or warehousing facilities
ii. beverage industry
iii. BuzzKola

Indicate experience in:
- *Project Management*
- *Engineering*
- *Procurement*
- *Site supervision*

The breakdown of Svensco personnel is shown below. Because of the rapid changes in our business and numerous client projects, employees frequently move between Svensco companies and countries.

Our policy is to locate and assign the most qualified individual available.

Some of the classifications also overlap. Engineers often serve as project managers or supervise sites.

Svensco Worldwide

Discipline	Manufacturing or Warehouse	Beverage Industry	BuzzKola Facilities
Project Management	330	63	10
Engineer	952	295	6
Procurement	212	44	12
Site Supervision	623	114	8
Total Per Category	2,117	516	43
Total Technical Personnel Worldwide	**5,532**		

(27)

Figure 5-1. Beverage Storage and Distribution Center. *Scandia Beverage needed an energy-efficient distribution center to support European markets. Scandia selected Svensco as the . . . best value approach. Svensco completed a large underground storage, distribution center, and warehouse in Sweden on time and within budget.*

SVENSCO

1

Local simplicity in a complex world

❶ Open a major section with a theme statement, followed by a short section summary to provide perspective for evaluators that primarily are forced to focus on details.

See **Question/Response Proposals.**

❷ This sentence is an introduction designed to reassure evaluators that all questions are answered in the order listed in the bid request.

See **Question/Response Proposals.**

❸ Each bid request question is repeated in the left margin adjacent to the bidder's answer.

NOTE: Document 13 used left-justified text for callouts while right-justified text is used here. Left-justified text is easier to read; however, right-justified text is more easily associated visually with the response. Select a preferred style and be consistent in the same bid.

❹ Each question is answered directly in the first sentence. All additional text supports or substantiates the initial answer. Placing the answer in bolded text makes the answer easier to spot.

See **Question/Response Proposals.**

Proposal to Provide Database Software Development Services for GIBM, Inc.

4.0 SOFTWARE MAINTENANCE

❶ **ISI offers GIBM comprehensive, trouble-free software maintenance at no additional cost for 10 years following software installation.**

ISI's Client Services Organization is widely acknowledged as one of the finest service organizations in the information services industry. We provide 24-hour-a-day, 7-day-per-week support and are able to resolve most problems within 1.57 hours. The software maintenance plan we offer meets all of GIBM's needs in a convenient, low-cost manner.

❷ Below are our responses to your specific questions regarding software maintenance: ❹

❸

Is software maintenance available?

1. **Yes.** ISI provides regular software maintenance on all system software used by the Master Control system.

If yes, is the price included in the price of the software?

2. **Yes.** Software maintenance is included in the price of the software. GIBM would incur NO additional costs for maintenance.

If priced separately, what is the price and how is it paid? (monthly, yearly, other?)

3. **Maintenance costs are not priced separately.**

How long will the vendor maintain the system?

4. **ISI will maintain the system at no cost for 10 years** following installation. Following the 10-year maintenance period, GIBM can purchase an ongoing maintenance contract from ISI. Currently, such a contract costs $500/day on a time-and-materials basis.

Can a user maintain the software?

5. **Yes.** Under initial guidance from ISI software engineers and maintenance personnel, GIBM personnel can develop the expertise necessary to maintain system software and install periodic upgrades.

How does a user receive a new version of release of the product to which he is licensed?

6. **Uncustomized system software is upgraded at least once annually.** New software versions or releases are announced 6 to 8 weeks before becoming available. During that period, users can request upgrading for a nominal installation fee. Customized software is upgraded 4 to 12 weeks following release of upgraded uncustomized software. Costs depend on the amount of upgrading and the extent of customization. Upgrading is priced on a case-by-case basis.

How long is a user covered by a maintenance contract after a new release/version is available if he does not upgrade?

7. **Users are covered by the original maintenance contract for 10 years** following installation if software is not upgraded. Each software upgrade extends the maintenance contract to 10 years following installation of the upgrade.

I·S·I Information Systems, Inc. • 8700 South State Street • St. Louis, MO 33701 • 573.222.2222 • 573.222.4747 (fax) • www.infosys.com

NOTE: Dotted lines indicate material eliminated for brevity.

❶ Capture plans, like any document written for senior management, should have an executive summary of one page or less.

See **Executive Summary** *and* **Organization.**

❷ This bullet list summarizes the executive summary.

See **Lists** *and* **Organization.**

❸ This short setup and summary provides the necessary context and summarizes the immediate opportunity.

See **Organization.**

❹ The numbered list previews how the capture plan is organized. The numbers and titles are identical to the subsection titles to eliminate confusion.

See **Lists.**

❺ Notes the need for reviews and updates.

See **Capture Planning.**

❻ Establishes the market need for those unfamiliar with the market.

❼ Previews the organization and purpose of a seven-page section.

See **Organization.**

Fiberdyne Capture Plan | **DOT Bridge Composites Research**

❶ Executive Summary

❷
- ***$200 million annual market***
- ***Entry controlled by FHWA***
- ***Available now: $1–$3 million applications research and demonstration contract.***
- ***Probable teaming partner required***
- ***Commit resources early***

❸ Fiberdyne has the opportunity to position itself to capture a significant portion of a potential $200 million market. The Department of Transportation (DOT) is sponsoring the initial applications demonstrations to prove the viability of using fiber reinforced composites in bridge construction and renovation.

We have prepared this capture plan to efficiently focus Fiberdyne's limited marketing resources on capturing the DOT's initial $2 million demonstration program. Our capture plan consists of four major sections:

❹ 1.0 External Analysis

2.0 Internal Analysis

3.0 Capture Strategy

4.0 Implementation and Control

❺ We look forward to the planned monthly senior management reviews and will update this plan to include both management suggestions and new information.

1.0 External Analysis

❻ The poor condition of bridges in the U.S. and internationally and the fierce competition for funding has encouraged industry experts to explore the use of innovative methods and improved materials. The Department of Transportation's (DOT) Federal Highway Administration (FHWA) establishes the specifications that must be met to receive Federal funding. Fiberdyne materials must be reviewed, tested, and approved by FHWA officials to be accepted in bridge building applications.

❼ Our external analysis examines the customer, the situation, key program requirements, and probable competitors. Our purpose is to identify potential opportunities for Fiberdyne materials and threats to acceptance of our materials in bridge building applications.

Fiberdyne Capture Plan | **DOT Bridge Composites Research**

(8) 1.1 The Customer: FHWA guidelines drive bridge building and repair specifications

(9) ***Organization and Key People***

(10) Within the DOT, the "road guys" are in the FHWA. The FHWA sets standards for road and bridge construction and repair. While states do all of the contracting for work, the Feds kick in various percentages of funding for projects that meet FHWA specifications. The FHWA regularly investigates new materials and methods that will use the Federal funds more efficiently.

(11) The Research Division of the FHWA headed by Assistant Undersecretary of Transportation, Dr. Brown, is charged with new materials research and testing. The key members of Dr. Brown's organization are sketched in figure 1.

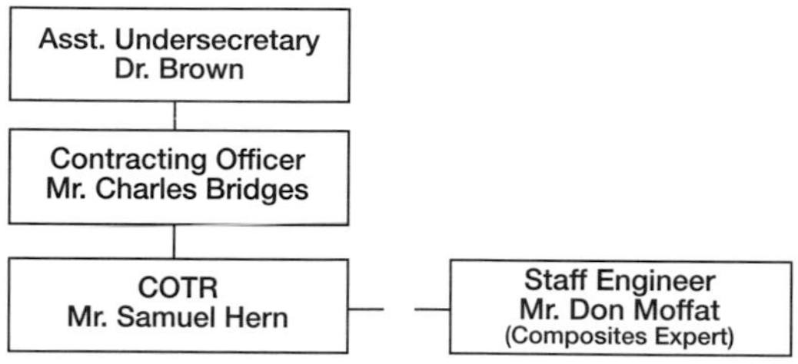

(12) **Figure 1. FWWA Research Division Structure.** *These FHWA employees have been assigned to the proposed project to research high-performance bridge materials.*

Acquisition Process

(13) Mr. Charles Bridges, the PCO, said that the research budget is set, but internal competition for the funds within the DOT continues. He expects a minimum of $1 million and a maximum of $3 million to be budgeted, depending on the extent of the demonstration. Mr. Samuel Hern, the COTR, is reluctant and primarily concerned about something going wrong on his watch. Dr. Brown, a strong supporter of developing improved materials, will push the project through the DOT funding cycle. Mr. Don Moffat, a relatively new FHWA staff engineer, has been our best source of information. To date no company seems to have the inside track.

Evaluation Process

(14) We expect Bridges, Hern, and Moffat will be evaluators. Dr. Brown will probably not evaluate formally, but will be involved as much as his schedule permits. We expect at least three more people to be added to the evaluation team. As long as the total contract stays below $3 million, the PCO is likely to evaluate the cost proposals.

---

(8) Uses informative headings where headings are not dictated. Most organizations have an established, required organization for capture plans.

See **Capture Planning** *and* **Headings.**

(9) Subtitles within sections are placed in the left margin to permit readers to immediately understand how the section is organized and to skip to any section of immediate interest.

See **Page and Document Design.**

(10) The immediate customer is established within the context of the large customer organization.

(11) Only the key people are listed. The diagram instantly shows their organizational relationships, while the action caption indicates their assignment.

See **Action Captions** *and* **Graphics.**

(12) This is a two-part action caption with a heading and full-sentence caption. Note that the graphic is introduced in the prior text.

See **Action Captions.**

(13) The funding is established and might increase. Note the sources of information are identified.

See **Capture Planning.**

(14) The anticipated role of specific individuals in the evaluation permits the seller to focus on individuals' issues and perceptions.

16–MAJOR PROGRAM, TEXT FORMAT (CONTINUED)

⑮ A disciplined effort was made to analyze the key individuals, understand their motivations, and suggest potential marketing actions.

⑯ A bulleted list was used for added emphasis.

See **Lists.**

Fiberdyne Capture Plan **DOT Bridge Composites Research**

⑮ We have identified several experiences of key FHWA people in figure 2 and linked those experiences with potential Fiberdyne marketing actions.

Type of Experience	Customer Result	Goal	Potential Marketing Action	Reasoning
Don Moffat has unique expertise with composites in bridges.	Led to current job at FHWA. Employed and promoted.	Build his technical credibility in FHWA.	Keep Moffat informed. Share technical information. Learn more about his Golden Gate Bridge experience. Dr. Hats to participate in sales call.	Primary influencer, likely evaluator, build familiarity with our proprietary fibers.
Sam Hern has seen careers tarnished by risky projects.	Avoids new technology whenever possible. Minimizes risk.	Emphasize proven materials and low risk approach.	Emphasize bridge application experience, management, scheduling approach. Stay practical, simplify technology. Keep composites techies away.	Build comfort, acceptance. Wary of new technology.
Charles Bridges is a contracting pro.	Promoted by following the rules.	Build idea that FDyn follows the rules.	Indicate FDyn interest. Obtain permission to discuss with FHWA employees.	Build familiarity, acceptance.
Dr. Brown developed reputation as an innovator.	Rapid advancement.	Innovation to draw attention w/low risk.	Presentation by Dr. Hats (technical) and FDyn CEO (management). Introduce project manager.	Build acceptance of FDyn's tech. and management competence.

Figure 2. FHWA Experience. *Key FHWA emplyee experiences are listed along with potential marketing actions.*

Issues and Hot Buttons

We have identified the following customer issues and hot buttons:

⑯
- Low risk
- Advanced materials, especially with composites
- Dual-use technology
- Bridge building experience and expertise
- Respected image as a leader and trend-setter with consulting engineers, constructors, suppliers, Federal officials, and academia
- Ability to contribute some portion of the project costs, not to exceed matching the Federal contribution
- Proven ability to manage costs and meet schedules

⑰ The informative heading both creates interest and focuses on the buying officials.

⑱ The bulleted list quickly establishes market context.

⑲ The customer history focuses on the decision maker, not the entire organization.

⑳ The source of the requirements establishes the customers' ownership. All items in the list are parallel in structure.

See **Customer Focus** *and* **Lists.**

Fiberdyne Capture Plan | **DOT Bridge Composites Research**

Environmental Factors

⑰ **1.2 Situation: FHWA officials are interested in proving the viability of improved materials.**

Some facts about the U.S. bridge building market:

⑱
- $30 billion is spent on public highway construction annually.
- $6 billion is spent on bridges—70 percent is for new construction, 20 percent is for alterations and reconstruction, and 10 percent is for maintenance and repair.

Even though many bridges are off-system, Federal approval of Fiberdyne's proprietary materials will be required before many others accept them. Our successful entry of a potentially $100 million domestic market and subsequent international market requires FHWA sponsored applications testing. The opportunity to obtain partial Federal funding for the applications testing is attractive.

⋮

Customer History

⑲ Dr. Brown has a history of identifying innovative opportunities, pushing them through, being recognized, and then getting promoted. His primary motivation seems to be to make the project a success, and he appears willing to maintain an accessible approach.

Dr. Brown is aware of the rival Corps of Engineers program and would like to beat them.

1.3 Program Requirements

While a statement of work and RFP have not been written, we have identified several requirements in our conversations with FHWA personnel. We are not certain which ones will actually be included:

Key Requirements

⑳
- Evaluate the economic and technical feasibility of using composite materials in bridge building applications.
- Test and evaluate various types of advanced composite materials.
- Analyze the impact of composites on design parameters.
- Survey current relevant applications of composites.
- Investigate applications to cables and structural members.
- Evaluate production methods.

16–MAJOR PROGRAM, TEXT FORMAT (CONTINUED)

㉑ Sellers in concentrated markets can identify specific competitors. The breadth of competitors led the writer to analyze competitors by type. Much competitor analysis can be lifted from business, market, and sales plans.

See **Capture Planning, Process,** *and* **Strategy.**

㉒ The graphic is introduced in the prior text.

See **Action Captions.**

㉓ This is a bidder comparison matrix, comparing potential bidders or types of bidders against the customer's requirements.

See **Strategy.**

㉔ All types of graphics should have action captions to help the reader interpret the graphic as the writer intended. Placement is consistently below the graphic when space permits.

See **Action Captions** *and* **Page and Document Design.**

Fiberdyne Capture Plan **DOT Bridge Composites Research**

- Develop designs for representative components, then construct and test the components.
- Prepare a detailed final report and publish it in an appropriate industry journal.
- Present and discuss results at appropriate industry forums.

1.4 Competitor Analysis

Numerous potential competitors exist and are classified by type:

Five Types of Competitors ㉑

- Research companies like ourselves, interested in royalties
- Raw material producers, producing fiber and resin
- Converters, who manufacture composite products
- Bridge builders
- Consulting engineers

We have examined the typical factors that could affect the FHWA's buying decision against each type of competitor in figure 3.

Note: Figure 3 not included for brevity.

⋮

Competitive Comparison of Program Requirements ㉒

We next examined the program requirements identified in section 1.3, slightly rearranged and consolidated. The result is shown in figure 4.

FHWA Program Requirements	Fiberdyne	Research Companies (Sterling)	Material Producers (R. Horning)	Converter (Franklin Fiberglas)	Bridge Builder (American Bridge)	Consulting Engineers
⋮	⋮	⋮	⋮	⋮	⋮	⋮
Present results at industry forums	3	3	3	2	4	4
Total	**41**	**40**	**41**	**31**	**29**	**37**

Figure 4. Analysis of Competitive Factors. *Program requirements currently identified are ranked on a 1-(lowest) to 5-scale (highest). The results change significantly as the comparison becomes more specific, but the strengths and weaknesses are similar.*

㉕ Anticipating the probable competitive strategy of competitors is the purpose of a black-hat team.

See **Process, Reviews,** *and* **Strategy.**

Fiberdyne Capture Plan **DOT Bridge Composites Research**

Competitive Strategy

We next examined the competitive strategies typically used by our competitors. The result is shown in figure 5.

㉕

Typical Approach or Competitive Strategy	Research Companies (Sterling)	Material Producers (R. Horning)	Converter (Franklin Fiberglas)	Bridge Builder (American Bridge)	Consulting Engineers
1. Type of Markets	Royalties, contract R&D	Large production contracts	Large components in large quanties	Builds bridges	Sells services at a fixed rate
2. Leader/follower	Fiber development leader	Production methods leader	Leader in new product application	Construction leader	Follower
3. Commitment to FHWA opptnty.	Establish own fibers	Positioning for volume sales	Positioning for product sales	Seeking discriminators: Comp. experience and mfg adv.	Positioning for design edge
4. Flexibility	Good	Limited	Limited	Limited	Limited
5. Pricing	High on own fibers	Invests in new markets	Invests in new markets	Aggressive	High
6. Probable sales approach	Emphasize R&D aspects, composites expertise	Will hire experts and/or team	Will hire experts and/or team	Emphasize bridge construction expertise, composites experience, and fabrication facility	Cite "big names" and use "little names"

Figure 5. Analysis of Competitive Strategies. *The probable competitive strategies of the different competitors are shown here. This matrix will be updated as more is learned.*

16–MAJOR PROGRAM, TEXT FORMAT (CONTINUED)

㉖ The second major section opens with a summary and introduction.

See **Organization.**

㉗ The informative heading states the most important point, much like a theme statement in a proposal.

See **Headings** *and* **Themes.**

㉘ Specific requirements are compared to specific capabilities rather than general strengths and weaknesses. Potential actions that require management support are clearly identified.

Fiberdyne Capture Plan — **DOT Bridge Composites Research**

2.0 Internal Analysis

㉖ The focus of our internal analysis is to develop a winning solution. We clearly want to emphasize our strengths. We must also identify our weaknesses, the gap between to the FHWA's needs, competitors' approaches, and our current capability.

We have used gap analysis to develop a competitive solution.

Our internal analysis will also look at our financial resources, pricing, and potential risks.

Determine Solution

㉗ **2.1 Fiberdyne Solutions: Fiberdyne Must Be Seen as the Obvious Choice to Demonstrate the Viability of Composite Materials.**

We analyzed the gaps between the requirements and our currently available solution in figure 6.

㉘

FHWA Program Requirements	Available Solution	Gap	Action Required
Evaluate economic feasibility	None internal	Must know bridge building economics	Hire consultant or team
Evaluate technical feasibility	Dr. Hats and his staff	None	Emphasize unique capability of Dr. Hats
Evaluate materials	Dr. Hats and his staff	None	Emphasize broad look, beyond Fiberdyne's materials
Analyze design impact	Non internal	Need bridge designer	Subcontract
	⋮	⋮	⋮
Present results at industry forums	Dr. Hats and staff	None	List recent industry forum presentations

Figure 6. Gap Analysis. *Major program gaps can be closed by subcontracting or teaming.*

(29) An informative heading was added to highlight the overriding point of the section.

(30) Subheadings in the left margin permit readers with waning interest to get the main point of each paragraph without reading the paragraph.

(31) The stated assumptions and apparent agreement from several methods of analysis increases the credibility of the estimate.

(32) Placing the proposal budget in the context of the potential net contribution margin offers a basis for comparison.

See **Presenting Cost and Pricing Data.**

(33) The informative heading summarizes the greatest risk.

(34) All risk is limited to a high-level treatment of strengths, weaknesses, opportunities, and threats.

See **Risk Management.**

Fiberdyne Capture Plan | **DOT Bridge Composites Research**

(29) **2.2 Financial Resources and Pricing: Fiberdyne Must Be Seen as the Company Offering the Best Value for Their Expenditure**

(30) Fiberdyne lacks the financial resources offered by other, much larger companies. A Rowens Horning or Franklin Fiberglas . . .

.
.

Team to Reduce Costs — We should team with a larger company that will have or can hire the bridge building expertise that we lack. If we choose to go alone, hiring the appropriate consultants in bridge building would be costly.

Overheads Covered — For the project, all facilities and personnel can be charged at our full overhead rate, but our profit margins will have to be acceptably small, probably under 5 percent.

(31) ***Conservative Capture Budget of $60,000*** — Assuming the contract is written at $2 million, Fiberdyne normally budgets 1.5 percent of sales to capture business, or $30,000. Our normal win rate is 25 percent, but if we . . .

.
.
.

(32) Considering the annual net contribution margin potential of $1.75 million, budgeting $60,000 to win the business seems quite conservative . . .

.
.
.

(33) **2.3 Risk Analysis: Fiberdyne's greatest risk is missing the opportunity to position our proprietary fibers in the bridge building market**

Strengths — (34) Our strengths include Dr. Hats reputation, testing capabilities, leading edge fiber development record, and familiarity with . . .

.
.
.

Weaknesses — Our weaknesses include limited experience with bridges and bridge design, limited record with the DOT, reputation for poor . . .

.
.
.

Opportunities — The greatest opportunity is to obtain FHWA endorsement . . .

.
.

Threats — We have identified several threats:

- FHWA could require a waiver of royalties on proprietary fibers
- Component failure of a bridge component could cause . . .

16–MAJOR PROGRAM, TEXT FORMAT (CONTINUED)

(35) Like earlier sections, it opens with a summary and introduction.

See **Organization**.

Fiberdyne Capture Plan — **DOT Bridge Composites Research**

3.0 Capture Strategy

(35) Our capture strategy sets specific objectives that we must accomplish to win. The Integrated Customer Solution Worksheet uses the prospect's stated requirements to develop implied issues, our baseline solution, our discriminators and gaps and suggests potential strategies and actions. Readers with limited time may go directly to the bulleted lists of potential strategies at the end of section 3.1. Our approach to achieving the objectives is detailed in a series of action plans:

3.2 Intelligence Collection Plan

3.3 Call Plan

3.4 White Papers

3.5 Advertising and Promotion Plan

3.6 IR&D and Trade Studies

3.7 Contingency Plan

All action steps are not included, pending management review. Actions will be reviewed monthly.

Overall Capture Strategy Objective

3.1 Fiberdyne Strategy: We must establish in the eyes of six key FHWA employees that Fiberdyne is the most capable, qualified, and unbiased organization to demonstrate the viability of composite materials for bridge building applications

The large Integrated Customer Solution Worksheet in figure 7 should be read row by row horizontally. We will reexamine this worksheet monthly to track progress towards positioning Fiberdyne as the organization preferred by the FHWA. The trackability of items within the worksheet helps ensure that no key requirements, potential solutions, and strategies are lost.

(36) When time is limited, complete this worksheet and omit other portions of the capture plan. Maintain the horizontal relationship between items.

See **Capture Planning.**

Fiberdyne Capture Plan **DOT Bridge Composites Research**

(36)

# (1)	Customer Issue (2)	Program/Product Requirement (3)	Available Solution (4)
1	Reduce bridge maintenance costs	Evaluate economic feasibility	None internal
2	Will it work?	Evaluate technical feasibility	Dr. Hats and his staff
3	Are proven materials available?	Evaluate materials	None internally
4	Will bridge designers accept composites?	Analyze design impact	Dr. Hats' staff
5	Risky? Fund "dual-use" technology	Survey relevant applications of composites	Dr. Hats and his staff
6	Are uniform qualtiy materiels available in sufficient quantity?	Evaluate production methods	Dr. Hats and his staff
7	Testing must be reliable and realistic	Develop component designs	Design engineering group
8	Bridge designers and builders must accept results	Prepare final report	Dr. Hats' staff
9	Findings must be seen widely	Publish findings	Dr. Hats and his staff
10	Must obtain industry acceptance	Present results at industry forums	Dr. Hats and his staff

Figure 7. Integrated Customer Solution Worksheet. *Read this worksheet horizontally. Potential strategies and actions are summarized in the bulleted lists on the following pages.*

16–MAJOR PROGRAM, TEXT FORMAT (CONTINUED)

Fiberdyne Capture Plan **DOT Bridge Composites Research**

Discriminators (5)	Gap (6)	Strategy (7)	Action Required (8)
Negative—lack bridge building expertise	Must know bridge building economics	Hire consultant or team	Identify partner Negotiate contract
Dr. Hats Golden Gate cables Corps of Engineers in MT	None	Emphasize unique capability of Dr. Hats	Introduce to prospect Submit past professional papers
Dr. Hats and staff	None	Emphasize broad look, beyond Fiberdyne's materials	Collect client comments Cite fibers we have evaluated and recommended that were developed by others
Negative—need a bridge designer	Need bridge designer	Subcontract	Identify subcontractor
Recognized composites expertise; Developed many of leading applications	None	Emphasize previous similar experience	Try to arrange site visits Include samples List materials and tasks completed
Experience in all areas of contract manufacturing; have survey experience	None	Emphasize employees with similar experience	Invite prospect for plant tour and reception with staff
In-house test capability and facilities, especially for large components	None	Feature extensive component design experience	Show examples on tour Put photos in proposal
None perceived—we are unknown	Perceived gap	Emphasize recent training	Include current samples
Extensive associations with technical journals	None	Emphasize publications expertise	List all staff publications
Extensive presentation experience	None	List recent industry presentations	Include copies of forum programs in our presentations & proposals

(37) All strategy elements are elaborations from the final two columns of the Integrated Customer Solution Matrix.

See **Capture Planning** *and* **Strategy.**

Fiberdyne Capture Plan | **DOT Bridge Composites Research**

Emphasize Strengths

(37) We must emphasize the following strengths:

- Stress our fiber and composite superiority
- Stress our prestigious principal investigator, Dr. Manny Hats
- Stress our depth of experience by emphasizing the Golden Gate Bridge cables and the Corps of Engineers project in Montana
- Emphasize our ability to connect materials expertise, component production, and applications
- Emphasize our in-place laboratory and ability to test full-scale components
- Emphasize how we have successfully pioneered composites in other markets like aerospace

Mitigate Weaknesses

- Mitigate our weaknesses in cost control by implementing a new inventory control system and training our people
- Mitigate past weaknesses in project definition by developing a clear, comprehensive WBS and SOW that the FHWA can use
- Mitigate lack of bridge design expertise by teaming with the Brooklyn Bridge Company
- Mitigate our scheduling weaknesses by purchasing, implementing, and demonstrating an integrated project management system

Highlight Competitors' Weaknesses

- Highlight difference between typical fiber composite applications and high strength applications of composites
- Stress that the typical high volume production methods casue voids, incomplete fiber wetting, and fiber damage; all lead to long-term failure
- Stress the unique R&D nature of the project
- Stress the limited availability of seasoned high-strength composites experts, such as Dr. Hats
- Point out the critical lessons learned at Windy Canyon, Montana
- Stress the difficulty in finding quality, full-scale test apparatus, justifying why Fiberdyne had to develop our own

16–MAJOR PROGRAM, TEXT FORMAT (CONTINUED)

(38) An informative heading summarizes the most important point in each action plan.

See **Headings.**

(39) All actions plan tasks require the same elements: objective, action, person assigned, timing, and measure to assess completion.

Fiberdyne Capture Plan — **DOT Bridge Composites Research**

Neutralize Competitor's Strengths

- Stress our solid team management approach
- Emphasize our team's ability to fully cost share as planned
- Emphasize Brooklyn Bridge's bridge design group and their leadership in the applications of new materials
- Deemphasize the importance of high-volume production expertise to a demonstration project
- Stress our prestigious principal investigator, Dr. Manny Hats, will manage the engineering; Mr. Adams of BB will manage the project

Objective

(38) **3.2 Fiberdyne Intelligence Collection Plan: Our primary need is to learn more about our FHWA customer.**

Supporting Actions

(39) **Learn the FHWA history with similar purchasing decisions.**

Schedule meetings with Dr. Brown, Charles Bridges, Sam Hern, and Don Moffat. Ask them.

Who: Y.A. Title

When: Within 30 da.

Measure: Update plan and report during next plan review

.
.
.
.

Objective

3.3 Fiberdyne Call Plan: Our primary need is to establish our capabilities with key FHWA officials and influence the RFP.

Supporting Actions

Establish Fiberdyne as the industry leader with the FHWA.

Invite Dr. Brown and his staff to Fiberdyne to review our latest research and tour our laboratory facilities.

Who: Y.A. Title

When: Within 60 da.

Measure: Update plan and report during next plan review

.
.
.
.
.
.
.
.

Fiberdyne Capture Plan | **DOT Bridge Composites Research**

⋮

Objective

3.4 Fiberdyne White Papers: Our focus is to be first to stake our claim to industry leadership in applying composites to bridges.

Supporting Actions

Establish our composites expertise in bridge building applications and counter the view that we do not understand bridges.

Combine our economic analysis of bridge building with our Golden Gate and Montana experience in a single white paper.

Who: Dr. Hats will supervise preparation

Y.A. Title will circulate it among key FHWA people.

When: Within 60 da.

Measure: Review draft as soon as it is complete

⋮

Objective

3.5 Advertising and Promotion: Our focus is to be first to stake our claim to industry leadership in applying composites to bridges.

Supporting Actions

Advertising has little application because our target audience is small. Limited promotion activities could be helpful.

Support and participate in the FHWA's semiannual industry forum. Offer to discuss applying high strength composites to support cables and large structural components. Display samples from the Golden Gate and Montana projects.

Objective

Secure FHWA approval to join the program.

Supporting Actions

Who: Y.A. Title

When: Within 30 da.

Measure: Report in next update meeting

Prepare presentation.

Who: Dr. Hats

When: After approved by FHWA and 30 da. before the program.

Measure: Update plan and report during next plan review

16–MAJOR PROGRAM, TEXT FORMAT (CONTINUED)

(40) Only major risks are included in the capture plan rather than every identifiable risk.

See **Capture Planning** *and* **Risk Management.**

Fiberdyne Capture Plan — **DOT Bridge Composites Research**

3.6 IR&D and Trade Studies: Our projected image of industry leadership in applying composites to bridges must be based on accurate facts.

Objective

The FHWA project is partially a trade study. Fiberdyne's credibility will be enhanced if we appear to have an early start.

Supporting Actions

Quickly survey public domain information and our files on competitive materials and products. Summarize the findings for internal use. Whether and how the information is used outside Fiberdyne will depend on our findings.

Who: N.O. Norganic

When: Within 15 da.

Measure: Report in next update meeting

3.7 Contingency Plan

Four threats were identified as part of our internal analysis. Each risk and our recommended risk management approach is summarized below.

(40)

Major Risk	Priority	Management Approach
FHWA requires bidders to waive royalties	1	Stress that the fiber offering best value should be used. Royalties must be justified economically. If not acceptable, we will have to risk taking exception, waiving the royalty, or not bidding.
Teaming could lead to loss of our proprietary advantages	2	Negotiate acceptable teaming agreement. Our partner is not a composites company.
Tests of our fibers by others could be biased	3	Win. Establish fair testing guidelines with the FHWA and get them written into the RFP.
A bridge component could fail during testing	4	Our company liability insurance will cover potential financial losses. The greater impact is on our long-term market success. Yet the risk is no different than our other types of business. Our normal design review processes are adequate. We will also ask our teaming partner to review and approve all designs.

41 All contributors need to know that senior management has approved the plan.

See **Capture Planning.**

42 Near term events are identified.

43 The roles of key managers of the capture plan are identified as well as the review process. Obsolete or outdated plans offer little value and prompt participants to lose interest.

See **Capture Planning.**

Fiberdyne Capture Plan — **DOT Bridge Composites Research**

4.0 Implementation and Control

41 The draft of this capture plan was reviewed, revised, and approved by a team of Fiberdyne managers:

M.R. Big - CEO
B.L. Suit - V.P. Finance
I.M. Slick - Sr. V.P. Marketing
K.E. Blunt - V.P. Manufacturing and Engineering

42 A kick-off meeting for the capture team participants is scheduled for mm/dd/yy.

The purpose of the kick-off meeting is to reinforce top management support and to assign tasks.

Each participant will receive the portion of the plan that defines their tasks.

43 The capture team manager is Y.A. Title. If the opportunity proceeds as expected to the proposal state, A.B. Clark will be the proposal manager. The capture team will meet weekly. The capture manager will review progress monthly as a regular agenda item in the monthly management meeting. All capture plans are reviewed in greater detail as part of our quarterly marketing review.

The schedule of tasks follows. The schedule is maintained on scheduling software and will be updated weekly.

All implementation questions should be addressed to Y.A. Title, Capture Manager.

17–MAJOR PROGRAM, PRESENTATION FORMAT

❶ Begin with your top points that everyone should accept and remember. Assume a key person might leave after the first slide.

See **Oral Proposals** *and* **Organization.**

❷ Preview the organization of your presentation to help managers focus on content rather than trying to discern how your presentation is organized.

❶

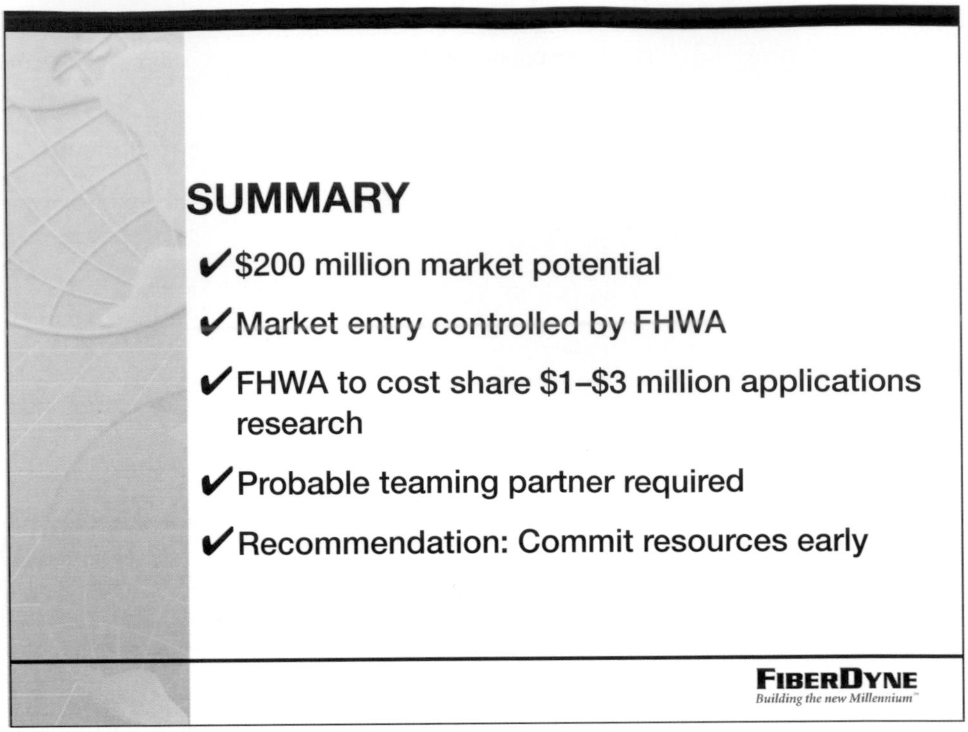

❷

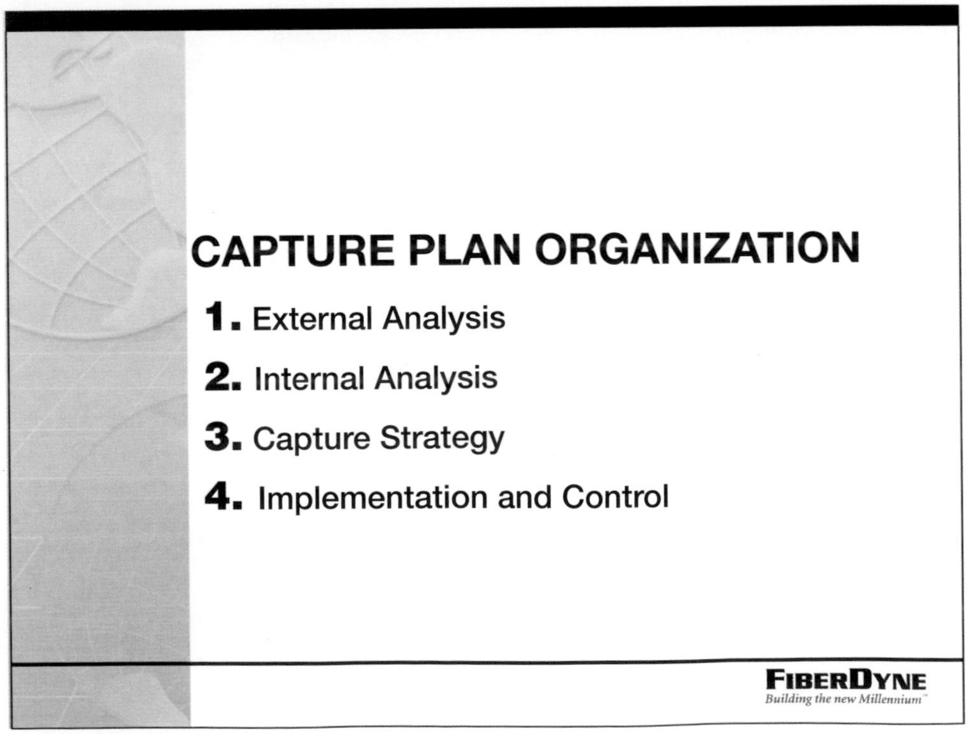

NOTE: This capture plan is identical to the previous text-format plan. Only the first three slides are presented to show how essential content is summarized. Capture plans in a presentation format are faster to prepare and are recommended when busy managers lack the time to read capture plans in text format.

❸ The heading indicates the section of the capture plan.

❹ The same graphic as in the written plan shows organizational relationships. The graphic has been adjusted for the presentation. The presenter covers the information from the text and action caption.

❸

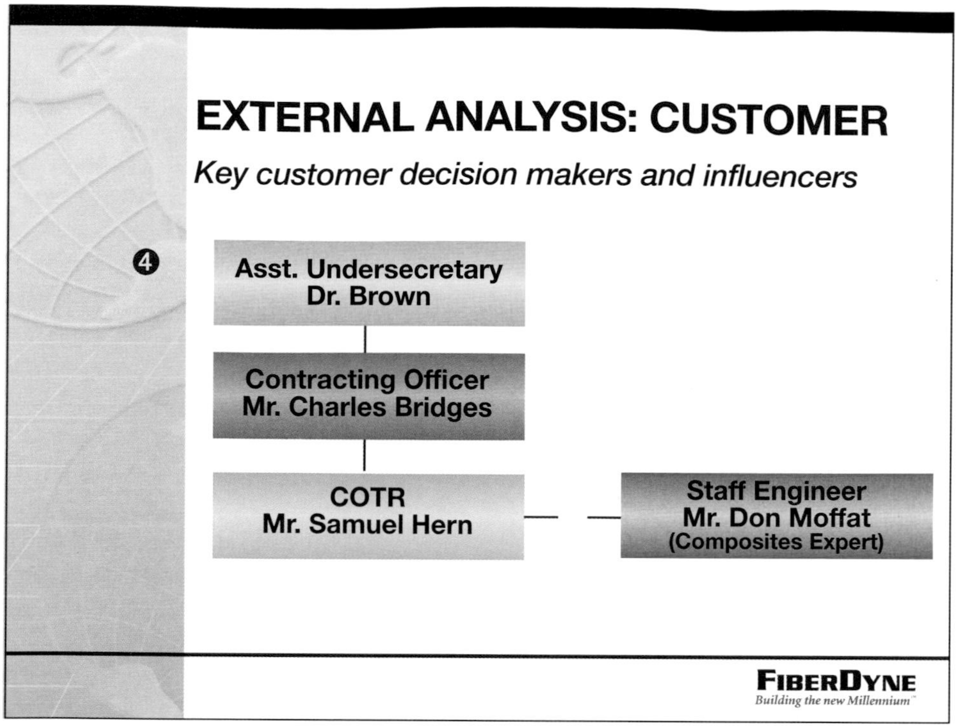

The following conventions were used in this index:

- Main entries or topics in the Guidelines section are printed in large capital and small capitals. For example, ACTION CAPTIONS, APPENDICES, and BID DECISIONS.
- Following the title of a main entry, the page number(s) in boldface refer to the main alphabetically arranged entries, as in this example: CUSTOMER FOCUS, **32-34.**
- Cross-references with only *See* and a page number indicate that what your are looking up appears under the *See* reference. For example, if you look up ***document format,*** you will find the following *See* reference: *See* PAGE AND DOCUMENT DESIGN, 103-110.
- Cross-references with *Also see* and a page number indicate that you will find extra information on the pages listed, but that this information in not the main discussion. For example, under ACTION CAPTIONS appears this reference: *Also see* FEATURES, ADVANTAGES, AND BENEFITS, 50-52. You will find that the entry for FEATURES, ADVANTAGES, AND BENEFITS includes additional information relevant to ACTION CAPTIONS.
- Model documents on p. 229-276 are not indexed in detail. They are listed by title and type of document. References to model documents are in boldface followed by a page number, as in this example: **Prospecting (model), 230.**

A-4 paper, 70, 105, 145
Account plan, 134, 146
relationship to other plans, 13
relationship to PROPOSAL MANAGEMENT PLAN, 146
Acronyms, 20
in international proposals, 19-20
maintaining list of, 142
in pre-submission checklist, 140
ACTION CAPTIONS, **1-5**
Also see FEATURES, ADVANTAGES, AND BENEFITS, 50-52
Also see GRAPHICS, 53-62
in boilerplate, 114
in daily reviews, 37
in executive summaries, 48
format, placement, and style, 4-5, 103, 104, 109
in grant proposals, 226
in international proposals, 69
in letter proposals, 79
in question/response proposals, 152
referencing in prior text, 4
reviewing, 166-167, 177
similarities and differences to theme statements, 214
in storyboards and mock-ups, 193
in support tools, 135
Added value, 127
Also see VALUE PROPOSITIONS, 215-218
forcing readers to discover, 119, 130
as a pricing strategy, 127-130, 136
in grant proposals, 225
quantifying, 127-130, 199
in question and response proposals, 172
supporting claims of 120, 127-130
visualizing, 23, 90
Alpha-numeric numbering systems. *See* NUMBERING SYSTEMS, 83-84
APPENDICES, **6-7**
in document organization, 92
in a letter proposal, 79
in grant proposals, 227
placement in bid requests, 97
placing graphics in, 60
when planning proposal production, 140
to Proposal Management Plan, 71, 147
in storyboards, 88, 190
Annexes. *See* APPENDICES, 6-7
Annotated outlines, 187
Association of Proposal Management Professionals (APMP), 41
Attachments. *See* APPENDICES, 6-7
Attention lines.
See informative headings, 75-76, 175-177
See signal words
—in executive summaries, 47
—in letter proposals, 75, 77
—in sales letters, 175-177
Audience
for a capture plan, 12
when choosing colors, 24-25
for grant proposals, 219-225
for oral proposals, 86-91
when organizing documents, 95
for presentations to prospects, 116-118

Baseline solution, 35, 134, 179
Begin with important ideas, 93-94
Best practice
aligning process and strategy, 195
business development processes, 131-138
graphic tracking numbers, 114
managing proposals as a strategic project, 205
measuring business development capability and maturity, 132
preparing cost volume summaries, 121
preparing executive summaries, 49
pricing approaches, 128
Proposal Management Plan, 146
quantifying benefits in theme statements, 218
retrieving graphics and action captions, 3
style sheets for writers, 104
supporting risk management approach in a table, 170
tailoring resumes, 157
"Why us?" section graphic, 30
BID DECISIONS, **8-11**
in business development process, 134-135
in capture planning, 12-16
Bid Decision Tree, 10
Bid Request Compliance Matrix, 29
Bid Request Response Locator, 30
Bidder Comparison Matrix
to analyze teaming combinations, 206-207
in capture plans, 14-15
in Sales Proposal Planner, 189
to develop strategy, 195, 198, 200
to evaluate potential teaming combinations, 206-207
in executive summaries, 45
as kickoff meeting handout, 73
as recommended template, 95
Bid/no bid decisions. *See* BID DECISIONS, **8-11**
Bid validation, 16, 133, 135.
Also see BID DECISIONS, 8-11
Also see PROCESS, 134-135
relationship to proposal kickoff, 71
Binding proposals (covers and packaging), 43, 44, 62, 103-105, 136, 140-145
Blue Team, 142, 162-163. *See* CAPTURE PLANNING, 12-16
Also see REVIEWS, 162-168
Boilerplate
action caption files, 4
checking for computer viruses, 42
graphics, 57, 109, 111, 114, 137
influence on proposal review time, 166, 168, 181
as input for bid validation decision, 11
as output from bid decision, 27
for proposal planning, 35, 134, 135, 146, 149, 180
for question/response proposals, 151-152
resumes, 158-159
reviewing and maintaining, 138
tailoring,57, 66, 75, 81-82, 93, 185, 188, 192, 194, 195, 213
Book boss. *See* volume manager, 72
Black Hat Team, 163-164
British English, 69
Broad Agency Announcements (BAA), 220
Bullets
coloring, 25
in lists, 80-82
Buyers, types of, 197

Callout, 94, 104, 167-168
Also see pull quote, 213-214
Captions. *See* ACTION CAPTIONS, 1-5
Capture plan, 8, 11, 134, 163
Also see CAPTURE PLANNING, 12-16
Also see STRATEGY, 195-202
Blue Team review of, 163
organization of, 95, 146
Presentation Format (model), 274-275
Text Format (model), 258-273
use in proposal planning, 146-148
CAPTURE PLANNING, **12-16**
Also see Process, 131-138
Also see Strategy, 195-202
Integrated Prospect Solution Worksheet, 197
review of, 163
relationship to bid decisions, 8
relationship to executive summaries, 45
relationship to kickoff meetings, 71-72
relationship to proposal cover letters, 31
template, 95
Capture strategy, 111, 164, 195, 200, 202, 203
Charts, 1-2, 25, 54-60, 63, 109, 120, 156, 170
in foldouts, 105
in grant proposals, 221-222
"meatball," 165
in oral proposals, 87
for scheduling, 179
in service proposals, 185
in strategy statements, 201
in team proposals, 207
Checklists
for bid decision, 8-11
for Black Hat Team, 163
for Blue Team, 163
to brainstorm theme statements, 209
compliance, 26-30, 73, 87, 88, 189-190
for Lessons Learned, 166
for Pink Team, 164
pre-submission, 140
printing and delivery, 140
for Red Team, 164
requirements, 178, 182, 189
response, 101
for reviewing executive summaries, 49
CHOOSING CORRECT WORDS, **17-22**
in grant proposals, 222
Clinchers, 17, 20-21
Cliches, 17-21, 31, 175
in graphics, 54
COLOR, **23-25**

adjusting to medium, 24-25
copying, 114
as a discriminator, 38
emotional impact, 24-25
for emphasis, 107-109, 114, 177, 211
as a feature, 50, 52
in graphics, 58-59
in headings, 66
overly expensive or elaborate, 114
in page and document design, 103
in photographs, 111
in presentations, 90, 117
printing, 53, 113, 139-144
standards, 24
in style sheets, 104
Color-blind, adjusting for, 24-25
Columns, 60, 107-110
in mock-ups, 193
for resumes, 158
for risk management charts, 170
Competitive range, 130
COMPLIANCE AND RESPONSIVENESS, **26-30**
Also see OUTLINING, 96-102
in cost proposals, 123
in daily team management, 36-37
echoing in theme statements, 213-214
in grants, 220-227
in headings, 64
in numbering systems, 83
in page design, 133
in presentations, 116
in process design, 133-138
in production, 139-142
proposal organization, 93
in reviews, 162-167
in scheduling, 179
statements of compliance, 47, 76-79, 94
who prepares, 204
Sales Proposal Planner, 188-189
Compliance Checklist, 73
preparation shortcuts, 28
in oral proposals, 87
in storyboards, 88, 189-192
Compliance Matrix, 36, 64
Compliance Requirements Checklist. *See* Compliance Checklist, 73
Consolidated Prospect Solution Worksheet, 46
Cooperative Research and Development Agreement (CRADA), 220
Cost and price data. *See* PRESENTING COST AND PRICE DATA, 119-126
Cost bogey, 128
Cost volume summary, 119-126
Cover Letter Models. ***See*** **Model Documents, 241-243**
To Buyer for Formally Solicited Government Bid, 243
To Decision Maker with Buying Criteria, 241
To Decision Maker without Buying Criteria, 242
COVER LETTERS, **31**
in grant proposals, 222
organization of, 95
when planning production, 140, 142
as a sales letter, 172
as transmittal letter, 142
Covers for proposals
color, 23
designing, 103, 105
placing summary information in a cover pocket, 119, 121
planning and scheduling production, 140, 144-145
Competitive range, 130
CUSTOMER FOCUS, **32-34**
cliches, 18
in daily team management, 35
in executive summaries, 44
in grant proposals, 221-227
measuring, 44, 138
in page and document design, 103, 105
in presentations to prospects, 116-117
in process design, 133, 135
in Proposal Development Worksheets, 88
in sales letters, 172, 175, 177
in theme statements, 210
when developing proposal outlines, 96
Customer focused writing process, 173-177

DAILY TEAM MANAGEMENT, **35-37**
Also see PROPOSAL MANAGEMENT PLAN, 146-150
Also see SCHEDULING, 178-182
display lists. *See* LISTS, 80-82
Decimal numbering systems. *See* NUMBERING SYSTEMS, 83-84
Desktop publishing. *See* PAGE AND DOCUMENT DESIGN, 103-110
estimating the time required, 180
DISCRIMINATORS, **38-46**
Also see CHOOSING CORRECT WORDS, 19
Also see FEATURES, ADVANTAGES, AND BENEFITS, 50
in bid decisions, 9
in cover letters, 31
emphasizing, 23, 30
in executive summaries, 45-49
in grant proposals, 224-227
in graphics, 53-55
in headings, 64-65
in Integrated Prospect Solution Worksheet, 14-15, 45-46
in letter proposals, 77-78
in oral proposals, 88
as page allocation tool, 101
people as, 157
in photographs, 111-114
in presentations, 116
related to strategy, 73, 128, 148, 197-198
reviewing, 165-168
risk as a discriminator, 170
in service proposals, 184
in storyboards, 189, 191
in theme statements, 209-213
Document-based reviews, 135
Document format. *See* PAGE AND DOCUMENT DESIGN, 103-110
Double-sided printing, 105, 107, 114, 141

ELECTRONIC SUBMITTALS, **41-43**
international proposals, 70
related to page and document design, 107-108
scheduling, 178, 181
with graphics, 143
with oral proposals, 91
with photographs, 113
Eligibility Guidelines
for grants, 220
Eligibility Rules
for grants, 220
Emphasis
in action captions,1 ,5
of benefits, 50, 52
of compliance, 98
of costs and pricing data, 118, 121
of discriminators, 38, 40
of relevant experience/past performance, 153-156
in resumes, 157-161
of risk management, 170
in sales letters, 175-177
in service proposals, 184-185
in storyboards and mock-ups, 191
in strategy statements, 44-47, 89, 148, 199-202
in theme statements, 210-214
using color, 23
using graphics, 53-62, 79
using headings, 66
using lists, 80-82
using page and document design, 103-110, 133
using photographs, 111-114
using repetition, 1, 17, 20
using signal words, 77
when presenting, 87, 122, 125
Envisioning. *See* Vision statements. *Also see* Visualizing, 154
Estimating guidelines, 126-129
Exhibits
See ACTION CAPTIONS, 1-5
See GRAPHICS, 62
EXECUTIVE SUMMARY, **44-49**
cliches in, 18
creative forms, 23, 104
emphasizing discriminators, 40
for grant proposals, 223
including pricing in, 119-121, 126-130, 133
length of, 79, 101
mocking up, 188-189
organization of, 94, 95, 133
as part of kickoff package, 73
preparation tools, 135
presenting value propositions in, 217-218
production of, 140, 142
related to letter proposals, 75-76
relationship to cover letters, 31
relationship to hot buttons and strategy, 196-198
relationship to oral proposals and presentations to prospects, 87, 91, 116

relationship to Proposal Management Plan, 146-150
relevance to bid decisions, 11
reviewing, 166
risk management, 169-170
role in Question/Response proposals, 151-152
as a telegraphic heading, 63
using color in, 23, 114
using graphics in, 53, 57, 60, 112
when prepared, 51, 134, 179
when to submit, 133
Executive Summary Models. *See* **Model Documents, 236-240**
Formally Solicited Government Proposal, 240
Incumbent's Informally Solicited Services Proposal, 238-239
Informally Solicited Commercial Proposal, 236-237

FEATURES, ADVANTAGES, AND BENEFITS, **50-52**
Also see ACTION CAPTIONS, 1-5
Also see CUSTOMER FOCUS, 32-34
Also see THEME STATEMENTS, 209-214
in action captions, 1-5
discriminators, 38-40
in executive summaries, 44, 47
in graphics, 54, 56, 59, 62
in headings, 63-66
naming lists, 80-82
in Oral Proposal Planners, 88-89
in photographs, 111
reviewing, 162-168
role in unsolicited proposals, 27
in sales letters, 172-178
storyboards and mock-ups, 187-194
strategy, 195-204
in value propositions, 215-218
visualizing, 154
when developing pricing, 128
Figures
See ACTION CAPTIONS, 1-5
See GRAPHICS, 62
Foldouts
appropriate and inappropriate applications, 60
influence on page count, 104
production issues, 141, 145
response matrix, 105
Format, *See* PAGE AND DOCUMENT DESIGN, 103-110
Also see **Model Documents, 230-275**
of capture plans (models), 258-275
of cover letters (models), 241-243
of executive summaries (models), 236-240
of proposal sections (models), 236-247
of sales letters (models), 230-235
of storyboard (model), 244-245
of action captions, 1-5
of capture plans, 13-14
cover letters, 31
electronic submittals, 41-43
executive summary, 47-48
grant proposals, 222
graphics, 53-62
headings, 63-66
international proposals, 67-69
oral proposals, 90
presentations to prospects, 116
of Proposal Management Plans, 146-150
of question/response proposals, 151-152
of resumes, 158-161
of sales letters, 173-177
storyboards and mock-ups, 188-193
theme statements, 211
value propositions, 215-218
Four-box organization
applications, 95
for executive summaries, 47-48
for letter proposals, 75-79
for presentations to prospects, 116
to present value propositions, 217
for sales letters, 172-177
Funders, 219-227
Funding instruments, 219-220

Ghosting
in cost volume summaries, 122, 124
planning, 163, 166, 184, 195, 201-202
in presentations, 89, 126
in resumes, 157
reviewing, 37
in risk management, 170
in storyboards, 191
Goals for grant proposals, 223-225
Gobbledygook, 17-20
Gold Team
See Reviews, 162-165, 178-179
Grant applications 219-227
Grant guidelines, 219-227
Grant proposals. *See* WRITING FOR GRANTS, 219-227
Grant Writing. *See* WRITING FOR GRANTS, 219-227
GRAPHICS, **53-62**
Also see ACTION CAPTIONS, 1-5
Also see COLOR, 23-25
Also see PHOTOGRAPHS, 111-114
estimating cost, 27, 138, 143
in executive summaries, 48-49
in grant proposals, 225-227
in international proposals, 67-70
in letter proposals, 75
managing and reviewing, 36-37, 72-74, 102, 114, 135, 137, 166-168
in oral proposals, 86, 90
in page design, 103-110
to present cost and pricing, 119-125
to present experience and performance, 153-156, 161
in presentations, 124
production of, 42, 139-143
in question/response proposals, 152
to sell services, 183-185
in storyboards and mock-ups, 187-192
in strategy statements, 200-201
submitting electronically, 41-43, 74
tailoring to the evaluator, 92-94
Graphic or visual association, 4, 105-106
Grouping similar ideas, 92-93, 222

HEADERS, 106-107, 114, 142, 210, 213
HEADINGS, **63-66**
in action captions, 5, 62
as an alternative to theme statements, 214
in color, 25
defining production style, 142
as a *grabber*, 20, 22
in lists, 81
matching the introduction, 34
numbering, 84-85
in outlines, 73, 84-85, 96, 100
in page design, 103-110
reviewing, 167-168
role in organization, 93
in sales letters, 75-78, 173-177
in storyboards and mock-ups, 187, 192
Hierarchy of business plans, 13
Also see PROCESS, 131-138
Horse titles or captions. *See* ACTION CAPTIONS, 1-5
Hot buttons, 196
as basis for page allocation, 101
as basis for proposal outline, 98
in capture plans, 14
customer focus aspects of, 32-34
discussing in kickoff meeting, 71, 73
in letter proposals, 75-79
organizing executive summaries around, 44-49
organizing presentations around, 116
organizing sales letters around, 173, 176, 177
in proposal management plan, 148, 150
treating sub-value propositions as, 217-218
ways to address, 112, 119
Hyperlinked proposal files, 43, 136

Illustrations. *See* GRAPHICS, 53-62
Inch stones, 36, 149, 178
Informally solicited or unsolicited proposals, 27, 101-102, 139
Also see LETTER PROPOSALS, 75-79
Informative headings
for action captions, 62
Also see HEADINGS, 63-66
to answer bid request questions, 93
establishing styles, 108
reviewing, 168
in sales letters, 173, 177
for short executive summaries, 79
similarity to theme statements, 214
when developing proposal outlines, 96, 100
International business English. *See* INTERNATIONAL PROPOSALS, 67-70
INTERNATIONAL PROPOSALS, **67-70**
developing proposal outline for, 96-102
how evaluated, 167
for oral proposals, 86
production of, 144-145

question/response proposals, 151
remote kickoff meetings, 74
using color, 24-25
using correct words, 20-22
Introductions. *See* ORGANIZATION, 92-95
to cost volume, 125, 129
in executive summaries, 18, 47
in grant proposals, 222
of graphics, 59-60
in letter proposals, 76, 78
to lists, 81
to oral proposals, 87-91
of proposal sections, 65-66, 84, 171, 192-193
to proposals, 97
to question/response proposals, 151
reviewing, 167
of sales letters, 173-177
versus summaries, 44
Issues, 33, 50-54
addressing in presentations, 116
to allocate time to question/response proposals, 151
in bid decisions, 10
in capture planning, 14-15
communicating at kickoff meeting, 73-74
in developing strategy,196-200
in developing value propositions, 215-217
in executive summaries, 45-49
in grant proposals, 220
identified in daily team management, 36
in proposal production, 140-142
in proposal team selection, 203-205
quantifying, 128-130
reviewing, 163, 165
in sales letters, 173-177
in storyboards, 88-90, 189-194
in teaming, 208
visualizing, 111-112
Italics, 108, 117, 177

Jargon, 17-22
avoiding in strategy template, 174, 175
avoiding in theme statements, 211, 212, 214
avoiding in grant proposals, 222
keeping a list of acceptable standards, 142
using "partner", 34
Justifying text, 110

Keeping setups short, 18, 78, 81, 173, 175, 177
KICKOFF MEETINGS, **71–74**
relationship to bid decisions, 8, 10, 12
in capture plans, 14, 16
materials required for
—compliance checklists, 27
—executive summary, 49
—inviting the Red Team, 164
—proposal ground rules, 142
—Proposal Management Plan, 35-36, 146, 149
—security needs, 142
—storyboards, 189-192
—strategy, 202
—style sheet, 104
—timing, 134, 178-182

Labeling Graphics. *See* ACTION CAPTIONS, **1-5**
Landscape format, 43, 60, 104, 117
Lead Compatibility Grid, 9
Leading, 108
Lessons learned, 3, 134
when presenting experience, 156
reviewing, 166
neutralizing competitors' strengths, 170, 201
in oral proposals, 91
in theme statements, 211-212
Letter Models. *See* Model Documents, 230-235, 241-243
Cover Letter: To Buyer for Formally Solicited Government Bid (model), 243
Cover Letter: To Decision Maker Without Buying Criteria (model), 242
Cover Letter: Informally Solicited Commercial Proposal (model), 241
Sales Letter: Follow-up to a Phone Call (model), 231
Sales Letter: Follow-up to a Meeting (model), 232
Sales Letter: Invitation to a Sales Event (model), 233
Sales Letter: Prospecting (model), 230
Sales Letter: Request RFP Modification (model), 234-235
LETTER PROPOSALS, **75-79**
Also see COVER LETTERS, 31
Also see EXECUTIVE SUMMARIES, 44-49
Also see ORGANIZATION, 92-95
Also see SALES LETTERS, 172-177
including support, 153-154
page design, 107
templates, 95
unsolicited proposals, 27
Letter of transmittal. *See* COVER LETTERS, 31
Levels of headings. *See* HEADINGS, 64-66
LISTS, **80-82**
as an emphasis device, 103-109, 115, 117, 156
of headings, 65
introducing headings, 65
role in organization, 92, 175
in sales letters, 175, 177
Listing figures/tables in proposal contents, 140, 142

Management overview
See EXECUTIVE SUMMARY, 44-49
See PROCESS, 131-138
See REVIEWS, 162-168
Management summary. *See* EXECUTIVE SUMMARY, 44-49
Master book, 139, 144, 192
Metrics, for business development, 131-138,
Metrics, for proposal development, 180
Milestone reviews.
See PROCESS, 131-138
See REVIEWS, 162-168
Motivators, 196

Naming conventions, 96-98, 142
Naming individuals for positions, 100, 157-158,
Naming lists, 81
Numbering
appendices/attachments/annexes, 7
figures, graphs, and tables, 2, 62
headings, 64,-65
lists, 82
pages, 106
NUMBERING SYSTEMS, **83-84**
Also see OUTLINING, 96-102

Objectives
outcome objectives, 223
process objectives, 223
ORAL PROPOSALS, **85-91**
Also see GRAPHICS, 53-62
Also see ORGANIZATION 92-95
Also see PRESENTATIONS TO PROSPECTS, 115-118
based upon executive summary, 49
presenting cost and price data, 120
presenting services, 183
presenting strategy, 199
selecting backgrounds for graphics, 109
using color, 23-25
using Four-Box organization, 47
using *grabbers*, transitions, and clinchers, 20
ORGANIZATION, **92-95**
of action captions, 2
Also see COMPLIANCE AND RESPONSIVENESS, 26-30
Also see LISTS, 80-82
Also see NUMBERING SYSTEMS, 83-84
Also see OUTLINING, 96-102
Also see PAGE AND DOCUMENT DESIGN, 103-110
of business development process, 131-138
of capture plan, 14
of cost volume summary, 121-124
of executive summaries, 46-49
of grant proosals, 222
of kickoff meeting, 71-74
of letter proposal, 75-79
of oral proposal, 85-91
of proposal management plan, 147-150
of question/response proposals, 151-152
of resumes, 158-160
of reviews, 162-168
of sales letters, 175
of storyboards, 190-191
of U.S. Federal bid requests, 97
of value propositions, 216
OUTLINING, **96-102**
Also see COMPLIANCE AND RESPONSIVENESS, 26-30
Also see NUMBERING SYSTEMS, 83-84
in capture plan, 16
discussions in daily standup meeting, 36
discussion of kickoff meeting, 73
grant proposals, 221-222
in kickoff package, 73
an oral proposal, 87-91
placing the executive summary, 44
in proposal management plan, 147-149, 182
proposal sections, 181, 187-194

question/response proposals, 150-151
reviewing, 164-166
solution, 197-199
when prepared, 133-134, 178
who prepares, 204

PAGE AND DOCUMENT DESIGN, **103-110**
Also see ORGANIZATION, 92-95
of action captions, 1-5
of electronic submittals, 41-43
of headings, 63-66
of lists, 80-82
for question/response proposals, 145-146
of resumes, 157-161
of theme statements, 203
using mock-ups, 190-193
Page size, 105
Parallel tasks, 179
Parallelism
in headings, 65
in lists, 80-81
Past experience. *See* RELEVANT EXPERIENCE/PAST PERFORMANCE, 153-156
PDF (Portable Document Format), 41, 43, 136, 143
Peer review for grants, 221
Peer Review Template, 176
Persuasion, 25, 44, 47, 75, 195, 203
in action captions, 1-4
in document design, 103-110
in grant proposals 223-227
in graphics, 55
in headings, 65
in lists, 81
in photographs, 111
in presentations, 86, 87, 122-124
in question/response proposals, 152
in sales letters, 173-176
in theme statements, 210, 213
in value propositions, 218
PHOTOGRAPHS, **111-114**
action captions for, 1-5
Also see COLOR, 23-25
Also see GRAPHICS, 53-62
to convey experience, 154, 184-185, 200-201
in electronic submittals, 42
in executive summaries, 45
in grant proposals, 225-227
in letter proposals, 78-79
printing on, 109
production and scheduling impacts, 141-143, 180
in resumes, 161
Pink Team, 36, 102, 134, 142, 162-164, 170
Placing action captions, 4-5
Pompous words. *See* CHOOSING CORRECT WORDS, 17-22
PRESENTING COST AND PRICE DATA, **115-121**
Also see ACTION CAPTIONS, 1-5
Also see COLOR, 23-25
Also see GRAPHICS, 53-62
Also see PRICING, 124-128
Also see VALUE PROPOSITIONS, 215-218
in executive summaries, 48-49, 76, 133
in grant proposals, 225
in sales letters and letter proposals, 76
PRESENTATIONS TO PROSPECTS, **122-125**
Also see COLOR, 23-25
Also see CUSTOMER FOCUS, 32-34
Also see EXECUTIVE SUMMARY, 44-49
Also see GRAPHICS, 53-62
Also see ORAL PROPOSALS, 85-91
based upon executive summary, 49
organizing, 123
presenting services, 183
presenting strategy, 199
selecting backgrounds for graphics, 109
setting color standards, 24
using color, 23-25
using Four-Box organization, 47
using *grabbers*, transitions, and clinchers, 20
Pre-submission checklist, 140
PRICING, **126-130**
Also see PRESENTING COST AND PRICING DATA, 115-121
analysis in capture planning, 14
discussing at kickoff meeting, 72
in executive summary, 18-19, 76, 133
in letter proposals, 78-79
strategy, 148, 197-202
when to develop, 133-134
who develops, 203-205
Print dummy. *See* print mock-up, 141
Print mock-up, 141
Printing and delivery checklist, 140
PROCESS, **131-138**
Also see BID DECISIONS, 8-11
Also see CAPTURE PLANNING, 12-16
Also see KICKOFF MEETING, 71-74
Also see PROPOSAL MANAGEMENT PLAN, 146-150
Also see REVIEWS, 162-168
Also see SCHEDULING, 178-182
to clarify features, advantages, and benefits, 50-52
to develop action captions, 1-4
to develop compliance checklist, 26-30
to develop electronic proposals, 41-43
to develop executive summary, 44-49
to develop graphics, 53-62
to develop responses for question/response proposals, 151-152
to develop risk management responses, 169-171
to develop strategy, 195, 202
to develop value propositions, 215-218
documenting, 136-137
metrics, 137-138
owner of, 137
to prepare letter proposals, 75-79
to prepare oral proposals, 85-91
to prepare proposal outlines, 96-102
to prepare theme statements, 209-214
to refine discriminators, 39-40
PRODUCTION, 139-145
appendices, 6-7
costs, 42, 61, 180
of electronic deliverables, 41
impact of color, 23, 25
impact of foldouts, 60
impact of page and document design, 103-108
of international proposals, 67-70
link to kickoff meeting, 72, 74
managing graphics, 53-62
of photographs, 111-114
in proposal centers, 138
of resumes, 157-158
scheduling and task assignments, 36, 178-182, 203-205
testing systems, 42
Program Research and Development Announcement (PRDA), 220
Proposal covers
color printing, 23
designing, 103, 105, 144-145
producing, 140, 144-145
using pockets for summaries, 115, 117
Proposal Development Worksheet, 35, 73, 85, 87-89, 189-194
Proposal project summary. 73, 147
Proposal Section. *See* **Model Documents, 246-257**
Casually Solicited Commercial Bid, 252-255
Formally Solicited Government Bid, 246-251
Question and Response Proposal, 257
Prototypes, *See* STORYBOARDS AND MOCK-UPS, 187-194
Pull quote, 213-214
Pursuit decision, 8-11, 12, 14-16, 133-136, 138
defining sales objective, 196-197, 215, 218
reviewing, 163, 165
PROPOSAL MANAGEMENT PLAN, 146-150
items required for
—executive summary, 44-49
—for kickoff meeting, 71-74
—for oral proposal, 85-91
—pricing, 126-130
—proposal ground rules, 36
—proposal outline, 96-102
—proposal schedule, 178-182
—storyboards and mock-ups, 187-194
—strategy, 195-202
—theme statements, 209-214
planning reviews, 162-165
relationship to capture plan, 13
when teaming, 203-205
when to prepare, 133-134, 178-182
Proposal specialist, 72, 136, 138, 189, 204-205
Proposal strategy. *See* STRATEGY, 195-202
assigning development responsibility, 203
based upon capture strategy, 16
extending into storyboards, 189, 191
influence on page allocation, 100
at major milestones, 11
for oral proposals, 88
in Proposal Management Plan, 147-148
required for kickoff meeting, 71, 73
strategy statement template, 46
when to develop, 134
Proposal plan, planning. *See* PROPOSAL MANAGEMENT PLAN, 146-150

relationship to capture planning, 16
Punctuation
of action caption, 5
of display lists, 82
of international proposals, 67-70
reviewing, 173, 177
of run-in heading, 64

Quantifying benefits, 4, 39, 50, 116, 191, 224, 225
Also see Value Propositions, 215-218
in theme statements, 210-211, 214, 218
Question/response proposals, 151-152
inserting summaries, 92-95
using graphics in, 53-62

Red Team
conducting, 162-168
planning and scheduling, 102, 134, 140, 179-180
quality of document expected, 143
Redundant words, 17, 21
Relevant Experience/Past Performance, **153-156**
emphasizing graphically, 23-25, 53-62, 111-114, 226
Repeating key points
in action captions, 1
in different proposal sections, 93
for emphasis and retention, 18, 214
in executive summaries, 79
in graphics, 23, 59
in introductions and headings, 63
in oral presentations, 87
Repeatable process
for business development. *See* Process, 131-138
to write sales letters, 173
Requirements checklist, 101
Also see Compliance and Responsiveness, 26-30
Research and development proposals, 219-220
Response locator, 30
Response matrix
Also see Compliance and Responsiveness, 26-30
format, 105
in outlining, 97, 99
scheduling, 178, 182, 190
Resumes, **157-161**
Also see Page and Document Design, 103-110
Also see Photographs, 111-114
Also see Relevant Experience/Past Performance, 153-156
Reviews, **162-168**
Also see Compliance and Responsiveness, 26-30
Also see Process, 131-135
scheduling, 178-180
standards for
—action captions, 1-5
—color, 23-25
—cover letters, 31
—customer focus, 32-34
—executive summary, 44
—graphics, 53-62
—headings, 63-66
—organization, 92-95
—theme statements, 209-214
—value propositions, 215-218
Risk management, **169-171**
Also see Relevant Experience/Past Performance, 153-156
Also see Strategy, 195-202
presenting graphically, 53-62
Run-in headings, 64
Sales Letter Models. *See* **Model Documents, 230-235**
Follow-up to a Meeting, 232
Follow-up to a Phone Call, 231
Invitation to a Sales Event, 233
Prospecting, 230
Request RFP Modification, 234-235

Sales Letters, **172-177**
Also see Executive Summary, 44-49
Also see Letter Proposals, 75-79
Also see Organization, 92-95
maintaining customer focus, 32-34
relationship to business development process, 131-135
using action captions, 1-5
using graphics, 53-62
using headings, 63-66
using lists, 80-82
Sans-serif fonts, 66, 108, 117
Schedules. *See* Scheduling, 178-182
Scheduling, **178-182**
acceptability in foldout format, 60, 105
capture plan actions, 12, 16
in Sales Proposal Planner, 189
in cost proposal summary, 123
daily team management, 35-36
as a discriminator, 38
in grant proposals, 225
inserting photographs in, 113
international proposals, 67, 70
as kickoff meeting handout, 71-74
in letter proposal, 76, 79
managing, 203-205
oral proposals, 86
presentations to prospects, 118
production, 139, 142
in Proposal Management Plan, 134, 147, 149
in proposal storyboard, 191
Red Team, 164, 166
required for pricing, 129
reviewing, 162, 167
as a services discriminator, 185
who develops, 203
Sentence length, 68, 177
Sequential tasks, 179
Serif fonts, 66, 108
Service Proposals, **183-186**
Also see Resumes, 157-161
Also see Writing for Grants, 219-227
developing theme statements for, 209-214
discriminators for services, 40, 202
features, advantages, and benefits, 50
informally solicited, 27
naming individuals in, 157
as part of WBS (Work Breakdown Structure), 150
presenting costs, 120
presenting relevant experience and past performance, 153-156
pricing, 128-129
question/response style, 151-152
using color in, 23
using graphics in, 54, 56, 59, 79, 111-112
visualizing impact, 111-112
Setting capture objectives, 16
Setups, 18, 175, 177
Should-costs, 128
Signal words, 47, 75, 77, 175-177, 218
SOW (Statement of Work), 29-30, 99, 100, 124, 129, 165, 225
Stand-up meetings. *See* Daily Team Management, 36
Storyboard: Formally Solicited Government Bid (model), 244-245
Storyboards and Mock-ups, **187-194**
Also see Graphics, 53-62
Also see Outlining, 96-102
action captions in, 1-5
applied to question/answer proposals, 151
assigning, 73-74, 142
daily reviews, 35-37
headings, 63-65
in kickoff meetings, 73
as a management tool, 192, 204
for oral proposals, 86-90
as an organizational tool, 93-95
as part of strategy development, 202
Pink Team reviews of, 142, 164
in proposal responsibility matrix, 102
scheduling, 36, 134, 179
Strategy, **195-202**
to allocate pages, 100-101
for bid decisions, 11
in capture plans, 12-16
communicating to proposal team, 71-74, 147-150
costing, 119, 126, 128-130
emphasizing, 23, 53-62, 111-114
impact on compliance and responsiveness, 26
in executive summaries, 44-49
for grants, 220-227
influence on page and document design, 104, 109
to mitigate risks, 155-156, 169-170
in oral proposals, 86-91
refining, 36, 51
in resumes, 157-161
reviewing, 142, 144, 162-168
role of discriminators, 39, 51
in sales letters, 172, 174-177
in storyboards, 37, 189-194
in theme statements, 209-214
when developed, 133-134, 136, 178-182
when teaming, 206
Strategy statements
developing, 195-202

in storyboards, 189
using to prepare executive summary, 45-46
in written proposal plan, 142, 148
Strategy template, 172, 174-177
Streamlining proposals
Also see GRAPHICS, 53-62
using appendices/attachments, 6
SWOT (Strengths, Weaknesses, Opportunities, and Threats) analysis, 14, 88, 189-190
Subject lines, 47, 75-77, 175-177, 218
Success stories, 95, 153-154, 209
Summaries
Also see EXECUTIVE SUMMARY, 44-49
in appendices, 7
choosing correct words for , 19
of cost volume or cost proposal, *See* PRESENTING COST AND PRICING DATA, 119-125
in cover letters, 31
differentiating section summaries and theme statements, 212
emphasizing discriminators in, 40
establishing length of, 101
in grant proposals, 222-223
in international proposals, 69
keeping customer focused, 32-34
labeling with telegraphic heading, 63
in letter proposals, 75-79
placement when organizing a document, 92-95
in presentations, 87, 89-91, 116, 118
of price in executive summary, 130
in question/response proposals, 151-152
of risk management approach, 170
role in evaluation, 104-105
of skills in matrices, 184
using color in, 23
using graphics in, 53,57, 60
using photographs in, 112-114
of value proposition, 215-218
of where to find your response, 30
Summary resumes, 159
Supporting claims
in action captions, 1-5
Also see VALUE PROPOSITIONS, 215-218
in appendices, 6-7
in cost proposals, 122-125
in grant proposals, 224-227
in graphics, 23-24, 53-62, 78, 109, 111-113, 151-152, 161, 170
in linked files, 43
in oral proposals, 87, 89, 91
in presentations, 115-118
of quantified benefits, 52
of relevant experience/past performance, 153-156
in sales letters, 172-177
in strategy statements, 199-201
in storyboards, 189-191
in text, 78, 93, 151-152, 171, 199-202, 210-214

TEAM SELECTION AND MANAGEMENT, **203-205**
Also see PROCESS, 131-138
Also see PROPOSAL MANAGEMENT PLAN, 146-150
Also see SCHEDULING, 178-182
TEAMING, **206-208**
communicating roles, 148
daily stand-up discussions, 36
internationally, 67
kickoff meetings, 71-73
photographs of teams, 113, 184
presenting capabilities, 161, 184
production, 143
selecting partners, 14
when to arrange, 134
Team Management
See TEAM SELECTION AND MANAGEMENT, 203-205
See DAILY TEAM MANAGEMENT, 35-37
Also see PROPOSAL MANAGEMENT PLAN, 146-150
Also see SCHEDULING, 178-182
international proposals, 70
kickoff meetings, 71, 74
oral proposals, 91
outlines, using to manage team, 102
of presentations, 91, 115-118
of pricing, 128-129
of process. *See* PROCESS, 131-138
of production, *See* PRODUCTION, 139-145
of question/reponse proposals, 151
of reviews, 166-167
of storyboards, 188-194
Telegraphic headings, 100, 108
Also see HEADINGS, 63-66
Templates
Bidder Comparison Matrix, 198
Sales Proposal Planner (contents), 188-189
electronic, 135-137
Four-box, 47, Also see Four-box organization
Integrated Prospect Solution Worksheet, 197-198
Proposal Development Worksheet, 190-191
Proposal Management Plan, 146-150
success story, 154
value proposition, 216
Theme litmus test, 214
THEME STATEMENTS, **209-214**
Also see FEATURES, ADVANTAGES, AND BENEFITS, 50-52
converting advantages to benefits, 51
as *grabbers*, 20
in grant proposals, 224
in proposal management plans, 148
mitigating risk in, 171
reviewing, 37, 168
similarity to action captions, 4-5
similarity to headings, 63-64
similarity to value propositions, 215, 218
Thumbnails. *See* STORYBOARDS AND MOCK-UPS, 187-194
Tone, 31, 34, 71-74, 97, 152, 166
Trade-offs, 116, 123, 170-171, 195-197, 201-202, 216
Trade studies. *See* Trade-offs, (above)
Transitions
in documents, 20-22, 33, 68
in presentations, 90-91, 123
Translating proposals, 70
Transmittal letter. *See* letter of transmittal, 142

Underlining for emphasis, 66, 108, 177

Value Propositions, 215-218
developing, 199
presenting, 217
quantifying, 4, 52, 127
in grant proposals, 225
in sales documents, 48
when developed, 134, 195, 215-218
Version control, 145, 192
Viruses, 42
Vision. *See* Vision statements
Also see Envisioning the final document, 139, 205
Vision statements
in capture plans, 13-14
in customer focus, 32-33
to determine prospects' discriminators, 40
developing collaboratively, 50-52, 134, 183-184
in executive summaries, 44, 47-49, 94, 150
in grant proposals, 223-224
location in different sales documents, 76-78
in presentations, 116
presenting in photographs, 111-114
reengineering, 97, 128
when teaming, 206, 208
Visual aids
See GRAPHICS, 53-62
See ORAL PROPOSALS, 85-90
See PRESENTATIONS TO PROSPECTS, 115-118
Visual or graphic association, 4, 105-106
Volume manager, 72, 125, 148, 181, 189-190, 194, 203-205

WBS (Work Breakdown Structure), 29, 73, 100, 123-125, 140, 147, 150, 204, 206, 208
White space, 63, 103, 105-110, 177, 201, 210
Win strategy, 11, 14
Also see STRATEGY, 195-202
Word choice. *See* CHOOSING CORRECT WORDS, 17-22
Word problems. *See* CHOOSING CORRECT WORDS, 17-22
Wordy phrases. *See* CHOOSING CORRECT WORDS, 17-22
Writer's packages, 73
WRITING FOR GRANTS, 219-228